LOOKING AT LIVES

*For Jackie,
It's been great
working with you for
the past 14 years!
Best wishes,
Erin*

LOOKING AT LIVES

American Longitudinal Studies
of the Twentieth Century

ERIN PHELPS
FRANK F. FURSTENBERG JR.
ANNE COLBY

EDITORS

Russell Sage Foundation / New York

The Russell Sage Foundation

The Russell Sage Foundation, one of the oldest of America's general purpose foundations, was established in 1907 by Mrs. Margaret Olivia Sage for "the improvement of social and living conditions in the United States." The Foundation seeks to fulfill this mandate by fostering the development and dissemination of knowledge about the country's political, social, and economic problems. While the Foundation endeavors to assure the accuracy and objectivity of each book it publishes, the conclusions and interpretations in Russell Sage Foundation publications are those of the authors and not of the Foundation, its Trustees, or its staff. Publication by Russell Sage, therefore, does not imply Foundation endorsement.

Library of Congress Cataloging-in-Publication Data

Looking at lives: American longitudinal studies of the 20th century / Erin Phelps, Frank F. Furstenberg Jr., and Anne Colby, editors.
    p. cm.
    Includes bibliographical references and index.
    1. Social sciences–Research–United States–Methodology. 2. Social sciences–Longitudinal studies. I. Phelps, Erin. II. Furstenberg, Frank F. III. Colby, Anne.

H62.5.U5 L665 2002
300′.7′2–dc21

2001055715

The paper used in this publication meets the minimum requirements of American National Standard for Information Sciences–Permanence of Paper for Printed Library Materials. ANSI Z39.48-1992.

Text design by Suzanne Nichols

RUSSELL SAGE FOUNDATION
112 East 64th Street, New York, New York 10021
10 9 8 7 6 5 4 3 2 1

In memory of Robert B. Cairns

Contents

Contributors

Erin Phelps is associate director for technical services at the Henry A. Murray Research Center, Radcliffe Institute for Advanced Study, Harvard University.

Frank F. Furstenberg Jr. is the Zellerbach Family Professor of Sociology and research associate in the Population Studies Center at the University of Pennsylvania.

Anne Colby is a senior scholar at the Carnegie Foundation for the Advancement of Teaching and former director of the Henry Murray Research Center, Radcliffe Institute for Advanced Study, Harvard University.

Karl L. Alexander is the John Dewey Professor of Sociology at the Johns Hopkins University.

William G. Axinn is professor of sociology and senior research scientist at the Survey Research Center and Population Studies Center of the Institute for Social Research at the University of Michigan, Ann Arbor.

Ann F. Brunswick is senior research scientist in public health and sociomedical sciences at Columbia University, New York.

Beverley D. Cairns was director of the Social Development Research Laboratory at the University of North Carolina at Chapel Hill.

The late **Robert B. Cairns** was the Boshamer Professor of Psychology and director of the Center for Developmental Science at the University of North Carolina, Chapel Hill.

Greg J. Duncan is professor of education and social policy and a faculty associate in the Institute for Policy Research at Northwestern University. He is also director of the Northwestern University/University of Chicago Joint Center for Poverty Research.

Glen H. Elder Jr. is the Howard W. Odum Distinguished Professor of Sociology and director of the Carolina Consortium on Human Development at the University of North Carolina, Chapel Hill.

Doris R. Entwisle is professor emerita of sociology at the Johns Hopkins University.

Ronald Freedman is Distinguished Emeritus Professor of Sociology and emeritus research associate of the Population Studies Center at the University of Michigan.

Janet Zollinger Giele is professor of sociology at the Heller School for Social Policy and Management at Brandeis University in Waltham, Massachusetts.

John H. Laub is professor of criminology and criminal justice at the University of Maryland, College Park, and affiliated scholar at the Henry A. Murray Center, Radcliffe Institute for Advanced Study, Harvard University.

John Modell is professor of education, human development, and sociology at Brown University.

Frank L. Mott is a senior research scientist and adjunct professor of sociology in the Center for Human Resource Research at Ohio State University.

Linda Steffel Olson is a senior research assistant in the Department of Sociology at the Johns Hopkins University.

Robert J. Sampson is the Lucy Flower Professor of Sociology at the University of Chicago and senior research fellow at the American Bar Association.

Arland Thornton is professor of sociology and senior research scientist at the Survey Research Center and the Population Studies Center of the Institute for Social Research at the University of Michigan, Ann Arbor.

George E. Vaillant is professor of psychiatry and director of the Study of Adult Development at Harvard Medical School, and senior physician at Brigham and Women's Hospital.

David P. Weikart is president emeritus of the High/Scope Educational Research Foundation in Ypsilanti, Michigan.

Emmy E. Werner is a developmental psychologist and research professor in human development at the University of California, Davis.

Acknowledgments

Many people worked on this project over the past five or six years, and we are grateful for their support. We especially appreciate the efforts of key individuals in organizations that provided financial support for their guidance through the funding process and their encouragement of our work. Special thanks to Emelyne Otey of the National Institute of Mental Health, Eric Wanner at the Russell Sage Foundation, Lonnie Sherrod formerly of the William T. Grant Foundation, Ruby Takanishi of the Foundation of Child Development, Idy Gitelson of the John D. and Catherine T. MacArthur Foundation, and Steven Breckler from the National Institute of Science. We would like to express our appreciation to Annabel Panopio of the Murray Research Center for her years of administrative support in this work, and Suzanne Nichols of the Russell Sage Foundation for her continuous encouragement and help in seeing this volume through to publication.

PART I

MULTIPLE INTERSECTIONS

Introduction

Looking at Lives:
American Longitudinal Studies
of the Twentieth Century

ERIN PHELPS AND ANNE COLBY

A NNE COLBY and Frank Furstenberg attended a meeting in the spring of 1996. During a walk at the lunch break, their conversation turned to the rigors of conducting lifelong studies, the singular benefits of following participants' lives through time, and the curious ways that a longitudinal perspective transforms the research process. They had discussed these sorts of issues before, but this time a spark was lit. Anne Colby recruited her colleague Erin Phelps to join the process of writing a proposal that resulted in a conference at the Henry A. Murray Research Center in the spring of 1999. The papers in this volume are products of that conference.

What transpired over the course of the project—developing an attractive idea, acquiring funding, producing the papers, and the resulting exchange of common observations and experiences during the conference—is itself, in miniature, what transpires in the process of conducting academic research. It is impossible to recount in detail what happened between inception and completion, but we want to give those who were not at the meeting some sense of the excitement of bringing together, in a single room for several days, many of the leading lights in longitudinal studies.

The development of the conference and the proposal seeking support for it were sustained by an energy that drew on the end-of-the-millennium fever that was gripping the nation, but it was the result even more of our own excitement about the importance and timeliness of the project. Long-term longitudinal designs have been one of the great advances in the

3

social and behavioral sciences in the twentieth century, producing insights about human development that would have been obscured by any other method. These studies had been published individually and even integrated to some extent within subject areas, but they had never been pulled together across widely different areas, and earlier reports have focused on either substantive findings or technical aspects of their methods. We were interested in something quite different. We wanted to ask the researchers to reflect on their experiences from the inside, to give us their stories of success and failure, and to look at their intellectual lives and work in the historical context of the decades in which they were conducting these studies. We also wanted to be able to share these insider accounts with the other researchers, with students just embarking on their professional lives, and with observers who share our fascination with studies that track people's lives over long periods of time.

Ideally, we would have brought together investigators from major prospective studies across the world to reflect on their work with a larger group of social scientists, graduate students, and journalists—perhaps even to create a documentary film about these historic studies. Available resources were limited, however, so we settled on a much smaller, invitational conference. In the end this proved an advantage, in some ways, because the format afforded an intimate exchange of ideas and life stories that might not have been possible in a larger, more public setting.

Six sources of funding combined to support the meeting. Each of the six foundations or government agencies has made important contributions to the field of life-course studies, and each has benefited from the leadership of at least one key individual who has lent his or her support to this kind of work. Conference funding from the John D. and Catherine T. MacArthur Foundation, the National Institute of Mental Health, and the National Science Foundation were drawn from larger institutional grants to the Henry A. Murray Research Center. We are grateful to Idy Gitelson of the MacArthur Foundation, Lynne Huffman and Emelyne Otey of the National Institute of Mental Health, and Steven Breckler from the National Science Foundation for their support of both the Murray Center and this meeting. We are also grateful to Eric Wanner of the Russell Sage Foundation, Ruby Takanishi of the Foundation for Child Development, and Lonnie Sherrod of the William T. Grant Foundation for their confidence in and support of this work.

We chose fourteen long-term longitudinal studies—which we originally called "landmark studies"—to be represented in the conference and the resulting book, asking participants to prepare papers for presentation at the conference so we could capture their reflections not only in conversations during our time together but also in a book that would reach a wider audience. Among long-term studies of critical importance in their fields, we chose studies that would represent a wide range of disciplines, problems addressed, and approaches to instrumentation and design. We deliberately included both large, quantitative panel studies and more focused, qualitative prospective studies of individual development. All but two of those invited agreed to participate, in spite of their already heavy publishing commitments—an indicator of the group's enthusiasm for the project. We regret that some important studies are not represented here—some because of limitations in our resources and two because the investigators (Jack Block, Byron Egeland, and Alan Sroufe) had particularly intense prior commitments so could not accept our invitation to participate.

For the purposes of identifying studies, we cast a wide net in the fields of psychology, sociology, and education and then used stringent criteria for selection. Our criteria included a long age span, broad scope in terms of the kinds and amounts of information collected on participants, a large sample size, and an impact that extends beyond the original research plan. Five of the twelve studies presented here were started before 1950, and five more had been initiated by 1982. Finally, we looked for samples that included a range of ethnic groups.

Because of funding restraints, we had to limit ourselves to American researchers. This is indeed a serious limitation because some of the most important long-term longitudinal studies have been conducted outside the United States. Since the 1950s, interest in this method has been as evident in Europe as in the United States. Several European institutions for social science research played leadership roles in this movement. For example, in England, the Economic and Social Research Council was established in 1967 to collect and make available data, including longitudinal data, about social economic affairs from university, government, and commercial sources. Two studies with a developmental focus that were supported by the Economic and Social Research Council are the National Survey of Health and Development, which was initiated in 1946, and the National Child Development Study, begun in 1958. Both studies began observing newborns and continued to follow them for many years. In Sweden, David Magnusson launched the Study of Individual Development and Adjustment in 1964 with subjects who were ten, thirteen, and fifteen years old. The youngest cohort was followed for more than twenty-four years (Magnusson 1988). The Berlin Aging Study, initiated more recently (in 1989), focuses on the oldest members of German society, thus presenting a unique view of the end points of development (Baltes and Mayer 1999). Information about more than five hundred longitudinal studies conducted in Europe is available in an inventory published by the European Science Foundation (Schneider and Edelstein 1990).

Additional important long-term studies have been done outside Europe. For example, the Dunedin Multidisciplinary Health and Development Study is a twenty-one-year investigation of a representative birth cohort of infants born in 1972 and 1973 in Dunedin, New Zealand. Perinatal data for 1,139 births were obtained at delivery, and cohort members were reassessed every other year from the ages of five to fifteen and again at eighteen and twenty-one (Silva and Stanton 1996). Longitudinal researchers, at least those working on related issues, form an active international network, sharing information through visits by staff and important international meetings as well as through awareness of one another's published reports. The international connections and influences constitute a fascinating story in themselves. Unfortunately, it is beyond the scope of this book to tell that story.

Each of the studies represented in this book has been a complex and ambitious project undertaken over many years' time. The rich and shifting textures of these and other long-term longitudinal studies result from the dynamic interplay of many factors, some of which play a role only in studies of long duration. Because they track human lives over time, they are complicated by the many contexts in which people's lives are lived—within institutions (schools, families, workplaces, the military), in ongoing and evolving connections with other people, in a world that impinges on them and with which they interact. Mediated by these and other life contexts, demographic shifts and historical trends and events play important roles in shaping their lives, whether or not the studies tracking them explicitly investigate those influences.

However, longitudinal studies are not entirely determined by the nature of the phenomena they are tracking and trying to understand. Paralleling the complexity of people's lives, they also depend on the secular trends in research fashions, tools, funding opportunities and constraints, institutional arrangements, and so forth. The investigators' intellectual histories, theoretical understandings, professional commitments, shifting interests, goals, and motivations, and career concerns and contingencies play significant roles, which are often invisible to consumers of the research. The primary topics of concern and major findings of the studies collected here are widely familiar, but their inner workings have not been explored. To our knowledge, no one has tried before to explicate the complicated patterns of relationships that underlie them, and that is the special contribution of this book.

With this goal in mind, we asked principal investigators, before the conference began, to reflect on their experiences in carrying out their long-term studies, to think about the interplay between the shape and progress of the study and the relationship of this to their professional and personal lives and to the lives of the study participants. We also asked them to consider what they had learned over the course of doing the work, in somewhat broader terms than the usual research paper would capture. We suggested that they might want to comment on their observations about the participants' lives, the changing historical, cul-

tural, and scientific contexts of the work, and theoretical and methodological changes in the field. In addition, we solicited their observations
about the policy effects and implications of the research.

This rather unusual approach to describing their research would, we
hoped, serve two purposes. The first was to document for other social
and behavioral scientists, including young investigators, at least an ap-
proximation of the "inside stories" of these well-known studies—what
circumstances and forces made them possible and determined their
shape and direction. We hoped this documentation would render more
explicit and visible some critical factors that ought to be recognized and
taken into account by researchers collecting or reanalyzing longitudinal
data, interpreting the findings of longitudinal studies, or exploring the
significance of these studies in the landscape of twentieth-century social
and behavioral science.

The second reason for structuring the task as we did was our desire
to explicate some of the many ways in which the knowledge generated
by these studies cannot be separated from the history through which it
was produced. Longitudinal research is not unique in being interpretable only in historical, social, and intellectual context; but studies
that extend over several decades involve an especially complex interplay of shifting contexts, and for this reason they provide vivid examples of the ways in which scientific truths are best understood as context
dependent, partial, and provisional. Conventional modes of reporting
research tend to obscure these complexities, so a different approach is
needed to throw them into relief.

Because of the Murray Research Center's commitment to longitudinal research, its advisory committee includes many distinguished longitudinal and developmental researchers. Some of them joined the
meeting and added insights from their own work to the already rich
mix. We have been able to capture two of these contributions as chapters in this book. Advisory committee members who acted as discus-
sants were John Modell, Janet Giele, Jack Block, Carol Tomlinson-
Keasey, Ellen Bassuk, and Abigail Stewart. Ruby Takanishi from the
Foundation for Child Development, Emelyne Otey from the National
Institute of Mental Health, and Laura Steppe from the *Washington Post*
further enhanced the meeting with their comments from the perspectives of funders and reporters of social science research.

We have organized the fourteen chapters into five sections, based on
some of the central ideas in the task we set for the authors. All of the
chapters take on the same challenge, and several could have been placed
equally well in other sections. The emphasis varies from one chapter to
the next, however, making it possible for us to organize them in a way
that highlights several different aspects of our perspectives on both the
developmental issues and on the nature of longitudinal research.

The two papers in the first section, "Multiple Intersections," look directly at the complex interplay from which these studies emerge and evolve. Janet Giele draws on her long career in life-course developmental theory and research to develop insights that cut across all of the studies in this collection, setting the stage for the chapters that follow. In a sense, Frank Furstenberg's thoughts about his own research were the original impetus for the conference and this book and provide the exemplar for the remaining chapters.

The four papers in the next section, "Lives and Studies in Social Historical Context," emphasize a critical dimension of these investigations: they are studies done during a particular time period of particular people who lived and developed during that period, and not some other, and who must be understood within their historical contexts. These studies were thus doubly shaped by history—tracking lives lived in real time and shaped (both investigators and studies) by the contingencies of their contexts.

The importance of timing—in the lives of the study participants and in the studies themselves—is a central theme of the next four papers. It is well understood that the timing of data collection is extremely important in longitudinal studies. In some studies many years go by between contact with participants, whereas for others successive waves of data collection are more frequent and regular. These decisions about timing are driven partly by scientific and theoretical considerations—for example, by hypotheses about developmental mechanisms that may be operating—but they are also driven by external contingencies. To complicate things further, the timing in individual lives interacts with the timing in studies. The careful or fortuitous conjunction of timing can yield insights that would otherwise have escaped notice.

Lives are lived in complex interplay with others—families, community members, demographic cohorts, and the like. The three papers in the fourth section, "Connecting Lives," highlight, with different approaches, the difference the social context of lives can make. Longitudinal studies are also shaped by the many ways the investigators are connected with others in the field and with institutions, including most notably their employers and their funders. In addition, in studies that follow individuals over several decades, important relationships develop between investigators and study participants, and these relationships affect the studies as well.

Finally, in the last section, "Reflections," John Modell reflects on the unusual and challenging questions these authors have addressed and the answers they give. As a historian and an astute observer of developmental research, Modell brings a broad and long view to the task. Stepping back yet one more level, he places the project of this conference and book into the context of the history of social science research, considering its meaning and importance from that point of view.

It may seem that the people conducting major, well-known longitudinal studies in the United States would know one another. To some extent this is true, but the linkages tend not to extend across discipline and major differences in approach unless there are large areas of shared substantive focus. For this reason, many of the researchers at the conference knew of one another's work in a general way and knew they had been doing long-term studies over the same period of time but had not been acquainted. We hope this book will convey some of the excitement of the meeting, which resulted in discoveries of common ground and common dilemmas and the establishment of new relationships that promise to fill the gaps in the net of interconnections.

Because of the commitment needed to keep a long-term study alive, it is perhaps not surprising that the group we gathered was a passionate lot. In every case, their life's work was an effort to understand a serious social problem, with the explicit aim of contributing to the improvement of people's lives. The investigators were deeply respectful of the study participants, showing a degree of humility in their effort to learn from participants, which is unusual when human beings become the subject of scientific study. Our initial sense that this might be true was one of the reasons we wanted to learn more about the connections among the life course of the investigators, the participants, and the studies.

We chose not to group the papers according to shared content themes, because we wanted to underscore the fact that this book is not meant as a compendium of longitudinal research findings. Even so, it is worth pointing out some themes that cut across several studies, because these themes are intimately related to the investigators' reasons for conducting the studies and the special value this kind of work can have. Perhaps many of the studies focused on lives of disadvantage because of a passion for social justice that moves many of these investigators. Some of the studies began as assessments of interventions designed to address a social problem and, as they proceeded through second and then further follow-ups, shifted to the broader explication of the life course and later life outcomes of people who had had insufficient resources earlier in their lives. Despite their diversity, many of the studies shared a goal of illuminating the experiences and conditions that protect individuals against the potentially devastating effects of disadvantage.

Contrary to some common conceptions of the roots of psychological adaptation, the protective experiences often occur well past early childhood. This is evident, for example, in John Laub and Robert Sampson's efforts to uncover the factors that seem to have a long-term positive impact on the lives of juvenile offenders, especially those factors that lead them away from crime later in life. Through new analyses of archival longitudinal data collected from a group of men in Boston beginning in the 1940s, combined with newly compiled criminal career histories on the men and follow-up interviews with many of them, who were then in their sixties and seventies, Laub and Sampson find that differences in the men's childhood experiences and temperament were not sufficient to predict differential patterns of adult crime. The critical turning points came later, generally in connection with adult roles. Military service was a positive turning point in the lives of many of the men, offering structure, a chance to contribute to society, and educational opportunity. In addition, stable marriages and connections with the workforce were important predictors of desistance from crime.

This finding is echoed across time and place by two other studies that investigated resilience in the face of disadvantage. In a group of children born on the Hawaiian island of Kauai in 1955, thirty years after the samples Laub and Sampson used, Emmy Werner found military service and marriage to a stable partner to represent positive turning points in the lives of many of the boys and girls she followed through conditions of economic hardship, parental substance abuse, and family disruption. Glen Elder's research findings with the Berkeley Guidance Study men who grew up in deprived families during the Depression also mirror these results to a large degree. For these children, higher education, a good marriage, and military service offered effective exits from disadvantaged and risky life situations. Although both Werner and Elder also found some experiences in childhood and adolescence to be predictive of positive adaptation in many ways, all three studies make clear the important lesson that over time, people's lives often take dramatic turns that cannot be predicted from their early patterns. If these studies had ended in adolescence or early adulthood, we would have been left with a misleading and more pessimistic picture of the potential for overcoming early disadvantage.

Long-term data yield a more complex and often more optimistic picture than do "snapshot" surveys or short-term studies. As with medical research that demonstrates the benefits of a drug in the short run only to discover no benefits (or possibly harm) with longer-term longitudinal research, many of the studies described in this volume suggest that long-term effects may be quite different from those one would extrapolate directly from static correlational associations. In addition, and not coincidentally, longer-term studies show many common assumptions to be incorrect. When these incorrect assumptions become widespread myths, they can influence social policy to the detriment of the populations in question. Three studies with poor African American samples illustrate this point.

In 1959, David Weikart was interested in changing the practices of education to enable disadvantaged children to attain greater personal, social, and economic success. He was new to a segregated school system, in which students in the African American school scored in the tenth percentile or below while students in a white school across town invariably scored in the ninetieth percentile or higher on standardized achievement tests. Using ideas that were novel at the time, Weikart started a broadly based preschool intervention project for the disadvantaged African American children, with the goal of improving their intellectual and academic abilities. The prevailing view at the time was that three- and four-year-olds were not mature enough to benefit from a school-based program and that disadvantaged children, in particular, would be unable to handle any program of this kind.

Against this backdrop, the High/Scope Perry Preschool Project was designed and launched. At the end of two years, the outcome was an extraordinary increase in children's IQ. Later, however, at the end of early elementary school, the intervention effects on IQ had disappeared. If the study had ended at this point, the conclusion would have been that the program had not been able to provide any lasting advantage. The study did not end, however, and by the third grade achievement test scores and classroom behavior ratings were significantly higher for the program group than for the control group, a difference that remains decades later. This finding has been the basis of critical policy decisions to invest in the early education of disadvantaged children, which results in dramatic cost savings in the long run owing to a reduction in serious problems, such as criminal behavior later in life.

Results of Frank Furstenberg's long-term study of teen mothers also run counter to common expectations of dire outcomes. Teen mothers and their children have long been considered simultaneously at risk for and the cause of a continuing, multigenerational cycle of poverty. In the 1960s, Furstenberg became involved in a service program in Baltimore that was designed to support mothers and children by providing schooling, counseling, and contraceptive services—controversial at the time because they were thought to encourage childbearing outside of marriage.

Seventeen years later, the mothers were reinterviewed, and their children were interviewed at about the same age their mothers had been at the beginning of the study. Contrary to the predictions of popular myth, only a minority of the mothers remained on welfare. Most had returned to school and become self-supporting, and most were deeply committed to their children's well-being. Furthermore, most had finished high school or received a certificate of General Educational Development (GED), and only one-third of the daughters had become teen parents themselves.

Despite this general picture of outcomes for teen mothers that are less uniformly disastrous than we have been led to expect, there is still great variation, and some do much better than others. To understand why this is so, it is important to look not only at the effects of single predictors in isolation from one another but also at the interactions among the predictors. In her study of Harlem teenagers born in the 1950s, Ann Brunswick found that drug use helps to explain which teen mothers become self-supporting and which do not. Her study began in 1968 as a cross-sectional survey of a representative sample of thirteen- to seventeen-year-olds from Harlem designed to provide a comprehensive description of health problems and health care needs in an underserved teen population. Five years later, the study became longitudinal as Brunswick recontacted the sample in an effort to understand the health consequences of substance use. She continued to reassess the sample; by 1993, participants were in their late thirties. Consistent with Furstenberg's descriptions of the outcomes of teen motherhood for African American inner-city adolescents, Brunswick found that neither early childbearing alone nor drug use alone had significant negative consequences for later education, employment, or health. It was the combination of teen pregnancy and substance abuse that predicted negative consequences for the women in her study.

Methods for doing research about human lives have changed dramatically since the early 1900s. The Terman and Oakland and Berkeley studies were among the earliest studies of child development to be conducted in the United States. Their goals were modest, and samples were limited to residents of California. Travel options limited the sampling frames, as did available technologies for communicating with participants. Measures were scarce, and duplicating was arduous. Changes in technology during the twentieth century expanded the research arena. Theoretical advances in research design, sampling, and statistical analysis have altered our understanding of the validity and generalizability of findings and how best to approach questions of causality. Finally, widespread availability of high-speed computers and more complex statistical models such as structural equation and hierarchical models have allowed us to develop and test more complex models of human development and the contexts in which development occurs.

As interest in studying change or growth over time or in antecedent-consequent relationships grew, new statistical methods were needed. Similarly, particularly in schooling research, the variability among schools and students needed to be disentangled, and this required models that could manage the multiple levels of data and effect. Beginning in the 1970s, along with rapid developments in computer technology, statistical software began to appear that could begin to address some of these questions. Event-history analysis, structural modeling, sequence analysis, and, a little later, hierarchical modeling became available to researchers; most of these required maximum likelihood estimation and iterative routines that are not practicable without high-speed, capacious computers. This in turn allowed us to increase the complexity of the questions that could be addressed empirically and thus affected our theoretical models.

The effects of changing technology were probably most dramatic in the 1960s. Policy concerns led the government to fund a series of large-scale longitudinal studies in the 1960s and 1970s that continue to the present, such as the Panel Study of Income Dynamics (PSID), the National Longitudinal Survey (NLS), and the National Longitudinal Survey of Youth (NLSY). These were nationally representative samples intended to tell us something about the entire U.S. population. Samples were constructed in the most scientific ways known at the time. Computers were used to manage and analyze the very large (for the time) volumes of data and information. Travel and long-distance communication had improved tremendously since the 1920s, facilitating greater ease of data collection. The enterprise of conducting research in the social sciences saw a substantial shift in scope, in part as a result of these inventions and advances. They also permitted the extensions of these studies into long-term projects of which we are the benefactors today.

In his paper, Greg Duncan discusses the PSID, and Frank Mott's chapter is based on his many years' experience with the NLS, the NLSY, and the newer Children of the NLSY. With thousands of respondents, these panel studies have permitted researchers to chart the life courses of representative cohorts of adults as they move from early to later adulthood. Although lacking the rich detail of some of the smaller studies, these larger studies have allowed researchers to investigate a wide array of social and economic phenomena, such as human capital formation and its impact on later earnings. These studies have also prompted the development of innovative statistical modeling techniques that have greatly advanced our understanding of causal processes and the interaction and the timing of events that shape economic, social, and psychological careers. Moreover, these large-scale studies have provided an opportunity for a great number of social scientists to have access to longitudinal data sets through a number of data banks that offer national sample survey data for secondary analysis.

Several papers in this book illustrate how productive it can be to mine longitudinal data collected by other investigators. Elder, Vaillant, and Laub and Sampson have all based their research on existing archives. Many longitudinal studies undergo shifts in personnel over the course of their multidecade lifetimes, and all longitudinal investigators reanalyze data collected at earlier times by their younger, less experienced selves, if not by others. In this sense, secondary and primary analyses in longitudinal research are less different than they may seem and confront many of the same challenges. Insofar as use of archival data throws some of these challenges into bolder relief, it can help us better understand the nature of any study that builds on data collected many years earlier. Similarly, we hope that by offering readers the "inside stories" of twelve major studies collected here, we will make it easier for investigators of the twenty-first century to make new sense of these twentieth-century data.

References

Baltes, Paul B., and Karl U. Mayer. 1999. *The Berlin Aging Study: Aging from Seventy to One Hundred.* Cambridge: Cambridge University Press.

Magnusson, David. 1988. *Individual Development from an Interactional Perspective: A Longitudinal Study.* Hillsdale, N.J.: Lawrence Erlbaum Associates.

Schneider, Wolfgang, and Wolfgang Edelstein. 1990. *Inventory of European Longitudinal Studies in the Behavioural and Medical Sciences.* Munich: European Science Foundation.

Silva, Phil A., and Warren R. Stanton, eds. 1996. *From Child to Adult: The Dunedin Multidisciplinary Health and Development Study.* Auckland: Oxford University Press.

Chapter 1

Longitudinal Studies and Life-Course Research: Innovations, Investigators, and Policy Ideas

JANET ZOLLINGER GIELE

THE SIGNIFICANT studies of the life course that are represented in this volume can be seen as markers of a general intellectual movement that took place in developmental psychology, sociology, and history after World War II. This new perspective was apparent in four key trends. First, development of the individual began to be more widely understood as resulting from a combination of ontogenetic unfolding of the organism and socializing influences from the environment (Brim and Kagan 1980). Second, the potential for change in a person's life was increasingly seen as extending across the whole life span, from childhood and adolescence into adulthood and old age (Brim and Wheeler 1966). Third, understanding of the possible dimensions of growth and development (intelligence, attachment, achievement, self-concept, and so on) became at once more complex and specialized—and more integrated—and scholars began to see interconnections across these different domains within the life course and within the historical and cultural context (Baltes 1983). Finally, new longitudinal methods, group comparisons, and analytic strategies emerged that made it possible to distinguish between continuity and change, to assess the magnitude of the change, and to sort out the causal factors involved (Baltes, Lindenberger, and Staredinger 1998; Colby 1998).

Although all of these improvements built on long-standing principles of psychology and other social sciences, the new synthesis spelled out four key explanatory elements that were interconnected in a new

15

and more encompassing framework for understanding the shape of the individual life course: namely, the location of the person in time and place, that person's membership in a surrounding family and community, the agency and actions of the individual, and the timing and patterning of the person's major life events and their relationship to the timing of events in the larger community and society (Elder 1998; Giele and Elder 1998).

Against this conceptual backdrop, the accounts in this volume invite reflection that is guided by the very life-course perspective that they embody. For example, how do the studies presented here illustrate these four key conceptual elements of the life-span framework—location, membership, agency, and timing? What do these authors reveal about the ways in which their own personal background, social location, and biographical history have influenced the focus and design of their studies? Is there any evidence of a link between their motivation and ideals and the practical use and policy purposes that they envisioned for their research? In posing these questions, I am looking for links between the lives of the investigators and the shape of their craft that I believe a life-span perspective leads us to expect but which up to now have been only implicit in the stories told here.

To formulate these questions in this way, I have relied heavily on the sociology of knowledge and the pioneering contributions of Thomas Kuhn (1962), in his study of scientific revolutions, and Robert Merton (1957), in his demonstration of the connections between the social origins of scientists and the nature of their scientific inventions. The sociology of knowledge is useful, first, for understanding the scientific revolution by which the investigators moved beyond older forms of inquiry and, second, for discerning the links between the investigators' lives and the research, programs, and policies that grew out of that research. The lives of the investigators and of their projects thus provide a window on the gradual intellectual revolution that has occurred over the past half century in the study of lives and in the use of that knowledge to serve larger social ends.

Construction of the Life-Course Perspective

In his study of scientific revolutions, Thomas Kuhn (1962) describes repeated instances of a reigning theory that is eventually deposed by discrepant findings that do not fit the theory. Eventually a new paradigm develops that better accounts for the anomalous findings. Following World War II, something similar to this happened in the behavioral sciences with respect to the understanding of human development. The nature of the anomalies and their resolution depended, however, on the discipline (Colby 1998). Psychologists, for their part, began to note that trajectories of growth and development could vary considerably depending on the social location or ethnic identity of the individual (Kagan 1980). Sociologists, on the other hand, began to question the tendency of their discipline to give greater weight to social context and behavior typical of the average person rather than to dynamic processes within the individual case (Mishler 1996). The upshot was that behavioral scientists interested in the study of lives began to look beyond disciplinary boundaries to a larger organizing scheme for explaining continuity and change and for describing the integration of ontogenetic and cultural change. According to Paul Baltes (1983, 99) the result was the study of cohort effects and intergenerational differences in a longitudinal framework that permitted observation of "at least two streams of interactive changing systems: the individual and the society broadly defined."

The conceptual and methodological challenge in observing the interaction of these two systems was to find a way to follow the individual over time and at the same time provide a means of disentangling the effects of the age-related development of the individual, the influence of historical period, and the interaction with a particular set of social institutions and groups at any given time of life. Longitudinal methods and the large panel surveys provided a way of capturing a snapshot of concurrent events at a single point while also making it possible to link a series of these snapshots of the same individual and his or her surrounding circumstances over time. Such a technique addressed both Jerome Kagan's point that more attention needs to be paid to the social context and Elliot Mishler's observation that it is critical to follow the dynamics of change as it occurs in individual cases, not just in aggregate cross sections.

According to Merton, the sociology of knowledge flourishes in a climate of value diversity in which there has been a loss of a common cultural consensus. It distrusts simple answers and searches for underlying meaning. Using this framework to analyze the life-course perspective, such questions can be asked about the studies presented in this volume: Why were the seeds of the life-span perspective planted in the 1950s and 1960s, when many of these important longitudinal studies originated? Why were the objects of study such a wide array of socially diverse groups—people of different races, social classes, and ages? What was the significance of their being followed over time in many dimensions of their lives, such as school success, income and poverty, drug use, and prosocial or antisocial behavior?

It seems reasonable to suggest that prevailing social conditions helped to shape the nature of these research inquiries. For example, many of the large longitudinal studies reported in this volume originated in a climate of social ferment and profound concern for racial and economic justice, changes in the roles of youth and women, and the inexorable movement toward an even more urban and individualistic society.

In their overview of change in major academic disciplines since 1950, Thomas Bender and Carl Schorske observe that a key challenge was the growing diversity of the value base of American society following World War II. Although some fields like economics and philosophy took a positivistic turn, others, like English and American studies, met the challenge by attempting to give voice to many different cultural perspectives and to find "a new, nonexclusionist commonality, . . . a task in which, consciously or otherwise, all America is engaged" (Bender and Schorske 1997, 326). In analogous fashion, perhaps it can be said that the life-course perspective came out of value diversity both in the relevant academic disciplines and in the larger society. Psychology, sociology, history, and economics accorded the individual and the social context different weight in the process of human development and social change. In addition, cultural ferment and increasing diversity in American society as a whole demanded a new, more comprehensive analytic framework for understanding the course of human lives.

How did the four key elements of a life-span perspective provide the potential for a common theoretical outlook that could bridge academic disciplines as well as cultural variation within American society? Attention to historical and cultural location in time and place revealed both the importance of environmental factors and the diversity within American culture as well as the influence of changing historical conditions over time. Consideration of membership and participation in particular social networks and institutional settings was another way of recognizing the impact of apparent differences by age, race, gender, and family background on the life and development of the individual. The concept of agency, on the other hand, accorded a key place to the choices, decisions, adaptations, and goals of the individual and provided an intellectual foundation for explaining innovation and protests like those that erupted in the social movements of the 1960s. Finally, observation of the timing of events captured the specific points at which the interaction of historical period, social networks, and individual action occurred and helped make sense of the departure from tradition that was suddenly being experienced after a period of postwar calm.

Location in Time and Place

Paul Baltes (1983), along with many other scholars of the aging process, has noted that those life experiences that occur in a particular historical period, such as military service or unemployment, are especially important for shaping adult behavior and development. Certainly such major historical events as the civil rights movement or President Lyndon Johnson's War on Poverty had a profound influence on the investigators' own choice of their subject matter and also legitimated decisions by government agencies and private foundations to fund their studies. Thus, for example, David Weikart's study of the Perry Preschool in Ypsilanti, Michigan, began in an atmosphere of growing public concern about racial inequality and efforts to redress unequal educational opportunities for children of color. The Panel Study of Income Dynamics was inaugurated in the wake of the War on Poverty to follow the economic fortunes of a representative group of five thousand families.

Recognition of the importance of historical and cultural location also helped spur methodological innovation. If a person's historical and cultural location is a decisive factor in his or her being at risk or having an opportunity to succeed, it is important to compare different groups in ways that will reveal the effects of historical period or cultural ideals. Cultural effects can be studied by comparing two different racial or ethnic groups of similar chronological age during the same historical period. Historical or period effects show up in the differential life experience of different cohorts who are compared when they are at similar ages. Ann Brunswick, for example, found that a much higher proportion of Harlem teenagers born in 1952 had used heroin (28 percent) than those born only five years later (3 percent), when drug enforcement policies and the choice of drugs had changed.

Membership in Social Networks and Institutions

Orville Brim and Jerome Kagan (1980, 2) contend that the dominant Western view of human ontogeny is of a fairly unvarying sequence of development. As they point out, however, the studies of middle-aged and older people indicate that personality and behavior are more malleable than most people think. The longitudinal studies keep this an open question by following individuals over time and at the same time noting the shifts in the surrounding social context. For example, as Arland Thornton surveyed Detroit families over several decades by interviewing mothers about childbearing, household membership, and other related matters, he discovered that family norms were changing. Not everyone followed the time-honored pattern of courtship, marriage, parenting, empty nest, and retirement. There was instead a significant amount of divorce, remarriage, childbearing out of wedlock, cohabitation, and moving in and out.

Age and gender roles were also changing rapidly during the 1960s and 1970s, and Herbert Parnes and Frank Mott's National Longitudinal Surveys of mature women (aged thirty to forty-four) and young women (aged fourteen to twenty-four), begun in the late 1960s, were set up precisely to document the lives of those at the leading edge of women's massive movement into the labor force. At the micro level, household composition and detailed educational and employment histories were also to be observed because they contained variables that could shift the life course of the individual in a number of possible directions.

Investigations of less traditional populations frequently entailed new measures, new kinds of data, and new ways of collecting data that took various social networks into account. Way ahead of her time, Brunswick used age and gender matching of her interviewers with her respondents. Robert and Beverley Cairns made a great effort to be accepted in the community and the school where their studies were going forward to retain the very youngsters they were most concerned about. Frank Furstenberg took on a quite nontraditional sample of teenage unmarried mothers in inner-city Baltimore and learned how to win their trust, interviewed them, and returned over the next couple of decades to question not only the original sample but their daughters and male partners as well.

Human Agency

Yet even in the face of these larger cultural and social forces and the influence of their families and friends, the investigators using a life-span perspective understood that individuals are not simply automatons totally at the mercy of either their heredity or their environment. Rather they are actors or agents whose goal-oriented behavior is part of the cause of the behaviors to be explained (Abbott 1992; Jessor 1996; Mishler 1996). Given the right conditions, it seemed that the self has considerable capacity to change the direction of the life course and to dampen the effects of early development and early social relations.

In his High/Scope Perry Preschool Project, Weikart found that the right kind of early education could raise IQ and school performance of black children who had always scored poorly. An individual trait such as intelligence, then, is not entirely stable but may be mutable. Emmy Werner discovered in her longitudinal study of children in Kauai that early intervention worked with a significant number of children who were at risk for alcoholism, poverty, mental illness, or social dysfunction. A number would "recover" and lead happy and productive lives when given the right kind of help and support along the way. In similar fashion, Glen Elder (1974) found that the children of the Great Depression who came from poor families were not necessarily fated to remain poor but, under certain conditions (such as war service and access to the GI bill), could become upwardly mobile.

Timing of Events

Although the contextual and developmental aspects of the life-course perspective were already familiar to social and behavioral scientists, it probably is safe to say that its pivotal attention to timing was much less so. Yet timing of events was the common denominator by which to record interaction of the individual's historical and cultural location, social membership, and personal decisions and choices. Dates could simultaneously represent a historical period, a duration of time, the nature of events in a specific domain such as marriage or employment, or the chronological age of the person experiencing those events.

Because they all shared in some form of longitudinal design, the studies in this volume were able to collect (or, in the case of the archival studies, to reorganize) date-marked information for individual cases over time in such fashion that it became possible to make observations about the overall amount of change or stability and the impact of timing on life-course outcomes. At the outset of studies like the Panel Study of Income Dynamics, there was surprise at the amount of dynamism and turmoil between one survey wave and the next. Greg Duncan reports that such evidence of continuous change ran entirely counter to the reigning economic theories of the 1960s. Arland Thornton makes similar observations on American families, and one can imagine the difficulties such a booming, buzzing confusion would give to the neat functionalist theories of sociologists (for example, Parsons and Bales 1955) who had explained the traditional family division of labor by age and sex as more or less inevitable and necessary.

To confidently make any observations that translated into larger generalizations about human behavior, however, it became necessary to devote enormous energy to the preservation of balance in the sample being studied and to be thoughtful about the timing variable as it entered into the research process itself. The biggest challenge was to follow up on and retain respondents and to make sure that the sample maintained its representativeness. For example, the Intergenerational Panel Study of Parents and Children, reported on here by Arland Thornton, Ronald Freedman, and William Axinn, went to great lengths to follow respondents across state borders, collect names of persons who would know where the respondent could be found, and so on. The Cairnses similarly emphasized the crucial importance of trying to keep the hardest-to-retain aggressive youths in the sample so that the findings could be generalized appropriately to the group of greatest concern. All kinds of technical improvements resulted: telephone callbacks, intensive training methods, the maintenance of a loyal and committed staff, streamlined instruments, and the like.

The timing variable also created its own challenges. How could events be best recorded? For Elder and for John Laub and Robert Sampson, the first steps were to recast the existing data in a meaningful way to discover patterns related to family or work histories or delinquent careers. When they did so, all sorts of possible interconnections began to emerge between major life events, career histories, and different life-course outcomes.

Another methodological question related to timing was whether the timing of data collection made any difference. Doris Entwisle found that poor children's test scores were lower at the end of the summer, when their social resources were fewer, but were virtually equal to the test scores of middle-class children during the school year, when school made their learning opportunities more nearly equal. Entwisle also opened up other issues in the treatment of time, such as differences between institutional clocks of schools and employers and individual timetables of social or biological development. These issues not only pose challenges for data collection and measurement, they also suggest a theoretical insight to Entwisle: that the persons whose social and individual clocks were at variance were also those at greatest risk of difficulty later in life.

Social Characteristics of the Investigators

In describing the way the sociology of knowledge is practiced, Merton (1957, 487) notes that one of its goals is "to seek out the perspectives of scholars and relate these to the framework of experience and interests contributed by their respective social positions." The biographical accounts in this volume give us only a partial glimpse of the full persons who mounted these various important longitudinal studies, but they are nonetheless valuable subjective reports by the investigators themselves on what they see as connections between their backgrounds and experience and the studies in which they engaged. Each of these stories illustrates a connection between the salient events of a particular time and place and the moment in the lives of the investigators when they turned their attention to the current issues that would become the central focus of their research careers. To impose some order on these partial and sometimes fragmentary accounts, I have used the four main elements of the life-course perspective to suggest that, across the group as a whole, there is an orderly and congruent pattern in the connections between the investigators' lives and their research.

Location in Time and Place

Many of these landmark longitudinal studies were begun in the turbulent 1960s by a generation of investigators, born between 1930 and 1950, who were just launching their careers. The purpose of many of their studies was to understand a new social phenomenon that was of widespread concern. We repeatedly observe a distinct confluence between the events of the period and the investigators' need to identify an interesting and promising topic for research. Thus, for example, David Weikart launched his study of early intervention in a black elementary school in Michigan in the 1950s just after the Rosa Parks incident and the Montgomery bus boycott but before the civil rights movement had yet begun.

Frank Furstenberg, fresh from graduate school at Columbia, went to Baltimore, where he was offered the opportunity to conduct a study of teenage mothers. The opportunity occurred just as the Moynihan Report (see Rainwater and Yancey 1967) appeared, with its controversial explanation of an especially high incidence of unmarried motherhood in African American families. As the topic of teenage pregnancy gradually evolved into a growing concern for an economy that was inhospitable to urban black males, Furstenberg took this shift into account in his research and reaped the benefits of rising interest in what had originally been an unorthodox and risky set of topics for sociological research.

Glen Elder, born during the Great Depression when his mother lost her job as a teacher and his father began a medical career, went to his first job at Berkeley in the 1960s to work for the Institute for Human Development. He found the world changing all around him. There was a massive entry of women into the labor force, the country was involved in the Vietnam War, and many other patterns of work and family life were being transformed. In this atmosphere of change and turmoil he discovered that the concept of the life cycle was inadequate, that career was too unitary a concept to fit existing frameworks, and that he needed a new way to think about the lives of the Oakland and Berkeley children beyond that provided by the old developmental models. In the process Elder became one of the key architects and spokesmen for the new life-course perspective.

Ann Brunswick was living and working in New York with her two teenage daughters, twelve and fifteen years old, when she undertook her study of drug use in Harlem in the 1960s. Although her account does not address just how she came to work on this topic, we can surmise that it had some personal relevance. She admits to using her daughters as "guinea pigs" for developing her interview items on health, self-esteem, personal efficacy, and task orientation.

Each of these stories illustrates the sociological significance of location in time and place. They trace the connection between the salient events of the 1960s, with all its social ferment, and the moment in the lives of the investigators when they turned their attention to the current issues that would become the central focus of their research careers.

Academic Institutions, Social Networks, and Family Background

All of these investigators were original and pioneering in their topics and initial insights, but they did not embark on their enterprises entirely alone. Rather, to the extent that each has told us the story, they appear to have been accompanied by what Robert Kahn and Toni Antonucci (1980) have termed a "social convoy" that provided social support and gave meaning to the enterprise. In addition, they learned how to stretch the institutions of academic research to advance their innovative studies.

For Weikart, working among the skeptical administrators of the Ypsilanti schools, the "social convoy" was made up of three reform-minded principals in his district, his loyal research staff, and strong ties to graduate school at the University of Michigan and his mentors there, who helped him persevere against self-doubt and resistance. The head of the Spencer Foundation later provided financial support and a fledgling legitimacy to the project.

In recounting his recourse to institutional precedent, Furstenberg harkens back to his Columbia training in sociology and recalls the work of Richard Cloward and Lloyd Ohlin (1960) on deviance and that of William J. Goode (1960) on illegitimacy in the Caribbean. Closer to home, he reports, it was his mother, a social worker, who helped him to get involved in the Sinai Hospital study of pregnant teenagers, not only because of her professional contacts but also because of her professional appreciation of the topic itself. Furstenberg also acknowledges his debt to well-known principals in the life-course field, such as Orville G. "Bert" Brim, at that time president of the Russell Sage Foundation and later president of the Foundation for Child Development. Brim, like Paul Baltes, Matilda White Riley, and Glen Elder, had long been involved in the research committees of the Social Science Research Council and later, like many of them, with the various research networks on human development of the MacArthur Foundation. Such connections to a behind-the-scenes research community helped to foster the new life-course perspective as well as to ensure that its pioneers would stay at the leading edge of the social science community.

In the mid-1970s, analogous institutions and personal ties supported the work of the new panel studies. Greg Duncan, Arland Thornton, and Frank Mott began their careers, respectively, as directors of the Panel Study of Income Dynamics, the Intergenerational Panel Study of Parents and Children, and the National Longitudinal Surveys. Duncan followed in the footsteps of James N. Morgan, the economist who in the 1960s launched the Five Thousand Family Study (later known as the Panel Study of Income Dynamics), and thereby found himself at the University of Michigan's Survey Research Center with a whole team of innovative people from a wide variety of disciplines. Similarly, Thornton took over the Detroit-based Intergenerational Panel Study from Ronald Freedman and not only benefited from the ongoing continuity of a devoted research staff but also helped to foster its continuance and spectacular success with excellent sample retention and continued high response rates over a thirty-year period.

Also in the 1970s, Frank Mott was trained as a demographer and worked in government before assuming direction of the National Longitudinal Surveys begun in the previous decade. The older and younger male cohorts of the surveys were eventually dropped, but surveys of mature women continued into the 1990s, and the surveys of youth, begun in the 1970s, continue to this day. In each of these cases it was not only staff who provided a network of social support but also a grand intellectual convoy of economists, sociologists, and demographers all over the country who intensively used the National Longitudinal Survey data and made its continuation indispensable to the progress of empirical and policy-oriented social science.

A dramatic variation on the social convoy theme is the story of Sheldon and Eleanor Glueck and their quite brilliant departure from the conventional social science of the 1930s and 1940s in launching their pioneering studies of juvenile delinquents. Laub and Sampson tell us little about their own biographies in relation to reanalyzing the Gluecks' data, but they give us a wonderfully illuminating account of the Gluecks themselves. It is a painful story of a pair of creative Jewish scholars excluded from the Harvard establishment. Sheldon Glueck, a lawyer with a doctorate in social ethics, finally secured a professorship at Harvard Law School, but his wife, Eleanor, with a doctorate in education, never held a title above research associate. They were excluded from the Harvard sociology department and its successor, the Department of Social Relations. Fortunately, they found friendship and support from renowned lawyer Felix Frankfurter at Harvard Law School and psychologists William Healey and Augusta F. Bonner at the Judge Baker Guidance Center, with its working ties to Harvard Medical School and Boston's psychiatric community. As Everett Stonequist (1961) found in the case of persons on the margins of groups who were sometimes especially original in their approach, the Gluecks were perhaps able to take such a fresh approach to their topic because they were not in the center of the intellectual establishment. The social support they did have enabled them to move forward nonetheless.

Personal Agency, Crossing Boundaries, and a Social Ethic

A deeper analysis of the personal goals and values of these pioneer investigators would ideally be based on a systematic set of qualitative interviews. In their absence, however, we can put together bits and pieces from the accounts in their chapters here and from informal knowledge of the authors' backgrounds and careers. Even on such a sketchy basis as that, it is possible to see a connection between the investigators' values and motives and the topics of their research. Two themes stand out:

a desire to help others by using their scientific expertise and a willingness to cross intellectual boundaries and barriers in search of truth.

Bob and Beverley Cairns began their professional lives with a particular interest in the psychology of education and the kind of teaching that would help aggressive kids. They built on Bob's experience as a researcher and Beverley's as a teacher to construct their studies of adolescents at risk and used their knowledge of psychology and teaching to develop practical interventions that would have a beneficial effect. Greg Duncan began his career as an economist wanting to learn how to alleviate poverty. After an undergraduate exchange in which he participated in a cooperative work project among poor people in Central America, he went to the University of Michigan for graduate work in economics with the idea that it would help him serve that end. He delved through the records of families in the Panel Study of Income Dynamics to learn what specific events or programs had helped them climb out of poverty. Frank Furstenberg concedes several times in his story that he tried to get away from the topic of teenage pregnancy but kept being pulled back to it because it was so compelling. From what he tells us, we gather that something about his upbringing and his mother's profession as a social worker made this topic important to him and made him comfortable working in a social service setting.

David Weikart, born in Youngstown, Ohio, a Methodist who went to Oberlin College, tells us explicitly that he wanted to do something that would work against social and racial inequality, but in a theoretically informed and scientific way. Like Furstenberg's mother, Weikart's parents were social workers, and his mother later became a teacher. He links his willingness to take up his unorthodox research to several kinds of past experience. The exchanges at home around the dinner table with his parents' wide range of friends made him comfortable with all kinds of people. Military service in the Korean War, he notes, taught him to take a "disciplined approach" to solving problems (which, judging from his attention to controls in his study, we might well understand to mean a "scientific approach").

The theme of being able to cross intellectual boundaries reminds us again of the creativity that Stonequist (1961) associates with the "marginal man." Just as the person who is marginalized by established social networks may thereby be enabled to make unorthodox observations and discoveries, so too the person who feels at ease in crossing intellectual boundaries and academic disciplines may be aided in the process of creative and innovative thinking.

Several of our authors crossed intellectual, disciplinary, or cultural boundaries in one way or another, which may have spurred their creativity and originality. Doris Entwisle started out in mathematics and was an assistant to the eminent statistician Frederick Mosteller at Harvard, then proceeded to Johns Hopkins, getting a sociology degree and working in the 1960s and 1970s with James Coleman on his famous study of American public schools (Coleman 1966). Entwisle's penetrating ability to reframe questions and findings evidently helped her to see not only that testing children in the summer rather than the winter makes a difference in the findings (showing that children from lower socioeconomic backgrounds did less well in summer) but also that the findings should be interpreted according to her original insight about social resources (that they remain "on" during the summer for middle-class kids but are turned "off" for poor kids).

The Gluecks brought together expertise from law, education, psychiatry, sociology, and criminology. Their eclecticism enabled them to devise an ingenious study comparing social background data on juvenile delinquents with their nondelinquent peers matched by age, neighborhood, and ethnicity. In addition they compared the records on these boys kept by schools, social service agencies, and the courts. Rather than being confined to the techniques and thought patterns of only one discipline or institutional setting, Sheldon and Eleanor Glueck were thus able to transcend professional and institutional boundaries to understand how the boys experienced all these worlds as interconnected.

Emmy Werner not only crossed intellectual boundaries between mental health, psychology, and education, she also literally crossed national and cultural boundaries, leaving her native Germany shortly after World War II and emigrating to the United States, where she lived first in Minnesota and then in California. Two strong themes in her work are most likely the result of this personal history: First, she reveals an abiding interest in recovery and resilience. Not only does she find it; she has reason to believe in it, given her own origins in a war-torn country. Second, her chapter, of all those in this volume, shows the greatest explicit international concern. Not satisfied to stay within the comfortable bounds of her adopted country, she keeps pressing ever outward to help poor and sick children in the rest of the world.

Timing: Opportunity, Coincidence, and Continuity

At last we come to what often seems an undetermined or accidental feature of the life course that also affects invention and prominence. This is the timing of events—what seems to be pure coincidence between events in an investigator's life and opportunities or barriers in the larger world of social science research. When things go well, as in the case of the studies represented here, the results are seen in the efficient staffing of projects, the successful launching of careers, and the maintenance of quality and continuity in longitudinal designs.

One of the most striking themes in many of these accounts is the good fortune that can result from joining or beginning a major longitudinal study. With the right match one can find enough work to last a lifetime, and indeed a number of the investigators included here have had careers that are almost coterminous with the studies they have managed. This is especially true for studies begun when the researchers were relatively young, like Weikart's preschool project in 1957, Brunswick's study of adolescent drug use in Harlem in the 1950s, the Cairnses' follow-up study of aggressive adolescents in several communities, Werner's tracking of the Kauai children, Entwisle's study of twenty Baltimore elementary schools, and Furstenberg's work on teenage pregnancy.

A similar observation can be made about those who took charge of an ongoing study at the beginning of their careers. By the 1970s, George Vaillant had revived the importance of the Grant Study of Human Development, a health study of Harvard alumni begun in the 1940s. Glen Elder came to the Berkeley and Oakland children of the Depression in the 1960s and wrote the best-known work about them in 1974. Greg Duncan came to the Panel Study of Income Dynamics as a graduate student in the 1970s and eventually became its director. Also in the 1970s, Arland Thornton became the director of the Intergenerational Panel Study, and Frank Mott took over the National Longitudinal Surveys. John Laub and Robert Sampson, although they modestly keep their own stories in the shadow while focusing on the Gluecks, have almost single-handedly saved the Gluecks' data from oblivion and at the same time used their creative reconstruction and analysis of the data to build their own careers in criminology and sociology, respectively. Although it has been said that "a 'ten-year' study does not a 'tenure' study make" (because it will not be ready in time), most of these longitudinal studies have helped establish their investigators' careers.

An outstanding longitudinal study can launch the career of the investigator, but it can also create obstacles that are indirectly related to its long time span. These challenges include preserving the data, keeping the study going, updating the content appropriately, getting grant support, maintaining the records and updating the files, and finding another investigator who will take up the baton when the first retires. Preserving existing data is the first requirement. Vaillant tells of how he helped ensure that both the Grant study of Harvard men and the Gluecks' data on delinquency were preserved at Radcliffe's Murray Research Center— though it appears from his story to have been a close call. If there had been no such knowledgeable person to come to the rescue, the records could have been lost or destroyed.

Once a study is converted into an ongoing enterprise by restoring old records or instituting a second wave of a new study, it becomes necessary to maintain the records and update the files. The principal investigator, as Ann Brunswick testifies, is likely to be the only one who knows where everything is and how it all fits together. Furthermore, recording tasks involve not only paper records but also tapes and electronic files that have to be updated from punched cards to tapes to compact disks, with all the attendant puzzles related to obsolescence of succeeding generations of hardware and software.

Then there is the question of how to keep the study timely. Thornton and Furstenberg add the children of their original samples and update the questions and content. Brunswick moves from the study of drug use to the study of human immunodeficiency virus (HIV). Duncan migrates from a focus on work and family income to issues of child development and the role of poverty. Elder sees the children of the Great Depression age and then studies parallel questions concerning hardship in the Iowa farm sample and military service in the males of the Terman study.

Finally, there is the question of a successor. Who will take over the study? How does an investigator groom an heir? Will the study continue? Entwisle provides an inside picture of the timing of the Baltimore Beginning School Study and the point at which she found a successor in the person of Karl Alexander. Alexander studied with Elder at the University of North Carolina. Doctoral degree in hand, he then went to Baltimore, where he served as an apprentice on Entwisle's project; he published, took more responsibility, got tenure, and finally "made partner." For a number of other investigators, however, the challenge of finding a successor appears to be still unresolved. The issue is one that will undoubtedly become more visible with the aging of the life-course field as well as of its pioneers.

Connections to Social Policy

The longitudinal studies considered here, beginning as many of them did in the 1950s and the 1960s, not only helped American society cope with its new awareness of cultural diversity, they also held out the possibility of using the social sciences in ways that might help solve social problems. In fact, the organizers of the conference, recognizing the potential relevance of the landmark studies for addressing important questions in child rearing and education, asked the contributors to comment on possible applications of their studies to policy questions.

My purpose here is to suggest that the potential policy relevance of these studies does not occur entirely after the fact but is inherent in the very nature of the studies from their inception up to the present. As is clear from the biographical accounts, the values and social consciousness of the investigators were an integral part of the design and purpose of their studies. Apart from the motivation and intentions of the investigators, however, the very nature of the longitudinal studies, in examining how previous experience is linked to outcome, makes it possible to suggest how the direction of the life course is changed for better or for worse by experience over time. The logic in and of itself suggests that something can be done, that change is possible.

When the earliest of these longitudinal studies first came into the world, however, the culture of the social sciences was by and large positivistic and "value free." In anthropology and sociology, the cultural relativism of Ruth Benedict and Margaret Mead had made large inroads. Sociologists in the leading departments at Columbia, Harvard, and the University of Chicago tended to focus more on "pure" research than on social problems. One of the leading critics of these attitudes was C. Wright Mills, who made fun of the turgid writing of grand theorists and abstract empiricists. Mills called for the younger generation to draw on their own experience and turn their knowledge to the purpose of freedom in seeing how things might be changed. "It is the political task of the social scientist," he wrote, "continually to translate personal troubles into public issues, and public issues into the terms of their human meaning for a variety of individuals" (Mills 1959, 187). The most important role of the social scientist, in Mills's view, was to be "advisor to the king."

Because a number of the important longitudinal studies were directed at understanding current social issues, they helped to point questions in the direction that Mills had indicated. Studies like the National Longitudinal Surveys (funded by the Labor Department) or the Panel Study of Income Dynamics (launched during the War on Poverty) expressed a growing societal consensus on the goal of alleviating poverty. Furthermore, government support made clear society's interest in funding social research to understand and help in the solution of social problems.

Longitudinal studies by their very nature could illuminate the immense amount of dynamism and turmoil in American economic, family, and educational life. As particular attention was given to how individual and social changes were brought about, the distinction between pure and applied social science blurred. The findings of the landmark studies had clear implications for education, employment, family, and health care, and they also posed important explanatory questions about why different life patterns were associated with specific times, places, and populations. This review touches on only some of the most obvious links between the study findings and what might be generalized from them.

Educational Programs and Policies

C. Wright Mills (1959, 174) propounded the view that the social scientist can help society to "find points of effective intervention, in order to know what can and what must be structurally changed if the role of explicit decision-making in history is to be enlarged." Mills's principle of maximizing freedom by finding the points at which human decision could intervene is perhaps most often seen in longitudinal studies of education. In the High/Scope Perry Preschool Project, Weikart was deliberately looking for ways to save poor minority youngsters from a fate of chronic low performance in school. The potential benefits were enormous if society could prevent the seven-to-one ratio of costs to society for kids who did not get into preschool programs compared with those who did. No wonder there was widespread application of Weikart's findings, not only to early intervention programs such as Head Start in the United States but also to similar programs around the world.

Entwisle's long-running Beginning School Studies also compared the educational outcomes for children in poor and middle-class schools. A key factor was the immense differentiation in resources between children from families of high and low socioeconomic status in their access to nursery school, kindergarten, play resources, and parenting skills. The differences between homes, schools, and neighborhoods helped the middle-class children and held back the poor and working-class youngsters. Yet although Entwisle drew a clear implication that summer enrichment programs (rather than summer school) are needed for poor children, recent social policy still seems to have supported an increase in summer school programs to the exclusion of enrichment programs (Randal C. Archibold, "Without Much Data on Success, Mandatory Summer School Grows," *New York Times*, June 17, 1999, 1). For children who are at particular risk of mental illness or extreme aggression, work by Werner on children in Kauai and by the Cairnses in North Carolina showed remarkable evidence that educational interventions can make a big difference in deflecting a child from a path toward mental illness, alcoholism, substance abuse, or violent acting out. Some of this recovery might be attributed to resilience in the individual; but much of the credit seems attributable to social support and school and community efforts that surrounded the child with help and led toward acceptance and success rather than rejection and failure.

Poverty Programs and Employment

Although the nation discovered persistent poverty during the 1960s, one of the repeated findings of the life-course studies was the relatively small number of people who remained in poverty over a long period. Elder's tracking of the children who experienced greatest hardship during the Depression of the 1930s revealed remarkable upward mobility. The men from deprived families were found to have benefited especially from service in the military. They learned new skills and were able in some cases to get higher education through the GI bill. The Civilian Conservation Corps during the New Deal and military service during World

War II helped to pull the Depression generation out of disadvantage and thus suggested to Elder the importance not only of large period effects such as depression, war, and economic boom but also the efficacy of programs that build discipline and open up opportunity. The fact that these benefits were more significant for the deprived than the non-deprived would appear applicable to contemporary programs for disadvantaged youth, such as YouthBuild or AmeriCorps.

Similar possibilities of recovery emerged from the longitudinal studies begun during the 1960s to understand employment and income. Although the Moynihan Report of 1964 had uncovered a surprising phenomenon of long-term welfare use that was passed on from mothers receiving Aid to Families with Dependent Children (AFDC) to their children, the nationally representative Panel Study of Income Dynamics put this phenomenon into perspective. Based on repeat survey waves spaced a year or so apart, the study showed that women receiving AFDC were typically in the program for relatively short spells, and only a minority were long-term recipients. One implication was that people needed support mostly to get on their feet through training programs, a minimum wage, food and housing supplements, child care, health insurance, and disability coverage. Only a relatively small number needed supported work programs to provide their basic incomes (Ellwood 1988).

The National Longitudinal Surveys (directed by Frank Mott) provided data showing the nature of work and health conditions that make older men more likely to retire, middle-aged women to go to work, and younger women and men to make the transition to adulthood in a number of alternate ways. The surveys themselves, which focused on several different age-gender cohorts and covered a variety of predisposing variables such as health, education, age of children, child care, and level of family income, helped to delineate the multivariate determinants of labor market entries and exits as well as alternative activities such as going to school or having a baby. These findings could then be made "policy relevant" by attempting to link their implications to specific programs for education and training, family planning, child care, flexible work schedules, and retirement. Over time the "relevant" policies also shifted from concern with the fate of older men and mature women to the impact of younger mothers' employment on the quality of parenting and outcomes for their children.

Family and Children's Issues

As is true of any social or political issue, questions of family structure and the optimal upbringing for children are draped in heavy moral and ideological overtones. Is unmarried teenage pregnancy immoral, or is it a marker of an alternative family form? Is cohabitation a sign of decline in the family, or is it a new stage in the transition to marriage? Whether such phenomena turn out to be behaviorally deviant or merely further signs of a changing social order is important for social policy. If the former, special programs will likely try to prevent or inhibit the behavior; if the latter, they will more likely treat the phenomenon as a reasonable alternative for the persons who have chosen it. The policy question then becomes what alternative the actors in question would have chosen if better options had been open to them and how these could be made available.

The Intergenerational Panel Study that began in 1961 in the Detroit area was one of the first longitudinal studies of families to reveal the true nature of household formation, childbearing choices, and sexual norms as distinguished from moral strictures about what they should be. After their mothers had married, children who were listed as nieces and nephews at an earlier point came to be acknowledged as daughters and sons. Divorce, cohabitation, and movement in and out of the household were all on the increase, suggesting that the structure of the family was indeed changing to become more diverse.

Furstenberg has pinpointed the shift from moralizing to the new understanding that began to emerge around the issue of teenage pregnancy and out-of-wedlock births. The longitudinal data suggest that fertility and "loose morals" were the effect, rather than the cause, of poverty. Instead of stimulating out-of-wedlock births, social programs for pregnant teenagers helped prevent them by providing fresh opportunities for training and employment.

Over the past thirty years, interest has gradually shifted to a greater focus on what types of family situations are best for children. On the basis of data from the Panel Study of Income Dynamics, Duncan concludes that the timing of financial assistance to families has different effects depending on the age of the child. Although sufficient economic resources are important at any age, they are most critical during infancy. Duncan concludes that society needs to reorder its priorities in terms of children's needs for healthy development.

Elder, extending his understanding of findings during the Depression to a study of farm families during the Iowa farm crisis of the early 1980s, found that the resilience and recovery of the children were related to farmwork, academic discipline, emotional support from parents, and ties to community institutions such as school and church. Despite their experience of severe economic crisis, the farm children had better high school grades than children from nonfarm homes. Although the policy implications of these findings are not explicit, they suggest that current efforts toward helping parents to integrate work and family life and to have time for involvement in the community may do more good for their children's development than any other single intervention or remedial program ever could.

Health Behaviors and Mental Health

Not unlike the matters of family behavior that were formerly construed as entirely moral questions, certain health-related behaviors such as use of alcohol, drugs, and tobacco have moved from the realm of preachers' warnings to the category of addictions or illnesses to be treated or prevented. Longitudinal data can show incidence, prevalence, and change over time as well as long-term outcomes. Many recent studies contribute to this end, but the work by Vaillant and Brunswick was pioneering in both documenting the use of various substances and drugs and suggesting long-term adverse effects. Vaillant followed alcohol and tobacco use in the Grant study of Harvard men and concluded that cigarettes and alcohol are more dangerous than fat. Brunswick compared drug-use patterns across succeeding cohorts of Harlem adolescents and tracked them into adulthood, most recently adding the study of HIV.

Two main lessons for mental health emerge from longitudinal studies: early intervention makes a difference in averting a child with predisposing factors from risk of getting sick, and recovery is possible and occurs in a fair number of cases. The Cairnses, in working with highly aggressive youngsters, found both precepts to be true. Laub and Sampson, in their follow-up of the delinquents studied by the Gluecks, also observed recovery that could usually be attributed to such later events as military service, a stable marriage, and a steady job. Emmy Werner had such strong confirmation that intervention and recovery were possible that she was successful in getting Hawaii to establish special mental health services for troubled children and youth. Even now she is working in California, training her graduate students to bring that knowledge to the attention of state legislators and to make them aware that in the new welfare-to-work programs, there is a great need to buffer the negative impact of the repeal of AFDC on the most vulnerable families and children.

Conclusion

In 1959, in *The Sociological Imagination,* C. Wright Mills heralded the end of the modern period, with its waning hopes of a reign of democracy, freedom, and reason and its growing faith in grand theories and abstract empiricism. He counseled students to eschew such empty academic exercises and instead "to use your life experience in your intellectual work" (Mills 1959, 196). In the longitudinal studies of the changing life course that have been considered here, we see how a generation of social scientists who were coming of age and launching their careers at the very time of Mills's advice were indeed using their own life experience in their intellectual work. Drawing on their particular historical location in a period of cultural turmoil, they constructed a new conceptual framework that combined the ontogenetic and contextual factors in development to emerge with a new life-course perspective that incorporated time and place, social networks, human agency, and the dynamic flow of specific events. Their new longitudinal methods and studies provided data that not only helped them to develop the new framework but also confirmed it with evidence that varied by cohort, race, and socioeconomic group.

The knowledge they acquired was relevant to the social problems of their era and could also be used to inform social policy. A number of investigators would qualify as what Mills called "advisors to the king." Many of their studies were funded by government agencies interested in solving significant social problems, and almost all dealt with some threat to development such as poverty, out-of-wedlock births, poor school performance, and other maladaptations. Together these studies suggested—if only implicitly—some ways to prevent such problems. It seems fitting that it was longitudinal methods that made these insights possible and, by the same token, that it will be against life-course data that proposed new theoretical paradigms and preventive policies will ultimately be evaluated.

References

Abbott, Andrew. 1992. "What Do Cases Do? Some Notes on Activity in Sociological Analyses." In *What Is a Case?*, edited by Charles Ragin and Howard Becker. New York: Cambridge University Press.

Baltes, Paul B. 1983. "Life Span Developmental Psychology: Observations on History and Theory Revisited." In *Developmental Psychology*, edited by Richard M. Lerner. Hillsdale, N.J.: Lawrence Erlbaum Associates.

Baltes, Paul B., Ulman Lindenberger, and Ursula M. Staredinger. 1998. "Life-Span Theory in Developmental Psychology." In *Theoretical Models of Human Development*, edited by Richard M. Lerner, vol. 1 of *Handbook of Child Psychology*, edited by William M. Damon. New York: Wiley.

Bender, Thomas, and Carl E. Schorske. 1997. *American Academic Culture in Transformation: Fifty Years, Four Disciplines.* Princeton: Princeton University Press.

Brim, Orville G., and Jerome Kagan, eds. 1980. *Constancy and Change in Human Development.* Cambridge, Mass.: Harvard University Press.

Brim, Orville G., and Stanton Wheeler. 1966. *Socialization After Childhood: Two Essays.* New York: Wiley.

Cloward, Richard A., and Lloyd E. Ohlin. 1960. *Delinquency and Opportunity: A Theory of Delinquent Gangs.* Glencoe, Ill.: Free Press.

Colby, Anne. 1998. Foreword to *Methods of Life Course Research: Qualitative and Quantitative Approaches*, edited by Janet Z. Giele and Glen H. Elder Jr. Thousand Oaks, Calif.: Sage Publications.

Coleman, James S. 1966. *Equality of Educational Opportunity.* Washington: U.S. Government Printing Office for U.S. Department of Health, Education, and Welfare, Office of Education.

Elder, Glen H., Jr. 1974. *Children of the Great Depression.* Chicago: University of Chicago Press.

———. 1998. "The Life Course and Human Development." In *Theoretical Models of Human Development*, edited by Richard M. Lerner, vol. 1 of *Handbook of Child Psychology*, edited by William M. Damon. New York: Wiley.

Ellwood, David T. 1988. *Poor Support: Poverty in the American Family.* New York: Basic Books.

Giele, Janet Z., and Glen H. Elder Jr. 1998. "Life Course Studies: Development of a Field." In *Methods of Life Course Research: Qualitative and Quantitative Approaches*, edited by Janet Z. Giele and Glen H. Elder Jr. Thousand Oaks, Calif.: Sage Publications.

Goode, William J. 1960. "Illegitimacy in the Caribbean Social Structure." *American Sociological Review* 25(1): 21–30.

Jessor, Richard. 1996. "Ethnographic Methods in Contemporary Perspective." In *Ethnography and Human Development: Context and Meaning in Social Inquiry*, edited by Richard Jessor, Anne Colby, and Richard A. Shweder. Chicago: University of Chicago Press.

Kagan, Jerome. 1980. "Perspectives on Continuity." In *Constancy and Change in Human Development*, edited by Orville G. Brim Jr. and Jerome Kagan. Cambridge, Mass.: Harvard University Press.

Kahn, Robert L., and Toni C. Antonucci. 1980. "Convoys over the Life Course: Attachment, Roles, and Social Support." In *Life-Span Development and Behavior*, edited by Paul B. Baltes and Orville Gilbert Brim Jr. Vol. 3. New York: Academic Press.

Kuhn, Thomas. 1962. *The Structure of Scientific Revolutions.* 2d ed. Chicago: University of Chicago Press.

Merton, Robert K. 1957. *Social Theory and Social Structure.* New York: Free Press.

Mills, C. Wright. 1959. *The Sociological Imagination.* New York: Oxford University Press.

Mishler, Elliot G. 1996. "Missing Persons: Recovering Developmental Stories/ Histories." In *Ethnography and Human Development: Context and Meaning in Social Inquiry*, edited by Richard Jessor, Anne Colby, and Richard A. Shweder. Chicago: University of Chicago Press.

Parsons, Talcott, and Robert F. Bales. 1955. *Family, Socialization, and Interaction Process.* New York: Free Press.

Rainwater, Lee, and William L. Yancey. 1967. *The Moynihan Report and the Politics of Controversy.* Cambridge, Mass.: MIT Press.

Stonequist, Everett V. 1961. *The Marginal Man: A Study in Personality and Culture Conflict.* 1937. New York: Russell and Russell.

Chapter 2

How It Takes Thirty Years to Do a Study

FRANK F. FURSTENBERG JR.

L ONGITUDINAL research is ineluctably reflexive. Investigators must confront the errors or misdirections in their studies that have occurred in the past even as they take steps to correct them in the future; they are compelled to wrestle with the changing historical and social context in which they and their subjects are situated; and ultimately they must take account of personal ideas and ambitions altered by the passage of time and career transitions. It is this intersection between the history and lives of subjects and the researcher that gives longitudinal research its distinctive mark. Investigators find themselves in the position of being participant observers in a strand of history partly of their own making. The intertwined and intersecting experiences between subject and researcher are the subject of this paper about my longitudinal study of teenage mothers in Baltimore.

Without my being fully aware of it at the time, the Baltimore study began in 1965 when I was a graduate student at Columbia University. My mother, a social worker in a newly established program for teenage mothers at Sinai Hospital of Baltimore, phoned me one day to ask if I would write some questions for a grant proposal to evaluate the program. She had volunteered the services of her son, the sociologist in training, to the doctors who had created one of the nation's first programs to provide prenatal and postnatal care for "adolescent mothers." I patiently explained to my mother why I could not comply with her request. Evaluation of a program, I had recently learned in a course, required intimate knowledge of its goals and procedures. It could not be done from afar. Not deterred in the least by my professional scruples, my mother reappealed on grounds of filial piety. So I sent her a list of questions, accompanied by a letter replete with pedantic protest. The codirectors of the program, two very able pediatric researchers, invited me to Baltimore to present a plan for evaluating the program, and thus the Baltimore study commenced.

Had it occurred to me that I would have been occupied and preoccupied with this study for several decades hence—indeed throughout my entire professional life—I would never have had the audacity to begin the research. Once begun, longitudinal research can become addictive. One acquires a thirst for drinking from a particular fountain of information. Just a few more sips, it seems, and that knowledge will be complete. This belief is, of course, an illusion, for the social world is continually transformed, as are the subjects of one's research. The investigator keeps changing, too, bringing to bear ever more exacting standards of knowledge and casting doubt on what he or she thought was already known.

The Issue of Teenage Childbearing in Historical Perspective

It is easy to forget that teenage childbearing did not exist as a social issue in 1965. There was no shortage of teenage parents, of course, but they had not yet been rendered problematic in the social worlds of academics, politics, and the media. For this to occur would require a series of demographic and social changes that were already in the making but had not yet become publicly visible. The most important of these was the rapid decline in the rate of marriage, especially among the young. The so-called marriage rush that followed World War II suddenly came to a screeching halt in the mid-1960s as educational careers were prolonged, job prospects for youth declined, and the process of deindustrialization in the United States commenced. In the early 1960s, nearly half of all women were married by the age of twenty. By 1970 the average age at first marriage had risen to nearly twenty-one, and today it is nearly twenty-five. Teenage marriage, once common, has become a rarity.

A good many marriages in the 1950s and 1960s were preceded by a pregnancy. Indeed, some sociologists argue that in certain segments of the population, pregnancy was virtually a part of the courtship system (Rubin 1976; Vincent 1961). Certainly the "shotgun wedding," a term that has nearly disappeared from our lexicon, was commonplace. Just as the earning power of younger men began to decline, in the 1960s, women were beginning to enter the labor force in larger numbers. Marriage simply was not as good a bargain for women as it had been in earlier decades (neither was it for men, who were beginning to lose power in their dealings with women). Once the centerpiece of early adulthood, marriage no longer commanded the same cultural salience for women, who became increasingly unwilling to put their eggs in a single basket.

As it happened, my study began at just the right time to witness this turn of events, particularly as it affected African Americans, who were the first group to lose confidence in early marriage. The women I began to follow were faced with the dilemma of getting married and setting up a household or remaining unmarried and staying with their families. I can still remember the aggravating problem of trying to draft an interview schedule to capture the multiple contingencies of life events for the predominantly African American population who were eligible for the service program. It did not take a demographer or sociologist to recognize the sharp differences that emerged between the minority of white teenage participants and most of their black counterparts. The pregnant white teens continued to marry (or to give up their children for adoption), while the pregnant black teens divided fairly evenly between those who remained in school and those who married. Although a few took neither route and simply became full-time mothers supported by public assistance, that pattern was unusual and remained so, despite widespread public perceptions in the following decades that teens were getting pregnant in order to go on the dole.

This changing scenario in the life course of teenage mothers is certainly clearer to me now than it was at the time. My task was to evaluate the service program at Sinai Hospital, designed to mitigate the adverse consequences of early childbearing for mother and child by providing prenatal care, parenting classes, and contraception to prevent second births. Until the mid-1960s, teens who became pregnant typically were forced out of school, and their only viable alternatives were marriage or adoption. (Abortion did not become legally available in the state of Maryland until 1970.) Thus this comprehensive program, designed to support young mothers regardless of whether they married or not, was a daring innovation. The Sinai Hospital program, along with a special high school for pregnant teens in Baltimore that was started at about the same time, marked the point at which social institutions started to acknowledge that marriage alone might be an insufficient response to an unplanned pregnancy. These measures of providing schooling, counseling, and contraceptive services to teenage mothers were controversial at the time and remained so, for they were thought to encourage out-of-wedlock childbearing. (See, for example, the published exchanges that I had with June Sklar and Beth Berkov [1973] and later with Maris Vinovskis and Lindsay Chase-Lansdale [1988] on the issue of whether services to teenage mothers promoted unwed parenthood by discouraging marriage [Furstenberg 1988a].)

The first set of interviews, conducted at Sinai Hospital with the pregnant teenagers and their mothers in the mid-1960s, supplied abundant evidence that early marriage was on its way out. This was most apparent in the black community, where unemployment rates for teenagers and young adults reached high levels. A growing number of African American parents, I discovered, were counseling their children to wait to wed until they had graduated from high school and could be assured of being able to support themselves in the event that the father of the child failed to live up to his responsibilities. More and more fathers in the black community were deemed to be unsuitable mates because they lacked stable employment and prospects for the future. Large numbers of young women were eschewing marriage as a solution to a premarital pregnancy.

The new pattern of out-of-wedlock teenage childbearing in the black community was a departure from the recent past. In hindsight scholars attributed the rising rates of "illegitimacy" to long-standing stresses among blacks resulting from slavery, urban migration and dislocation, and, later, a cultural predilection for a matrilineal family brought from Africa. The inclination to regard this new practice as a characteristic of blacks was understandable: in 1960, black teens were nearly twice as likely as white teens to have children out of wedlock, and the ratio of nonmarital to marital births was almost six times as high for black as for white teenagers (Furstenberg and Brooks-Gunn 1986). However, the perception that early and unwed childbearing was unique to blacks later proved to be wrong. Young black couples were merely the first to experience disenchantment with marriage. In the following decades, young whites and then older women of all races became more reluctant to marry when facing a pregnancy. By the 1990s, unwed parenthood had become far more common among white teens and, indeed, among white women of all childbearing ages (Furstenberg 1991; Luker 1996; U.S. Bureau of the Census 1999).

Earlier age at first intercourse certainly helped to undermine marriage practices. We can speculate that the rising age of marriage may have encouraged the young to have intercourse earlier, as it became more difficult to wait until marriage was a realistic possibility. A series of surveys in the 1970s indicate that premarital sexual behavior was becoming more common even as it was less likely to be a prelude to marriage. By the late 1970s, the historical link between sex and marriage had been largely severed, creating a new life-course scenario for youth. Again, black youth led the way but were soon followed by whites, who were in growing numbers having sex long before they were in a position to marry (Zelnik, Kantner, and Ford 1981).

These changes in sexual practices forced policy makers to reconsider the ban on providing contraception to unmarried women and especially to teenagers. Beginning in the mid-1960s and throughout the decade that followed, a grudging shift occurred in the provision of services to the young, the poor, and minority groups, who were increasingly having unplanned pregnancies that did not eventuate in marriage. In the 1970s, the legalization of abortion, hitherto largely the last resort of the wealthy and the desperate, offered another alternative to marriage (Luker 1996; Nathanson 1991; Vinovskis 1988).

Each of these demographic and social trends, all of which led to the creation of teenage childbearing as a social problem, was amplified by the sheer size of the teenage population. The changes in marriage timing, sexual norms, and the cultural ambivalence about contraception were spotlighted as the huge baby-boom cohort entered its teens. The ratio of births to teenagers to all births shot up in the mid-1970s, as did the ratio of teenage out-of-wedlock births to all births, in large part because of the phenomenal increase in the adolescent age group (Furstenberg 1991).

These demographic and social changes occurred against a backdrop of rising moral apprehension about youth in the 1960s and early 1970s (Coleman 1974). During the Vietnam War era, social constraints on the young appeared to be breaking down. Among the most conspicuous of these were the sexual practices of youth, who seemed disinclined to observe traditional norms upholding virginity (which, in any case, were largely fictional by the 1950s). Liberalization of abortion laws and high government expenditures for public assistance benefits helped ignite a fierce political debate over what seemed to be a growing disregard for time-honored family formation practices. By linking these public concerns, teenage childbearing came to symbolize social breakdown, especially in the black community. Nowhere was this argument more dramatically framed than in the famous report by Daniel Patrick Moynihan (1965), the assistant secretary of labor under the Nixon administration, expressing a deep foreboding that the black family was being caught in "a tangle of pathology" (29).

Launching an Academic Career

Unbeknownst to me when I began my modest evaluation, I had stumbled onto one of the momentous sociological issues of the day: the social consequences of teenage childbearing. I cannot say that I was totally oblivious to where I was heading, even from the start. My training at Columbia with Robert Merton, Richard Cloward, Lloyd Ohlin, and especially William J. Goode had prepared me to locate my research as a study of anomie and illegitimacy. Although the study was cast as an evaluation, my earliest papers referred to the question of the "process of unplanned parenthood" as a response to blocked opportunity and sought to challenge the proposition that teens were becoming pregnant because they held "distinctively different attitudes and values about family formation" ("Unplanned Parenthood: The Social Consequences of Teenage Childbearing," Furstenberg 1976, chapter 3).

The first pair of papers, written just after I had completed my thesis (on a different topic), attempted to locate the research as an investigation of competing explanations for the growing pattern of teenage childbearing (Furstenberg 1970; Furstenberg, Markowitz, and Gordis 1969). The research was framed as a study of unwed parenthood as a form of "deviant behavior," a term linking my research with a field of sociology that was lively at the time but that has now largely been incorporated into criminology. I discovered that I was also in a strategic position to test the validity of controversial ideas about the existence of "a culture of poverty," the widespread conviction of social conservatives that poverty was generated by the distinctive value system of the poor (Banfield 1970; Lewis 1968). In fact, this intellectual debate has continued, or some would say resumed, in the 1980s in the guise of research on the "urban underclass" (Wilson 1987). Viewing the poor as deviants has never appealed to me, and my early work represents a struggle to escape from the language of social stigma. However, as I reread my work in later years, I found that it was deeply embedded in local disciplinary debates even as I searched for a language freer from the heavy-handed moral discourse about the poor that prevailed in the 1960s and early 1970s.

In 1967, I arrived at the University of Pennsylvania with a freshly minted doctorate and an ongoing evaluation project. Set loose from my graduate school mentors, I found myself very much on my own in a sociology department at the time that provided little intellectual guidance for my line of work. Although Penn's reputation was strong in both demography and criminology, my sociology training at Columbia had ill prepared me for fitting comfortably into either of these fields. Young— I was twenty-six when I first arrived at Penn—and more than a trifle arrogant, I was disdainful of what appeared to be the narrow empirical work of some of my more distinguished colleagues. Two years after entering the department, I resigned to work for the government, believing that I had made a mistake in becoming an academic. It took me about a month in the government to reverse that misapprehension. A year later I gratefully returned to Penn, having decided that the academic life was truly for me. It was time to get down to the business of showing my colleagues (and myself) that I was serious in this resolution.

My academic reputation in sociology was not going to be made on evaluation research, which has never been accorded the respect it might deserve. In 1970, when I returned to Penn, I wrote a research proposal to follow up the teen mothers beyond the year-long evaluation that was just concluding. At a conference in the summer of 1968, I had met Glen Elder who, though only five years my senior, was beginning to work on his classic study, *Children of the Great Depression* (Elder 1974). Ever a proselytizer for adoption of the life-course perspective, Elder's ideas influenced the shape of my follow-up study, and he became my academic "older brother." Miraculously, the proposal I wrote upon my return received funding both from the Population Council and the Children's Bureau, the federal agency that had funded the initial evaluation. I called Charles Gershensen, the kindly director of the Children's Bureau, to explain that I had already received funding. To my great surprise, he did not want me to return the grant. Instead, he allowed me to reshape it so that I could follow the partners of the young mothers in my study as well as a group of classmates who had not become pregnant in their teens. This addition greatly enhanced the research design.

The attempts to interview the fathers opened my eyes to the problems of family formation among the young couples. I began to observe the tenuous ties between unmarried and formerly married fathers and their children, topics that were later to become central to the Baltimore study and related research that I would conduct on fathers two decades later (Furstenberg 1988b, 1995; Furstenberg and Harris 1993). At the three-year follow-up, I managed to interview barely half the fathers. Finding the classmates proved more successful, albeit enormously time consuming. The tenure clock (then set at five years, including my year in Washington) was ticking away. By 1972, the year of my tenure review, I had amassed far more data than publications.

To my colleagues at Penn, understandably, I seemed like a questionable case. I had produced only a dozen articles on a variety of unrelated topics; I appeared to be unfocused and unfulfilled. With limited sponsorship and a spotty record, I barely squeaked by, receiving a promotion only because academic standards were still relatively loose and discretionary. My first book was still four years away; I had not even completed the third wave of data collection, much less written about it. Several years of data analysis and writing would pass before I could justify my promotion.

With the tenure review behind me, I went to work, but the process was unremittingly painful, and progress was slow. I began to suffer agonizing doubts about the entire enterprise in 1974, when I started to write a book about the Baltimore study. On one of my darker days, I compiled a lengthy list of all the reasons I was unqualified to undertake the task: I lacked the knowledge and authority to draw conclusions from the data; the data itself were flawed; and I was only writing what others either already knew or would not accept. Entire days passed during which I would hardly write a paragraph. Finally, in an act of desperation, I decide to abandon writing a book. Instead I would simply fulfill my requirement to my sponsors by doing a "report."

In 1975, I finally completed a report entitled "Unplanned Parenthood: The Social Consequences of Teenage Childbearing" and submitted it to the Children's Bureau. The summer of that year went by before I dared to show it to any of my colleagues. In the fall of that year, I sent it to several mentors, including Glen Elder and Melvin Kohn, who had provided encouragement and advice from the time I was a graduate student. I also sent the report to Gladys Topkis, an editor at the Free Press, whom I had known during my years at Columbia. Within a matter of weeks, she offered me a contract, and Glen Elder agreed to write a foreword to the volume, which required only a modest revision of my report. *Unplanned Parenthood* was published the following year, still some years before the issue of teenage childbearing reached its zenith as a public issue.

The Baltimore Study Revisited at Midcareer

I had confidently predicted just the opposite—that teenage childbearing would recede in importance—in the concluding chapter of my book (Furstenberg 1976). Demographic changes, I contended, would reduce the problem of early childbearing as the baby boom gave way to the baby bust. Indeed, the numbers of teenage parents did dramatically decline in the decade following the publication of my book; however, the perception of the problem heightened for reasons that I have alluded to earlier in this paper. Just as I thought I had concluded my study, I suddenly found myself in the position of being one of the nation's experts on a topic about which little had been written.

Almost perversely, I was determined to turn to other areas of research. I remember saying to a colleague at the time that I hoped never again to study a teenage mother. In the decade after my book was completed, I embarked on a series of studies seemingly unrelated to teenage parenthood. I started to do historical demographic research in the mid-1970s and became interested in undertaking qualitative work, thinking that I would abandon survey research because of its severe limitations. In the late 1970s, I even undertook an observational study of families (albeit with teenage parents) under the guidance of Salvadore Minuchin, an eminent family therapist. For a time, I considered getting training in that field. The urge to venture into new areas (or leave the one I knew best) was powerful.

Despite my resolution to stake out new and different territory, I also found it difficult to resist the security that comes with knowing a subject well, not to mention the blandishments of attention and funding that come with expertise. I discovered that funding was now readily available for investing in a number of problems related to my data, ones I had left unexplored. These motives led me to continue my research on teenage parenthood, extending it in directions that had not been developed in my book. I wrote several pieces about the impact of teenage childbearing on the extended family of young mothers, as well as a paper on teenage fathers (Furstenberg 1980; Furstenberg and Talvitie 1979).

Worse yet (as I saw it then), even when I worked on other topics I found myself thinking about how they related to the families in my Baltimore study. Historical research on African Americans in Philadelphia, demographic work on the changing life course, and a new longitudinal study of transitions from divorce to remarriage all cast reflections on what I thought I knew about teenage parenthood. It was as if this stratum of knowledge was being altered by ideas that percolated from new and different areas of research.

Human development, as I have come to understand the term, presumes that skills, knowledge, and beliefs are altered by ongoing experience in the social world as well as by internal psychological changes arising both from aging and life encounters. *Unplanned Parenthood* was the book of a young sociologist limited by a rudimentary mastery of the tools of his trade and incomplete knowledge of his discipline, let alone other related disciplines that might inform his intellectual perspective. My sociological imagination, too, was confined by the historical times in which the study had been set. As the years passed, I began to mature professionally and personally: I became historically more aware, the revolutions in gender and the family had affected my thinking, and I was becoming more confident about my ability to address difficult issues. Moreover, the topic of teenage childbearing had become intellectually fashionable; new research was being published in sociology, demography, economics, psychology, and even history. Finally, the times they were a-changing in ways that Bob Dylan had never contemplated, requiring that I take account of the sharp political swing to the right that occurred in the decade following the publication of my study.

Politics in America became meaner in the post–Vietnam War years. The ambitions of the Great Society were first abandoned and later repudiated. Attempts at redressing racial injustice through redistribution and reconciliation were rejected in favor of "benign" neglect and outright racist appeals. The poor went from being viewed as victims of the American economic changes to being seen as villains who were freeloading off the backs of the working poor and middle class. President Ronald Reagan regaled the country with stories about "welfare queens," and Charles Murray (1984) rewrote the history of the 1960s as the cause, not the consequence, of American inequality. Teenage parents became an identifiable social category, signifying much that was wrong in America's inner-city communities. Increasingly, there was public discussion of the "self-perpetuating cycle of poverty" generated by families on welfare, especially those who began family life as teenage parents.

Despite my efforts to show the diverse effects of early childbearing on teen mothers and their children, the findings of the Baltimore study were sometimes cited as evidence that early childbearing produces calamitous effects on the life chances of mothers and their children. In fact, the results seemed to suggest that many women did surprisingly well in the aftermath of early parenthood. Yet those reading the results focused on the differences, not the similarities, between teenage mothers and their classmates who had postponed parenthood.

In 1981, Orville "Bert" Brim, one of the master impresarios of innovative research in the social sciences, convened a seminar consisting mainly of younger behavioral scientists to discuss the links between childhood and adulthood studies. Over several days of work and play, I began to talk with Jeanne Brooks-Gunn, whom I met there for the first time, about reinterviewing the Baltimore families a decade after the five-year follow-up. Although only five years had elapsed since the publication of *Unplanned Parenthood*, it was a significant span of years in my professional career. By then, I had published a series of papers on social history and had nearly completed a study of the transition from divorce to remarriage. I felt that I had managed to put some distance between myself and the Baltimore study. I was emotionally and intellectually ready to return, especially if I could be joined by a talented developmental psychologist of the likes of Brooks-Gunn.

Potential granters were intrigued, although most were skeptical about our ability to locate the families after so long a passage of time. Brooks-Gunn and I put the challenge to the Institute of Survey Research at Temple University. In a matter of a month or so, they managed to locate 90 percent of a random subsample. On that encouraging finding, we received funding from both the Commonwealth Fund and the Robert Wood Johnson Foundation to conduct a follow-up in 1984, when the offspring of the teen mothers would be approximately the same age as their mothers had been at the time of the initial interviews seventeen years earlier. Interviewing two generations at the same point in time created an appealing research design: it permitted us to examine the parents and offspring at the same point in the life course. Equally important, we would be able to observe how the teen mothers were faring in their midthirties.

Working collaboratively has its special pleasures and its inevitable challenges. Brooks-Gunn and I had to learn a common language to connect our disciplines. Nothing—perhaps not even political or religious ideology—rivals the strength of disciplinary preferences and prejudices. Nothing uncovers these predilections so quickly and completely as collecting, analyzing, and interpreting data. By the time the data collection was completed in 1984, I had learned a lot about thinking developmentally. With the able collaboration of S. Phillip Morgan, then a young colleague of mine at Penn, Brooks-Gunn and I attempted to address the question of how the mothers' developmental trajectories affected their children's course of development. Although our data were limited and our methods imperfect, the resulting analysis broke new conceptual ground by linking the parallel life courses of two generations observed over time (Furstenberg, Brooks-Gunn, and Morgan 1987).

The findings, supported by a large number of later studies, greatly reinforced the conclusion that teenage parents hardly lived up to their popular stereotype. Whereas 60 percent of the women had been on welfare and only a tiny minority were (still) married to the fathers of their first children, by their midthirties most teen mothers had become self-supporting and were deeply committed to their children's well-being. Only a minority had gone on to have large families that kept them on public assistance. To the contrary, most had returned to school at some point to advance their education and improve their labor market prospects. Their conjugal relations had, however, been less successful. Many of the women moved in and out of relationships; many others had, by midlife, dropped out of the marriage market altogether, turning their attentions to advancing their careers and caring for their families.

Funding had been unavailable to relocate the classmates, but we compared the Baltimore study women with their counterparts in the National Longitudinal Survey. In most respects, they appeared to be comparable to a nationally representative sample of teen mothers living in metropolitan areas of the country. When compared with women of similar age and race who had borne children later in life, they were generally not doing as well, although the differences were relatively modest, especially among African Americans. Moreover, as we could not adjust for many unmeasured differences in the two populations, these findings almost surely overstated the effects of early fertility itself. Early parenthood, we argued in our book *Adolescent Mothers in Later Life* (Furstenberg, Brooks-Gunn, and Morgan 1987), was at least as much of a marker as a source of social disadvantage. According to their personal accounts, some mothers benefited from having had a child; others clearly were not up to the responsibility; most fell somewhere between these two extremes. In almost all cases, the teen mothers wished that they had begun their families later, feeling that they might have done more with their lives. Yet it is not completely evident that these perceptions are entirely accurate. For women highly disadvantaged from birth, teen parenthood does appear to alter the sequences of life events, but not always for the worse.

The circumstances of the offspring of the teen mothers also did not conform to the public imagery. Consider the following facts: virtually all of the children grew up in families headed by single parents, and nearly all of the mothers had been economically disadvantaged in early childhood; all but a small number of their parents had not chosen to become pregnant when they did; most of their parents had made difficult adjustments to parenthood, involving a period on either welfare or family assistance or both or a hasty and often unsuccessful marriage followed by welfare or family support or both; and the mothers of most of the children were themselves second-generation teen mothers, second-generation single parents, and second-generation welfare recipients. How might we have expected the children to fare under these circumstances? When I pose this question to most observers, predictions are rarely on the positive side. Typically, people guess that upwards of two-thirds of the next generation will also become teenage mothers and that most of the children will suffer severe disadvantages in adulthood.

When we first examined the children in the preschool years, they were not functioning poorly. The majority were being adequately cared for, and parents reported relatively few behavioral problems. However, the results of the 1984 interview were less encouraging. At midadolescence, many of the children were experiencing some amount of turmoil. Compared with the offspring of older mothers in the National Longitudinal Survey of Youth, their educational attainment was lower, and they had higher rates of teen parenthood. Even so, the majority were still in school, had not become teenage parents, and had not been incarcerated— three gross indicators of well-being. Surprisingly, even at this "unflattering" stage, most seemed to be heading for reasonably stable and productive lives. Yet it was still too early to tell. We decided to revisit the youth in 1987, when we could get a better reading on the outcomes of schooling and family formation. By then, all but a few were in their early twenties.

The twenty-year follow-up was something of a departure for me. For the first time since the study had begun, I started interviewing some of the families myself. To get a better feeling of how the youth were doing, Brooks-Gunn and I began talking to a subsample of the young people. This also gave us an opportunity to talk to family members, because virtually all were still living with parents or kin. This venture into qualitative case studies finally brought me in touch with the families that I had been studying for two decades. Although these discussions did not undermine the survey results as much as I had feared they might, they amplified the findings in a variety of ways that deepened my understanding of the everyday living situations of the young adults. For the past ten years, I have stayed in touch with a dozen or so young people, talking with them every few years. Although I am unschooled as a fieldworker, this qualitative research has helped me enormously in keeping a focus on individuals and the contexts in which they live. I have become increasingly skeptical of statistical models that examine discrete variables in an effort to isolate causal processes.

Although useful for some purposes, these efforts lead us away from understanding how people actually behave in varied situations and contexts, because people frequently can resort to a variety of strategies that are neither mutually exclusive nor entirely redundant. The packaging of qualities or the configuration of situations is not well captured in the multivariate models that are so popular in contemporary sociology and developmental psychology. In short, our science does a poor job of mimicking social process.

The 1987 interviews yielded a much clearer impression of how the children of the teenage mothers were doing. Close to two-thirds of the young women had not become teenage parents themselves. Most had finished high school or earned a certificate of General Educational Development (GED). The picture of the young men was less positive, however. Close to half had gotten caught up in the justice system by early adulthood, and consequently more had failed to complete high school, enter college, or make it into the labor force by their early twenties. Whereas three-fourths of the young women seemed to be managing successfully in early adulthood—according to the most conventional measures of success—fewer than half of the young men were on a successful trajectory.

By the late 1980s, the situation of young black males in urban America had probably deteriorated to its lowest ebb in recent times. Staggering rates of unemployment, linked with high levels of substance abuse, violence, and school dropout, made Moynihan's controversial predictions two decades earlier seem prescient. Indeed, the sharp differences in the success of young men and women in the study pointed to the influence of contextual differences in the family, school, and community experiences of boys and girls in the urban ghettos. Both poor opportunities and weakened social institutions were affecting young men and young women who were growing up in similar economic circumstances in different ways. In the family, males were more likely to be given a freer reign, saddled with less responsibility, and, perhaps, subject to less monitoring; at school, they were treated more harshly by their teachers, probably because they were more likely to act out when faced with tasks for which they were unprepared; and in the local environment they were more subject to negative peer influences and the risk of being hassled by authorities. When they got in trouble with the law, the males were more likely to suffer adverse consequences. In short, males showed all the earmarks of a developmental course of low investment, low expectations, and low levels of control along with high stigma and negative response by authorities.

The vulnerable position of males showed up not only in the survey data but also in the qualitative interviews that Brooks-Gunn and I conducted in 1987. The males were more likely to be floundering as they tried to make their way into adulthood. Those carrying the burden of having dropped out of high school or involvement in the criminal justice system were finding it difficult to obtain employment and frequently were unwilling or unable to hold low-wage jobs. Quite a few had drifted into the illegal economy. By contrast, the majority of the young women, especially those who had avoided early parenthood, seemed to be doing well.

The disparity in the situation of males and females aggravates the problem of family formation in the African American community. Most males in their early twenties were not deemed to be eligible partners because they possessed limited resources for sustaining a household. The marginalization of men resulting from the negative opinions of women, their families, and the wider society thus becomes an important ingredient in the etiology of nonmarital childbearing. Women did not, and probably could not, restrict their sexual relations to potentially eligible partners, especially because young men in the Baltimore study frequently exaggerated their willingness to support children in the event of early childbearing.

Following the publication of *Adolescent Mothers in Later Life,* I carried out a series of interviews with both male and female children of teenage mothers who had themselves become parents. If the possibility of marriage had still been in play for their parents in the mid-1960s, that possibility had all but disappeared for the offspring by the late 1980s. Only one or two of the second-generation teenage parents had married. Most of the couples who considered eventually marrying had lived together for a short time before the relationship dissolved. Only rarely did early parenthood result in a stable family. I observed a high degree of gender distrust among young couples, who were wary of one another's reliability, faithfulness, and commitment (Furstenberg 2001). Women frequently spoke of the immaturity of men, their jealousy and possessiveness, and the fact that they could not be counted on as trustworthy caregivers. Men in turn complained about women's insatiability, unwillingness to permit them sufficient freedom, and constant carping about their inadequacies. Both economic circumstances and family experiences created a legacy of uncertainty, making it difficult for the young adults to settle into permanent relationships. Marriage remained an ideal, but an ever elusive one, in the minds of many of the young adults (Furstenberg 2001).

An ongoing debate exists between conservatives and liberals over the sources of poverty and its recurrence across generations. Conservatives point to individuals who rise from poverty by dint of talent, will, and solid family support, highlighting the weaknesses inherent in single-parent households; liberals note that structural barriers limit access to the middle class and point to the values shared by poor and nonpoor alike. Data from the Baltimore study support both these positions. There is little doubt that two-parent families, especially those in which parents successfully collaborate in raising their children, are more effective in promoting social mobility; children do suffer when their fathers provide inconsistent support or even negative influence. However, the findings from the study to date show that many, if not most, families overcome these disadvantages, although their ability to rise to middle-class status is severely truncated by the absence of adequate preschool, school, and after-school programs, recreational programs, and the wide array of resources that middle-class families take for granted. The polarization of our national dialogue about family values in the 1980s and 1990s symbolized the inability to reach a public consensus on how to blend social responsibility and social opportunity. As one of the young men that I have gotten to know over the years once remarked to me, "It is obvious. You got to have both opportunity and responsibility."

The Latter Part of an Academic Career: Studying Adolescent Mothers at Midlife

Following the publication of *Adolescent Mothers in Later Life,* I made no effort to escape, as I had previously, from being an expert on teenage childbearing: no longer had I an interest in fleeing from the professional responsibilities that come with conducting policy-related research. Accepting grants from the government or foundations to carry out studies of social problems brings obligations: to educate, to speak out on issues about which you have special knowledge, and even to propose and promote policies that may address the needs of the populations who have offered information (and presumably expect a fair hearing in return). In short, I came to understand that academics cannot remove themselves from the worlds they study, any more than can environmental scientists or geneticists who work on policy-related issues.

Finally, I also began to appreciate that the Baltimore study—as they say in the communication business—had legs. It had survived the fate met by most research, even longitudinal research, of dying prematurely before realizing its potential to reveal how lives are structured over time. Rather than suffering an embarrassment by working on the same project year after year, as I had once felt about the Baltimore study, its longevity had become a source of pride and of personal identity. I was not afraid of doing research that was graying and had more than a few wrinkles: it seemed downright distinguished to carry on. So the study continues even to this day. As this paper is being written, I am beginning to harvest the data from the seventh or eighth wave (depending on how you count it) of the Baltimore study, a thirty-year follow-up conducted in 1995 and 1996. If I am fortunate enough, I may be one of the few investigators to publish papers from the same study over a span of four or perhaps even five decades. Some of the students who have worked with me on the Baltimore study are now entering the senior ranks of academia; others are still in graduate school. We have become an extended family of sorts, resembling the major participants in the study, some of whom are grandparents and even great-grandparents (Elo, King, and Furstenberg 1999; Furstenberg and Foley 1999; Furstenberg, Hughes, and Brooks-Gunn 1992; Furstenberg, Levine, and Brooks-Gunn 1990; Furstenberg, Masnick, and Ricketts 1972; Furstenberg and Weiss 2000; Harris 1997).

The impetus for the thirty-year follow-up came from several directions. In 1989 and 1990, Brooks-Gunn and I spent a year at the Russell Sage Foundation looking at our data on young adults. To be sure, the additional interviews allowed us to gain more purchase on the situation of youth, but it was still too early to chart the direction of the offspring's lives because they were still on the cusp of adulthood. We were getting some glimmerings from our work on the second-generation teenage parents, but more time would elapse before the young adults really came of age.

In the early 1990s, I joined the Research Network on Successful Adolescence in High Risk Communities sponsored by the MacArthur Foundation and designed to promote interdisciplinary research on the social context of adolescent development in disadvantaged communities. Supported by this network, I began to launch a series of new projects designed to explore neighborhood and school influences during adolescence (Furstenberg et al. 1999). Some of this work seeped into occasional pieces I wrote about the families in the Baltimore study, and I continued to stay in touch with the young adults I had first interviewed in 1987 (Furstenberg 1995, 2001). Consequently, it occurred to me to shift the focus of the study and to do more intensive work on the younger generation, with the aim of understanding the pathways and barriers to opportunity among urban black youth.

However, the genesis of the thirty-year follow-up once again must be credited to my lifelong mentor and friend, Bert Brim, who in 1992 was organizing another MacArthur Foundation Network on Successful Midlife Development (MidMac). One day over lunch, Bert asked whether I had any interest in examining the Baltimore study mothers at midlife. His network had been considering augmenting longitudinal studies with an eye to following participants into midlife. Unable to resist the offer, I began to lay plans to reinterview the teen mothers in 1993. With support from the network to follow up one generation of the Baltimore families, I approached the William T. Grant Foundation about their interest in funding another round of interviews of the young adults and their offspring. Jeanne Brooks-Gunn agreed to manage the interviews of the fourth generation. (We referred to the parents of the teen mothers as the G1s and the focal subjects, the teen mothers, as the G2s. Their offspring are called G3s, and the grandchildren of the teen mothers are G4s.)

Remarkably, we have been able to follow up close to two-thirds of all the women who had had live births, participated in the original prenatal and postnatal programs at Sinai Hospital, and were believed to be alive in 1996. Some attrition occurred at the beginning of the study, as we did not follow women who moved from Baltimore until the three-year follow-up, when the study was converted from an evaluation to a life-course investigation. Thus we lost a disproportionate number of white women who had married and moved out of the city. Among the African Americans, our follow-up rate reached nearly 70 percent of those still living.

The thirty-year follow-up incorporated a number of questions taken from Midlife in the United States (MIDUS), the national midlife survey instrument. Thus we are able to contrast the former original teenage mothers with women of comparable age in the national survey. Our analysis is still in process, but some interesting findings have already emerged. Although the physical health of some of the women is deteriorating, their mental health may actually be improving as they reach midlife. Certainly, the G2s, the cohort of teen mothers, generally feel better about their current economic and social circumstances than they did in earlier years. Many feel as though they have accomplished a great deal despite their rocky beginnings. Teenage mothers, in contrast with the largely middle-class and affluent women in the MidMac study, are, I suspect, aging more rapidly in a psychological sense. In their midforties, they have become the family matriarchs, strong women who are prepared to lend a guiding hand to the younger kin. A remarkable metamorphosis has taken place as they have gone from being "social problems" to figures in the black community revered for their strength and wisdom.

It would be wrong to suggest that this transformation invariably occurs. Some teenage mothers displayed a sense of competence, confidence, and coping skills from the first time they were interviewed; others seemed to have them at first but saw them erode over time; and some women never had nor gained these attributes. Indeed, one of the goals of the analysis under way is to understand these developmental trajectories and their relation to the educational, occupational, family, and child-rearing careers of the teenage mothers. We do know that substantial gains in occupational success occurred in midlife. The majority of the women managed to rise to the working class or the lower middle class, and a fortunate few eventually completed college and entered the middle class. In the aggregate, they hardly measure up (or I should say down) to their stereotypes, though to be sure, a quarter to a third of the women were still living on the margin.

Their children's experiences are even more variable. Huge differences persist between the women and men in their late twenties. Finally, it seems evident from the findings on educational attainment that a minority of the G3s are forging middle-class futures; however, a majority are situated in the "forgotten half," to use a phrase that describes non-college-bound youth. A surprising number (15 percent) of the youth in their late twenties, like their parents at a similar age, were still in school on a full-time or part-time basis. We see the same sorts of patterns developing when we look at patterns of childbearing. A majority of both the women and men have delayed having children, but a sizable minority are repeating the experiences of their parents. The dark side of the picture concerns the nearly half of the young men who have spent time in correctional institutions; most of these men seem far from finding employment or establishing families whom they can help to support. It is important, however, not to make the common mistake of some who study the situation of disadvantaged minorities—especially the young—of assuming that disadvantage is permanent. One lesson that looms from this project is that huge changes occur over the life span from adolescence to maturity. Events, even those as consequential as teenage childbearing or incarceration, have neither unique nor uniform consequences.

Reflections at Late Midlife in an Academic Career

I could never have envisioned that the Baltimore study would have figured so prominently in my life. It has never let go of me professionally, and I am grateful for that. The families in the study have been a continuous source of knowledge as well as inspiration. They have shared their lives with me. My project has involved understanding those lives in the larger context in which these families resided and the historical circumstances that have influenced this context. I have tried to share these lives and my understanding of them with those even further removed from the daunting challenges faced by those young women. Little did I imagine what might become of those "girls," who almost seemed to be pretending to be pregnant when I first observed them, sitting in the waiting room of the prenatal clinic at Sinai Hospital in 1965. That I would see these frightened "children" become mature women and even grandparents—watching them become parents first of toddlers, then teenagers, and finally young adults—was unimaginable. Perhaps my greatest disappointment is that I did not come to know them even better over this period. They might have seen me change from an eager graduate student to an anxious but aspiring young faculty member to a more secure and, I would like to believe, wiser senior academic had I taken them more into my confidence from the start.

My efforts to reduce the social distance between researcher and research subject, even if sincere, have been paltry. Sometimes I have been delighted by a letter sent by one of the subjects or an expression of gratitude for listening to their "stories." My tokens of reciprocation have been all too modest, however, in return for the time they spent in building the Baltimore study. They have shared their stories in hopes that policy makers will be persuaded that poverty is neither a disease nor a form of deviance. Indeed, for most of the families that I have come to know, poverty has resulted from an insufficiency of resources and not from an emotional problem or a deficit of character.

During the last round of interviews, on a hot summer's day, I interviewed a G3 mother who had several children. Through the window, in a yard strewn with weeds and trash, I could see a couple making love on a sun-baked porch. The young mother was telling me about her efforts to return to school and raise her children right. She was living with her sister and her sister's two children in a tiny row house, and children were spilling out of the front of the house. When the children came into the room where we were sitting, she told them in a firm but calm voice that she was not to be interrupted. The seven-year-old was instructed to watch the two younger children until their father showed up. The mother recounted how, after taking a course in the local community college, she had started to take her children with her to the library and to read to them every evening. By the time I left the interview I was close to tears as I thought about this woman's attempt to pull herself out of poverty. Driving across town to the cool, stately house, surrounded by greenery, where my parents lived did nothing to reduce the knot in my chest. In my heart of hearts, I knew that my efforts to communicate the unjust plight of this young mother and her children might win me academic kudos but was unlikely to change her situation or improve the life chances for her children.

Lifelong studies can transform an academic's view of the research process and undermine his confidence in the limited set of tools available for gaining lasting knowledge. Lifelong studies resolve some complexity while revealing others. In the best of all worlds, longitudinal research improves our understanding of lives through time, but it only rarely establishes certain conclusions. Hard as it is to arrive at certainties, long-term studies demonstrate the even greater difficulties of eroding popular stereotypes, destroying conventional wisdom, or combating political contrivances. Sadly, it seems that longitudinal studies surely have a greater capacity to change the lives of researchers than of altering the lives of the participants.

References

Banfield, Edward C. 1970. *The Unheavenly City: The Nature and the Future of Our Urban Crisis.* Boston: Little, Brown.

Coleman, James S. 1974. *Youth: Transition to Adulthood.* Chicago: University of Chicago Press.

Elder, Glen H., Jr. 1974. *Children of the Great Depression: Social Change in Life Experience.* Chicago: University of Chicago Press.

Elo, Irma T., Rosalind Berkowitz King, and Frank F. Furstenberg. 1999. "Adolescent Females: Their Sexual Partners and the Fathers of Their Children." *Journal of Marriage and the Family* 61(1): 74–84.

Furstenberg, Frank F. 1970. "Premarital Pregnancy Among Black Teenagers." *Trans-Action* 7(7): 52–55.

———. 1976. *Unplanned Parenthood: The Social Consequences of Unplanned Parenthood.* New York: Free Press.

———. 1980. "Burdens and Benefits: The Impact of Early Childbearing on the Family." *Journal of Social Issues* 36(1): 64–87.

———. 1988a. "Bringing Back the Shotgun Wedding." *Public Interest* 90(winter): 121–27.

———. 1988b. "Good Dads, Bad Dads: The Two Faces of Fatherhood." In *The Changing American Family and Public Policy*, edited by Andrew J. Cherlin. Washington, D.C.: Urban Institute Press.

———. 1991. "As the Pendulum Swings: Teenage Childbearing and Social Concern." *Family Relations* 40(April): 127–38.

———. 1995. "Fathering in the Inner City: Paternal Participation and Public Policy." In *Fatherhood: Contemporary Theory, Research, and Social Policy*, edited by William Marsiglio. Thousand Oaks, Calif.: Sage Publications.

———. 2001. "The Fading Dream: Prospects for Marriage in the Inner City." In *Problem of the Century: Racial Stratification in the United States at Century's End*, edited by Elijah Anderson and Douglas S. Massey. New York: Russell Sage Foundation.

Furstenberg, Frank F., and Jeanne Brooks-Gunn. 1986. "Teenage Childbearing: Causes, Consequences, and Remedies." In *Applications of Social Science to Clinical Medicine and Health Policy*, edited by Linda H. Aiken and David Mechanic. New Brunswick: Rutgers University Press.

Furstenberg, Frank F., Jeanne Brooks-Gunn, and S. Philip Morgan. 1987. *Adolescent Mothers in Later Life.* New York: Cambridge University Press.

Furstenberg, Frank F., Thomas Cook, Jacquelynne Eccles, Glen H. Elder, and Arnold Sameroff. 1999. *Managing to Make It: Urban Families in High-Risk Neighborhoods.* Chicago: University of Chicago Press.

Furstenberg, Frank F., and Kathleen A. Foley. 1999. "Paternal Involvement and Children's Health: A Longitudinal Study." Paper presented at the first biannual conference of the Harvard University Urban Seminar Series on Children's Health and Safety, Conference on Fatherhood. Cambridge, Mass. (April 23–24).

Furstenberg, Frank F., and Kathleen Mullan Harris. 1993. "When and Why Fathers Matter: Impacts of Father Involvement on the Children of Adolescent Mothers." In *Young Unwed Fathers: Changing Roles and Emerging Policies*, edited by Robert Lerman and Theodora Ooms. Philadelphia: Temple University Press.

Furstenberg, Frank F., Mary Elizabeth Hughes, and Jeanne Brooks-Gunn. 1992. "The Next Generation: The Children of Teenage Mothers Grow Up." In *Early Parenthood and Coming of Age in the 1990s*, edited by Margaret K. Rosenheim and Mark F. Testa. New Brunswick: Rutgers University Press.

Furstenberg, Frank F., Judith A. Levine, and Jeanne Brooks-Gunn. 1990. "The Daughters of Teenage Mothers: Patterns of Early Childbearing in Two Generations." *Family Planning Perspectives* 22(2): 54–61.

Furstenberg, Frank F., Milton Markowitz, and Leon Gordis. 1969. "Birth Control Knowledge and Attitudes Among Unmarried Pregnant Adolescents." *Journal of Marriage and the Family* 30(1): 34–42.

Furstenberg, Frank F., George Masnick, and Susan A. Ricketts. 1972. "How Can Family Planning Programs Delay Repeated Teenage Pregnancies?" *Family Planning Perspectives* 4(3): 54–60.

Furstenberg, Frank F., and Kathie Talvitie. 1979. "Children's Names and Paternal Claims: Bonds Between Unmarried Fathers and Their Children." *Journal of Family Issues* 1(1): 31–57.

Furstenberg, Frank F., and Christopher C. Weiss. 2000. "Intergenerational Transmission of Fathering Roles in At-Risk Families." *Marriage and Family Review* 29(2–3): 181–201.

Harris, Kathleen Mullan. 1997. *Teen Mothers and the Revolving Welfare Door.* Philadelphia: Temple University Press.

Lewis, Oscar. 1968. *The Study of Slum Culture: Backgrounds for La Vida.* New York: Random House.

Luker, Kristin. 1996. *Dubious Conceptions: The Politics of Teenage Pregnancy.* Cambridge, Mass.: Harvard University Press.

Moynihan, Daniel Patrick. 1965. *The Negro Family: The Case for National Action.* Washington: U.S. Government Printing Office for the U.S. Department of Public Policy and Planning.

Murray, Charles. 1984. *Losing Ground: American Social Policy, 1950–1980.* New York: Basic Books.

Nathanson, Constance A. 1991. *Dangerous Passage: The Social Control of Sexuality in Women's Adolescence.* Philadelphia: Temple University Press.

Rubin, Lillian B. 1976. *Worlds of Pain: Life in the Working-Class Family.* New York: Basic Books.

Sklar, June, and Beth Berkov. 1973. "The Effects of Legal Abortion on Legitimate and Illegitimate Birth Rates: The California Experience." *Studies in Family Planning* 4(11): 281–92.

U.S. Department of Commerce. U.S. Bureau of the Census. 1999. "Births: Final Data for 1997." *National Vital Statistics Report* 47. Washington: U.S. Government Printing Office (April).

Vincent, Clark E. 1961. *Unmarried Mothers.* New York: Free Press.

Vinovskis, Maris A. 1988. *An "Epidemic" of Adolescent Pregnancy? Some Historical and Policy Considerations.* New York: Oxford University Press.

Vinovskis, Maris A., and P. Lindsay Chase-Lansdale. 1988. "Hasty Marriages or Hasty Conclusions?" *Public Interest* 90(winter): 128–32.

Wilson, William J. 1987. *The Truly Disadvantaged: The Inner City, the Underclass, and Public Policy.* Chicago: University of Chicago Press.

Zelnick, Melvin, John F. Kantner, and Kathleen Ford. 1981. *Sex and Pregnancy in Adolescence.* Beverly Hills, Calif.: Sage Publications.

PART II

LIVES AND STUDIES IN SOCIAL HISTORICAL CONTEXT

Chapter 3

Looking Backward: Post Hoc Reflections on Longitudinal Surveys

FRANK L. MOTT

T HE CONCEPT of a career is far from unique, as it can be viewed in so many ways in a longitudinal context. Indeed, in important respects, a career can best be defined retrospectively, once one can look backward and turn a continuing series of events into an intellectual whole. Even then, one must be careful not to inadvertently reconstruct a disconnected work history into something it is not.

In my case, although there was significant intellectual continuity, there also has been considerable serendipity. The continuity has to do with my having an essentially quantitative and social science orientation. The serendipity relates to where I happened to be at particular points in my life cycle. For example, many years ago, having completed a master's degree in economics at the University of Pennsylvania and hoping for a break from academia, I was offered two jobs, one at the U.S. Bureau of the Census and one at the U.S. Department of Labor. I chose the Department of Labor because it appeared the work there would draw on both my technical and social research inclinations.

Shortly thereafter came one of the serendipitous events: I happened to be on staff when the director of my department, Howard Rosen, initiated the National Longitudinal Surveys (NLS). Rosen arranged for the surveys to be run by Herbert Parnes at the Ohio State University. As it later turned out, this represented a very good match for me, though if anyone had told me at that time that I would still be connected with longitudinal surveys almost thirty-five years later, I would not have believed it.

After a number of years in what was then known as the Manpower Administration of the U.S. Department of Labor, I returned to Brown University to pursue a mixed program of sociology and demography, essentially the same intellectual track I had been on, and ultimately received my doctorate. A brief return to the Labor Department and the NLS followed. Feeling I had had enough of Washington, I accepted an appointment with the Population Council in Lagos, Nigeria, at the Human Resource Research Unit of the University of Lagos. There I taught courses, conducted research, and ran surveys on population and topics related to human resources. Being young, and not a good planner, I found myself in Nigeria two years later, wondering how, from this faraway location, I could find an academic job in the United States. (This was well before e-mail—indeed in a location where even telephone and mail were not very effective.) I wrote to Herb Parnes at Ohio State, whom I knew well through my work on the National Longitudinal Surveys and respected personally and professionally. Parnes offered me a job.

My research agenda over the years has united my intellectual inclination with the practicalities of data availability. Of course, these are not entirely distinct, in that I played a role in determining what data was collected. In the early years the primary focus of the NLS was the collection of economic data, including some demographics. My typical analytical orientation was somewhat different. Indeed, for many years I have considered myself an ombudsman for the social science community, broadening the data collection to include inputs and outcomes essential to the research needs not only of economists but also of sociologists, psychologists (particularly those in child development), health researchers, and others. My performance of this role has not always been smooth, as the remainder of this paper illustrates. However, it has been satisfying and consistent with the intellectual orientation of the National Institute of Child Health and Human Development, the agency that has been a pivotal sponsor of the NLS for almost two decades.

The research focus of my work over the past twenty-five years has been integral life-course events, their determinants, and their consequences. This includes marriage and divorce and their consequences for women and children; women's transitions in and out of the labor force, particularly in relation to childbearing; adolescent substance use and sexuality; and most recently, issues associated with fatherhood and child development. Contemporary national longitudinal data collection frequently focuses on data relevant to questions of current interest, and so my work with the NLS has often permitted me to explore major issues of contemporary social concern. The dynamic nature of the various surveys has usually made it possible for me to explore research issues of personal interest without going far afield. A deliberate secondary goal of much of this work has been to publicize the available data and to encourage other researchers to use the NLS data. The intersection of interests—my personal ones, those of society, and those of the broader research community wishing to use the data—is a major factor in my longevity in this field and the reason I can claim, in a psychological and intellectual sense, to have had a "career."

I would be remiss not to emphasize the fact that others have played an equally important part in this career—namely, my wife and our two children. We have had and continue to have a family life incorporating two careers, which sometimes intersect, and two other "transitions to adulthood." The inertia responsible for my remaining in the same career after all these years comes not only from strong positive feelings about my own professional life but equally strong positive feelings about the life trajectories of these other family members.

I have alluded to a number of points at which my personal orientations and the vicissitudes of my career have crossed paths. My long and close connection with the National Longitudinal Surveys affords me the role of historian, not so much in detailing the surveys as in illuminating how, for better or worse, longitudinal surveys cannot be separated completely from their historical context.

Social, political, and economic contexts are all essential ingredients in explaining why longitudinal surveys, particularly those with long time lines, can evolve in a variety of intentional, as well as serendipitous, directions over time. Indeed, it is perhaps fair to say that the longer a survey's time line, the greater the likelihood that the ultimate data collection will differ substantially from the original intent. A long-term panel survey is much like a small boat making a long journey, continually being buffeted by gentle winds or other outside forces. The original intentions are rational, but owing at least partly to external forces, the final destination may or may not conform with the journey's intended outcome. In the case of longitudinal data collection, the reasons for this veritable laundry list of both exogenous and endogenous forces are many. Some reasons for changes in direction are unfortunate, many are intentional and positive, and at least as many have both positive and negative effects; indeed, many consequences cannot be evaluated until years after a survey has run its course.

A Social Historical Perspective

When I refer to the National Longitudinal Surveys, I am indeed referring to a series of surveys, some of which began in the 1960s and have continued for four decades. The world was a different place then, as was social science in both content and method. As noted earlier, the longer the time line for the data collection, the greater the likelihood that fundamental social transitions can alter the meaning or value of data collected earlier.

In the past several decades we have witnessed massive changes in our social fabric, as indicated by fundamental changes in both attitudes and behaviors. Although we have a long way to go to attain full racial equality, clearly we have made substantial strides toward bringing African Americans into the social and economic mainstream. The integration of millions of Hispanic Americans from many diverse cultures into American society is an ongoing process, as is the assimilation of Asian Americans. Perhaps the most dramatic changes have been in norms relating to the roles of women in society. From the perspective of longitudinal (panel) data collection, the presence of surveys such as the National Longitudinal Surveys is extremely fortunate, as it has permitted a wide range of careful social and economic analyses of many topics directly linked with these fundamental societal changes. However, the news is not all good; many of these changes have occurred at a pace far beyond our ability or willingness to change our data collection efforts. There is much evidence of this in national, particularly federally funded, data collection.

Typically, specific questions dealing with important topics do not enter into national data collection efforts until well after the attitude or behavior in question is well established within the normative structure. Although this is easy to understand, it makes the attempt to quantify and evaluate the significance of social changes, particularly at the "cutting edge," extraordinary difficult. For example, our contemporary ideas about what constitutes a family are undergoing rapid change as a growing variety of family forms have gained normative approval. This is not to say that many of these forms have not been in evidence for many decades but simply that contemporary social and political processes have perhaps made it easier for less mainstream relationship structures to gain a firmer foothold in American society. Similarly, societal notions regarding "acceptable" fertility behavior have surely undergone important reconstruction in recent decades.

Let me connect these two related normative notions to recent national data collections, beginning with a brief consideration of our recent decennial census. The concepts of household and family have been and continue to be fuzzy, often meaning different things to the Census Bureau and the average citizen. Moreover, in both cases they have been changing over time: for many decades, "head of household" arbitrarily referred to the "man of the house." This notion has been altered over the past two decades, although the evidence available so far suggests that the change has been of little pragmatic consequence (see Smith 1992). "Householder," the term now used, refers to an individual of either gender who rents or owns the dwelling unit. In practice, this person is typically male.

From an analytical perspective, however, the problems arising out of the official definition of "family" offer much greater cause for concern. The traditional and continuing official definition of family refers to two or more individuals living together who are related by blood, marriage, or adoption. Without belaboring this issue here (although I return to it later in this paper, in the context of the National Longitudinal Surveys), in many respects this is a limiting concept when examining the contemporary population of the United States from an analytical perspective. In part, the problem is the difficulty in defining relationships in a manner consistent with contemporary mores. The bigger issue, however, which becomes crucial when one is examining patterns over time, is that rarely have national data collection efforts collected data on basic characteristics (such as earnings, other relationship history information, or even basic fertility information) for anyone other than a respondent or a spouse. Indeed, in many instances, basic information has not been gathered for spouses because the respondent, typically male, was assumed to be the individual responsible for much of the family's relevant nonhome activities.

Thus from a longitudinal perspective, the fact that appropriate relationships and their characteristics have not been fully defined over time means that the data elements for reconstructing desired patterns of relationship after the fact are not available. Family income represents a typical, and excellent, example of this problem: it is generally infeasible to gather information on partners (regardless of gender) using much of the data currently being collected, and rarely possible for previous points in time. Sometimes this problem can be resolved by collecting the needed information retrospectively. Of course, this is possible only in a longitudinal data collection effort, and in studies of this kind, most attitudinal and behavioral information obtained retrospectively may be of a sensitive nature and is notoriously unreliable. As long as "family" continues to be officially defined in the traditional manner—for example, as long as income or earnings information is asked only for selected or traditional family members—the problem will persist. From the perspective of sample selection, one essentially mechanical suggestion is that all samples be defined in terms of individuals rather than a stipulated group of individuals whose boundaries may change conceptually over time.

Social norms can also constrain analyses of trends in situations in which certain kinds of questions can be asked only of certain kinds of people and in which the person deemed an appropriate respondent changes over time. The Current Population Survey—the monthly survey that not only collects basic employment and unemployment data but has also gathered information on topics such as marriage and fertility on an annual basis—provides a good example of this limitation. Until 1975, this census survey limited its lifetime fertility questions to women who had ever been married because of the presumed sensitivity of asking those questions of unmarried women. However, in a 1975 experiment, they found virtually no difference in the willingness of respondents to provide this information, regardless of marital status (U.S. Bureau of the Census 1976). Therefore, in 1976, these questions were additionally asked of all women who were at least eighteen years of age and had never married.

Furthermore, despite the fairly consequential number of single women under the age of eighteen who reported having given birth, the Current Population Survey did not begin collecting fertility information for these women until the early 1990s. Although vital statistics have always provided birth counts by age, the analytical utility of these records has been historically quite limited. Given the growing program and policy importance of issues associated with adolescent childbearing throughout the 1980s, it is interesting to note that the Current Population Survey, a primary data set for examining national fertility trends, did not include this important population subset in their data collection effort.

Official thinking has progressed slowly on this issue. For instance, in rationalizing the fact that the 1970 National Fertility Study was limited to an examination of women who had at some time been married, researchers have made note of the problems "inherent in asking questions about fertility and contraception of never-married young girls" (Westoff and Ryder 1977). In 1973 the first National Survey of Family Growth (conducted by the National Center for Health Statistics, data collection by the National Opinion Research Center at the University of Chicago) expanded this sample somewhat by including women who had never married and already had children. As Charles Westoff and Norman Ryder (1977) noted a few years later, "The profession may be close to considering this whole question" (4). To my knowledge, the 1982 round of the National Survey of Family Growth, carried out by the research company Westat, became the first in-depth national fertility survey to include a fully representative sample of all women of childbearing age.

It should be noted that the 1980 census indeed asked about the fertility behavior of all women, thus preceding the Current Population Survey by close to a decade. In retrospect, though the demography profession may have internalized the notion that proper fertility analysis requires fertility data for a full cross section of women of childbearing age, the federal infrastructure, with its power of the purse, was still ambivalent. Even more specifically, the Census Bureau, with its more stringent data collection rules and regulations, was somewhat schizophrenic in its willingness to ask questions on topics related to attitudes or behaviors that some nontrivial portion of the population might consider sensitive.

From the perspective of the conference from which this volume emerged, the bottom line is that the existence of scientific need, or program and policy relevance, are necessary but not sufficient conditions for defining national data collection. As a result, essential longitudinal (or cross-sectional) data may not become available until well after the behavior or attitude that requires examination has entered the normative mainstream. In part, the problem is that government agencies making many of the ultimate decisions on data collection are creatures of the body politic, and political considerations typically trump scientific considerations. This, of course, is a problem for cross-sectional as well as longitudinal surveys.

The National Longitudinal Surveys

Let me now shift gears and focus more specifically on how some of these issues have impacted data collection in the National Longitudinal Surveys. Some of the issues I highlight pertain directly to the willingness of a data collection agency to collect the data. With some embarrassment however, I acknowledge that some of the major data gaps are the result of errors on my part: my colleagues and I who were responsible for determining interview content at the Ohio State University's Center for Human Resource Research were not sensitive enough twenty-five to thirty-five years ago to know what data needed to be collected. The NLS currently includes a package of several national surveys that, to varying degrees, have been in process since the mid-1960s (U.S. Bureau of Labor Statistics 1998). The initial NLS cohort was what we termed the "mature" men, followed shortly thereafter by a survey of "young" men. The mature men's cohort covered men who were aged forty-five to fifty-nine when selected to be interviewed in 1966, the first survey year, and the young men's cohort covered men aged fourteen to twenty-four at the time they were selected for the first interview, which was initiated in late 1966.

Although these data were analytically useful for many purposes, at that time the rationale for collecting data on mature men rested heavily on the ongoing interest in programs and policies associated with potential job loss owing to automation, as well as to impending retirement. For the younger men, data collection focused primarily on issues associated with the transition from school to work. In 1967 an additional cohort of what was termed "mature" women, thirty to forty-four years of age, was initiated. This cohort was not part of the initial planning but was created in part because of internal pressures applied within the Department of Labor by individuals in the department's Women's Bureau. Even as late as 1967, a time when dramatic changes in the participation of women in the labor force were under way, the inclusion of women in a longitudinal data effort was not a given. Ultimately, inclusion of this cohort was attributed to the need to gain information about the dynamics of women's return to work when their children approached school age. Finally, in 1968, a fourth cohort of young women fourteen to twenty-four years of age was added for reasons paralleling those for the young men (Parnes et al. 1968). As it turned out, these data on young women were quickly and heavily utilized, because they constituted the first and only national data set for clarifying the many important linkages between education, family, and career for young women who were at the cutting edge of the female employment revolution.

As of this date, interviews continue to be carried out with the two cohorts of women. The two male cohorts have been terminated, largely for budgetary and attrition-linked reasons. For reasons I clarify further later in this paper, it is important to note that the data in these four surveys have been collected by the Census Bureau. The U.S. Department of Labor funded most of the core data collection for these cohorts, a fact that has impacted the kinds of data collected.

An additional cohort, the National Longitudinal Survey of Youth (NLSY79), was added to this package of data collection in 1979 (U.S. Bureau of Labor Statistics 1998). This data set, still in process, originally covered more than twelve thousand respondents aged fourteen to twenty-two when first interviewed in 1979, about equally divided between men and women. It also included an overrepresentation of African American (also true of the original 1960s cohorts), Hispanic, economically disadvantaged white, and military youth so that statistically meaningful cross analyses based on race and ethnicity would be possible. The Department of Defense requested and partially funded inclusion of the military sample. In 1982 the NLSY was substantially broadened to include a much wider range of demographic and health-related data. The additional data collected focused on the female respondents—in particular, on activities related to fertility behaviors and to prenatal and postnatal attributes and behaviors that could be predictive of and linked to healthy-child outcomes. Additionally, and perhaps most important, beginning in 1986 and continuing to this day the children of these female respondents have repeatedly been given a variety of cognitive and socioemotional assessment batteries, some self-administered and some completed by their mothers. (These child-linked data have been largely funded by the National Institute of Child Health and Human Development.) Since 1994, as they reached the age of fifteen these children are no longer tested but complete an interview schedule much like that completed by their mothers back in 1979.

One additional data collection effort should be noted. Beginning in 1997, a new youth cohort, termed the NLSY97 (the earlier youth cohort is now termed NLSY79) was initiated. This cohort originally constituted more than nine thousand youth, aged twelve to seventeen when first interviewed in 1997, with oversampling similar to that of the NLSY79. A fourth round of data has now been collected from these youth, and plans are to continue this newest survey indefinitely. It is important to note that whereas the data collection for the four original cohorts was completed by the Census Bureau, the data for the two newest cohorts have been gathered by the National Opinion Research Center at the University of Chicago. Thus, though all of the data collection efforts for all the cohorts have been funded by the federal government, the more recent data have not been directly collected by government agencies. Although all the data collection is subject to review by the federal Office of Management and Budget, the nonpublic data collectors typically are less constrained regarding the specific questions they are willing and able to ask and the data they are able to release. This is an issue that is of particular importance for a longitudinal survey, as the following discussion makes clear.

The Unique Value of the National Longitudinal Survey Data Collection

Longitudinal data, and panel data in particular, have unique strengths and weaknesses, and the unusual nature of the NLS magnifies them. The major weakness of a panel survey is that it is typically "cohort bound," so that, as in the case of any of the NLS cohorts, the data collection is limited to respondents who are a certain age in a certain year. The NLSY79 cohort, for example, was limited to men and women who were born between 1957 and 1964. This fact uniquely defines this group in terms of their own experiences since that date. The social norms and the political and economic environment these youth have experienced define their behaviors, attitudes, and general lifestyle in important ways. From an analytical perspective, any analyses carried out on these youth and their families must be qualified, to the extent that birth cohorts who preceded or followed them live in different milieus. Generalizations beyond this cohort are possible for some or perhaps even many analyses. It is usually assumed that such generalizations are possible; otherwise observations from a particular constrained cohort would be of limited value. On the other hand, the power of a panel data set rests in its ability to follow a cohort of individuals over time, clarifying micro- or individual-level processes. This clarification facilitates more meaningful life-cycle connections for individuals and families, but equally important it improves the likelihood of being able to infer causal connections.

If a panel data set includes a fairly wide age range (which the NLS does for some cohorts), then in some instances we can sort out period and cohort effects. For example, the 1967 mature women's sample is made up of women who were born between 1922 and 1937, a fairly heterogeneous period in American history. Depending on one's research interest, it thus can be treated as a series of birth cohorts, year-of-marriage cohorts, and so on.

An enormous strength of these data is the existence of a series of cohorts that overlap similar ages in different time periods. For example, as just noted, the mature women were born from 1922 to 1937, and the young women in the 1968 sample were born from 1943 to 1953. Our cohort of young women who were fourteen to twenty-two years of age in 1979 were born from 1957 to 1964. Finally, our latest cohort of young women, aged twelve through sixteen at the very end of 1996, were born from 1980 to 1984. This did not happen by chance; the planning for the temporally later cohorts was significantly conditioned by the presence of the earlier ones. The inherent limitations of a cohort sampling frame can be partially overcome if one has the foresight (or hindsight) and resources to replicate one's sampling and questionnaire design repeatedly over time.

Essentially, the NLS makes it possible to follow national cohorts of American women for all birth years from 1922 to 1964 (except the periods from 1937 to 1942 and from 1954 to 1956) well into adulthood. Ultimately, the newest cohort, born from 1980 to 1984, will enhance this analytical time line. Of course, to maximize the value of this time line one would wish to have as much comparability as possible over time, both in sample design and, more important, in data items and data concepts. However, the longer the time line, the more difficult this becomes, which leads us to a more careful discussion of these issues. These inherently complex issues are intimately linked to a multitude of social, political, and economic factors internal to the individuals and families we are studying, as well being closely tied to social and political issues of the day.

Data and Conceptual Inconsistencies over Time: Causes, Consequences, and Possible Resolutions

The problems discussed here have a variety of origins—political, economic, and intellectual. Sometimes they find effective solutions, sometimes ineffective solutions, and sometimes, unfortunately, they are beyond resolution. In some instances, the opportunity for resolution has passed one by for many different kinds of reasons. Cross-sectional surveys may encounter similar issues, but they tend to be magnified in longitudinal data collections. Let me begin with a few examples of why some of these issues arise and, in some instances, cannot be anticipated.

Maintaining respondent confidentiality is a critical issue for virtually all forms of data collection and particularly so for panel surveys. First, maintaining rapport with respondents is essential, as one wishes to contact them again (and maybe again and again and again). This cannot be done unless the respondents have the utmost confidence that what they tell the data collector will go no further. Second, and this is an issue that we became sensitive to early in the data collection game, the greater the volume of information a researcher has available about a person or family, the easier it becomes to identify that family. Certain forms of data collection make this particularly apparent. This problem has been of particular importance to the Census Bureau, which, because of its higher political profile, tends to be especially cautious in its data collection.

One example may illuminate this issue. When the 1960s cohorts were created, we included a variable identifying the state in which a respondent lived on the public-use data files. This soon became a concern to the Census Bureau because it opened the possibility, however remote, of identifying a specific individual. After a few interviews with a family, several state-level geographic identifiers would be available, the permutations of which might uniquely identify a particular household. This led to a decision to limit the geographic identification to the nine census divisions of residence. Similar logic prevailed, and after additional survey rounds, we were limited to identifying only the four census regions of residence. Ultimately, we have been reduced to providing users with only South or non-South residence. This identification problem was compounded by the fact that the data file included a number of area characteristics, such as categorical variables measuring the size of the labor force and the level of unemployment in the respondent's area of residence. It should also be noted that the federal confidentiality rules have become more stringent over the years, so that data that were considered acceptable in an early year may no longer have been so in later years. As this example illustrates, setting data collection priorities for longitudinal planning and maintaining comparability across variables over time becomes very complex, at least for certain data items.

This issue is more complex then I have implied, and in some instances leads to catch-22 situations. Over time, the reconstitution of confidentiality rules led, in some instances, to the Census Bureau's denying the release of data items that were already in the public domain. From our perspective, and given the long-term research objectives of users, changing decision rules in some instances resulted in our being less able to make rational priority decisions regarding which items would best be released. Indeed, as state and local policy issues become more important, the Census Bureau's stand on confidentiality vitiates the usefulness of any data that were collected when less restrictive rules applied.

Some of these issues may be endemic to national cross-sectional data collection. Others only become relevant, or perhaps become more cogent, in a panel survey. In terms of planning, it becomes extraordinarily difficult to anticipate changes in the political, bureaucratic, and legal decision-making process. Moreover, as noted later in this paper, it is difficult to anticipate social changes that make particular questions or wording more or less appropriate over time. Finally, it is often almost impossible to anticipate changes in the political landscape or in the importance of specific social issues, which invariably creates unintended pressures on data collection. This last point involves not just the issue of altering priorities in longitudinal data collection but also encountering pressure to incorporate data items that have high face validity but may have only cross-sectional analytical value in a survey intended primarily for analyses over time. In surveys that are cost constrained and, increasingly, time constrained, the cost of adding a one-time data supplement, which in all likelihood will be used only for cross-sectional analyses, is quite high.

Let me now provide a few examples in which our insensitivity to the currents of history resulted in seemingly incongruous gaps in data collection. I focus on issues that are closest to my particular research orientation. As I have already mentioned, the original young women's cohort (aged fourteen to twenty-four in 1968) was initiated with the prime objective of providing data to clarify the adjustment process from adolescence to adulthood in several life domains—school, work, and family. The desire to clarify the dynamics of this process, ideally from a causal perspective, was especially important. A particularly anomalous gap is evident when examining the young women's interview schedules for the early survey years, 1968 through 1977. It was only after ten years of data collection, in 1978, that the survey collected a birth history for the women.

A parallel but even greater analytical glitch may be found in the early rounds of the young men's survey. It was not until 1981, the last round for that survey, that a comprehensive birth history became available for the men in this cohort. In some respects, this was an even more significant analytical oversight than for the women, because a higher proportion of men than of women will live apart from their children at some point, and thus information about their children could not be accurately reconstructed from the household roster information. In contrast with this omission, the 1976 survey of young men included a complete roster of their siblings, regardless of residence. This is not to denigrate the importance of sibling information but rather to emphasize that given the primary objectives of specific longitudinal surveys, data collection processes are not always rational.

The primary objective of the surveys has always been to examine family labor force processes and dynamics, but it was not until many survey rounds had passed that reasonably comprehensive information related to family (in particular, spouse) employment was systematically collected in these surveys. Neither was information on child care gathered in any formal way for either cohort until many survey rounds had gone by. One might make the excuse that it was only in the 1970s that female employment analysis became mainstream, but such data had not been collected for the men, either. The blame for this omission can perhaps be attributed more directly to the limitations of economic theory at that time. Economists did not begin to analyze labor supply by considering the potential contribution of all family members until the middle or end of the 1960s (see, for example, Gary Becker's [1964] seminal work on the new home economics and Bowen and Finegan 1969). It was well into the 1970s before family economic modeling became the standard operating model (see overview in England and Farkas 1986).

Allowing for some time lags, it is thus not surprising that the principal labor force survey of the day did not become appropriately operational until many years later. There are a number of linked reasons for this time lag, some (but not all) of which are specific to the limitations of longitudinal data collection. First, more caution is always needed when making fundamental changes to a long-standing, ongoing, and successful data collection process. Second are issues of money and time: all surveys, including the NLS, are significantly time constrained. If one leaves a particular set of employment questions unchanged in order to maintain comparability over time, one invariably runs into a time barrier if one wishes to add an additional detailed series (for example, detailed employment experiences of other family members).

Often, the addition of an additional lengthy sequence of "essential" new questions requires the deletion of other items. Given the eclectic nature of an omnibus labor force survey, and the need to include at least a minimal package of explanatory information essential to understanding labor force processes, these trade-offs can be painful. As a result, there is rarely consensus among researchers of goodwill who sit around a table to set survey priorities, reflecting differences among them in research orientations and thus in their views of essential explanatory variables. In addition, the interest of the sponsors of the data collection effort must also be given great weight and are generally determined by the major program and policy issues of the day.

What I have just suggested is true for almost all surveys. What makes this issue particularly cogent for a panel survey is that over time there can be a major changing of the guard; and as the relevant actors in the agencies change, so too do their priorities. This, of course, is closely linked with the reality that funding for a longitudinal survey has been, and continues to be, provided on a relatively short-term basis and requires frequent periodic renewals. These renewals may not only alter some of the requested data collection; subject to funding constraints or shifts in funding priorities, they may also lead to rather sudden changes in samples. Although sample transitions are sometimes carried out with great thought, in other instances they may be quite precipitous and often beyond the control of the project officers or even the agency involved. In the case of the original NLS cohorts, when funds became constrained, the young men's cohort was terminated (at the point at which they had reached the ages of twenty-nine to thirty-nine), although in this instance an important contributing factor was substantial attrition, particularly of black men.

The sample of mature males was essentially ended in 1983, when the men were between the ages of sixty-one and seventy-seven. Although attrition for these older men was indeed significant, it owed largely to mortality, which, of course, does not introduce any real bias. An underlying reason for the sample termination was that, by virtue of its age, the sample was for the most part no longer of great interest to the Department of Labor. Thus, when funds became tight, it was relatively easy for the department to make the termination decision. From a longitudinal perspective, this was unfortunate, as this cohort had a seventeen-year track record including information on comprehensive employment, training, health, income, and family. Thus it represented an outstanding vehicle for examining the process of more and less successful transitions into retirement, a critical issue in an era in which issues associated with aging are so important. The vicissitudes of longer-term funding were certainly at play here. As important was the fact that specific government sponsors have specific interests that can change; in this case, the peculiar interests of an agency can certainly be life-cycle- and program-specific. (In the case of the mature men's survey, a one-time follow-up survey was completed in 1990, with funds obtained in a grant from the National Institute on Aging.)

Generating cooperation and encouraging overlapping interests across agencies is a solution that is being increasingly implemented. In some respects, this bodes well for longitudinal omnibus surveys that tend to be heterogeneous in their data collection elements and thus increasingly useful in meeting the data needs of agencies with diverse missions. It is fair to conclude here that the discrete manner in which much government-sponsored data collection has been agency specific, and thus topically specific, has resulted in many analytically constrained, sometimes misspecified, analyses. As a generalization, however, it is also perhaps fair to say that this mode of funding has changed substantially in recent years, as interagency cooperation and funding possibilities have snowballed. This bodes well for a more rational approach to the funding of omnibus panel surveys in the future. One downside to this is that the more eclectic the data collection, the more difficult it becomes to collect all "essential" data elements within a finite interview schedule.

The National Longitudinal Survey of Youth, initiated in 1979, illustrates some issues and problems that are unique to longitudinal data collection. The original cohort included a military oversample, which was funded by the Department of Defense. However, the military sample was terminated in 1984, when its funding expired, and the possibility for extended in-depth analysis of the effects of early military service on subsequent adjustment to civilian life was lost. Additionally, the NLSY originally involved oversampling of economically disadvantaged white youth, but this oversample was discontinued in 1991. Although the wisdom of the original oversampling is admittedly debatable, the fact remains that as of 1990 a vast amount of information about employment, education, and family had been collected for this population subgroup that was important from a policy perspective.

Discontinuing the data collection on economically disadvantaged white youth had another unintended negative effect. Beginning in 1986, a substantial body of information was collected on a biennial basis about the cognitive and socioemotional development of all the children of the female respondents in the NLSY, with the expectation that this information would provide important insights into the subsequent development of these children. Yet, reflecting short-term funding constraints, for reasons of financial expediency the large oversample of children of economically disadvantaged female respondents was dropped from the NLSY child sample, after having been followed longitudinally for only one assessment data collection follow-up.

The child "add-on" to the NLSY79 represented a major breakthrough both for cross-agency cooperative funding and data collection and for cross-disciplinary cooperation. This collaborative effort meant that certain analytical and programmatic priorities of the National Institute of Child Health and Human Development could be addressed better than ever before at the relatively marginal (albeit still very substantial) cost of supporting only one component of a large ongoing data collection effort. The Department of Labor has made a major financial investment in this cohort, in the collection of longitudinal data on employment, education and training, income, and many related topics for a large representative sample of younger American men and women. This survey has formed the basis of a great number of research efforts exploring issues of employment and employability of the American population.

In contrast, a major component of the National Institute of Child Health and Human Development's research agenda relates to children—in particular, their physical, emotional, and intellectual development. Over the years there had been little in the way of national data examining child development in a truly longitudinal context, which requires a lengthy family time line. The fortunate presence of a number of innovative thinkers both inside and outside of government led to a dramatic link between the agencies, resulting in a unique longitudinal data collection. The ready availability of the records of a respondent and the respondent's family from 1979 to 1986 could be linked with new data collection tests that were given to the children of all the female respondents in the NLSY79, beginning in 1986. These new tests instantaneously created a child development file that included a seven-year family history, at the marginal cost of the child-testing supplement. The children have continued to be tested every two years, as a supplement to the main NLSY79 data collection.

The Department of Labor and the National Institute of Child Health and Human Development have continued to be partners in this effort.

The net result has been a longitudinal data file that is meeting the needs of researchers in many disciplines. The richness and depth of the data collection has made it superior for many analytical purposes to a data set that would have included only one set of inputs. Regardless of one's research orientation, the longitudinal panel dimensions of the data permit causally oriented analyses that simply are not possible with cross-sectional data.

This process has not been as simple or as straightforward as the preceding paragraphs suggest. Clearly, in a time-constrained survey there will be tensions between the needs and interests of the different government agencies. Of perhaps even greater significance, there have been inherent tensions between the disciplines involved. It has not been easy to get many psychologists and members of the child development community, who typically use small, in-depth, purposive samples that they have collected themselves, to use a large anonymous set of data collected by others. To be fair, a data set like that of the NLSY cannot collect certain kinds of in-depth information as readily as a small intensive survey.

Second, significant disciplinary differences exist in how questions should be asked, as well as what questions can be asked. Typically—and there are significant exceptions—economists prefer highly quantified, behavioral questions, responses to which can be "unambiguously" obtained. In contrast, sociologists and social psychologists have a higher tolerance, and indeed need, for attitudinal and nonquantitative information. Over the years, this has led to several interesting discussions concerning what data should be collected. A longitudinal survey may be a preferable mechanism for collecting attitudinal information, because it more effectively collects information on a continuing, rather than a retrospective, basis. This somewhat reduces the risks of biased data associated with the reconstruction of history after the fact.

When these disciplinary differences are joined with the reality that the mix of actors in this cross-disciplinary drama changes over time, and that over time all disciplines experience changes in data priorities, it can be seen that longitudinal data collection intensifies the likelihood of discontinuities in the coherence of the data collection effort. Indeed, with every new round of data collection, it is possible to reopen discussions about what data should be collected. These include both the cross-disciplinary discussions already noted and input from sponsors who may be dealing with new programs and priorities. This represents a positive outcome when the data enhancement improves the overall analytical quality of the data set from a longitudinal perspective. In cases in which it results in the inclusion of a supplement that has essentially only cross-sectional analytical value, the addition may come at a high cost. Also, from a longitudinal perspective, there is some tendency for items intended only for short-term analysis to take on a life of their own and remain in the survey indefinitely, owing either to oversight or to an inherent inertia that discourages removal of items from a panel data set. In this regard, one suggestion is that those working with longitudinal data sets need systematically to consider data deletion as well as addition—not an easy task. It involves a careful consideration of which items have not been used and, additionally, have no apparent utility for future use.

Internal Data Evaluation and Data Reconstruction

The fact that certain questions may be asked repeatedly either in similar or slightly different form can be an important strength or weakness, depending on one's specific objectives. In the simplest case, an identical item may be repeated in successive or disparate survey rounds. This may be because it is easier to ask a question again than to search out and reword a question that could potentially alter its meaning. The upside of repetition is that it can permit one to gauge data quality as measured by consistency of response. The downside is that inconsistent response issues cannot always be resolved.

In the early years of the NLSY, there were many instances in which questions of fertility history were repeated with high levels of inconsistency. Not surprisingly, the likelihood of inconsistency increased the further removed one was from the date of the original event, for a number of reasons (Mott 1983, 1985). Reports on specific fertility events, both the dates of birth and the actual existence of specific children, not infrequently have changed from survey to survey. These fertility-related report inconsistencies are particularly prevalent for men but are also in evidence at a nontrivial level for women (Mott 1998). We presently have a substantial research evaluation project under way to quantify the magnitude of this issue.

A brief example from our ongoing male fertility data evaluation clarifies how substantial discrepancies can be. One of our ongoing evaluations involves a comparison of fertility reports for the men in the NLSY79 in 1984 with those interviewed in 1996. In this analysis, if the data are accurate, all births reported in 1984 should also appear in the 1996 birth record (limited to men interviewed at both points), and all youth aged twelve and older reported in 1996 should have appeared in the 1984 birth record. Here is what we found: Approximately one thousand men in the eligible sample reported at least one birth by 1984 or reported a child in 1996 that was born by the 1984 survey point. Of these one thousand purported fathers, sixty-six who reported a child in 1996 should have reported a child in 1984 but did not. Fifty-one reported a biological child in 1984 who should have been reported again in 1996 but was not. Fifty reported a change in at least one child's year of birth. All in all, substantial discrepancies between just those two years occurred in the reports of almost 25 percent of the men. As we examine reports across all the survey year possibilities, two things will happen: The number of anomalies will snowball, making us more aware of this major data issue. However, at the same time the longitudinal data will enable us to resolve many of the data discrepancy issues.

How do we resolve some of these discrepancies? Let me continue with a few examples and insights from earlier evaluations we have undertaken. First, a longitudinal survey can unambiguously improve some data. This is particularly true in cases in which there are dating inconsistencies. As one specific example that is especially important in our work with the NLSY, if there are discrepancies in reported birth years of a child from one survey to another, we can reasonably assume that the earlier report is more likely to be correct. This is a nontrivial occurrence, and the longitudinal nature of the data have permitted us to "clean up" many fertility records. As already noted, this has been a major problem in the fertility reporting by men, particularly younger and less educated men, who in many instances are no longer living with that child in subsequent years (and indeed, in a significant number of cases, may never have lived with the child). This of course does not guarantee that any of the dates are right; it simply indicates that one must be wrong.

Child dating information may be inaccurate because a parent, particularly an absent parent, simply cannot recall a date. Such longitudinal data, however, can provide useful inferences about family processes. This does not mean that resolution can always be obtained but merely that useful analytical clarification is sometimes possible. We are currently investigating this issue. Let me focus here specifically on the reporting of births and birth dates by male respondents. As mentioned earlier, men generally do a poorer job than women of remembering when their biological children were born. Part, although far from all, of this recall problem is related to the fact that men are much less likely to be living with their children. Indeed, when a relationship transition occurs, in the vast majority of cases—85 to 90 percent—children stay with their mothers, and often, for various reasons, fathers have little subsequent contact with their children.

In many instances, a long-term longitudinal survey offers insights into family processes even when data resolution is not possible. For example, we have cases in which a man will retrospectively redefine the status of a child—let us say, from biological child to stepchild, or vice versa—to match a relationship history more closely. As a relationship with a woman lengthens, a man might redefine children who live with the couple as biological, though the children were previously defined as stepchildren. Conversely, children who had been considered biological are sometimes redefined as stepchildren at some point after a relation-ship has ended. The longitudinal record does not necessarily tell us which is right and which is wrong, but it does provide important in-sights into family processes. The record can also tell us a bit about the social, if not the biological, reconstructions of parenthood.

There are parallel examples from a social perspective. Over the past decade, the NLSY has rostered all nonbiological children (mostly step-children) every other year, regardless of whether those stepchildren are in residence. Typically, those children tend to come and go with their bi-ological parents—that is, if a woman with children from a prior rela-tionship enters into a relationship with a male partner, those children typically follow the woman into the relationship and, from the man's perspective, can now be called his stepchildren—sometimes immedi-ately on entry and other times not until the woman and children have all been living with him for a while. Sometimes this social reconstruc-tion is clearly linked with the conversion of the relationship into a mar-riage, sometimes not. Interestingly, a symmetrical pattern is associated with the ending of relationships: sometimes a man disavows specific stepchildren when his relationship with their mother ends; in other cases, a man continues to identify his partner's children as his stepchildren in-definitely, even after the relationship ends.

Clearly, these disparate patterns have important social psychological meaning and may be important predictors of continuing affective links between these various actors, which, from the perspective of longitudi-nal analyses, may be important predictors of subsequent parent and child behavior patterns. It would be difficult to tease out these analyti-cal possibilities without continuing to maintain child rosters indepen-dent of residence, especially without a record of events over time. We are currently trying to sort out what measurable factors may be useful predictors of these different social connections.

My colleagues and I (Burchett-Patel, Gryn, and Mott 1999) have be-gun to quantify the potential responsibility that men may have over fairly lengthy time periods for nonbiological as well as biological chil-dren. This information is not typically available in surveys, as stepchil-dren in men's households come and go whereas, theoretically at least, biological children can be registered even if no longer present in the fa-ther's household. As has already been noted, the rostering includes at several time points acknowledged stepchildren who are present in the household as well as those who are acknowledged but not present. As an example, about one out of eight white and one out of five black men from our NLSY79 sample, who were thirty-one to thirty-nine years of age in 1996, indicated a connection with a stepchild in at least one sur-vey year from 1987 to 1996. In almost all instances, this child was pres-ent in the man's home at the time of at least one survey. The point I want to make here is that cross-sectional data collection cannot effectively provide a dynamic picture of complex family structures and how they change over time.

The foregoing example focuses on family social connections. A different kind of example, which was more prevalent in past decades, suggests that longitudinal records can change because of social norms and to be fully aware of this phenomenon one needs a longitudinal record. The NLS young woman's cohort that began in 1968 followed forward in time a national sample of women who were then fourteen to twenty-four years old. During the early years of the survey, many of the women began to have children, but not always within a marital relationship. Because we did not collect a fertility record until a number of years later, we could identify children born to these women only if they were living in their mothers' homes and therefore listed in the household records. Indeed, we used this household record information to construct an approximate fertility record, making the assumption that biological children in the household accounted for the large majority of children ever born to these women. In the process of constructing this record, we noted an interesting phenomenon.

By visiting the Census Bureau storage facility in Jeffersonville, Indiana, and examining the hard-copy records that included the actual names of all household members, we found that in a nontrivial number of cases, a younger child had been reported as, for example, the niece of a female respondent, but as the respondent aged, the child would be reported as her daughter. I use niece as an example, but the earlier reports could indicate any number of relationship possibilities. Although other interpretations are possible, we believe the dominant explanation is that the child was born to the woman when she was young and when no partner, certainly no spouse, was present. This was during a historical period when acknowledging a child outside of marriage, particularly for a younger woman, was, if not taboo, then far less socially acceptable than it is now. As these women aged, entered relationships, or formed their own households, the social stigma associated with the earlier birth event had substantially declined, thus creating the tendency to redefine relationships. Following these women over time permitted a clarification of these kinds of transitions.

A somewhat parallel example from our ongoing examination of respondent relationship records in the NLSY79 is informative. When this ongoing cohort was initiated in 1979, we included in the data collection an essentially continuous marital history, which allows a user to build a marital history for a respondent covering the entire time period from 1979 to the present. The record permits a user not only to identify a respondent's marital status on a continuing basis but also to identify whether or not the relationship has been with the same or a different spouse.

However, given the fact that other partnership relationships were less prevalent and also somewhat less socially acceptable at that time, we did not include partnership information in this relationship record, beyond noting whether or not a partner (regardless of gender) was listed in the household record. Only recently have we begun to include partnership information in the survey instrument, including dates on which such relationships began. However, even now, we have no on-going partnership record that would enable a researcher to integrate marriages and cohabitations in order to build continuous relationship profiles. A data user cannot tell from the annual household record information whether a cohabiting partner is the same person who was present during earlier surveys and, for the most part, cannot tell whether cohabitors and spouses are the same or different individuals. Because this is now a mainstream issue from the perspective of many kinds of analyses, we reconstructed relationship histories for the period from 1979 to 2000 to the extent the data permit. This is also part of the male fertility project described earlier in this paper. This project is feasible only because we have internally available the names of all the individuals on the household record.

For obvious reasons of confidentiality, we cannot release the names of the individuals to the public. We have matched the names of all spouses, other partners, and other appropriate-aged adults in the households of male respondents across the available eighteen waves of data. This enables us to ascertain whether reported spouses, cohabitors, and other adults are the same or different individuals from one year to another. Using this constructed record, we have prepared a set of variables that permit users to link these individuals over time while still maintaining individual confidentiality. Clearly this cannot be a perfect record, as individuals can come and go between survey rounds and thus might never appear on a particular survey date. Nonetheless, this may turn out to be the best available relationship history for a contemporary American cohort, as the data on relationships indicated at each survey point were collected contemporaneously and are probably less subject to post hoc relationship reconstruction. This is another example in which a reasonably accurate life-event history could be collected long after the event only because a panel record was available. This relationship record is now available to all interested users.

How does this parallel the foregoing fertility example? As with fertility, one can find a number of analytically useful examples of relationship transitions, suggesting how normative change, as well as personal preferences, may dictate the way such transitions are reported. As with fertility, some of the possible inferences one may make are not definitively verifiable. However, the data set does include complementary longitudinal information that may aid with the detective work.

First, what can this kind of longitudinal record tell us? With a reasonable degree of confidence it can tell us which categories of individuals maintain stable relationships regardless of marital status, which move from cohabitation into marriage with the same individual, and which show a history of many relationships with many individuals. This relationship time line permits a researcher to clarify, for example, which category of men first report themselves as married to a specific individual for a number of years and later redefine themselves as cohabiting with the same person. In at least some instances, this may be associated with the recent greater normative acceptability of acknowledging a cohabiting relationship. The main methodological point to be emphasized here is that this relationship identification is being provided on an ongoing basis, reducing the likelihood of a retrospective recreation owing either to recall error or to a conscious reconstruction of history. Equally important, any analyses of the determinants of relationship events or transitions can make use of a wide range of antecedent explanatory variables—behaviors as well as attitudes—that were asked about before the event rather than at the same (cross-sectional) point that the outcome measure of interest was queried.

In the same vein, it will be possible to construct parallel records of biological and nonbiological children that can be meshed with the relationship record, perhaps clarifying causal connections not only between the birth and relationship events but also between how these various events are socially constructed at the various time points. For example, as noted earlier, it will be easier to describe how redefining one's relationship from cohabitation to marriage (or vice versa, with the same or a different person) may be linked with a social reconstruction of one's relationship with children either in or outside the household.

One additional data issue is useful for describing how longitudinal data, while having unique strengths, may also leave one with problems that do not readily lend themselves to satisfactory resolution. I focus here on self-reports of early sexual activity and relationships of youth over time. Up to this point, our data collection on early sexual activity and related subject matter has largely been asked about in a paper-and-pencil self-report booklet (although we are now beginning to ask these questions using computer-assisted technology). Youth older than twelve years of age are asked a sequence of items relating to their early sexual behaviors. Until now, we had not found an easy, low-cost mechanism that would enable us to avoid repeatedly asking youth the same questions at successive surveys. As a result, we have repeatedly asked a large sample of youth whether they have ever had sex, the age at which they first had sex, and a variety of questions about early relationships.

This repeated sequence may be a methodologist's dream, but in many respects it is an analyst's nightmare. Not surprisingly, many youth change their responses from survey to survey (Mott 1985; Mott et al. 1996). They alter, sometimes significantly, the age at which they first had sex. They sometimes regain virginity status and sometimes alter a retrospective response in the other direction. Although we can speculate about why this happens, we are invariably left with some uncertainty. The kinds of reasons suggested for changing responses include, but are not limited to, youthful braggadocio, lack of understanding as to what constitutes sexual intercourse, a very early, perhaps involuntary sexual encounter that a respondent prefers to forget, or simply faulty memory. Youths may change their minds regarding what they are willing to report, not conceptually unlike adults' changing their minds about acknowledging a child or a prior relationship.

Clearly resolution in this situation is not always possible, although "rational" decision rules must be developed. For example, if a youth repeatedly, in several surveys, reports one (and the same) young age at first sex and then changes his or her mind to report a different age, the researcher might reasonably choose the first report as the more likely. At slightly older ages, if a youth provides an (inconsistent) age that temporally postdates an earlier reported relationship, the earlier dates might reasonably be chosen as the more accurate. A researcher can sometimes clarify misreports in the same manner that we clarified some fertility misreports, by noting the survey point and age at which the event was first reported. Other examples could be given, but the reality remains that no amount of data evaluation can completely resolve this problem. Some might argue that it would have been preferable not to have multiple reports, on the grounds that repeating identical questions (at least for those who have already acknowledged a loss of virginity) not only costs time but also invites ambiguity. Although these arguments may be valid, it remains somewhat valuable to clarify the characteristics of consistent and inconsistent reporters for several reasons already noted. Incidentally, clarifying the accuracy of a report on sexual activity (or, for example, substance use) can never be clarified as easily as a live birth event, for which the evidence of the event is tangible.

However, the whole issue of examining relationships—how and why they are entered into or left—almost requires high-quality panel data for appropriately measuring ongoing behaviors, attitudes, and linkages between the two in a temporal, potentially causal context. In particular, when activities or behaviors that explicitly have high emotional content are being examined, the likelihood of effectively collecting all the essential analytical inputs and outcomes retrospectively is, in my opinion, very low. This likelihood is reduced even further when the time line incorporating the whole process being examined is lengthy. Shifting back to the example at hand, an appropriate analysis of how different kinds of youth follow different relationship paths, how these paths may reflect differing earlier backgrounds, and how these paths, in turn, may lead to different subsequent attitudes and behaviors almost of necessity requires an ongoing data collection effort.

Concluding Thoughts

It should be apparent that longitudinal surveys are uniquely useful for certain kinds of analyses and for exploring micro-level family and individual processes. Longitudinal surveys are not preferable for all research objectives, however, and unique costs are associated with them. Except in selected circumstances (and in important respects the NLS is one of those exceptions), panel data are cohort bound; and although they can provide unique in-depth analyses, these may be constrained by time and place. Additionally, the inherent strength of a panel design as has been described above can lead to many instances of irresolvable data decisions. To the extent that the typical omnibus design of a large national longitudinal survey results in data collection "bandwagon effects," at some point "enough" can become too much. That is, the eclectic nature of a survey such as the NLS can ultimately result in data overload. On the other hand, from the perspective of a particular government agency, a modest investment in data collection can yield an enormous analytical payoff; for the price of a few questions, one gains access to the whole data package.

Based on the foregoing synthesis, what might one recommend for the future, at least with respect to forthcoming longitudinal data collection efforts? First, to the extent possible, funding guarantees that data will continue to be collected for specific topical areas over long intervals should be provided. Without some attempt to minimize uncertainty, there will be continuing pressures to alter course as new actors enter the stage. Omnibus surveys are particularly subject to these pressures. There will always be changes in the intellectual content of disciplines, which will, in turn, require changes in data collection inputs. However, these must be considered and introduced cautiously, reflecting the considered decision of representatives from those disciplines. In the government scheme of things, new programs and policies bring with them new pressures, and with concomitant money and political clout, these may be hard to resist. Before being incorporated, all potential new inputs must be carefully considered from at least two perspectives: do the proposed new inputs fall within the intellectual scope of the study, and does the introduction of new content jeopardize in significant ways essential content already in the study, bearing in mind overall time constraints.

Second, the longer a survey continues, the greater these tensions become—political pressures come and go, and the respondents themselves pass through new life phases. In these respects, rather then waiting for outside pressures to force serendipitous change it is important for those most closely connected with the study to formally build into the structure regular and systematic discussions regarding the relevance of change for the study. This includes issues relating to specific content as well as more generally the efficacy of strengthening the breadth and depth of the intellectual content. It is much preferable to search for funding that fits than to wait for interested outsiders to appear with funding that creates pressure for unwanted content. All of this of course presupposes an overriding intellectual premise for the overall data collection effort.

Finally, when push comes to shove, from a longitudinal perspective, maintaining sample size and sample representativeness is absolutely critical in a long-term survey. This is no mean feat, as the major costs of a survey are driven by the number of interviews and not by the length of the interview. Losing selected oversamples, as has happened several times with the NLSY, has huge consequences because those lost cases, for most intents and purposes, are lost forever and hence retain little value. Clearly it is now much more difficult to maintain respondent cooperation than was true in past decades. This trend, and thus the average cost of each completed case, continues to rise substantially. One implication is that it may be preferable, if one has a known sum of money for a known period, to decide in advance to sample fewer cases, thus increasing the assurance that funds will remain available for maintaining a higher completion rate. Better a smaller number of cases for a sample that is fully maintained than perhaps even a larger number of completions in a sample that has lost significant numbers from its inception. The longer the survey time line, the more critical this issue becomes.

The intellectual return for each dollar spent on longitudinal data collection can be enormous, and the set of national longitudinal surveys I have described constitutes perhaps the best example of this. Because of the breadth of the surveys and the vast intellectual output over the years, it is impossible to synthesize in any meaningful way how effectively these data have been used from a programmatic perspective. As with any academically oriented data set, most of the return is intellectual.

Over the decades an enormous amount of information has been gained about how human beings behave and think with respect to employment, education, family, and many other issues. Since the inception of the NLS, its research track record includes more than 3,600 items, including more than 1,500 peer-reviewed journal articles, almost 500 doctoral dissertations, and numerous books, conference papers, and so on. Reflecting the heterogeneity of the data sets, there are well over 100 papers in the area of child development, about 250 on welfare-related issues, many of which focus on the consequences for children, almost 200 focusing on retirement issues from various disciplinary perspectives, and, of course, large numbers examining employment and unemployment issues, many focused on female employment—to mention just a few of the topics investigated. Although on occasion specific findings from this research may make it directly into the program and policy domain, the overriding value of this research is to inform the research community and the larger public about contemporary facts and issues of concern to all of us. Indeed, it is through such a scientific evolutionary process that most social science research ultimately is translated into social and economic programs and policies.

References

Becker, Gary. 1964. *Human Capital.* New York: National Bureau of Economic Research.

Bowen, William G., and T. Aldrich Finegan. 1969. *The Economics of Labor Force Participation.* Princeton: Princeton University Press.

Burchett-Patel, Diane, Thomas A. Gryn, and Frank L. Mott. 1999. "The Families of Men: Exploring Relationship Dynamics with the National Longitudinal Survey of Youth." Paper presented at the annual meeting of the Population Association of America. New York (March 25–27).

England, Paula, and George Farkas. 1986. *Households, Employment, and Gender.* New York: Aldine Publishing.

Mott, Frank L. 1983. "Fertility-Related Data in the 1982 National Longitudinal Surveys of Work Experience of Youth: An Evaluation of Data Quality and Some Preliminary Analytical Results." Final report prepared for the National Institute of Child Health and Human Development. Columbus: Ohio State University, Center for Human Resource Research.

———. 1985. "Evaluation of Fertility Data and Preliminary Analytical Results from the 1983 (fifth round) Survey of the National Longitudinal Surveys of Work Experience of Youth." Final report prepared for the National Institute of Child Health and Human Development. Columbus: Ohio State University, Center for Human Resource Research.

———. 1998. "Male Data Collection: Inferences from the National Longitudinal Surveys." Columbus: Ohio State University, Center for Human Resource Research.

Mott, Frank L., Michelle Fondell, Paul Hu, and Elizabeth G. Menaghan. 1996. "The Determinants of Sex by Age Fourteen in a High-Risk Adolescent Population." *Family Planning Perspectives* 28(1): 13–18.

Parnes, Herbert S., Belton M. Fleisher, Robert C. Miljus, and Ruth S. Spitz and Associates. 1968. *The Pre-retirement Years,* vol. 1. Columbus: Ohio State University, Center For Human Resource Research.

Smith, Daniel S. 1992. "Meanings of Family and Household: Change and Continuity in the Mirror of the American Census." *Population and Development Review* 18(3): 421–56.

U.S. Department of Commerce. U.S. Bureau of the Census. 1976. "Fertility of American Women: June 1975." *Current Population Reports,* series P20, no. 301. Washington: U.S. Government Printing Office.

U.S. Department of Labor. U.S. Bureau of Labor Statistics. 1998. *NLS Handbook 1998.* Columbus: Ohio State University, Center for Human Resource Research.

Westoff, Charles F., and Norman B. Ryder. 1977. *The Contraceptive Revolution.* Princeton, N.J.: Princeton University Press.

Chapter 4

Sheldon and Eleanor Glueck's Unraveling Juvenile Delinquency Study: The Lives of 1,000 Boston Men in the Twentieth Century

JOHN H. LAUB AND ROBERT J. SAMPSON

S OCIAL BEHAVIOR occurs in particular times and particular places, in concert with particular social actors. The implication of this fact is that individual development can be understood only in the specific historical context in which it occurs. Extending this idea further, it can be argued that social science studies and the principal investigators of those studies need to be situated in historical contexts as well. Yet the thrust of current social science research is seemingly just the opposite. National samples, generalization, and invariant causal imageries dominate the landscape. Researchers almost appear embarrassed to situate their studies or themselves in history, as if that signals a limiting weakness. Adhering to what Dale Dannefer (1984, 100, 103) terms the "ontogenetic" model, the prevailing view of development has been one of "maturational unfolding" irrespective of context. That is, environment and history are thought merely to form the stage on which life patterns are played out and as such have no real bearing on understanding development.

What is missing in much contemporary social science research, then, is an appreciation of how lives develop in time and space in distinctive or contingent ways. As a result, most explanations of human behavior are generalizing, not temporal or contextual, in their logic

(Griffin 1993, 1099). This contrasts dramatically with the time-place orientation of the old Chicago school. As Andrew Abbott (1997, 1152) puts it, "Chicago felt that no social fact makes any sense abstracted from its context in social (and often geographic) space and social time. Social facts are located." The researchers of the Chicago school thus stuck closely to the contextual underpinnings of their subject material. The stuff of this era included maps, dots to pinpoint location of events, and thick descriptions of places—railroad yards, abandoned buildings, street corners, taverns, brothels, and much more. Indeed, a study's locale was clear to all readers, and its historical context was easily identified. In contrast, it is not at all clear whether social science's current embrace of generalized logic and decontextualized, abstract variables are an improvement over the Chicago focus (see Sampson 1993).

Therefore, in this paper, we step back and take seriously the need to contextualize or situate one's study in history. For several years, we have been working with a longitudinal study of crime causation originated by Sheldon and Eleanor Glueck (see Glueck and Glueck 1950, 1968; Sampson and Laub 1993). This study collected data on one thousand white males who grew up during the late 1920s, the 1930s, and the early 1940s in the city of Boston, Massachusetts, and reached adulthood in the late 1940s, the 1950s, and the early 1960s. We believe the historical time and place of the Gluecks' study—the last three quarters of the twentieth century in Boston—is an especially interesting one in which to think about crime and deviance as well as more general developmental patterns over the life course, such as the transition from adolescence to adulthood. Drugs like crack cocaine were not even known in this time period, for example, and criminal violence, especially gun use, was far less prevalent than it is today. The role of pervasive alcohol abuse coupled with the virtual absence of other drug use thus suggests a strong period effect. With respect to developmental trajectories, the likelihood of military service, coupled with the expanding employment opportunities and the normative expectations surrounding early marriage, makes this a distinguishable and important context to examine.

In short, we believe that the historical context in which the Glueck study was conducted serves as a useful baseline for identifying areas in which research findings are consistent across time and, equally important, areas in which the findings of contemporary research differ. Indeed we argue that precisely because these data are "old" they provide an unusual opportunity to assess whether and in what ways the causes of juvenile delinquency and adult crime are specific to a historical period. The "age" of the Glueck data thus becomes a strength, not a weakness (see also Clausen 1993, 528–29).

The Unraveling Juvenile
Delinquency Study

For more than forty years, Sheldon Glueck and Eleanor Touroff Glueck performed fundamental research on crime and delinquency at Harvard University. Their primary research interests were the causes of juvenile delinquency and adult crime and the overall effectiveness of correctional treatment in controlling criminal careers. For their period, the Gluecks' research projects were unusually large empirical investigations that included extensive follow-up periods. Their major studies included the Massachusetts Reformatory study (Glueck and Glueck 1930, 1937, 1943), the Women's Reformatory study (Glueck and Glueck 1934a), the Judge Baker Foundation study (Glueck and Glueck 1934b, 1940), and the Unraveling Juvenile Delinquency (UJD) study (Glueck and Glueck 1950), plus later follow-ups (Glueck and Glueck 1968). From these studies the Gluecks generated four relatively large data sets and more than 280 articles and 13 books during the course of their professional careers (for an overview, see Glueck and Glueck 1964, 1974).

Undoubtedly the work for which the Gluecks are known best is *Unraveling Juvenile Delinquency* (Glueck and Glueck 1950). The UJD project, a study of the formation and development of delinquent behavior, began in the fall of 1939. The Gluecks originally planned for a delinquent sample to be drawn from the juvenile court (see letter to Dr. Elizabeth Hincks, February 14, 1938, Glueck Papers); they faced a major obstacle, however, in finding a court that would grant access to subjects without interference. Five hundred officially delinquent boys were eventually selected from the Massachusetts youth correctional system. The sample of "persistent delinquents" contained white males, aged ten to seventeen who had recently been committed to one of two correctional schools— the Lyman School for Boys in Westborough, Massachusetts, and the Industrial School for Boys in Shirley, Massachusetts (see Glueck and Glueck 1950, 27).

Five hundred nondelinquents, also white males aged ten to seventeen, were chosen from the Boston public schools. Nondelinquent status was determined on the basis of official record checks and interviews with parents, teachers, local police, social workers, and recreational leaders as well as the boys themselves. The Gluecks' sampling procedure was designed to maximize differences in delinquency—an objective that by all accounts succeeded (see Glueck and Glueck 1950, 27–29).[1] Still, as Jancis Long and George Vaillant (1984, 345) note, although the nondelinquent boys were certainly different from the Boston youth remanded to reform school, compared with national averages the nondelinquents "did not represent a particularly law-abiding group." The nondelinquents were not atypical "saints" but rather "normal" youth who had not been involved in official or serious, persistent delinquency as reported by parents, teachers, and others at the time of the study. Although clearly not a random selection, the samples appear representative of the populations of persistent official delinquents and generally nondelinquent youth in Boston at the time.[2]

The matching design was a unique aspect of the UJD study. The five hundred officially defined delinquents and five hundred nondelinquents were matched case by case on the basis of age, race or ethnicity (as indicated by the birthplace of both parents), neighborhood (socioeconomic status), and measured intelligence (see "Social Case Histories: Policy Memo," November 1939, Glueck Papers). When the study began the average age of the delinquent group was fourteen years and eight months, that of the nondelinquents fourteen years and six months. Regarding ethnicity, 25 percent of both groups were of English background, another fourth Italian, a fifth Irish, less than a tenth American, Slavic, or French, and the remaining were Near Eastern, Spanish, Scandinavian, German, or Jewish. As measured by the Wechsler-Bellevue test, the average IQ of delinquents was 92 and nondelinquents 94. The matching on neighborhood ensured that both delinquents and nondelinquents lived in lower-class neighborhoods of central Boston. In other words, both groups grew up in similar high-risk environments with respect to poverty and exposure to antisocial conduct.

The one thousand male subjects in the UJD study were matched on key criminological variables thought to influence both delinquent behavior and official reactions by the police and courts (Sampson 1986). That half of the boys were persistent delinquents and half had avoided delinquency in childhood thus cannot be attributed to residence in urban slum areas, age differences, ethnicity, or IQ.

Data Sources and Follow-Up

A wealth of information on social, psychological, and biological characteristics, family life, school performance, work experiences, and other life events was collected on the delinquents and nondelinquent controls from 1939 to 1948. Some key items regarding families were parental criminality and alcohol use, economic status, family structure (divorce or separation), family relations, and the patterns of supervision and discipline by parents. Items on grades, school-related behavior, and educational and occupational ambitions were included as well. There were also numerous indicators of recreational and leisure time activities, peer relationships, church attendance, and complete psychiatric profiles gleaned from psychiatric interviews.

The Gluecks' research team collected these data through detailed investigations that included interviews with the subjects themselves, their families, employers, school teachers, neighbors, and criminal justice and social welfare officials. Interview data were supplemented by extensive record checks across a variety of social agencies. The Gluecks were especially concerned with independent sources of measurement and hence provided a means to validate many of the key concepts. Most of the social variables (family income, parental discipline, and the like), for example, were collected from a variety of sources such as home interviews conducted by the Gluecks' research team along with independent visits by social welfare agencies. This level of detail and the range of information sources are unlikely to be repeated, given contemporary research standards on the protection of human subjects.

The original sample in the UJD study was followed up at two different points—when subjects were aged twenty-five and again at age thirty-two. This data collection effort took place from 1949 to 1965 (see Glueck and Glueck 1968 for more details). As a result, extensive data are available for analysis relating to criminal career histories, criminal justice interventions, family life, school and employment histories, and recreational activities for the matched subjects in childhood, adolescence, and young adulthood. Data are available for 438 of the original 500 delinquents (88 percent) and 442 of the original 500 nondelinquents (88 percent) at all three age periods. When adjusted for mortality, the follow-up success rate is approximately 92 percent—very high by current standards (see, for example, Wolfgang, Thornberry, and Figlio 1987). The low attrition is testimony to the Gluecks' rigorous research strategy but also to lower residential mobility and interstate migration rates in the 1940s and 1950s as compared with today. It should be noted, though, that the follow-up of criminal histories and official records covered thirty-seven states, particularly California, New York, New Hampshire, Florida, and Illinois (Glueck and Glueck 1968, xix). Overall, then, criminal history data from first offense to the age of thirty-two were gathered through extensive record checks of police, court, and correctional files.

Information from interviews and record checks was collected on key life events over the time of the follow-up period, as well. Of particular interest are items such as the nature and change of living arrangements as an adult—including marriage, divorce, frequency of moves, number of children, and military experiences; employment history and work habits (for example, number and type of jobs, weekly income, unemployment, reliance on public assistance); and schooling history (age at final academic achievement, reason for stopping schooling, adult education, and the like). There were also a host of survey items on factors such as participation in civic affairs, aspirations, types of companions, and nature of leisure time activities.

Historical Context of the UJD Project and the Principal Investigators

The historical context and institutional affiliations of the original investigators of the UJD project, Sheldon and Eleanor Glueck, had an important effect on their research program, especially their methodological stance toward the study of crime and its causes.[3] The Gluecks' educational background was eclectic and interdisciplinary in nature. Sheldon Glueck, in particular, was an academic maverick. He first attended Georgetown University (in 1914 and 1915) and then transferred to George Washington University, from which he received his bachelor's degree in the humanities in 1920. He went on to receive bachelor's and master's degrees in law from National University Law School in 1920.[4] After being denied admission to Harvard Law School, he entered the Department of Social Ethics at Harvard University, an interdisciplinary precursor to the sociology department (see Potts 1965 for a description of that department). There he received a master's degree in 1922 and a doctorate in 1924. Reflecting this diverse educational setting, Sheldon Glueck's (1925) doctoral thesis crosscut the interests of sociology, law, and psychiatry in its focus on criminal responsibility, mental disorder, and criminal law.

Eleanor Glueck's academic terrain was similarly eclectic. After attending Barnard College (from which she received a bachelor of arts degree in English in 1920) and the New York School of Social Work (in 1921) and working in a settlement house in Dorchester, Massachusetts, she enrolled in the School of Education at Harvard. She received her master's in education in 1923 and a doctorate in education in 1925. Eleanor Glueck's early research focused on the sociology of education, especially the relation between schools and the community, and evaluation research methods in social work (Glueck 1927, 1936; see also Gilboy 1936).[5]

Overall, then, the Gluecks were not beholden to any one discipline in an a priori sense, and as a result they published extensively in the leading journals of criminology, social work, psychology, sociology, education, law, and psychiatry. The price they paid for such an interdisciplinary outlook was steep (see Laub and Sampson 1991). Indeed, as Gilbert Geis (1966, 188) recognized more than twenty years ago, "The Gluecks belong to no single academic discipline, and they are suffering the déclassé fate of aliens and intruders." (1966, 188).

The Gluecks' social positions within the academic community were also unique at the time and would be even today. After teaching a few years in the Department of Social Ethics at Harvard, in 1929 Sheldon Glueck was appointed to the Harvard Law School as assistant professor of criminology. He became a full professor in 1932 and was appointed the first Roscoe Pound Professor of Law in 1950 (Laub 1995). Glueck's position as a professor of criminology in a law school was an unusual institutional arrangement that led him to a somewhat isolated and outcast perspective. Although law professors and students do not often conduct (or reward) social science research, that was his specialty and main interest. Moreover, research on the causes of crime was a particular anomaly in a law school setting—though during the 1930s the Harvard Law School had a tradition of research on the administration of justice (for example, the Cleveland Crime Survey and the Harvard Crime Survey). Glueck's institutional arrangement was also a structural constraint in another crucial respect: he had no opportunity to train doctoral students who might carry on the Gluecks' research agenda.

Perhaps more salient was the institutional treatment accorded Eleanor Glueck. Although armed with a doctorate in education and a prolific publishing record,[6] Eleanor Glueck was unable to secure a tenured faculty position or any teaching position at Harvard. From 1930 to 1953 she was employed as a research assistant in criminology at the Harvard Law School.[7] She was "promoted" in 1953 to research associate in criminology, a position she retained until 1964. At the same time, from 1929 to 1964, she was codirector of the project on the causes and prevention of juvenile delinquency.[8] In short, Eleanor Glueck's entire career at Harvard University consisted of a social position akin to what many students working toward doctorates face today before graduation. As such, she was an outcast from mainstream academia at Harvard University and the academic field at large.

The Gluecks' intellectual mentors were a diverse group drawn from a variety of disciplines, each an unusual thinker in his or her own right. The group included such figures as Roscoe Pound, Felix Frankfurter, Richard Cabot, Bernard Glueck, William Healy, Augusta Bronner, and Edwin B. Wilson. This diversity of intellectual influence is evident throughout the Gluecks' research careers. Early on, the Gluecks were influenced personally as well as professionally by Sheldon Glueck's older brother, Bernard, a forensic psychiatrist at Sing Sing prison with a long-standing interest in crime (see Glueck 1916, 1918). Equally important, it was Bernard Glueck who arranged the first meeting between one of his graduate students, Eleanor Touroff, and his brother Sheldon.

At Harvard the Gluecks were influenced by Richard C. Cabot, a professor in the Department of Social Ethics. It was in a seminar with Cabot that the idea for a study of five hundred offenders from the Massachusetts Reformatory originated. Cabot's own research had utilized the follow-up method in assessing the accuracy of diagnoses of cardiac illnesses (Cabot 1926). Sheldon Glueck noted that in the field of penology no studies had been done assessing the posttreatment histories of former prisoners. Excited by the prospects of such research, Cabot arranged financing for the Gluecks' research, which culminated in *Five Hundred Criminal Careers* (Glueck and Glueck 1930). Felix Frankfurter served as director of the Harvard Crime Survey in 1926 and was also influential in the Gluecks' early studies. In fact, the Harvard Crime Survey, of which the Gluecks' *One Thousand Juvenile Delinquents* (Glueck and Glueck 1934b) was the first volume, can be seen as an early model of scientific inquiry in the social sciences. According to Frankfurter (1934, xii), the survey was "not an agency for reform" but rather a contribution of scientific knowledge to society in the areas of criminal behavior and social policy that "heretofore had been left largely to improvisation, crude empiricism, and propaganda." Moreover, Frankfurter believed, the formulation of the problem and use of the scientific process to address the problem would eventually lead to prudent social policies. This general viewpoint can be found in all the Gluecks' research.

William Healy and Augusta Bronner were probably most influential in the Gluecks' intellectual history. The Gluecks had met Healy and Bronner, directors of the Judge Baker Foundation, when they first arrived in Boston, a meeting facilitated in part by Bernard Glueck. The Gluecks had read Healy's (1915) *The Individual Delinquent* and were favorably disposed to his research. Healy was also interested in issues relating to Sheldon Glueck's doctoral thesis and was one of the reviewers who encouraged its publication by Little, Brown (Glueck 1964, 319). Most important to the Gluecks was the "scientific attitude" of Healy and Bronner, and in a memorial address for Healy, Sheldon Glueck (1964, 319) stated that Healy had been "a major catalyst of our work." Like the Gluecks, Healy focused on the individual as the most important unit of analysis, embraced a multiple-factor approach in the study of crime causation, and utilized knowledge across a variety of disciplines (see Healy 1915; Healy and Bronner 1926). In fact, Jon Snodgrass (1972, 326) has referred to *Unraveling Juvenile Delinquency* as "essentially a modernized *Individual Delinquent*."

Three factors thus worked together to develop a fiercely independent and even iconoclastic outlook on the Gluecks' part: Interdisciplinary educational training combined with Sheldon Glueck's unusual position in the Harvard Law School and apparent gender discrimination against Eleanor Glueck served to create in them an almost bunker mentality, especially regarding the discipline of sociology.[9] The Gluecks were also constrained by their lack of involvement in the training of graduate students. Added to this was the intellectual diversity of a set of colleagues who fostered empirical research beyond the confines of any one discipline. It is only within this context that we can now understand the distinctive theoretical and methodological perspective the Gluecks brought to bear on their classic study of crime causation.

The Macro-Level Historical
Context of the Study Participants

The boys studied by the Gluecks in the UJD study were born between 1924 and 1935. A period marked by the Great Depression, the rise of Adolf Hitler and Nazism, and extraordinary unrest and instability around the world. The Gluecks' research team began gathering data on the subjects of the UJD study in 1939 and 1940—the initial stages of World War II. This first wave of data collection continued through 1948. Data collection for the second and third waves continued throughout the 1950s and into the first half of the 1960s, a time of postwar prosperity and unprecedented economic opportunity in the United States.

Table 4.1 displays the key historical events influencing the lives of the subjects in the UJD study and anchors these events with respect to age for the oldest and youngest cohort members of the study. Because of the age variation among the subjects, key historical events influenced cohort members at different points in the life course. This suggests the importance of considering cohort effects, a main feature of life-course analysis. According to Glen Elder (1999), a cohort analysis is essential to understanding the effect of social change on lives by linking individuals to a specific social context (see also Ryder 1965). Furthermore, John Modell

Table 4.1   Age of UJD Study Men at Time of Selected Historical Events, by Age Cohort

Date	Event	Age of Older Cohort (Born in 1925)	Age of Younger Cohort (Born in 1932)
1929 to 1930	Great Depression, onset	4 to 5	—
1933	New Deal launched	8	1
1939 to 1940	World War II mobilization, initial stage	14 to 15	7 to 8
1945	World War II ends	20	13
1950 to 1953	Korean War	25 to 28	18 to 21
1950 to 1957	First follow-up by the Gluecks	25	25
1957 to 1964	Second follow-up by the Gluecks	32	32
1973	Vaillant's follow-up of criminal records	49	41
1995 to 1997	Third follow-up by Laub and Sampson	70 to 72	63 to 65

Source: Adapted from Sampson and Laub 1993, 60. For full citation see references.

(1989, 22) argues that "a social-historical approach to the life course might be no less interested in the way those altered individual experiences aggregated to constitute a new context for others living through these changes" (see also Elder, Modell, and Parke 1993).

Although the Gluecks' study was initiated after the end of the Great Depression and during World War II, these macrohistorical events are not even mentioned in *Unraveling Juvenile Delinquency*. They wrote several articles on delinquency in wartime, before the book appeared, (see Glueck and Glueck 1964 for details), but they apparently did not consider these historical events of major relevance in their own research project (either in data collection or data analysis). As a result, we cannot precisely determine the effects of the Great Depression and World War II on the subjects and their families as they grew up. The Gluecks did collect detailed information on the military experiences (in World War II and Korea) of those participants who served in the military.

Great Depression

In 1929, the U.S. stock market collapsed, and an economic crisis, which would become known as the Great Depression, was experienced over the next several years in the United States and around the world. Approximately one-third of the American workforce was unemployed in 1933. Countless families suffered severe income loss; the average family income dropped by nearly 40 percent in 1933. Manufacturing, industrial activity, and building construction, especially housing starts, saw major declines during the early 1930s as well (see Elder 1999 for details).

The conventional wisdom is that cohorts born during the 1920s were molded by the joint trauma of the Great Depression and World War II. As revealed in table 4.1, the Glueck men experienced the Great Depression at significantly different ages: the older cohort subjects were four years old at the start of the period of severe economic hardship; the youngest cohort members, born in 1932, were one year old at the peak of the Depression. As Elder (1999) points out, the timing of historical events across cohorts is crucial to understanding historical influences on individual development; this is the major premise of the life-stage principle.

World War II and Military Experiences

Given the time period during which the Glueck study was conducted, a majority of the men served in some branch of the military (67 percent overall). This time span covered specific military actions, such as the last few years of World War II and the stationing of troops in Japan and West Germany (in 1944 and 1945) and the Korean War (from 1950 to 1953) (Glueck and Glueck 1968, 131). Data on military experience were collected for each of these subjects during the second-wave investigation (at the age of twenty-five). The sources of information included records from the specific branch of military service in question (Army or Navy, for example), the Selective Service, the State Adjutant General, the Veterans Administration, and the Red Cross, in conjunction with interviews with the subject.

The availability of rich data on military experience reflects the unique historical circumstances of the Gluecks' study. The military is a particularly important area because it represents a relatively homogeneous social environment in which to explore differences in behavior. Moreover, World War II provided full employment for delinquents and nondelinquents alike and thus represents "a natural experiment" of the hypothesis that relates crime to unemployment (Gottfredson and Hirschi 1990, 164).

In a previous work (Sampson and Laub 1996), we examined the social mechanisms by which military service in the World War II era fostered long-term socioeconomic achievement. Our findings provide support to the theory of military service as a turning point in the transition to young adulthood: overseas duty, in-service schooling, and GI bill training between the ages of seventeen and twenty-five generally enhanced subsequent occupational status, job stability, and economic well-being, independent of childhood differences and socioeconomic background.

Moreover, our data indicate that the benefits of the GI bill were larger for veterans stigmatized with an officially delinquent past, especially those who served in the military earlier rather than later in life. When we account for military service, training under the GI bill, and the interaction of this training with age at entry into service, a striking pattern emerges: the proportion of delinquents in the UJD study who achieved skilled or professional jobs is only 15 percent for those who never served in the military, 21 percent for those who served but received no training under the GI bill, 54 percent for GI bill veterans, and fully 78 percent among those delinquents who had entered the military before the age of eighteen and had received GI bill training. In the control group, 71 percent of veterans receiving GI bill training were eventually employed in skilled or professional occupations, compared with 50 percent of both nonveterans and veterans with no training. Early entry coupled with later utilization of the GI bill thus eliminated the large differential in socioeconomic achievement among adult men with disparate criminal backgrounds.

Several life histories we examined from the Gluecks' files pointed to the military as a "settling influence" or turning point in the life course (see also Elder 1986; Clausen 1993, 310). At the same time, we also found continuity of antisocial behavior from adolescence into adult domains, including misconduct in the military (Sampson and Laub 1993). However it is not inconsistent that the military can serve to turn some men's lives around even as it disrupts other men's lives (Elder 1986) or provides yet another setting for some men to continue their deviant behavior. For example, one subject who spent his career in the Navy (more than thirteen years) joined up while on parole from the Lyman School for Boys, one of two reform schools in the state of Massachusetts. He stated that his enlistment in the military had changed his outlook on life: "In the Navy I was thrown in with guys from all over the country; some of them were well educated and had good backgrounds. I began to see that my thinking was way out of line and that I was probably wrong. I began to do things their way, and things have gone well ever since." His experience parallels that of several other subjects in the study who reported that they had "matured in the service" or that the "Army taught me a few things." Like Elder (1986), we thus find that for some men, serving in the military can help surmount childhood disadvantage (see also the life histories in Laub and Sampson 1993).

The Micro-Level Historical Context

The micro-level historical context of the Gluecks' study is equally important. Five distinct dimensions are particularly significant: the neighborhood setting in which the study subjects grew up, the nature of crime and deviance, the response of the juvenile justice system, employment experiences for the sample members as adults (aged seventeen to thirty-two), and marriage.

Boston Neighborhoods

Boston was first settled in 1630 and was incorporated as a city in 1822. Boston is the capital of Massachusetts, and some refer to it as the capital of New England. In 1925, the city's population was 779,620 (Harrison 1934, 173). Like comparable American cities of that time, Boston contained a relatively large proportion of foreign-born whites, primarily from Ireland. The largest group from non-English-speaking countries was Italian. Interestingly, compared with other cities of its size (for example, Baltimore, Cleveland, Detroit, and St. Louis), the proportion of black residents grew at a much slower rate (Harrison 1934, 174). As noted by Leonard Harrison (1934, 11) in the early 1930s, "Boston's population is characterized by the absence of extraordinary or sudden changes in number or composition."

What was true in 1925 and remains true today is that Boston is a city of neighborhoods separated by race and ethnicity. The UJD study took this aspect of the city into account by matching participants on neighborhood and ethnicity, ensuring that delinquents and nondelinquents of the same ethnic group had grown up in the same kinds of neighborhoods of central Boston. The neighborhoods included Roxbury, East Boston, Charlestown, South Boston, Dorchester, the West End, and the South End. Using census tract data, property inventory data for the city of Boston, and personal observation of the areas themselves, the Gluecks targeted "underprivileged neighborhoods"—slums and tenement areas—for selection in the study. These areas were regions of poverty, economic dependency, and physical deterioration and were usually adjacent to areas of industry and commerce—what Clifford Shaw and Henry McKay (1942) would have termed "socially disorganized neighborhoods" (see also Glueck and Glueck 1950, 29). One such neighborhood is described more vividly in interviewer notes found in one subject's case file:

> The neighborhood is a congested area; main streets all around are heavy with traffic; factories, businesses, and second-class tenements all around; no play places. [In relation to the subject's home, there is] street life (1 block); barrooms (1 block); alleyways (all around); gangs (men and boys, 1 block); dumps and empty lots (1 block); railroad yards and tracks (6 blocks); vice, i.e., prostitution (1 block, all around); cheap commercialized recreation, i.e., burlesque shows and dance halls (5-minute walk); supervised indoor recreational facilities (none); and supervised outdoor play places (none).

The physical homes of the participants also revealed the underprivileged character of the neighborhoods. In general, their homes were crowded and often lacked basic necessities like sanitary facilities, tubs or showers, and central heating. Interviewer notes found in the case materials for one of the subjects describe more graphically the physical conditions of the household: "The family lived in the cellar of a two-story building. The house was very old and in poor condition. It was a rickety wooden house in an alley. Living conditions in the house were crowded—two bedrooms for six people. There was an oil burner in the parlor and in the kitchen. No gas. There was an ill-smelling toilet in the hall."

Interestingly, despite widespread poverty, there is a sense that poor neighborhoods in Boston at early midcentury were considerably more cohesive and socially integrated than poor neighborhoods today. This is just the sort of contextual change that is hypothesized to have altered the social organization of concentrated poverty areas in the inner city (Wilson 1987).

The Nature of Crime and Deviance

The delinquent subjects in the Gluecks' study generated more than sixty-three-hundred arrest charges from first arrest to the age of thirty-two. The general patterns are consistent with current research. For example, criminal participation peaks from the ages of seventeen to twenty-five and declines from twenty-five to thirty-two for all offense types (Gottfredson and Hirschi 1990, 124–37). However, what is most striking about the criminal patterns of the men from this historical period is that there is relatively less violent crime compared to today, and there is virtually no drug use (see also Schlossman and Cairns 1993, 117). On the other hand, over the course of the study many of the subjects were arrested for drunkenness as adults. In fact, during the 1930s in Boston the offense of drunkenness constituted a relatively large number of the overall arrests and prosecutions (see Warner 1934, 7).

Even though the data are more than fifty years old, we also uncovered two crimes that have recently received contemporary focus. The first is domestic violence, including what is now referred to as stalking, the second concerns bias or hate crime. The following account is taken from narrative data recorded in the interview schedule (see Sampson and Laub 1993, 207–9).

In one case it appeared that the subject had grabbed his wife by the throat. Moreover, he had repeatedly threatened her with violence. His wife stated that she was afraid of him, and the subject was later arrested for assault and battery on his wife as well as child neglect. The case was eventually dismissed in court because his wife was reluctant to move forward on the charges. At the age of thirty-two, the subject was being sought as a fugitive from justice. He was formally divorced, but he lived with his wife after the divorce, and they had a second child. The ground for the divorce was cruel and abusive treatment based on neglect of children and the subject's bouts with drinking. Between the ages of twenty-five and thirty-two, the subject had also been arrested for destroying property (a door) at his mother-in-law's house. The subject also threatened his wife on the street and at the secretarial school she attended, forcing her to eventually leave the school.

As to the case of hate crime, we interviewed Charles Eliot Sands, a probation officer who worked with the Glueck delinquents, who told us that "a lot of kids used to exploit the 'fairies.' They would go to North Station and pick somebody up and get some money from him and maybe beat him up. It was profitable and treated like a sport. They used to do it because it was fun." Another probation officer, Louis Maglio, recounted that "there were serious assaults on homosexuals. We had one gang in Boston, these are kids now, that operated on the Boston Common. They would go into the Common and entice homosexuals into their apartments and once they were there they would steal everything and assault them very severely. The gang leader of that group was later sent to state prison for one of these vicious assaults." In 1943 the governor of Massachusetts organized a statewide committee to focus on juvenile crime, "which was sharply accentuated by a number of incidents of anti-Semitic attacks on persons of all ages in some sections of Boston by young hoodlums" ("Massachusetts Sets Up State-wide Youth Committee" 1943, 1).

It is also important to examine how deviance was defined in this historical period. The Gluecks collected detailed information on "bad habits" for all subjects from the age of twenty-five to thirty-two. Their list of bad habits included "occasional and frequent drunkenness; occasional and frequent gambling and betting; adultery and illicit sexual relations (begetting); pathological sex practices (homosexual acts, sodomy, other unnatural acts) and loafing, vagrancy." Reflecting the dynamic nature of deviance, when they interviewed subjects at the age of thirty-two (roughly from 1957 to 1965) the Gluecks added "drug addiction" to the list of bad habits.

A focus on data from the 1920s to the present leads to several interesting questions relevant to an understanding of current patterns of crime and deviance: Are the risk factors associated with crime similar across different structural contexts? Were characteristics of today's underclass (for example, chronic joblessness, family disruption, poverty, criminal behavior) in fact found among earlier immigrant and ethnic groups? In our previous analyses of the Gluecks' data, we have argued that crime in the Gluecks' era was not all that different from crime today in terms of its structural origins and underlying nature (see Sampson and Laub 1993 for details). The men in the Gluecks' delinquent sample were persistent, serious offenders, yet all were white ethnics in structurally disadvantaged positions in a major urban center. Moreover, even though drugs like cocaine and heroin were not pervasive, crime and alcohol abuse were widespread, and violence—especially among family members—did occur. The fact that sample members were all white provides an important comparative statement on current concerns with race, crime, and the underclass. (For an interesting within-race comparison across historical periods, see Lane 1992.) Definitions of deviance reveal behavioral concerns as well as concerns about what is considered "morality" (see Schlossman and Cairns 1993, 125). Thus, definitions of deviance—more so than definitions of crime—highlight the dynamic nature of historical context with respect to disrepute. More generally, it appears that historical context structures both the definition and behavioral manifestations of deviant conduct.

The Response of the Juvenile Justice System

By design, the delinquent subjects in the Gluecks' study were residents of either the Lyman School for Boys or the Industrial School for Boys. The Lyman School was the first state reform school in the United States. George Briggs, the governor of Massachusetts, stated the reformatory's mission at its opening in 1846:

> Of the many and valuable institutions sustained in whole, or in part, from
> the public treasury, we may safely say, that none is of more importance,

or holds a more intimate connection with the future prosperity and moral integrity of the community, than one which promises to take neglected, wayward, wandering, idle and vicious boys, with perverse minds and corrupted hearts, and cleanse and purify and reform them, and thus send them forth in the erectness of manhood and in beauty of virtue, educated and prepared to be industrious, useful and virtuous citizens. (Quoted in Miller 1991, 69.)[10]

Drawing on work by Jerome Miller (1991), Lloyd Ohlin, Robert Coates, and Alden Miller (1974), an autobiography by a former Lyman inmate (Devlin 1985), and other correctional research at the time, we found the reality of the Lyman School to be quite different from the lofty vision expressed by Governor Briggs (for further details and references, see Laub and Sampson 1995).

During the 1940s, the Lyman School was a large custodial institution housing 250 to 350 boys, primarily thirteen to fifteen years old. The institution was organized around a cottage system in which the units were segregated by age and supervised by houseparents. The structure of the institution was extremely regimented: inmates marched from their rooms to meals, and the day's activities were segmented and marked by a series of bells and whistles. Good behavior earned subjects credits for privileges like cigarettes and, ultimately, parole. If an inmate misbehaved, a master could subtract any amount of credit from the boy's total. Physical punishment and verbal humiliations were common: Boys were kicked in the rear, for instance, for minor infractions, such as talking. Inmates were hit with wooden paddles or straps on the soles of their bare feet. Cold showers and haircuts were used by the masters as a form of punishment, intimidation, and punitive discipline (see Miller 1991, 96).

The staff also imposed unusual and downright cruel punishments. For example, boys were forced to sit at their lockers for hours. Jerome Miller (1991, 94–95), the former director of the Massachusetts Department of Youth Services, writes of staff reporting the need to "hit the little bastards for distance." He describes "programs" that included "kneeling in a line in silence, scrubbing the floors with toothbrushes, or being made to stand or sit in odd, peculiarly painful positions." Along with these clearly "demeaning rituals," there were examples of sadistic discipline—forcing the boys to drink from toilets or to kneel for hours on the stone floor with pencils under their knees.

Employment

In the United States, the occupational role provides structure, content, and meaning to most men's lives (Clausen 1993, 259). When the subjects were interviewed at the age of thirty-two, 42 percent of the original delinquents and fifteen percent of the original nondelinquents were employed in unskilled positions; in contrast, 57 percent of the nondelinquents and 27 percent of the delinquents held skilled positions (Glueck and Glueck 1968, 91). Those holding unskilled jobs included factory workers, laborers or helpers, restaurant and hotel workers, longshoremen, and janitors. Some worked as laborers for the Civilian Conservation Corps or the National Youth Administration Project. The United States Maritime Service served as an employment outlet as well. Some of the men worked on a shipping line out of Boston and New York.

Given the employment opportunities and the nature of the sample, it is not surprising that few of the Glueck men worked in a professional capacity (as lawyer, doctor, dentist, or teacher). Some were public servants (postmen, firemen). Overall, however, the most attractive jobs were in the trades—plumber, electrician, mechanic, carpenter, bricklayer, painter, mason, baker, and cook. Yet between the second-wave (at the age of twenty-five) and third-wave (at age thirty-two) interviews, the Gluecks elaborated their coding scheme for "highest degree of skill." At the third-wave interview, new employment categories were added—running one's own business; managerial job, including supervisory and foreman; salesman; and clerk or office worker (for example, IBM operator)—reflecting the expanding economic opportunities, especially in the managerial and clerical areas, even for this group of men from disadvantaged neighborhoods in Boston. Given current debates regarding the nature of urban poverty and underclass populations (see Wilson 1987, 1996; Jencks 1992), the historical context of the Gluecks' data can serve as an important comparative baseline. The men in the Glueck sample were born in poverty-stricken areas of Boston during the Great Depression era (from 1925 to 1935) and experienced the critical transition to adulthood during the post–World War II economic period (from 1945 to 1965). This latter period saw a marked change in the occupational distribution of jobs—an increasing number of professional, managerial, and clerical workers in the labor force and a subsequent decline in the proportion of unskilled and semiskilled workers (Clausen 1993, 262). Equally important, the transition from adolescence to adulthood was disrupted by World War II (from 1941 to 1945) for older sample members and by the Korean War (from 1950 to 1953) for younger sample members (Clausen 1993, 252–54). This context raises interesting questions relevant to an understanding of current patterns of social mobility, especially the factors that facilitate exit from poverty over the life course (for a similar orientation, see Thernstrom 1973).

Perhaps more interesting is the role of education: overall fewer than 20 percent of the Glueck men graduated from high school, and only sixty-five of the thousand men went to college. That most of the men

were still able to achieve steady work as adults speaks to the conditioning effect of historical context on the meaning of educational attainment.

Marriage

John Clausen (1993, 171) states that "for any historical period, there is an
expectable life course in the sense that most people will follow a roughly
predictable set of developmental experiences." During this time period,
as John Modell (1989, 44) notes, marriage converged with the transition
from school to work and was normative for men between the ages of
eighteen and twenty-four. Fifty-five percent of the Gluecks' subjects had
married at least once by the age of twenty-five. Reflecting what Clausen
(1993) calls the "programming" of young women for marriage, the wives
of the Glueck men were even younger when they first married; 29 percent
of the wives were under the age of nineteen (Glueck and Glueck 1968,
81–82). Furthermore, divorce was not common: by the age of thirty-two,
only 21 percent of the original delinquents and 9 percent of the original
nondelinquents had separated or divorced (Glueck and Glueck 1968, 81).

More important, the language and structure of the variables the Gluecks
constructed reflect the views of marriage at the time. For instance, the
Gluecks collected data on "length of courtship," indicating the time
period in which a man attempted to gain the affections and love of a
woman before marriage. The Gluecks also collected information on
whether or not the marriage was "forced," owing to pregnancy, and
coded the "legitimacy" of the children. With respect to marital relationships, the Gluecks collected data on the nature of the conjugal relationship and the extent of material and emotional support by the subject. Because of the historical period during which these follow-up data were
collected (from 1948 to 1965), the available information often casts the
female in the role of subordinate to her husband. Husbands were characterized as "breadwinners," and wives were portrayed as providing
emotional support to assist the subject in achieving his ambitions. Fewer
than 20 percent of the wives worked steadily (part- or full-time) while
married (Glueck and Glueck 1968, 86). This resulted in what Modell
(1989, 269) refers to as "segregated marital roles" whereby women were
first and foremost homemakers while men focused on the world of work
(see also Clausen 1993, 172–73). Therefore, marriage in the Gluecks'
study has a particular social organization and meaning that may be
unique to this specific historical time.

Crime in the Making, 1985 to 1995

About fifteen years ago, we uncovered the original case files for the
delinquent subjects of the Gluecks' study in a dusty, dark subbasement

of the Harvard Law School Library. These data, along with the Gluecks' eighteen-year follow-up of the one thousand subjects from the UJD study, were given to the Harvard Law School Library by the Gluecks upon their retirement in 1972. The Gluecks also donated their personal papers, correspondence, books, photographs, and the like to the library. The papers and other items were sorted and fully cataloged as part of the Glueck archive; the cartons of data were simply stored in the subbasement of the library. These data were of immense importance, yet the obstacles to analyzing them were formidable. The data for the five hundred delinquent subjects alone were contained in more than fifty twelve-by-fifteen-inch cartons and seemed nearly impenetrable. How could these data possibly be recoded and computerized? Moreover, as we began to sort through the case files, we soon discovered that these were not conventional data. The boxes of data were moved eventually to the Murray Research Center, a data archive at Radcliffe devoted to the study of lives. Since 1987, we have been recoding, computerizing, and reanalyzing the Gluecks' data—in short, recasting the data for an extensive long-term study of crime over the life course.

While we were organizing and reconstructing the Gluecks' data, two important books rocked the field of criminology—*Crime and Human Nature*, by James Q. Wilson and Richard Herrnstein, and *A General Theory of Crime*, by Michael Gottfredson and Travis Hirschi. The thrust of these books was to redirect criminological attention to the importance of childhood factors in the explanation of crime. For example, Gottfredson and Hirschi (1990) argue that effective child rearing in the early formative years of a child's development produces a high level of self-control, which in turn is a stable phenomenon that inhibits criminal activity throughout the life course. Wilson and Herrnstein (1985) pushed the explanation of crime back even earlier in life to constitutional differences like impulsiveness and temperament in interaction with familial factors.

Ironically, then, as we were resurrecting the Gluecks' data, new life was breathed into the primary thesis of the Gluecks' research—that childhood temperament and family socialization matter most and thus the "past is prologue" (Glueck and Glueck 1968, 167). Although attracted to this renewed emphasis on the importance of children and families to the explanation of delinquency, we were also troubled by the profound questions raised by the childhood-stability argument. Are differences in child rearing and temperament all we need to know to understand patterns of adult crime? Are childhood differences in antisocial behavior invariably stable? Why does continuity in deviant behavior exist? Perhaps most important, what is the significance of individual change, salient life events, and turning points in adulthood?

Challenged by these and other questions, we set out to examine crime and deviance in childhood, adolescence, and adulthood in a way that recognized the significance of both continuity and change over the life course. To do so we synthesized and integrated the criminological literature on childhood antisocial behavior, adolescent delinquency, and adult crime with theory and research on the life course. By also rethinking the findings produced by longitudinal research, this strategy eventually led us to develop an age-graded theory of informal social control to explain crime and deviance over the life span. We then tested this theory on the longitudinal data reconstructed from the Gluecks' study (see Sampson and Laub 1993 for more details).

The first building block in our theory focused on the mediating role of informal family and school social bonds in explaining child and adolescent delinquency. The second building block incorporated the role of continuity in problem behavior that extends from youth into adulthood in a variety of life's domains (for example, crime, alcohol abuse, divorce, and unemployment). Having provided a role for continuity, we nonetheless believe that salient life events and social ties in adulthood can counteract, at least to some extent, the trajectories of early child development. Our third key idea was that an absence of adequate social bonds in the transition to young adulthood—especially attachment to the labor force and cohesive marriage—explains criminal behavior independent of prior differences in criminal propensity. In other words, pathways to both crime and conformity are modified by central institutions of informal social control in young adulthood (especially employment and marriage). Individual trajectories and transitions interlock in a dynamic process to generate turning points that modify one's subsequent life course. That is, despite the connection between childhood events and experiences in adulthood, turning points can redirect pathways.

One additional finding from *Crime in the Making* (Sampson and Laub 1993) deserves mention because of its relevance to current policy. We found that social bonds to employment were directly influenced by state sanctions—that is, incarceration as a juvenile and as an adult had negative effects on later job stability, and job stability was in turn negatively related to continued involvement in crime over the life course. Although we found little direct effect of incarceration on subsequent criminality, the indirect "criminogenic" effects appear substantively important (Sampson and Laub 1993, 162–68). One clear possibility is that current policies of incarceration are producing unintended criminogenic effects. From our perspective, lengthy terms of imprisonment appear to damage future prospects for employment and job stability. Our research supports the idea that nongovernmental institutions like families, schools, work settings, and neighborhoods must be the centerpiece of any crime reduction policy.

Following Up the Glueck Delinquents, 1995 to 2000

We recently launched a follow-up study of the juvenile delinquents from the Gluecks' study. In 1995, the men who were still living were between the ages of sixty-three and seventy. A major part of our follow-up study involved collecting life-history narratives from a subset of the delinquent subjects. These life-history interviews were combined with our collection of criminal histories to the age of seventy and death records for all five hundred delinquents. We draw on some of the narratives we collected that asked the men to reflect on historical events in their lives. These narratives help us better understand the long-term influence of historical events in later life.

The Great Depression

The conventional wisdom is that the trauma of growing up during the Great Depression shapes one's perspective for life (Brokaw 1998). We find this to be true in our life-history interviews. The reflections of Case 001 are a good example:

> I went through the Depression as a kid. Maybe some of these kids today couldn't go through it, like I went through it. . . . 1931 was the worst of it. I was like six years old at the time. And it wasn't that people didn't want to work—there was no work. I knew how tough it was. Oh yeah. I remember going out getting wood, going down to the railroad tracks and picking up coal, and getting a piece of ice, a piece of meat. Yeah, and picking up potatoes and eating them, and taking them home. You know, there was lines. Holy Christ. Lines of people were starving. I used to go down to get a loaf of bread. Lines for milk. When I went to school, there maybe were two kids who were all right, out of fifty. The other forty-eight were on welfare, because there was no work. . . . As soon as it became 1934, there was work, Roosevelt was in, my mother and father both got a job, and both went to work. In one year—the next year, the following year—we had all new furniture and a car. Because they went to work. They wanted to work, and they worked all their life, from there on. It was only during the Depression time there was no work. It's not that they didn't want to work. There was nothing.

This subject remarked that one of the lessons learned of the Great Depression is that "you know what a buck is."

Other subjects talked about being constantly hungry, lacking shoes without holes and basic clothing, like a coat to wear during the Boston winters. One said he had to learn how to have fun without money. Another stated that "unless you experience it yourself you couldn't really know" what the Depression was like. "It's nice to hear it from a lot of people—you get some insights—but experiencing it yourself is something. I try to tell my children that once in a while, but it goes over their heads. They just can't imagine it."

World War II and the Military Experience

As already noted, several of the Glueck men came of age during World War II. Serving in the military opened up new horizons for these men born during the Great Depression in Boston. Case 002 told us that:

> I went all over the world [in the military]. I went to quite a few foreign countries, and from what I learned I felt proud for being here from what I've seen. And we were well received wherever I went. I've been with the Navy occupation force in Japan—being in the Navy on a warship, we toured all the sea ships in Japan, and I enjoyed every bit of it. We've been in China—this was before the communists took over China—and I really enjoyed it.

Serving in the military was a turning point in the lives of many of these men (see Sampson and Laub 1996). As Case 003 told us, "Well, number one, you had guys coming out of the Depression. They got out of school and there were no jobs around, that was number one. A lot of guys [who] went into the service in World War II, a lot of them did not know what three squares a day was."

Of course, there is a downside to military service during wartime. When we asked Case 004 how military service had changed him, he responded matter-of-factly that he had "started to kill human beings." When asked if he had received any skill training in the service, he replied that he "learned to kill." In this subject's case folder for his interview at the age of thirty-two, the interviewer wrote that after subject came out of the service, he claimed that he " 'started to push people around just like we did over in Germany,' but he found out that he could not get away with it over here and so has stopped it." This man had physically abused his wife, engaged in excessive drinking, and experienced serious job difficulties during adulthood. At his interview at the age of seventy, this man told us that "the war destroyed him and he was just waiting to die." He described in vivid detail symptoms of post-traumatic stress disorder—night sweats, flashbacks, nightmares, and insomnia. He agonized that "the memories never leave you—the images of dogs eating dead babies and the smell of rotten, dead boys."

One other historical theme emerged in our life histories, and that concerns the difference between the World War II era and the Vietnam War era. One veteran of World War II said that he "wouldn't give you two cents for Vietnam." Another, who had fought in World War II, the Korean War, and the Vietnam War, told us, "Look what they did when we come back from Vietnam. Practically spit on us, killed the babies, and all that shit. Blowing up friggin' houses and all that stuff. That's what they were doing. We were murderers. Vietnam I'm talking about."

Lost Community

From our life-history interviews, we hear repeatedly that the "sense of community" has changed (also see Ehrenhalt 1995). One man observed that "there's no more neighborhoods anymore. That stuff's gone. It's a shame. It seems like everyone's in themselves today. There's no sense of belonging or something. It's hard to explain. In the olden days, there were neighborhoods. Everyone knew each other. They respected each other. . . . If you break down, everyone will stop to help you. If something happens in your house, everyone will come to help you, you know." Case 005 confirmed this sentiment:

> I can remember during the Second World War, I can remember no matter how hard times were, people were always helping people. There was always somebody around you could depend on. I think it was the bond between families—whether it was on your street or the neighborhood, they all felt the same. They were no different than you, you were no different from them, so you identified with them. It was a different generation in those days. People cared.

A Special Generation

We asked all of the men we interviewed if they thought their generation is a special one because they grew up during the Great Depression and came of age during World War II. The responses were interesting and varied. One man, Case 006, stated, "I think we were the best type of people at that time—the age. I don't think too much of the young today. They have no respect, period. A lot of people . . . I go in this place, the old place where I used to work the bar, I says 'I used to work here.' The young bartender says, 'Oh, who gives a fuck if you worked here.' " In a similar vein, Case 007 contended that his generation was unique "as far as family values. I think we're the last to have so-called family values, to be honest with you."

Case 008 articulated why his generation was "special": "Well, yes, I do. I think for what we went through, the Depression, not having anything, we turned out pretty good. And, of course, when you're a kid, thirteen, even up to sixteen, you really, you're under your parents' care, but there on in, that's when the whole world opened up for me." This subject's wife added,

> I think, though, that we made a big mistake, not us so much, we didn't spoil our kids with monetary things, because we didn't have it. We lived

paycheck to paycheck for the first—practically until we retired. All our lives, I've always had to worry about money. There's never been enough of it, but we managed to buy a home, several homes, and buy and sell them, and go up the ladder a little bit more each time. But I think that most parents of our generation were far too generous with their children, and I don't think it gave them the work incentive that our generation had. I think we took that away from them, and I think that's a sad thing. I think things come much too easy to my children's generation. It's much too easy for them to get themselves into debt. We couldn't have got ourselves into debt. They didn't have charge cards that I know of in our day, so if we wanted something, we had to save up for it. Or get it on time and have somebody cosign for us or something, you know.

On the other hand, several of the men we interviewed claimed that they were not at all special. Their one-word answer to our question was an emphatic "No!" One man, Case 009, elaborated,

I don't feel anything special. Big deal, I went and I fought a war. Somebody had to do it. I mean if I didn't go and do it and other guys like me didn't go and do it, we'd be under German rule by now, and it was something had to be done. Nothing special about it. We did what we had to do. That was it. I get a kick out of all these guys that went into Korea or Vietnam, they want this, they want that, and what have you, for what? They didn't do more than I did.

Case 010 pointed out that he wishes he were special—"I might have avoided doing a lot of stupid things. Maybe someone else sees it, but I don't." Case 011 was even more blunt. When asked if he felt that he was special, he responded, "No. A special fuck-up, maybe."

Conclusion

Our examination of the Gluecks' Unraveling Juvenile Delinquency study reveals that the life-course experiences of the study subjects were bound by their historical context. Although the specific historical context of this classic study suggests numerous avenues of theoretical exploration along the lines we have explicated, a key life pattern stands out: most of the male subjects came to young adulthood in Boston during a period of expanding economic opportunities during the 1950s and 1960s. They were also in a position to take advantage of numerous opportunities offered by the so-called GI Bill of Rights (see Modell 1989, 204–5). As Modell (1989, 162) has argued, "The dominant lasting effect of the war seems to have been the economic forces it unleashed, and the personal optimism and sense of efficacy that it engendered."

Thus we stress the importance of conceptualizing and measuring both structural context and secular change, especially through explicit cohort comparisons (Ryder 1965). In this regard we believe a central topic for future research is the study of crime over the life course in varying structural locations and historical contexts (see Jessor, Donovan, and Costa 1991; Hagan and Palloni 1990; Hagan 1991, 1993). For too long, individual lives have been examined in isolation even though it is now clear that historical time and geographic place are crucial for understanding lives in their full complexity (Elder, Modell, and Parke 1993). Longitudinal inquiries like the Gluecks' study provide the means to trace human lives over the long term in their varying historical and spatial contexts. An important question concerns the extent to which development is contingent on historical context or whether, on the contrary, general processes of development emerge across different historical eras.

The subjects of the Gluecks' study were bound by historical context, but the same was true for the Gluecks themselves. Their study was launched when social sciences were becoming more specialized and the sociological model of crime was ascending as the dominant paradigm in criminology. The intellectual training and institutional influences of the Gluecks heavily influenced the nature of the research design of the UJD study, their data collection strategies, and the subsequent analyses of those data. Indeed, to fully understand the Gluecks' data one must take into account the social, historical, and institutional context in which they worked (Laub and Sampson 1991).

In the end, there is no escape from historical context. History falls on investigators and subjects alike. What is needed is more explicit recognition of the influence of historical events and trends not only on the lives of study participants but on the lives of researchers as well. Only then will the full import and significance of our landmark studies be accomplished.

Portions of this chapter are adapted from John H. Laub and Robert J. Sampson (1995), "Crime and Context in the Lives of 1,000 Boston Men, Circa 1925–1955." In *Current Perspectives on Aging and the Life Cycle*, edited by Zena Smith Blau and John Hagan. Vol. 4. Greenwich, Conn.: JAI Press.

Notes

1. For example, approximately 30 percent of the delinquent group had had a juvenile court conviction at the age of ten or younger, and the average number of convictions for all delinquent boys was 3.5 (Glueck and Glueck 1950, 293). Furthermore, about two-thirds of the offenses were personal and property crimes (for example, burglary, larceny, assault) (Glueck and Glueck 1950, 29).

2. See also George Vaillant (1983, 245–47), who used the control group sample from the Gluecks' study in a highly regarded investigation of alcoholism.

3. For a detailed biography of Sheldon Glueck and Eleanor Glueck, see Laub 1995 and Laub and Smith 1995, respectively. See also Laub and Sampson (1991) for more information on the institutional and historical context in which the Gluecks worked.

4. National University Law School was affiliated with George Washington University and is now known as George Washington University Law Center. It appears that Glueck chose this school because it offered classes at night.

5. Both Sheldon and Eleanor Glueck were given honorary doctorates by Harvard University in 1958, the first husband-and-wife team to receive such an honor in the history of the university.

6. In 1925, when Eleanor Glueck received her doctorate, the Graduate School of Education was the only school at Harvard to admit women.

7. Harvard Law School did not admit women as students until 1950 and was the last Ivy League school to do so. Even then, it has been noted, during the 1950s and 1960s women at Harvard Law School were "treated like members of an alien species" (Abramson and Franklin 1986, 10).

8. Although the Gluecks' research was carried out under the auspices of the Harvard Law School, their research was funded by numerous private foundations. Eleanor Glueck spent an enormous amount of time on this fund-raising activity.

9. Harvard sociology in the 1930s has been described as "intellectually ill-defined" (Camic 1987, 425). Although Sheldon Glueck's criminology course was offered to sociology students, the powers that did exist (Pitirim Sorokin and later Talcott Parsons) certainly did not consider the study of crime to be central to the mission of sociology (see the 1954 Faculty Committee Report, *The Behavioral Sciences at Harvard*, in Glueck Papers, and Albert Cohen's interview with John Laub [1983]). It should also be noted that both Sheldon and Eleanor Glueck were Jewish. One can speculate that discrimination against Jews at Harvard University may have also contributed to isolating the Gluecks from the mainstream academic community (see Laub 1983, 185).

10. For a discussion of changing juvenile court practices on female status offenders, see Schlossman and Cairns 1993.

References

Abbott, Andrew. 1997. "Of Time and Place: The Contemporary Relevance of the Chicago School." *Social Forces* 75(4): 1149–82.

Abramson, Jill, and Barbara Franklin. 1986. *Where They Are Now: The Story of the Women of Harvard Law, 1974*. New York: Doubleday.

Brokaw, Tom. 1998. *The Greatest Generation*. New York: Random House.

Cabot, Richard C. 1926. *Facts on the Heart*. Philadelphia: Saunders.

Camic, Charles. 1987. "The Making of a Method: A Historical Reinterpretation of the Early Parsons." *American Sociological Review* 52(4): 421–39.

Clausen, John A. 1993. *American Lives: Looking Back at the Children of the Great Depression.* New York: Free Press.

Dannefer, Dale. 1984. "Adult Development and Social Theory: A Paradigmatic Reappraisal." *American Sociological Review* 49(1): 100–16.

Devlin, Mark. 1985. *Stubborn Child.* New York: Atheneum.

Ehrenhalt, Alan. 1995. *The Lost City.* New York: Basic Books.

Elder, Glen H., Jr. 1986. "Military Times and Turning Points in Men's Lives." *Developmental Psychology* 22(2): 233–45.

———. 1999. *Children of the Great Depression.* Boulder, Colo.: Westview Press.

Elder, Glen H., Jr., John Modell, and Ross D. Parke. 1993. *Children in Time and Place: Developmental and Historical Insights.* New York: Cambridge University Press.

Frankfurter, Felix. 1934. Introduction to *One Thousand Juvenile Delinquents,* by Sheldon Glueck and Eleanor Glueck. Cambridge: Harvard University Press.

Geis, Gilbert. 1966. Review of *Ventures in Criminology,* by Sheldon Glueck and Eleanor Glueck. *Journal of Criminal Law, Criminology, and Police Science* 57(2): 187–88.

Gilboy, Elizabeth Waterman. 1936. "Interview with Eleanor Touroff Glueck." *Barnard College Alumnae Monthly* 26: 11–12.

Glueck, Bernard. 1916. *Studies in Forensic Psychiatry.* Boston: Little, Brown.

———. 1918. "A Study of Six Hundred and Eight Admissions to Sing Sing Prison." *Mental Hygiene* 2: 85–151.

Glueck, Eleanor T. 1927. *Community Use of Schools.* Baltimore: Williams Wilkins.

———. 1936. *Evaluative Research in Social Work.* New York: Columbia University Press.

Glueck, Sheldon. 1925. *Mental Disorder and the Criminal Law.* Boston: Little, Brown.

———. 1964. "Remarks in Honor of William Healy, M.D." *Mental Hygiene* 48: 318–22.

Glueck, Sheldon, and Eleanor Glueck. 1930. *Five Hundred Criminal Careers.* New York: Alfred A. Knopf.

———. 1934a. *Five Hundred Delinquent Women.* New York: Alfred A. Knopf.

———. 1934b. *One Thousand Juvenile Delinquents.* Cambridge, Mass.: Harvard University Press.

———. 1937. *Later Criminal Careers.* New York: Commonwealth Fund.

———. 1940. *Juvenile Delinquents Grown Up.* New York: Commonwealth Fund.

———. 1943. *Criminal Careers in Retrospect.* New York: Commonwealth Fund.

———. 1950. *Unraveling Juvenile Delinquency.* New York: Commonwealth Fund.

———. 1964. *Ventures in Criminology.* Cambridge, Mass.: Harvard University Press.

———. 1968. *Delinquents and Nondelinquents in Perspective.* Cambridge, Mass.: Harvard University Press.

———. 1974. *Of Delinquency and Crime: A Panorama of Years of Search and Research.* Springfield, Ill.: Charles C. Thomas.

Glueck, Sheldon, and Eleanor T. Papers. Harvard Law School Library, Cambridge, Massachusetts.

Gottfredson, Michael R., and Travis Hirschi. 1990. *A General Theory of Crime.* Stanford: Stanford University Press.

Griffin, Larry. 1993. "Narrative, Event-Structure Analysis, and Causal Interpretation in Historical Sociology." *American Journal of Sociology* 98(5): 1094–1133.

Hagan, John. 1991. "Destiny and Drift: Subcultural Preferences, Status Attainments, and the Risks and Rewards of Youth." *American Sociological Review* 56(5): 567–82.

———. 1993. "The Social Embeddedness of Crime and Unemployment." *Criminology* 31(4): 465–91.

Hagan, John, and Alberto Palloni. 1990. "The Social Reproduction of a Criminal Class in Working-Class London, Circa 1950–1980." *American Journal of Sociology* 96(2): 265–99.

Harrison, Leonard V. 1934. *Police Administration in Boston*. Cambridge, Mass.: Harvard University Press.

Healy, William. 1915. *The Individual Delinquent*. Boston: Little, Brown.

Healy, William, and Augusta F. Bronner. 1926. *Delinquents and Criminals: Their Making and Unmaking*. New York: Macmillan.

Jencks, Christopher. 1992. *Rethinking Social Policy: Race, Poverty, and the Underclass*. Cambridge, Mass.: Harvard University Press.

Jessor, Richard, John E. Donovan, and Frances M. Costa. 1991. *Beyond Adolescence: Problem Behavior and Young Adult Development*. Cambridge: Cambridge University Press.

Lane, Roger. 1992. "Black Philadelphia Then and Now: The 'Underclass' of the Late Twentieth Century Compared with Poorer African Americans of the Late Nineteenth Century." In *Drugs, Crime, and Social Isolation: Barriers to Urban Opportunity*, edited by A. V. Harrell and G. E. Peterson. Washington, D.C.: Urban Institute Press.

Laub, John H. 1983. *Criminology in the Making: An Oral History*. Boston: Northeastern University Press.

———. 1995. "Sheldon Glueck." In *Dictionary of American Biography, Supplement Ten, 1976–1980*, edited by Kenneth T. Jackson. New York: Simon & Schuster and Macmillan.

Laub, John H., and Robert J. Sampson. 1991. "The Sutherland-Glueck Debate: On the Sociology of Criminological Knowledge." *American Journal of Sociology* 96(6): 1402–40.

———. 1993. "Turning Points in the Life Course: Why Change Matters to the Study of Crime." *Criminology* 31(3): 301–26.

———. 1995. "The Long-Term Effect of Punitive Discipline." In *Coercion and Punishment in Long-Term Perspective*, edited by Joan McCord. New York: Cambridge University Press.

Laub, John H., and Jinney S. Smith. 1995. "Eleanor Touroff Glueck: An Unsung Pioneer in Criminology." *Women and Criminal Justice* 6(2): 1–22.

Long, Jancis V. F., and George E. Vaillant. 1984. "Natural History of Male Psychological Health, XI: Escape from the Underclass." *American Journal of Psychiatry* 141(3): 341–46.

"Massachusetts Sets Up State-Wide Youth Committee." 1943. *Police Chiefs' News Letter* 10(11): 1.

Miller, Jerome G. 1991. *Last One over the Wall: The Massachusetts Experiment in Closing Reform Schools*. Columbus: Ohio State University Press.

Modell, John. 1989. *Into One's Own: From Youth to Adulthood in the United States, 1920–1975*. Berkeley: University of California Press.

Ohlin, Lloyd E., Robert B. Coates, and Alden D. Miller. 1974. "Radical Correctional Reform: A Case Study of the Massachusetts Youth Correctional System." *Harvard Educational Review* 44(1): 74–111.

Potts, David P. 1965. "Social Ethics at Harvard, 1881–1931: A Study in Academic Activism." In *Social Sciences at Harvard, 1860–1920,* edited by Paul Buck. Cambridge, Mass.: Harvard University Press.

Ryder, Norman. 1965. "The Cohort as a Concept in the Study of Social Change." *American Sociological Review* 30(6): 843–61.

Sampson, Robert J. 1986. "Effects of Socioeconomic Context on Official Reaction to Juvenile Delinquency." *American Sociological Review* 51(6): 876–85.

———. 1993. "Linking Time and Place: Dynamic Contextualism and the Future of Criminological Inquiry." *Journal of Research in Crime and Delinquency* 30(4): 426–44.

Sampson, Robert J., and John H. Laub. 1993. *Crime in the Making: Pathways and Turning Points Through Life.* Cambridge, Mass.: Harvard University Press.

———. 1996. "Socioeconomic Achievement in the Life Course of Disadvantaged Men: Military Service as a Turning Point." *American Sociological Review* 61(3): 347–67.

Schlossman, Steven, and Robert B. Cairns. 1993. "Problem Girls: Observations on Past and Present." In *Children in Time and Place: Developmental and Historical Insights,* edited by Glen H. Elder Jr., John Modell, and Ross D. Parke. Cambridge: Cambridge University Press.

Shaw, Clifford R., and Henry McKay. 1942. *Juvenile Delinquency and Urban Areas.* Chicago: University of Chicago Press.

Snodgrass, Jon. 1972. "The American Criminological Tradition: Portraits of the Men and Ideology in a Discipline." Ph.D. diss., University of Pennsylvania.

Thernstrom, Stephan. 1973. *The Other Bostonians: Poverty and Progress in the American Metropolis, 1880–1970.* Cambridge, Mass.: Harvard University Press.

Vaillant, George E. 1983. *The Natural History of Alcoholism.* Cambridge, Mass.: Harvard University Press.

Warner, Samuel Bass. 1934. *Crime and Criminal Statistics in Boston.* Cambridge, Mass.: Harvard University Press.

Wilson, James Q., and Richard Herrnstein. 1985. *Crime and Human Nature.* New York: Simon & Schuster.

Wilson, William J. 1987. *The Truly Disadvantaged: The Inner City, the Underclass, and Public Policy.* Chicago: University of Chicago Press.

———. 1996. *When Work Disappears: The World of the New Urban Poor.* New York: Alfred A. Knopf.

Wolfgang, Marvin E., Terence P. Thornberry, and Robert Figlio. 1987. *From Boy to Man: From Delinquency to Crime.* Chicago: University of Chicago Press.

Chapter 5

The Study of Adult Development

GEORGE E. VAILLANT

IN HIS introduction to Lewis Terman's four-decade study of gifted children, *Genetic Studies of Genius*, Robert Sears described the project thus: "Only among the chroniclers of the stars and the waters have such prolonged studies of individual objects been made heretofore. We can be grateful for the courage and the vision of the man who finally broke the barrier of the limited lifetime allotted to any one researcher and got underway a study of man that will encompass the life span of the subjects' lives, not just those of the researchers" (Sears 1959, ix). Forty years later, the Henry A. Murray Center reflects the vision of the women, especially Matina Horner, Abigail Stewart, and Anne Colby, who developed a means of preserving multiple studies of women and men that will, like Terman's study, encompass the life span of the subjects' lives, not just those of the researchers.

My relationship with the study of adult development began in 1960. As a medical intern I had dreamed of owning twenty black file cabinets containing the lifetime records of one thousand schizophrenics followed for twenty years. Like most dreams, mine was not fulfilled in the ways I had anticipated: I never owned even one file drawer of lifetime case histories of schizophrenics. However, after a residency at the Massachusetts Mental Health Center in Boston and a stint in the Public Health Service hospital at Lexington, Kentucky, from 1963 to 1965, I did own two black file drawers containing the histories of one hundred heroin addicts followed for twelve years and those of twelve schizophrenics followed for two to fifty years. With these data I could unambiguously document recovery—a phenomenon that many senior researchers believed did not happen in such disorders. By analyzing and publishing these files on my return to Boston, I found that I had made contributions not only to the social sciences but also to public policy (Vaillant 1998).

In 1966 I conceived the idea of interviewing a group of men who had been diagnosed as schizophrenic in college but who had later recovered and done well in life. Their twenty-fifth college reunion, I thought, would be an apt time to conduct such interviews, and the alumni of Harvard University an apt choice of subjects. As it turned out, the Harvard Health Service did not yet have a psychiatry department in 1941, but they had conducted a study of "normals." This was the Grant Study of Adult Development, whose subjects were Harvard sophomores selected for health (Heath 1945). I interviewed those men at their twenty-fifth reunion (Vaillant 1977) and a few years later, when I was appointed curator of these files, was able to save them from destruction.

On my return to Boston I also contacted Sheldon and Eleanor Glueck, whose groundbreaking study of delinquency shed light on my own follow-up of heroin addicts. As one of the first outsiders to gain the Gluecks' permission to examine their records, I was honored to later become (together with the head of the Harvard Law Library) the curator of the Glueck files. The files were thus rescued from disappearing into a dirty, dark subbasement of the Law School Library and installed in a first-floor room with a window where they could continue to be studied. Again, not only were paper files rescued from destruction but, equally important, contact was maintained with the surviving members of each cohort, permitting their follow-up into middle age and beyond (Vaillant 1995).

In the early 1970s Caroline Vaillant and I were married, and we both began interviewing the controls for the Gluecks' study of juvenile delinquency (Glueck and Glueck 1950, 1968). Thanks to the generosity of its director, Dana Farnsworth, the Harvard Health Services provided us, an unfunded junior couple, with "laboratory" space. I found myself, as a mere assistant professor at Tufts and then Harvard with no research funding, the unlikely guardian of two of Harvard's most distinguished longitudinal archives. Recognizing my fiduciary responsibility for a veritable Hubble telescope of human lives, in May 1974 I hosted a dinner at the University Health Services to seek advice from the Harvard community on how these records might be preserved for future researchers. None of the senior Harvard faculty that I invited offered any clear advice, but fortunately Matina Horner, the president of Radcliffe College, who had graciously joined us at the dinner, noted the interest of Radcliffe students in such studies and described some of the current work of the Radcliffe Institute for Advanced Study. She offered to look into possible space for the archives at Radcliffe and agreed to raise the subject of Harvard's archives at the next executive committee meeting of the institute.

In a very few years President Horner, with the philanthropic help of Nina and Harry Murray, created an institution for the study of lives. President Horner's administrative talent was then powerfully amplified by the generative leadership of Abigail Stewart and, later, Anne Colby, who together established the Henry A. Murray Center as an internationally known center for the study of lives. The Murray Center provided not only me but many other collectors of human lives a means of preserving and, more important, a means of passing on longitudinal studies to the next generation. In addition, the sponsorship of the Murray Center made it possible for me to become involved in still a third study of lives—the Terman study of gifted children. In 1986, Caroline Vaillant and I chose 90 women, a representative subsample of the original Terman sample of 672 gifted women, for reinterview. The Study of Adult Development now consists of twenty black file cabinets containing almost a thousand life histories of three diverse samples of women and men followed for sixty years or more.

The Study of Adult Development

The Study of Adult Development began in 1938 at the Harvard University Health Services and has expanded to include three cohorts: the sample of 90 gifted women, born around 1910, from the Terman study; the Grant study sample of 268 socially advantaged Harvard men, born around 1920; and the Glueck sample of 456 inner-city men, born around 1930. All three cohorts are still being actively followed, and most of their records are located at the Murray Center at Harvard University.

The Terman Sample

Perhaps the only prospective longitudinal study that is really comparable to the Grant Study—in terms of length, frequency of contact, and loyalty of study members—is Lewis Terman's life cycle study of children with high ability (Terman 1925; Holahan and Sears 1995). Lewis Terman and then his successors, first Melitta Oden, then Robert Sears (himself a member of the Terman study), and finally Albert Hastorf, have followed a group of gifted California children for almost eighty years. In 1986 after sixty-five years of follow-up, attrition for reasons other than death or invalidism was still less than 10 percent.

Between 1920 and 1922, Lewis Terman attempted to identify all of the children in urban California with IQs of 140 or higher. He chose to focus on three metropolitan areas: Oakland, San Francisco, and Los Angeles. In the 1920s these communities, though urban, were small; the schools had grassy playgrounds, and their worlds were closer to small-town America than to the blackboard jungle.

The original aim of Terman's crude selection net was to capture most of the intellectually gifted children in his three-city area. When he went back and checked entire schools, however, he found he probably had captured only 80 percent. Unattractive children and shy children had tended to slip through the net. In addition, Terman had arbitrarily included only children from public schools, excluding those who attended private schools or schools in which instruction was in Chinese. Nevertheless, the study has produced many significant findings, not the least of which was that the high intelligence of the sample members—whose mean IQ was 151—did not handicap them psychologically. Their mental health was, in fact, demonstrably better than that of their classmates. In personality traits, the gifted children showed significantly more humor, common sense, perseverance, leadership, and even popularity. They were as likely as their classmates to marry, and their physical health was better. At the age of seventy-eight, the mortality rate of the Terman women was only half that of white American women in their birth cohort.

In the 1920s, tuition at California colleges was cheap ($25 to $50 a term for both Stanford University and the University of California, Berkeley), and bright women were expected to earn college degrees. The Depression, which began when they were twenty years old, and World War II, which began when they were thirty, put pressures on these women to enter the workforce, but the jobs provided were usually menial and limited in scope and opportunity. When asked what occupational opportunities World War II had opened for her, one Berkeley-educated woman in the Terman study replied, "I finally learned to type." In contrast, the Terman men helped to found the Los Alamos and Livermore laboratories and to create Silicon Valley.

The women of the Terman study were part of their historical epoch. Until 1920, their mothers had been denied the right to vote. The Terman women were also the descendants of pioneers. One Terman woman's grandmother had saved her own life by killing an intruder with a tomahawk. Another woman's father, as a high school teacher in the rough mining town of Leadville, Colorado, routinely disarmed his students before the start of class.

In 1987, through the generosity of Robert Sears and Albert Hastorf and with the support of the Murray Center, my wife and I were permitted to conduct interviews with a representative subsample of 90 women from Terman's original sample of 672. Of these 90, 29 women had died, and another 21 were not seen, owing to poor health or their decision not to cooperate. We interviewed the remaining 40 women (Vaillant and Vaillant 1990), whose average age was seventy-eight. Most of the 50 women we did not interview had been closely followed for half a century, and so they could be included in most of the data analyses. Except for inferior physical health, the 50 uninterviewed women did not differ significantly from the 40 women whom we did interview.

The Grant Sample

The Grant Study of Adult Development was begun at the Harvard University Health Services in 1938 by two physicians, Arlie Bock and Clark Heath. The study was funded by a gift from the philanthropist William T. Grant, the founder of the Grant Department Stores, to redress what he saw as an appalling lack of research on successful adaptations to adult life. "Large endowments have been given and schemes put into effect for the study of the ill, the mentally and physically handicapped," Grant observed, "[but] very few have thought it pertinent to make a systematic inquiry into the kinds of people who are well and do well" (quoted in Heath 1945, 4).

In the original selection process, about 40 percent of each Harvard class had been arbitrarily excluded because there was some question as to whether they would meet the academic requirements for graduation. (Usually this meant a freshman grade average of C or lower.) The Health Service records of the remaining 60 percent of each freshman class were then screened, and half the remaining men were excluded because of evidence of physical or psychological disturbance. Each year the names of the remaining three hundred sophomores were submitted to the college deans, who selected about a hundred boys whom they recognized as "sound." About eighty of the one hundred students selected each year agreed to participate in the study—a demanding commitment to more than twenty hours of multifaceted scrutiny, with an implicit consent to be studied for the rest of their lives. The emphasis was on selecting men at the independent end of the independent-dependent continuum. The men, a majority of whom were first-born sons, had deliberately chosen to go to a difficult and competitive college. There they had been further selected for their capacity to master this situation. Selected for mental and physical health, the sample had also been chosen for its capacity to equal or to exceed its natural ability.

Over a four-year period, from 1939 to 1942, 268 sophomores were selected for study. Twelve of these students withdrew from the study while in college, and eight more men withdrew over the next half century. For nearly sixty years, the rest of the men have continued to participate with remarkable loyalty. After being accepted into the study, each man was seen by a psychiatrist for eight interviews. These interviews focused on the participant's family and on his own career plans and value system. The psychiatrists made an effort to get to know the men as people, not patients. No effort was made to look for pathology or to reduce interview data to rating scales.

By modern standards the study was old fashioned. Data were recorded into ledgers in ink and analyzed by manual counting. Data were not put onto punch cards until twenty-five years later. Ten years later still the data were transferred onto magnetic tape, and only fifty years after the study began were data transferred to a hard drive. All data are still available in the form in which they were collected.

The men of the Grant study were also seen by a family worker, Lewise Gregory Davies. Davies took a careful social history from each sophomore subject and then traveled the length and breadth of the United States to meet the parents of all subjects. In each boy's home she took a family history that included characterizations of grandparents, aunts, uncles, first cousins—and the furniture. She also obtained from the mother a history of the child development of each boy and a family history of mental illness.

Although they were no more intellectually gifted than their fellow Harvard classmates, in conventional terms the participants were far more successful: 61 percent of the men in the Grant study graduated with honors, in contrast with only 26 percent of their classmates; and 76 percent went on to graduate school. Socioeconomically, the men of the Grant study sample were drawn from a privileged group but not exclusively so. They had been adolescents during the Great Depression, and in 1940, one father in seven still made less than $2,500. Half of the men's parents had not graduated from college, and half were on scholarship or had to work during academic terms to earn at least part of their tuition fees.

Like the Terman women, the Grant study men have been unusually healthy. Compared with others in their age cohort, only one-seventh the number of Grant study men were rejected for military service on physical grounds, and only one-twelfth were rejected for psychiatric reasons. By the age of sixty-five, the mortality rate of the college sample was only half that expected of white males in their birth cohort and only three-quarters that of their Harvard College classmates. More than half of the subjects have or are about to become octogenarians.

Through their Harvard degree the men of the Grant study, whatever their social origins, were given a ticket of entry to the upper middle class. Returning from active military service in World War II, they benefited from high levels of employment, a valuable dollar, and the American GI bill, which virtually guaranteed these successful college students an affordable graduate education. The men themselves were also just young enough to participate in the secular trends of the 1960s through the 1980s, and thus participated in middle-aged physical fitness and smoking cessation. At the age of forty-seven, the average earned income of the college sample would have been about $90,000 in 1989 dollars, yet they were more likely to be Democrats than Republicans. They had the incomes and social status of corporate managers, yet they drove the battered cars and pursued the hobbies, politics, and lifestyle of college professors.

The Grant men's lives have been followed closely from their graduation up to the present through questionnaires administered every two years, physical exams every five years, and, in most cases, interviews every fifteen years. The questionnaires have paid special attention to employment, family, health, habits (for example, vacation, sports, alcohol abuse, smoking), and political views.

Selected for health and favored by society, the Grant men illustrate how the male adult life cycle progresses under favorable circumstances. As is true of all such longitudinal cohorts, all generalizations are limited to a single subculture and a single point in history.

The Glueck Sample

The 456 men of the Glueck study sample represented a very different cohort. To begin with, they were born in 1930. Their earliest memories were of grinding poverty, and a powerful theme in their adult lives was America's recovery from economic depression. As children of white immigrant parents, in the 1960s they passed on their minority status to urban African Americans and found themselves the political masters of Boston. This shift made the study of their lives a valuable means for studying paths out of the underclass (Long and Vaillant 1984).

These men had been chosen in junior high school as the controls for a prospective study conducted by Sheldon and Eleanor Glueck at Harvard Law School that led to a landmark book, *Unraveling Juvenile Delinquency* (Glueck and Glueck 1950). Like the Grant study college men, the inner-city men of the Glueck study were examined originally by a multidisciplinary team of physicians, psychologists, psychiatrists, social investigators, and physical anthropologists. The Glueck men have been interviewed at the age of fourteen, twenty-five, thirty-two (Glueck and Glueck 1968), and forty-seven (Vaillant 1995). Over the first thirty-five years of study, attrition owing to withdrawal held at 5 percent, and at least until the age of forty-seven no subject was permanently lost.

Between 1940 and 1944, the Gluecks selected the sample on the basis of their nondelinquent status. To match the control sample with the cohort of delinquent youths, the Gluecks had used four criteria: the subjects had to be of the same age, intelligence, and ethnicity and to have attended the same inner-city schools as the Gluecks' five hundred delinquents—all of whom had been committed to reform school. The majority of the parents of the inner-city sample were foreign born. Inexplicably, the Gluecks excluded African Americans, who in the 1930s still constituted a rather small fraction of Boston schoolchildren.

In childhood, half of the inner-city men had lived in clearly blighted slum neighborhoods. Half came from families known to five or more social agencies, and the families of more than two-thirds of the boys had recently been on welfare. The homes of half the boys had no bathtub or shower, and only one-third had hot water, central heat, electricity, and a tub and toilet. The inner-city men also suffered intellectual disadvantage: One-third had been selected because their individually tested Wechsler-Bellevue IQ scores were below 90. One inner-city youth in four had repeated two or more grades of school. Their low tested intelligence had denied them access to Boston's elite public high schools.

Nevertheless, as the inner-city men matured during the 1950s and 1960s they showed marked upward social mobility. Their lives often demonstrated that after the age of forty, "emotional IQ" (Daniel Goleman's [1985] EQ) was of far greater importance than IQ (Vaillant and Davis 2000).

John Mayer (a pseudonym), for example, had a performance IQ of 79 and a verbal IQ of 83 at the time he entered the study; his reading score on the Stanford test was 72. As expected, he completed only nine grades. However, Mayer had demonstrated advanced social skills from an early age. He was described at the age of fourteen as "conscientious," "likable, direct," and as having "very good poise . . . [and a] considerable sense of humor." In his adult life he has enjoyed an excellent marriage, and he has transformed his love for kids and skill at sports into a $60,000-a-year position as director of parks and recreation in a city of ninety thousand. For the past twenty-five years his city and his job have been slowly growing, allowing him to acclimate to expanding responsibility. His wife has always assisted him by keeping the books. Currently he has 160 people working for him, and after retirement he plans to run for the job of city commissioner. He loves his job, his wife, and his many grandchildren.

Comparison of the Three Samples

Each of the three samples in the Grant Study of Adult Development was relatively homogeneous, and each sample was very different from the other two. Thirty percent of the fathers of the Grant sample men, but none of the fathers of the inner-city men, were in what is defined in socioeconomic terms as social class 1 (physicians, successful lawyers, and businessmen). Thirty-one percent of the fathers of the inner-city men, but none of the fathers of the Grant men, were in social class 5 (unskilled laborers with less than ten grades of education). The parents of the Terman women were largely middle class or skilled laborers (social classes 3 and 4, respectively); few of their fathers were as privileged as those of the college men or as disadvantaged as those of the inner-city men.

The mean education of the Terman women's fathers was twelve years, in contrast with eight years for fathers of the inner-city men and sixteen years for fathers of the college men. Whereas none of the inner-city mothers had gone to college, a third of the mothers of the Grant men had graduated college—twice as many as mothers of the Terman women. The mean IQ of the Terman women was 151, that of the inner-city sample was 95, and the estimated mean IQ of the Grant sample was 130 to 135.[1] Two-thirds of the Terman women were college graduates, in contrast with 99 percent of the Grant sample and 10 percent of the inner-city men.

In contrast with the men in the Terman study, who as a group went on to distinguished academic or professional careers, the talents of the equally bright and nearly as well-educated Terman women were clearly underutilized by society. At least 253 of the Terman women, for example, had full-time jobs for most of their lives; but their mean maximum income was $30,000 (in 1989 dollars)—the same as that of the under-educated and often intellectually handicapped inner-city men.

Arguably, the three cohorts in the Grant Study of Adult Development include the longest prospective study of physical health (the Grant college sample), the longest prospective study of socially disadvantaged men (the Glueck inner-city sample), and a small subset of women from the longest prospective study of human beings (Terman study) ever conducted, though, as with the other studies at the Murray Center, none of the three cohorts can be viewed as representative of the general population. In social terms, however, the cohorts are vastly different from one another. Thus the between-group similarities and the within-group differences may be generalizable to other American Caucasian samples. A lesson that cultural anthropology and biology offer to both sociology and epidemiology is the need in multivariate problems to employ small, contrasting, but internally homogeneous populations. Small homogeneous samples permit control of confounding demographic variables, they permit control of attrition, and they provide rich idiographic data. The confounders involved in following a representative sample of a hundred thousand members of the world's population for a lifetime would defy statistical analysis, and the enormous attrition would compromise any conclusions reached. In contrast, after sixty years of follow-up not a single one of the 268 members of the Grant study has been completely lost, and after the first thirty years of follow-up not a single one of the 456 members of the inner-city sample had been lost.

Admittedly these studies are not perfect; but for the present they are the best available low-attrition lifelong studies of adult development in the world, and they allow a unique opportunity to address certain kinds of problems. The prospective study of individual lives facilitates a giant step in disentangling cause from association and biological from sociological causation, as the following examples illustrate. In one example, biology emerges as counterintuitively salient; in the other, sociology emerges as counterintuitively salient.

Sometimes Biology Is More Important than Sociology

The findings of our prospective study of alcoholism contradict a plausible sociological hypothesis. Although the Grant study sample of college men and the Glueck study sample of inner-city men cover only men from a narrow period in history, they permit an unusually thorough longitudinal view of the natural history of alcoholism. This is important because in cross-sectional studies alcoholism often gives an illusion of being largely the result of psychosocial disadvantage.

We followed the socially disadvantaged inner-city (Glueck study) men and the socially privileged college (Grant study) men forward in time from early adolescence into late middle age. Cross-sectional studies suggest that alcoholism is a symptom of alienation, depression, and unemployment, but longitudinal study reveals that alcoholics were not always that way. Short-term studies suggest that high socioeconomic status is a good prognostic factor in recovery from alcoholism. Our long-term studies, on the other hand, reveal that inner-city men were two times more likely to recover from alcoholism than the more advantaged college men. One plausible explanation for this finding is that severe alcohol dependence is correlated with the ultimate achievement of stable abstinence, and severe alcohol dependence was more common among the inner-city men. To our surprise, we found that men did not develop alcoholism because they came from multiproblem families or because they suffered from dependent personalities or because they were depressed or because they came from the lowest social class (Vaillant 1980, 1995). Rather, men became depressed, dependent, socially deprived, and the creators of multiproblem families because of alcoholism.

Figure 5.1 illustrates the influence of multiple problems within their families of origin and parental alcoholism on the rates of alcohol dependency among the men in the inner-city sample. Not surprisingly, men with multiproblem families and alcoholic parents were at high risk for alcoholism, and men with neither alcoholic parents nor multiproblem families were at low risk. This difference, commonly observed, has led many social scientists to posit the importance of social environment as a primary cause of alcoholism. However, the figure also looks at the likelihood of alcoholism in the two less common combinations: men from multiproblem families without alcoholic biological parents and men without multiproblem families but born of alcoholic parents, with whom they did not live. Men with alcoholic biological parents but without multiproblem families were three times more likely to develop alcoholism

Figure 5.1   Influence of Family Problems and Parental Alcoholism on Adult Alcohol Dependency

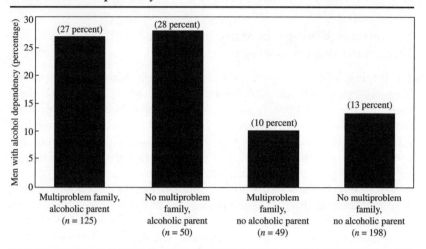

Source: Data from Glueck and Glueck 1950, 1968.
Note: Total *n* is 422, not 456, because of missing data.

than men from multiproblem families (that often did contain an alcoholic step-parent) without alcoholic biological parents. In short, the data presented in figure 5.1 suggest that heredity is more important to the development of alcoholism than social or psychological childhood hardship. Study of the Grant sample confirms these observations (Vaillant 1980).

Using the same strategy to study the Grant cohort we were able to closely observe the association between physical health in old age and strong social supports. Figure 5.2 presents our findings. Again, the world literature usually interprets the association between the two as suggesting that good social supports cause good physical health. However, longitudinal studies help us tease out the importance of other variables that intervene in the relationship. Alcoholism wreaks havoc on both physical bodies and interpersonal relationships. Heavy smoking, in addition to its bad effects on the heart, lungs, and circulatory system, is strongly correlated with (though not causative for) major depressive disorder—a disease that unequivocally erodes social supports. The prospective design of the study allowed us to identify the correlation: bad habits (heavy smoking and alcoholism) before the age of fifty were more than two-and-a-half times more common among the 59 men with the worst social supports at the age of seventy than among the 55 men with the best social supports. Figure 5.2 illustrates the importance of considering these bad habits as confounding factors in the relation between physical health and social support. Neither the protective effects of strong so-

Figure 5.2   Influence of Bad Habits and Strong Social Supports on Late-Life Physical Disability

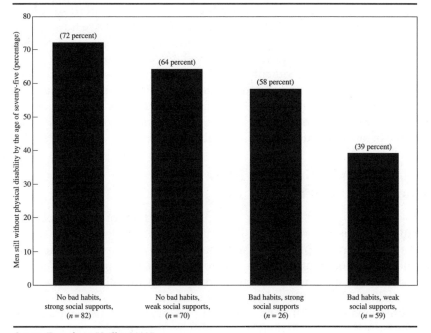

Source: Data from Vaillant 1995.
Note: Total *n* is 237, not 268, because of deaths and drops.

cial supports nor the deleterious effects of weak social supports on physical health in old age are as powerful when we control for a history of alcohol and tobacco abuse.

I certainly do not wish to suggest that social support has nothing to do with successful aging. The purpose of this example is only to illustrate that a longitudinal psychosocial study provides a means of disentangling association from cause. As in the example of alcoholism among inner-city men, however, collecting the evidence requires data from a multidecade longitudinal study.

Perhaps the most important social policy lesson to be learned from the preceding example is that alcohol abuse rivals cigarette smoking as the single most important health risk in the United States today. Although the data are derived from the two male cohorts, the same bad habits are, of course, detrimental to women as well. At present, this policy lesson is still absent from the five leading women's health magazines and from many leading journals of sociology and public health. The women's journals tell us that high-fat, low-fiber diets cause cancer and that high cholesterol causes heart disease. The importance of advertising revenues prevents these magazines from discussing the two far greater dangers to women's health: alcohol and tobacco abuse. The sociological and public health journals often put relatively more emphasis on smoking than on alcohol abuse because the former is easier to identify. Both sociology and epidemiology assess the risk to health of alcohol abuse through the cross-sectional assessment of alcohol consumption. Reported alcohol consumption over the past month correlates with alcohol abuse about as well as reported food consumption over the past month correlates with obesity—that is, very poorly. Alcoholics often imagine themselves to be currently "on the wagon," just as obese individuals usually imagine themselves to be currently dieting. Thus in many studies the importance of alcohol abuse remains invisible.

Sometimes Sociology Is More Important than Biology

In contrast with the foregoing example, the findings of our prospective study of societal forces in the lives of the women in the Terman study contradict a plausible biological hypothesis. In 1986 my wife, Caroline, and I set off for Stanford University to interview a sample of the Terman women with a clear hypothesis: women who were intelligent, well educated, and had achieved enough wealth (as was possible for young professionals in 1930) to have at least one servant should have had no trouble achieving brilliant careers. Studying these exceptional women's lives, we believed, might provide models for the current generation of women, including our daughters, for whom careers are far more accessible. All a woman needed, we reasoned, was a sufficient biological intellectual advantage over the average man to overcome existing inhibitory social forces. Longitudinal study reveals that our hypothesis was tragically incorrect.

Although even the best social interventions can usually increase IQ only about half a standard deviation, social forces have the capacity to destroy any intellectual potential that biology can create. The fate of the Terman women demonstrates the waste of much of the potential occupational contribution of 50 percent of society's most gifted citizens. In this example, to illustrate the power of longitudinal study I use idiographic case histories, rather than the multivariate statistics and nomothetic methods imbedded in the prior examples in figures 5.1 and 5.2.

The Terman women were blessed with high IQs—higher than Cal Tech graduates and roughly twenty points higher, on average, than the Harvard men in the Grant study. The most socially disadvantaged Terman women, those who never went beyond high school, scored as well at the age of forty on the Terman Concept Mastery Test as the average Stanford medical school graduate or the average Berkeley doctoral graduate with eight more years of higher education—especially remarkable in view of the test's sensitivity to years of education. Although many of the families of the Terman women were of limited means, most of the women we interviewed had graduated from Berkeley or Stanford.

Despite their intellectual and educational advantages, of the 672 women in the Terman study only thirty (5 percent) became tenured college faculty or enjoyed successful business or professional careers. Collectively, these thirty women gave birth to only seven children. The average Terman women enjoyed eight more years of education and a mean IQ almost three standard deviations higher than the men of the Glueck study, but those women who were fully employed received the same yearly income (in 1996 dollars) as the average inner-city man. In other words, in the face of concerted social forces, biological advantage meant next to nothing. These outcomes in the occupational and income-earning domain do not merely reflect differences in the women's aspirations for themselves. At the end of their lives, a third of the lifetime homemakers told us they wished they had also had careers. Fewer than 5 percent of the career and family women would have preferred to have just a family.

Only one woman of the forty Terman women we interviewed enjoyed a career as distinguished as perhaps half the women graduating today from Berkeley or Stanford. When we asked the Terman women themselves if society had given them a fair chance, however, thirty-nine of the forty replied in the affirmative. The problem, they explained, had been with themselves; they had lacked perseverance.

Had we done a cross-sectional study, society might have been held blameless. We could have retained our faith in biology and drawn the conclusion that gifted women in 1910 had not aspired to ambitious careers. However, the prospective record revealed uniformly high motivation and perseverance on the part of the Terman women and an implacably discriminative society. Indeed, at the age of forty the women could acknowledge the discrimination they faced. After all, they were not stupid. When asked the same questions at the age of eighty, however, most found it easier not to blame others—as if they had come to the psychological conclusion that continuing protest would have changed nothing.

Case examples illustrate the stunted occupational trajectories that were characteristic of so many Terman women. At the age of twenty-six, a gifted Berkeley Phi Beta Kappa wrote Lewis Terman of her "conviction that I am incapable of writing anything worthwhile. The realization that I lack the moral stamina to write has left me relatively content with an average domestic existence." Four years later she wrote that her "only ambitions are domestic ones. . . . Literary ambitions dropped either because of laziness or realizations of inability—I'm not sure which." Consulting her earlier record, however, we discovered that like most of the Terman women she had been singled out by her high school teachers for her extraordinary perseverance.

Lewis Terman himself had two gifted children in the study—a boy and a girl. They both graduated from Stanford, because in 1930 California, gender did not deny a bright student a good education. Both children got married, and both spent their lives working for Stanford. As far as I know, neither son nor daughter had mental illness. Their career paths, however, were decidedly different. Terman's son became provost of Stanford University and was an important creator of Silicon Valley industry. His career was even more creative and distinguished than that of his famous father. Terman's daughter also worked for Stanford—as the receptionist at a dormitory desk.

One woman had male doctors on both sides of her family for three generations; she had an IQ of 149, was good with her hands, and graduated from high school having taken both anatomy and psychology. At the age of thirty her score on the Strong Interest Inventory suggested that she become a nurse or a science teacher; apparently the original Strong Interest Inventory identified only males as surgeons. After college she put her dexterous hands and anatomic knowledge to use—first as a butcher and then as a cosmetologist.

Another Terman woman graduated from college summa cum laude with a degree in art. First, she fired pots for her husband's pottery business; at the age of forty she was earning $1.35 an hour as a nurse's aide. She later worked for Stanford for twenty years, as a brilliant technician in a particle physics laboratory. At retirement, she received a pension of $70 a month. Apparently moved by guilt, Stanford doubled her pension in 1985, to $140 a month. Thus, because of financial necessity she was still working at the age of seventy-seven. When asked if society had given her a fair chance, this woman replied with dead seriousness, "Oh sure, it was my fault. All this talk of equality of women . . . a great deal of it is their own fault." Besides, she went on to explain to us, there were physical reasons why women did not get ahead. Women, she explained, are "unable to overcome the physical aspects of being a female." They are "full of hormones" that lead to "flighty ideas." She then remarked, apparently unaware of the irony of her comment, that she had kept the books for both her husband and her adult children. "I was the smart one. I was always doing something responsible. My husband did not have the strength to handle finances."

Equally important, this woman never gave up her deeply rooted sense of career. Although she had spent her life working as a nurse's aide and a lab technician and always as a caretaker for three generations of her family, at the age of seventy-seven she still knew her vocational identity: "I was an artist from birth, I have always been an artist." Before we left we asked to see one of her paintings. It was beautiful.

In 1986, my wife asked another seventy-seven-year-old Terman woman how she had bridged the gap between her intellectual potential and a society that had prevented her from going to medical school and underpaid her for the work that she performed. "It was not like that," she protested. "You can't blame that on society. . . . If I had been determined enough. . . . Some women did go to medical school. I could have done it, you see. Just don't blame it on someone else. You know, if you really want to do something, you do, don't you? . . . come hell or high water . . . or at least most of the people I know do." When she saw her interviewer smile, she insisted, "We all believed in individual responsibility—that was actually the theme of the Puritan ethic, a crusade—for heaven sake, take responsibility for yourself. If you can subscribe to that to begin with, you can ride it with enthusiasm."

If society interfered with the Terman women's achieving occupational success, these brilliant and well-educated women were just as successful in achieving Eriksonian generativity as the more societally favored college men of the Grant study. If "career" can be defined as a sphere of competence to which one is committed and for which one receives significant compensation (monetary or otherwise), then it can be said that many of these women made careers as homemakers and family caregivers. Their ability to find meaningful ways of engaging life through their roles at home and in their communities was not necessarily compromised by their blighted performances in the public domain. The life histories of many of them, however, tell stories of underdeveloped and undervalued human potential. One senior California welfare official put it succinctly: "My income is not commensurate with my ability. I administer a budget of $10,000,000 a year, and I receive $6,000 a year as a human service official."

Of course the fate of the Terman woman is not news. For more than four generations women have labored to affect public policy to make it easier for the next generation of daughters to enjoy productive careers. The mothers of the Terman women had had to fight to get their daughters the right to vote. My point here is only to underscore the power of longitudinal idiographic research to alter individual prejudice and to provide a clear example of a case in which social factors proved more important than the hypothesized biological factors.

Conclusion

The Murray Center is an extraordinary resource for longitudinal researchers. It represents the fulfillment of a dream, and I hope that in the next millennium three of the center's most valuable features will be preserved. First, the Murray Center should continue to be an archive of individual lives connected to real people. The opportunity to attach real face-to-face interviews with the archival Terman data was invaluable to us. Second, for the Murray Center to focus on either biology or sociology to the exclusion of the other would be like trying to construct a building with bricks but no mortar. The study of lives binds together the biological and social sciences. Finally, perhaps what is most remarkable about the Murray archives is their extraordinary diversity of archived studies.

Note

1. The IQ scores of the Terman women were measured on the Binet scale, those of the Glueck men on the Weschler Adult Intelligence Scale (WAIS), and those of the Grant college men on the Army Alpha Test scale.

References

Glueck, Sheldon, and Eleanor Glueck. 1950. *Unraveling Juvenile Delinquency.* New York: Commonwealth Fund.
———. 1968. *Delinquents and Non-delinquents in Perspective.* Cambridge, Mass.: Harvard University Press.
Goleman, D. 1985. *Emotional IQ.* New York: Bantam Books.
Heath, C. 1945. *What People Are.* Cambridge, Mass.: Harvard University Press.
Holahan, C. K., and Robert R. Sears. 1995. *The Gifted Group in Later Maturity.* Stanford: Stanford University Press.
Long, J. V. F., and George E. Vaillant. 1984. "Natural History of Male Psychological Health, XI: Escape from the Underclass." *American Journal of Psychiatry* 141: 341–46.
Sears, Robert. 1959. Introduction to *Genetic Studies of Genius,* edited by Lewis M. Terman and M. H. Oden. Stanford: Stanford University Press.
Terman, Lewis M. 1925. "Mental and Physical Traits of a Thousand Gifted Children." In *Genetic Studies of Genius,* vol. 1. Stanford: Stanford University Press.
Terman, Lewis M., and M. H. Oden. 1959. "The Gifted Group at Midlife." In *Genetic Studies of Genius,* vol. 5. Stanford: Stanford University Press.
Vaillant, George E. 1977. *Adaptation to Life.* Boston: Little Brown.
———. 1980. "Natural History of Male Psychological Health, VIII: Antecedents of Alcoholism and 'Orality.' " *American Journal of Psychiatry* 137: 181–86.
———. 1995. *Natural History of Alcoholism Revisited.* Cambridge, Mass.: Harvard University Press.
———. 1998. "Poverty and Paternalism: A Psychiatric Viewpoint." In *The New Paternalism: Supervisory Approaches to Poverty,* edited by L. Meade. Washington, D.C.: Brookings Institution.
Vaillant, George E., and J. T. Davis. 2000. "Social/Emotional Intelligence and Midlife Resilience in Schoolboys with Low Tested Intelligence." *American Journal of Orthopsychiatry* 70: 215–22.
Vaillant, George E., and Caroline O. Vaillant. 1990. "Determinants and Consequences of Creativity in a Cohort of Gifted Women." *Psychology of Women Quarterly* 14: 607–16.

Chapter 6

The PSID and Me

GREG J. DUNCAN

A S PART of President Lyndon Johnson's War on Poverty, the Office of Economic Opportunity (OEO) directed the U.S. Bureau of the Census to conduct a nationwide assessment of the extent to which the new program was affecting people's economic well-being. This Census Bureau study, called the Survey of Economic Opportunity, completed interviews with about thirty thousand households, first in 1966 and again in 1967.

Interest in continuing this survey of economic "trajectories" (the other war going on at the time contributed its share of metaphors to the poverty debate), compounded by a desire to avoid Census Bureau bureaucracy, led James D. Smith and his OEO colleagues to approach James Morgan at the Survey Research Center (SRC) at the University of Michigan about interviewing a nationally representative subsample of approximately two thousand low-income Survey of Economic Opportunity households for five years.

With extensive prior experience in economic surveys, a proven ability to endear himself to sponsors by generating and then returning budget surpluses, coauthorship of the remarkably underappreciated 1961 book *Income and Welfare in the United States,* an unlimited supply of bright ideas, bad puns and funny phrases, and paternal genes inherited from a psychologist who wrote *How to Keep a Sound Mind,* Morgan, a professor of economics and the program director at the Survey Research Center, was a natural choice to lead the new study.

Morgan, however, was initially reluctant to take on the project because, according to its seriously flawed OEO design, the survey was to follow only low-income households.[1] Arguing the formidable virtues of complete population representation—pointing out, for example, that understanding why nonpoor households fell into poverty was at least as interesting as knowing why poor households climbed out—Morgan succeeded in talking the OEO into funding a design in which two thousand randomly chosen households that, by OEO standards, had initially been poor would be combined with a fresh cross section of about three thousand households from the SRC national sampling frame.[2] When weighted, the combined sample was representative of the entire population of the United States, including nonpoor as well as poor households. The disproportionately large number of low-income households, however, produced large analysis samples for black and other disadvantaged groups.

The year 1972 proved momentous for the PSID. As its original five-year tenure was coming to an end, President Richard Nixon dramatically abolished the OEO virtually overnight. Responsibility for the PSID was transferred to the Assistant Secretary for Planning and Evaluation (ASPE) of the Department of Health, Education, and Welfare (now Health and Human Services) where visionary ASPE officials such as Larry Orr saw the value of continued support of the panel survey.[3]

The year 1972 was also my first with the project. As a second-year economics graduate student at the University of Michigan, I was attracted to work at the Survey Research Center by Morgan's mile-a-minute course on survey methods and by the invaluable experience offered of spending my senior undergraduate year in Costa Rica as part of a field studies program. My research project focused on how efficiently Costa Rican farmers, truckers, and wholesalers brought to market basic agricultural produce. I conducted and analyzed data from interviews throughout the country. Fortunately, the data I collected over the course of my year in Costa Rica were much better behaved than I was.

I loved working on the PSID project and at the Survey Research Center. My first tour of duty was as a data editor, reading the often lengthy interviewer explanations of complications that rendered responses to the PSID's many closed-ended questions problematic, making sense of the demographic and economic data, observing the myriad events behind families' seemingly tumultuous economic fortunes, and learning which pieces of data deserved the greatest trust.

Morgan's first quantitative analysis assignment for me was to use as many as necessary of the 2,978 variables gathered over the course of the first five years of the study to understand responses to the fifth-year open-ended question: "We have been visiting you for five years now and asking a lot of questions, but we are also interested in your overall impression of this period. How would you say things have gone for you during the last five years?" The responses included precious few references to earnings, capitalist exploitation, family income, class solidarity, or any of the other economic and class factors I championed at the time. Almost nothing in the PSID's wealth of variables accounted for differences in reports of either the level or trends in well-being revealed by these open-ended responses. The assignment was hopelessly beyond my capabilities, but the process of flailing through data and literature planted a number of seeds that would later sprout in my mind.

Other, more manageable, analyses led to chapters published in the first of ten volumes of *Five Thousand American Families* (Morgan et al. 1974) and to my first published journal articles. With time, my work on the PSID came to include questionnaire development and proposal writing for future waves and assistance with the management of many of the other tasks associated with an annual panel survey.

Equally stimulating was the enterprise of the Survey Research Center itself. Dependent for 95 percent of its budget on the research grant "overhead" it generated, the SRC had developed a strong set of community-building norms, a sense of shared fate, and a democratic process for decision making. Its periodic staff lunches and, in time, some research collaborations reinforced my appreciation for the value of work being carried out in other disciplines. The dignity and wisdom with which researchers such as Angus Campbell, Robert Kahn, and Leslie Kish conducted themselves and their research—and, when called upon, their fulfillment of administrative duties—left a deep impression on me. Awarded my doctorate in 1974, I garnered a few job offers but found the option of staying with the PSID much more compelling—and indeed I remained with the study for the next twenty years.

By the late 1970s, after a decade of operation, the PSID's status properly evolved from a study of poverty into a unique longitudinal data resource for social scientists from several disciplines. This, combined with the ASPE's declining budget fortunes, led to a transfer of primary funding for the study from the ASPE to the National Science Foundation. President Ronald Reagan's attempt to all but eliminate social science research from the National Science Foundation budget in the early 1980s would have been the death knell for the PSID had it not been for three years of emergency funding from the Ford, Sloan, and Rockefeller Foundations, orchestrated by Tom Juster. Albert Rees of the Sloan Foundation remained deeply committed to the PSID and was an important sponsor well beyond the financial support he helped provide.

The intellectual agenda of the PSID's data collection has always been twofold. The first goal is to maintain a clean and consistent time series of core content—employment, family income, and family structure—based on the study's annual interviews. The second, dictated by our desire to maintain the PSID's capacity to address contemporary research issues and, eventually, dictated also by the study's funding structure, has been to complement the core content with question supplements.

The poverty focus of the PSID's early years led to the inclusion of an eclectic set of supplemental measures that might be expected to differentiate families who climbed out of poverty from those who stayed poor. Thus, the first five annual questionnaires are filled with measures of locus of control, future orientation, achievement motivation, employment barriers, entrepreneurial activity, trust and hostility, avoidance of unnecessary risks, access to sources of information and help, and a short sentence completion test. As explained toward the end of this paper, some of the measures have proved quite powerful in differentiating individuals according to their successes and failures in the long run, if not the short.

The surge of labor market research in the 1970s led us to eliminate the PSID's gender bias in the questions asked of married women and to add interesting supplement questions on work histories, labor market attachment, and on-the-job training.[4] In 1980, Morgan anticipated the interest in "social capital" by leading an effort to develop supplement questions on both past and potential exchanges of time and money between households. These were exciting times: we had the freedom to conceive and develop supplements on contemporary topics that, when coupled with the PSID's ever expanding time series of core content, would provide us—and a growing national network of analysts—with unique data drawn from our large national sample of households.

The nature of the PSID's operations changed somewhat when its major funding was taken over in the early 1980s by the National Science Foundation. A board of overseers began to review and pass judgment on PSID operations. Although many of their suggestions have improved the PSID considerably, the burdens of dealing with academic overseers proved considerable.[5] The creative elements of the PSID shifted more and more to the invention and design of question modules that supplemented the PSID's demographic and economic core. Because the National Science Foundation never funded more than 70 percent of what it took to collect and process the data, we became much more dependent on federal agencies and, occasionally, private foundations to fund question supplements that would help cover the PSID's $2.5 million (current dollar) annual cost.

Substantively, the question supplements developed in the 1980s and early 1990s, funded primarily by the National Institute of Child Health and Human Development and the National Institute on Aging, enabled the PSID to add many valuable questions on fertility, health, wealth, child development, and intergenerational transfers as well as a supplement sample of Latino households, funded by the Ford Foundation. We also found funding for projects establishing links between PSID sample members and the National Death Index and between the addresses given each year by PSID respondents and geographic identifiers such as census tracts, zip codes, and counties. This has enabled analysts to explore the nature of neighborhood effects by matching contextual information from the decennial census and other sources to the interview information.

Operationally, these supplemental activities required a great deal of proposal writing and other entrepreneurial effort, much of which I assumed when I joined Morgan as the study's codirector in 1982. Although burdensome, the process forced me to come up to speed on many topics that would eventually become part of my research and to develop a network of contacts in government agencies.[6] Reducing the burden during this period was an invaluable set of colleagues, in particular, Martha Hill, Dan Hill, Sandra Newman, Charlie Brown, and Jim Lepkowski. A remarkably capable and perceptive set of individuals working in the government agencies, particularly Daniel Newlon in the NSF, Jeffrey Evans in NICHD, and Richard Suzman in NIA, all understood both the research issues and, conditional on the enthusiastic scientific reviews we were able to garner, how to "work" their bureaucracies to secure the needed money. I was joined in 1993 by codirector Sandra Hofferth, who, with Frank Stafford, became the principal investigators of the PSID data collection activities.

A final set of burdens, which figured in to my willingness to leave the PSID in 1994, arose in 1992 when the National Science Foundation determined that PSID interviewing needed to be switched from paper and pencil to computer-assisted methods. This change was recommended by individuals who had enjoyed great success in implementing computer-assisted interviewing methods in cross-sectional surveys. Converting the PSID to computer-assisted methods was an unending nightmare, because we wanted to avoid creating a "seam" in the PSID's long time series. In addition, we had complicated sequences of questions on family relationship and faced situations every year in which newly formed families, discovered during the interviewing process, needed to be contacted and interviewed. None of these tasks could be accommodated with existing software. Our costs failed to fall as advertised, our careful manual editing of the data was eliminated in favor of much less satisfactory questionnaire-related programming, a programmer became part of the delicate questionnaire design process, and the lead time needed to develop the next year's questionnaire increased by several months. I am most decidedly a Luddite, at least when it comes to inserting technology into an ongoing panel study.

Some Important Lessons from the Panel Study of Income Dynamics

The PSID interviews provide a wide variety of information about both families and individuals collected over the span of the study. The central focus of the data is economic and demographic, with substantial detail on income sources and amounts, employment, changes in family composition, and residential location. In the early years, respondents were asked short sequences of questions designed to measure social psychological factors such as achievement motivation, locus of control, and future orientation. Question modules in some waves have covered neighborhood characteristics, child care, job training, retirement plans, military combat experience, health, kinship networks, and wealth.

The design of the PSID calls for interviews each year with families in the core sample, whether or not they were living in the same dwelling or with the same people as in the previous year. Fundamental to the success of the PSID are the often overlooked advantages of its following, and keeping as part of the sample, members of the families who moved away from their original households to set up new households, such as children who came of age during the study (Hill 1992). Because such individuals were originally chosen to be representative of the general U.S. population, the new families they form in the PSID sample are considered representative of new families formed in the larger U.S. population.[7] Furthermore, because children born to the PSID's representative sample families are themselves a representative sample of children, the study's design also provides continuous representation of births.

When played out over the course of thirty-two years, these design features enabled the PSID to provide a wealth of data. Four such categories are especially important: data on representative cross sections of families and individuals in 1968; data on representative annual cross sections of families and individuals between 1969 and 1999; thirty-year longitudinal data on individuals in the initially representative 1968 sample, including children observed both when they were living with their parents and long after striking out on their own in adulthood; and shorter-run comparative longitudinal data on representative cohorts of individuals at any point between 1968 and 1999.

In addition, four other design features of the PSID have been crucial to its ultimate success: the core content of the study's annual interviews has remained largely unchanged; response rates have been high and largely random (Fitzgerald, Gottschalk, and Moffitt 1998); remarkable effort has been expended on cleaning the data in exactly the same way in virtually every year of the study; and data have always been released to the larger research community as soon as they have been cleaned and documented. Unplanned but inevitable, given the stimulating and supportive environment Morgan created (and I tried to maintain), is the fact that many key support staff have remained with the study for decades.

The key role played by support staff in the success of the study cannot be overemphasized. Collectively, the support staff provided the institutional memory needed to keep the data comparable across waves. In their individual ways, they quickly discovered optimal methods for persuading reluctant respondents to continue with the study, wrote questions that could be understood by normal (that is, nonacademic) people, processed the data, and counseled the horde of young outside researchers who wanted to use the data—a small number of whom refused to read even the first page of documentation. The perfectionism of the staff caused more than a few headaches in meeting deadlines, but their single-minded dedication to getting things right has produced an extraordinarily detailed and accurate motion picture of American economic family life in the last third of the twentieth century.

These features have made the PSID one of the most widely used and influential data sets in the social science research community. As of 1996, PSID-based articles have appeared in more than one hundred different refereed journals; the bibliography on the PSID lists some twelve hundred publications in all. In the early 1990s, five PSID articles were published annually in the top four economics journals, six in the top labor economics journals, and five in the top five sociology and family journals.[8] I cannot hope to present a comprehensive summary of what has been learned from these many studies. In the spirit of this volume, my approach is decidedly selective and personal.

What a Family's Life Cycle Is Really Like

Despite the study's longitudinal nature, most analysts, myself included, typically approached the PSID's first decade of data as though they were drawn from a cross section. Longitudinal methods were not well developed in the 1970s, and the PSID questionnaire provided many novel measures that, when analyzed using cross-sectional methods, produced interesting and, most important, publishable articles. My own studies were inspired by my training as a labor economist and focused on such popular topics as earnings differences between men and women and between union and nonunion workers, economic rewards of on-the-job training, child-care decisions made by working parents, and, using retrospective reports, intergenerational models of completed schooling.

Lurking in the background, however, were persistently puzzling PSID data suggesting a striking degree of economic turbulence and perhaps genuine mobility at all income levels (see Morgan et al. 1974; Duncan et al. 1984). Incomes fluctuated a great deal from one year to the next, producing many transitions in and out of both poverty and affluence and on and off welfare rolls. Moreover, other important changes frequently took place: roughly one in five families changed composition from one year to the next, and a comparable fraction pulled up stakes and moved from one location to another.

What was going on? Were the income changes merely the result of measurement errors, or were families' economic fortunes really more volatile than previously believed? If the turbulence was real, what caused it, and to what extent was it voluntary or at least anticipated? How much of the turbulence reflected true mobility—permanent changes in economic and, perhaps, social position?

The prevalent academic conceptions of social and economic position in the 1970s were of unchanging social class, slowly building stocks of economically valuable (human capital) skills, or fairly predictable life-cycle changes experienced by individuals as they age. In the life-cycle view, early adulthood is usually seen as a period of relatively low income as career and marital arrangements are being sorted out. Income grows as careers stabilize and, in some cases, blossom and as multiple earners increase the household's total income. Retirement usually occasions a drop both in nominal income, cushioned by social security and private pension payments, and in work-related expenses.

Lenore Weitzman's (1985) sensational but erroneously overstated depiction of the dire economic consequences of divorce was still years in the future and had not yet been integrated into life-cycle theories. Glen Elder's (1974) landmark studies of the Great Depression provided a vivid picture of the consequences of severe macroeconomic disruptions, but few thought that these kinds of disruptions were a regular feature of many families' lives in the prosperous second half of the twentieth century.

This life-cycle view of income changes conforms closely to (and indeed has been developed from) family income data drawn from representative cross sections of the population showing higher levels of household income for older individuals until their late forties and then lower levels at older ages. If we succumb to the temptation to use these cross-sectional data on different families at various life-cycle stages to represent the likely economic path of individuals as they age, then we might view individual income trajectories as fairly smooth, with fluctuations occurring infrequently and at discrete points of the life cycle such as early adulthood and retirement.

The Panel Study of Income Dynamics as well as subsequent longitudinal household and administrative data reveal economic and social trajectories that are much more disparate and chaotic than envisioned by a life-cycle view. An idea of the scope of these fluctuations can be gleaned from table 6.1, which is taken from my PSID-based analysis of household income trajectories over the eleven-year period from 1969 to 1979 (Duncan 1988).[9] Because the longitudinal experiences of men and women are quite different, data are presented separately by gender.

The first row shows the average level of family income over the eleven-year period; the data display typical life-cycle patterns. Household incomes were highest for individuals who were in their prime earning years for the entire period, somewhat lower for those who were in their

Table 6.1   Level and Stability of Income, from 1969 to 1979, by Age and Sex

| | Age in 1969 | | | | | |
| | Twenty-Five to Forty-Five Years | | Forty-Six to Fifty-Five Years | | Fifty-Six to Sixty-Five Years | |
	Men	Women	Men	Women	Men	Women
Mean income level, in thousands of 1985 dollars	43.1	40.0	38.7	32.3	29.5	22.1
Percentage with rapidly rising income	35	32	22	21	7	6
Percentage with rapidly falling income	6	10	13	20	38	35
Percentage with large drop (50 percent or more) in income at least once	18	24	26	33	38	39
Of those with income drops, percentage expecting income loss	9	6	12	24	34	25
Percentage poor at least once	13	20	14	21	17	27
Percentage poor six or more years	2	5	3	6	4	9

Source: Data from Duncan 1988.

middle years when the survey began, (some of whom retired during the eleven-year period), and lower still for the next older cohort, who were between the ages of fifty-five and sixty-six at the start of the survey. The gap between the family incomes of men and women increases substantially over the life cycle as a result of the increasing proportion of women not living with spouses or partners.

To what extent do these averages conceal diverse individual experiences? The second and third rows of table 6.1 show the fractions of the sample in various age and sex groups with either rapid growth (more than 5 percent a year) or sharp declines (falling by at least 5 percent a year) in inflation-adjusted living standards over the period. Several startling facts emerge, the foremost of which is the prevalence of either large positive or negative trajectories. With the exception of the men of the middle age group (forty-six to fifty-five years old), at least 40 percent of all groups displayed either large positive or large negative economic trajectories. Figures for average income over the life cycle do indeed obscure a great deal of offsetting change at the individual level.

The direction of the trajectories varies predictably across the age groups. Rapid increases are concentrated in the early adult years, while the most rapid decreases are experienced by the retirement cohort. There are, however, many individual exceptions to these age patterns.

Duncan 1988 also provides estimates of the incidence of adverse income "events," defined as instances in which family-size-adjusted income falls by 50 percent or more in consecutive years. This yardstick is similar to that employed by Glen Elder and his colleagues in their studies of the effects of the Great Depression, which finds lasting effects of income drops of one-third or more.

The incidence of sharp drops in income-to-needs over the life course is shown in the fourth row of table 6.1. The overall risk is high: between 18 and 39 percent of the various groups are estimated to have experienced such a drop at least once during the eleven-year period. Most of these decreases left the individuals involved with, at best, modest incomes. Not shown in table 6.1 is the fact that 87 percent of the individuals experiencing these decreases saw their family incomes fall to less than $25,000.

Because the PSID questions respondents about their expectations of future changes in economic status, it is possible to calculate what fraction of the income drops of 50 percent or more were preceded in either of the previous two annual interviews by a report that the respondent expected his or her family economic status to decline.[10] The fifth row of table 6.1 shows that a majority of all income declines and the vast majority of income drops before retirement were unexpected.

Taken together, longitudinal PSID data show that it is a mistake to treat the "path" of average income as the typical income course of individuals as they age. Family incomes are quite volatile at nearly every point in the life cycle, making rapid growth or decline in living standards more the rule than the exception. We do not have to look, with Elder and his colleagues, to the Great Depression to find frequent instances of economic loss and hardship; the risk of sharp decreases in living standards is still significant at virtually every stage of life. Most of the losses are unexpected. These losses occur despite our system of government safeguards (unemployment insurance, Aid to Families with Dependent Children [AFDC]) and intrafamily transfers that might be expected to reduce or eliminate them.[11]

So What?

Should these newly discovered economic fluctuations be a concern? Elder's data provide compelling but historical evidence of circumstances in which economic shocks can have devastating effects on both adults and children. In *Falling from Grace,* Katherine Newman (1988) draws data from the 1980s to document the psychological and other damage brought about by downsizing, divorce, and other events. Countless more specialized studies focus on the consequences of individual events such as layoffs, divorce, and widowhood, with some showing an increase in the frequency of untoward events over the past quarter century (see, for example, Boisjoly, Duncan, and Smeeding 1998 on involuntary job loss). Contemporary economic dislocations are perhaps even more damaging than those of the 1930s, because there is currently much less of a sense that these events are shared by others.

On the other hand, some events producing economic losses may have benign or even beneficial effects. Children leave parental homes and older parents decide not to move in with their adult children, despite economic advantages they would otherwise enjoy, because they value their independence. Although their incomes are lower than before retirement, retired individuals may be better off because they have more leisure time than when they were working, and the predictability of retirement has allowed them time to prepare for its financial and psychological consequences. Despite their unstable incomes, construction workers may be reasonably well off because their higher rates of pay compensate them for the instability of their jobs, while the self-employed may value being their own bosses over a stable salary. In short, not all instances of income instability have similar negative implications. Indeed, some have argued explicitly that income variability over the life cycle is of little analytic and policy interest (for example, Murray 1986).

Because few data sets combine reliable longitudinal information on family income with well-measured subsequent physiological or psychological outcomes, it is difficult to conduct research on the consequences of economic fluctuation. One interesting exception using PSID data relates the level and stability of income to mortality (McDonough et al. 1997). The authors treat PSID data as if they were a series of independent ten-year panels, the first spanning calendar years 1967 to 1976, the second spanning 1968 to 1977, and so forth, with the last panel spanning the period from 1980 to 1989. Within each ten-year period they use the first five years to measure the level and stability of household income and the second five years to measure possible mortality.

Key results of the study are presented in table 6.2. They are taken from a logistic regression in which the dependent variable is whether the individual died between the sixth and tenth year of the given period. Income level and stability over the five-year period preceding the possible death are combined into a single classification among five categories: low and unstable income (mean of less than $20,000) and at least one big income drop over the given five-year period, low but stable

Table 6.2   Odds Ratios of Mortality for Individuals Aged Forty-Five to Sixty-Four Years, 1972 through 1989, by Level and Stability of Income

Five-Year Mean Income Level and Stability	Odds Ratio	95 Percent Confidence Interval
Income of less than $20,000 and one or more income drops	3.7*	2.4 to 5.7
Income of less than $20,000 and no income drops	3.4*	2.2 to 5.1
Income between $20,000 and $70,000 and one or more income drops	3.2*	1.9 to 5.5
Income between $20,000 and $70,000 and no income drops	1.5*	1.0 to 2.0
Income of more than $70,000 and one or more income drops	1.4	0.7 to 2.6
Income of more than $70,000 and no income drops[a]	1.00	—

Source: Data from McDonough et al. 1997.
Note: "Income drop" is defined as a situation in which size-adjusted family income fell by 50 percent or more in consecutive years. Odds ratios are adjusted for age, sex, race, family size, and period.
[a] Reference group.
* Coefficient is at least twice its standard error.

income, middle class (mean between $20,000 and $70,000) and unstable income, middle class and stable income, and affluent and unstable income. Affluent individuals with stable incomes served as the reference group.[12]

Consistent with a number of other studies, mortality risks fall with income level. Individuals with low incomes have, on average, three to four times the mortality risk of the affluent individuals in the reference group. New in the analysis is the result that unstable incomes also contribute to mortality risk, but only among the middle class. When compared with the consistently affluent reference group, middle-income individuals with stable incomes had a marginally significant 150 percent elevation of mortality risk. In contrast, an individual with middle-class but unstable income had a risk ratio more than three times that of individuals in the reference group and almost as high as individuals in the two low-income groups. Instability mattered neither at the low nor high end of the income distribution, perhaps because the disadvantages of low incomes and the advantages of affluence overwhelm the possible effects of instability. An important question for future research is whether it is the income fluctuations themselves or the events producing them (for example, unemployment, widowhood) that increase the mortality risks.

Poverty and Welfare Dynamics

In *Years of Poverty, Years of Plenty* (Duncan et al. 1984) my coauthors and I attempt to summarize the most important lessons from the first ten years of the PSID.[14] The book includes chapters on family economic and labor market mobility, labor market differences between African Americans and whites and between men and women, and poverty and welfare dynamics. It was intended to be an accessible summary of findings, and we are pleased by the extent to which it found its way into classrooms and policy discussions.

The interest generated by the book focused overwhelmingly on its findings on the dynamic nature of poverty and welfare use. As with the more general life-cycle results, there was a huge gap between popular perceptions of these phenomena and the data's clear message of turbulence and mobility. When the PSID began, there were widespread popular perceptions of the permanence of poverty and welfare receipt, perceptions that continue to the present. We speak easily of "the poor" as if they were an ever present and unchanging group. Indeed the way we conceptualize the "poverty problem," the "underclass problem" or "the welfare problem" seems to presume the permanent existence of well-defined groups within American society.

Much of our data on poverty is based on large annual Census Bureau surveys in which family annual cash incomes are compared with a set of "poverty thresholds" that vary with family size. In 1999, a three-person family with an income of less than $13,290 was designated as poor; the threshold for a four-person family was $17,029. Although the poverty rates calculated each year by the Census Bureau generate a great deal of publicity, they rarely change by as much as a single percentage point from one year to the next. Longer-run trends show jumps during recessions and a disturbing secular increase in the poverty rate among families with children.

Evidence that, for instance, one in five children was poor in two consecutive Census Bureau survey "snapshots" and that those poor children shared similar characteristics (for example, half of them lived in households in which their mother was the only adult) is consistent with an inference of absolutely no turnover in the poverty population; this evidence seems to fit the stereotype that poor families with children are likely to remain poor and that there is a hard-core population of poor families with little hope of self-improvement. However, the same evidence is equally consistent with 100 percent turnover—or any other percentage one might pick—assuming only that equal numbers of people with similar characteristics cross into and out of poverty.

In fact, longitudinal data from the PSID have always revealed a great deal of turnover both among the poor and among welfare recipients (Duncan et al. 1984). Only a little more than half of the individuals living in poverty in one year are found to be poor in the next, and considerably fewer than one-half of those who experience poverty remain persistently poor over many years. Similarly, many families receive income from welfare sources at least occasionally, but relatively few do so year after year.

Many descriptions of poverty experiences are possible with the PSID; perhaps the simplest is a count of the number of years in which an individual lived in a family with total annual income that fell short of the poverty threshold in that year. In the case of the eleven-year period used for table 6.1, if poverty were a persistent condition then the sample would cluster at one of two points—no poverty at all or poverty in all of the eleven years. If much contact with poverty is occasional, then we would expect that the persistently poor would be a small subset of the larger group that had at least some experience with poverty.

The last two rows of table 6.1 show what fractions of individuals in the various age and sex groups spent at least one of the eleven years below the poverty line and those who spent more than half of that time (at least six of the eleven years) in poverty. The difference in the sizes of these two groups at all stages of the life cycle is striking. Depending on the life-cycle stage, between 20 and 27 percent of adult women experienced poverty at least once during the eleven-year period. The risk of at least occasional poverty was considerably lower for adult men than for adult women. Persistent poverty, defined as living in poverty for more than half of the eleven-year period, characterized fewer than one-tenth of any of the subgroups. An older woman's chance of experiencing persistent poverty was roughly twice that of a young adult woman (aged twenty-five to forty-five) and nearly five times as high as that of a young adult man. Poverty rates for children, especially minority children, are much higher, with nearly one-quarter of black children living in persistent poverty (U.S. Department of Health and Human Services 2001).

By adopting event-history methods such as the life table and Cox regression (Tuma and Groeneveld 1979), Mary Jo Bane and David Ellwood (1986, 1994) furthered the transformation in how social scientists and policy analysts viewed poverty and welfare dynamics. These methods enable them to characterize the nature and determinants of poverty and welfare experiences by the length of a person's "spells" (that is, continuous periods) of poverty or welfare receipt.

Essential data from the Bane and Ellwood analyses are presented in table 6.3. In the case of poverty, they use the PSID to estimate what fraction of families who first begin a poverty experience do so for short (one to two years), medium (three to seven years) and long (eight or more years) periods of time. They find that although a clear majority of poverty spells are short, a substantial subset of poor families have longer-run experiences. Heterogeneity of experiences is thus key.

Table 6.3   Distribution of Duration of Poverty Spells and AFDC Receipt (Percentage)

Duration	Poverty Spells Among Nonelderly Persons	Total Years of AFDC Receipt
One to two years	60	36
Three to seven years	26	35
Eight or more years	14	29

Source: Poverty data from Bane and Ellwood 1986, table 2; AFDC data from Bane and Ellwood 1994, table 2.3.

Striving to discover the correct characterization of poverty—transitory or persistent—is fruitless, given that poverty experiences are always a mixture of transitory and long term. The policy implications of these data are profound, because the heterogeneous nature of poverty experiences demands a heterogeneous set of policies to address the needs they create. The short-term needs associated with short spells call for social insurance approaches in which fears of dependence need not be a concern. Long-term poverty spells are a different matter and call for policies that address the causes of the longer-run problems of the poor.

In the data presented in the second column of table 6.3, Bane and Ellwood (1994) calculate the likely total number of years of welfare receipt for families just starting to receive Aid to Families with Dependent Children (AFDC). They find a roughly even distribution of first-time welfare recipients across the three time intervals; approximately one-third have very short welfare experiences, another third medium-length experiences, and the final third long-term receipt.

With welfare, as with poverty, heterogeneity is a key feature. Before the welfare reforms enacted in 1996, AFDC operated simultaneously as a short-term insurance and a long-run support program. As shown in the final column of table 6.3, many families using AFDC did so for only a few years, after which they got back on their feet and never returned to welfare. However, a substantial fraction of recipients were dependent on welfare for a longer term, raising all of the inflammatory rhetoric that seems to surround contemporary discussions of welfare.

These data figured prominently in the mid-1990s debate over welfare reform. David Ellwood (1988) himself proposed time limits as a means of addressing some of the problems associated with long-run receipt, although in the context of a comprehensive package of supports designed to ensure that families who wanted work could get it and that the incomes of working families would remain above the poverty line. In fact, welfare reform is being implemented in fifty different ways across as many states, with some incarnations resembling Ellwood's desired policies but others quite different.

Road Trip

News of and use of data from the PSID soon spread to several European countries and generated interest in launching similar studies. The most ambitious and widely used are the German Socio-Economic Panel, which collected its first wave in 1984, and the British Household Panel Survey, which collected its first wave in 1990. Luxembourg, the Netherlands, and the Lorraine region of France ran panels in the 1980s; quite comparable household panels in all European Community countries began in the early 1990s.

Among the personal rewards to this work was one of particular serendipity: while returning from a 1981 trip to Sweden, standing in line in front of the TWA ticket counter at Kennedy airport in New York, I struck up a conversation with the woman who, eighteen months later, would marry me and, nineteen years later, is still willing to put up with my workaholic nature. Flying in and out on different planes but with just enough of a snow delay to give us a couple of hours to get to know one another—the improbability of it all leads me to attach a large stochastic component to people's fates.

There have been intellectual rewards to this work as well. One surprising result from comparative longitudinal analyses of income data is that the United States is far from alone in its high degree of economic mobility, particularly among the poor. This issue has important implications for the poverty debate in the United States.

Tim Smeeding's Luxembourg Income Study project documents the much higher rates of poverty prevailing in the United States than in other Western industrialized countries. Conservatives have argued that these uniquely high rates of U.S. poverty are the price we pay for our economic dynamism. Poverty is certainly less of a worry if the economy will ensure that prosperity is a year or two away. To what extent are the lower poverty rates of European countries associated with lower amounts of economic mobility?

With funding from the Russell Sage Foundation, I coordinated a project that examined poverty dynamics in nine Western countries (Duncan et al. 1995). Data from Canada, Finland, and Sweden came from administrative records; results for the Lorraine district of France, western Germany, Ireland, Luxembourg, the Netherlands, and the United States were collected from household panel surveys. Table 6.4 presents some of the findings of that project. Considerable effort was expended to ensure that all studies were based on representative and comparable samples and that they defined income levels and changes in comparable

Table 6.4   Poverty Rates, Poverty Transitions, and Income Changes of Low-Income Families in the Mid-1980s, Various Regions

Country or Region	Percentage of Families with Incomes Below 50 Percent of Median	Percentage of "Near Poor" Climbing Out of Poverty	Typical Percentage Income Change for Families in Bottom Decile
Canada	17	23	21
Finland	3	47	28
France (Lorraine)	4	32	10
Germany (West)	8	24	18
Ireland	11	22	22
Luxembourg	4	29	10
Netherlands	3	23	8
Sweden	3	45	9
United States	20	22	15
German foreign residents	18	23	12
U.S. blacks	49	15	8

Source: Data from Duncan, Gustafsson, et al. 1995.
Note: "Poverty" is defined by income less than 50 percent of median income in given country. "Near poor" are families with incomes at 40 to 50 percent of the median in base year. "Climbing out" is defined as income change from year 1 to year 2 from less than 50 percent to more than 60 percent of the median.

ways. To establish a comparable poverty line across countries, we used a relative threshold—50 percent of the median income of all households in the country.

The first column in table 6.4 presents a cross-sectional snapshot of poverty rates across the nine countries. Consistent with data from the cross-sectional Luxembourg Income Study project, the poverty rate is found to be much higher in the United States, particularly among African Americans, than in European countries, with Canada somewhere in between.

Poverty dynamics are gauged by the fraction of poor families (defined as those with incomes below 50 percent of the median in year t) that, in year $t + 1$, have incomes above 60 percent of the median.[14] If the poverty escape rates are calculated based on the entire poor population within each country (data not shown in table 6.4), then the U.S. poor rank near the bottom. However, this is largely attributable to the fact that the U.S. poor are, on average, much further away from the poverty line than the poor in other countries. If we take only those families with incomes in year 1 close to the poverty line (that is, with incomes between 40 and 50 percent of the median), then the poverty escape rates (second column of table 6.4) are remarkable similar across the countries. A more direct calculation of the degree of income instability among low-income families (third column of table 6.4) shows, if anything, less instability in the United States.[15]

Thus, the surprising result from this comparative study is that patterns of economic turbulence in other industrialized countries are similar to those in the United States. The extent of genuine economic mobility in these data is another matter. Most of the families climbing out of poverty do not end up in the middle class, and more than a few return to below-poverty-level incomes from time to time. A companion analysis of welfare dynamics (Duncan et al. 1995) finds that, if anything, the U.S. recipients had shorter-term experiences than recipients in most other countries.

Poverty and Child Development

As my work with the PSID continued, its fascinating data on family income and poverty dynamics began to take precedence over my interest in traditional labor economics topics. My research began to focus on understanding the patterns of change in family economic well-being. Because family structure itself figured so prominently in the income changes, a number of my studies were of the economic determinants and consequences of events such as divorce, widowhood, and out-of-wedlock childbearing. Economists such as Gary Becker had developed interesting models of these kinds of behavior, but so too had sociologists and psychologists.

By the mid-1980s, my attention turned to the "so what?" questions. Analysts working with the PSID were able to describe in exquisite detail the dynamic patterns of poverty, family structure, and social conditions but collectively knew little of the effects of these changes and events on the psychological and physical health of adults and on the life chances of individuals who experienced these events while growing up.

Addressing the "so what?" questions with the PSID's now thirty-two-year motion picture of economic, demographic, and social conditions and events has had the most profound impact on the evolution of my academic career. My early efforts to link economic and other events in the sample produced a mixed record of success, perhaps because older adults' formative years predated the PSID's first waves. Much more promising has been my research on child and adolescent development, which has been able to draw upon more complete information, much of it dating from birth and extending to the point in early adulthood at which developmental outcomes are assessed.

No single discipline monopolizes theoretical and methodological insights in this field of research, but there have been remarkably few collaborations among the relevant social science disciplines. Consequently, developmental studies designed by psychologists and sociologists attend to neither the economic dimension of family life nor economic aspects of the policy implications of the research. Moreover, economist-driven studies give short shrift to the idea of critical periods and to the careful measurement of outcome and process favored by psychologists and sociologists.

Although my mentoring by James Morgan, my SRC upbringing, and occasional contact with Glen Elder and some of the other major figures in human development predisposed me to read portions of the research literature in sociology and developmental psychology, it became clear to me that fruitful interdisciplinary collaborations require major mutual investments of time and energy. A meeting with the Social Science Research Council's (SSRC) Committee on the Life Course and Human Development led to a conference and volume (Elder 1985) on life-course studies using the PSID. My truly formative moments in the process, however, came over the course of my many meetings with the SSRC's Working Group on Communities, Neighborhoods, Family Processes, and Individual Development. Launched in 1989 as part of the SSRC's initiative on the underclass, this working group brought me into sustained contact with a stimulating set of developmental psychologists and sociologists.[16] Group interactions forced me to explain and reflect on the economic and policy underpinnings of links between child development and neighborhood and family processes and taught me approaches and insights from these other disciplines. My association with Jeanne Brooks-Gunn has proved particularly stimulating, fruitful, and enjoyable; our research collaborations continue to this day.

One thing has led to another; I now belong to a number of interdisciplinary research networks and committees and relish my role as the token economist. It enables me to ask naive questions without embarrassing myself and to contribute economic, econometric, and policy insights into the woefully insular studies of development by psychologists.[17] More important, these collaborations have borne fruit, as exemplified by my work with Brooks-Gunn, W. Jean Yeung, and others on links between poverty and child development.

Many studies, books, and reports have demonstrated correlations between children's poverty and various measures of child achievement, health, and behavior (for example, Duncan and Brooks-Gunn 1997; Brooks-Gunn and Duncan 1997; Children's Defense Fund 1994; Mayer 1997). As summarized in "The Effects of Poverty on Children" (Brooks-Gunn and Duncan 1997, table 1), the strength and consistency of these associations is striking. For example, poor children face higher risk than nonpoor children on a broad range of factors: 2.0 times higher for grade repetition and dropping out of high school, 1.4 times higher for learning disability, 1.3 times higher for parent-reported emotional or behavior problems, 3.1 times higher for teenage out-of-wedlock birth, 6.8 times higher for reported cases of child abuse and neglect, and 2.2 times higher for experiencing violent crime.

The literature on the causal effects of poverty on children has major shortcomings, however, the most important of which is that in many data sources that contain crucial information about child outcomes, family income is not reported. As a result, studies using these kinds of data have often used variables such as occupation, single parenthood, or low maternal education level to infer family income levels. Income and social class, however, are far from synonymous. As we have seen, family incomes are surprisingly volatile, which means that there are only modest correlations between economic deprivation and typical measures of socioeconomic background.

How can insights from economics and developmental psychology be best combined to understand the effects of poverty on children? Psychology emphasizes the importance of conditions surrounding developmental stages and transitions. In the context of poverty studies, the greater malleability of children's development and the overwhelming importance of the family (as opposed to school or peer contexts) lead to expectations that economic conditions in early childhood may be far more important in shaping children's ability and achievement than conditions later in childhood.

The possibility that the effects of economic conditions on children's development depend upon childhood stage is foreign to most economists, whose developmental models are simplistic, tend to focus on the role of "permanent" income, and tend to assume that families anticipate bumps in their life-cycle paths and can save and borrow freely to smooth their consumption across these bumps. Although some economists recognize the potential importance of credit and other constraints faced by poor families, none has attempted to gauge the implications of the bumps in the context of children's development.

The PSID's long-run scope and careful measurement of income enabled my colleagues and me (Duncan et al. 1998) to investigate the importance of childhood-stage-specific poverty to the completion of schooling. Their sample consisted of 1,323 children born between 1967 and 1973, who were observed in PSID families for the entire period between birth and the age of twenty to twenty-five and constitute a representative sample of children in these birth cohorts. To allow for the differential impact of income by childhood stage, they related years of children's completed schooling to measures of family income averaged over the first, second, and third five-year segments of the children's lives (see table 6.5).[18]

Taken as a whole, the results show that the timing of economic deprivation matters a great deal to schooling outcomes, with income early in

Table 6.5   Effects of Stage-Specific Parental Income on Completed Schooling

Age of Child	Family Income	Years of Completed Schooling
Birth to five years	Less than $15,000[a]	.00
	$15,000 to $24,999	.66*
	$25,000 to $34,999	.73*
	$35,000 to $49,999	.78*
	$50,000 and more	1.41*
Six to ten years	Less than $15,000[a]	.00
	$15,000 to $24,999	.16
	$25,000 to $34,999	.24
	$35,000 to $49,999	.44
	$50,000 and more	.33
Eleven to fifteen years	Less than $15,000[a]	.00
	$15,000 to $24,999	.34
	$25,000 to $34,999	.41
	$35,000 to $49,999	.36
	$50,000 and more	1.08*

Source: Data from Duncan et al. 1998, table 3.
Note: The regression controls for mother's schooling, family structure, race, gender, age of the mother at the birth of the child, total number of siblings, whether ever lived in South, number of geographic moves, and number of years mother worked for one thousand or more hours. Parental income is inflated to 1993 price levels.
[a] Reference group.
* Coefficient is at least twice its standard error.

life by far the most important. The coefficients reported in table 6.5 suggest that, controlling for income in other stages and other family conditions, children whose families' incomes were between $15,000 and $25,000 when they were youngest (from birth to five years old) average two-thirds of a year more schooling—about one-third of a standard deviation—than children in families whose income was less than $15,000 during the earliest part of childhood. In contrast, income from middle childhood and adolescence failed to strongly predict schooling outcomes.[19]

In short, economic deprivation occurring early in childhood appears to have the most pronounced and lasting effects on children's achievement. The lens of early childhood as the critical period with respect to economic deprivation leads to some important policy implications (see Duncan and Brooks-Gunn 1997). For example, the five-year time limits in the 1996 welfare reform legislation are not as worrisome as sanctions, because few families hitting five-year limits will include young children in the household, but many families sanctioned off Temporary Assistance for Needy Families (TANF) will. More generally, income support programs directed at families with young children are much less expensive than programs directed at families with children of any age.

Are There Undiscovered Dynamics in Noneconomic Phenomena?

John Modell has encouraged me to speculate about whether an annual or even more frequent panel study version of the General Social Survey, the National Election Study, or some of the landmark long-term developmental studies would revolutionize our thinking about the dynamic nature of attitudes or developmental pathways, as the PSID has done with respect to poverty, welfare use, labor supply, and other economic phenomena. Of course there are many examples of two- or three-wave panels involving noneconomic phenomena, some of which take their measurements at long intervals. None, to my knowledge, interviews frequently enough to provide the kind of motion picture that the PSID produces about its economic and demographic core.

Cast in event-history terms, such studies would enable us to ask whether attitudes, psychological states, or behaviors follow predictable "spell" patterns. Are changes gradual or sudden, perhaps in response to important individual or environmental events? How often and for what kinds of people do changes in attitudes and behaviors prove transitory? Such data would also enable us to investigate whether our conceptions of constancy and change should be supplemented with a focus on instability. Is instability in domains other than income a predictor of important health and other significant outcomes?

John Nesselroade and David Featherman (1997) argue that developmentalists' preoccupation with stability has led them to ignore powerful theoretical and empirical reasons for needing to understand the nature and determinants of change at the individual level. They point out that the focus of the life-span perspective on changes in individuals' capacity and performance as well as adaptations to changing environments should lead us to view variability as the norm and stability as the exception.

Yet most developmental research focuses either on relatively stable differences between individuals or on changes in a given individual that occur between measurement points that are months or even years apart (Alwin 1994, Costa and McCrae 1980) but almost never on duration or stability. Lacking panel data, we are tempted to infer life-cycle change by comparing individuals of different ages from cross-sectional data, which is precisely the mistake made in life-cycle studies of economic well-being.

Even with panel data, however, which are increasingly being used in developmental studies, we refuse to take instability and short spells seriously. We compute test-retest correlations from panel data gathered over short intervals to measure reliability rather than instability, which reflects our belief that most of our constructs are stable over at least short periods of time. Measures that exhibit instability are discarded by this process rather than seen as potentially valuable examples of short duration or unstable phenomena. Few developmental or attitudinal analyses are cast as event histories.[20] Think of how much less would now be known about subatomic processes if scientists required that particles, in order to be accepted as such, live for at least one second. Analogously, consider the fact that we would miss at least half of the action in understanding welfare receipt if only spells of at least three years' duration were studied. What are we missing in the absence of a PSID-type motion picture of developmental processes?

Some intriguing evidence suggests that turbulence matters in other than economic domains. Dara Eizenman and colleagues (1997) have gathered measures of locus of control and perceived competence over twenty-five consecutive weeks from a sample of elderly residents of a Pennsylvania retirement community. They derive measures of both the level and the stability of these two constructs and then relate both dimensions to the mortality status of their sample five years after their final measurement. As Peggy McDonough and colleagues (1997) have found in the case of income instability, Eizenman and colleagues discover that the instability of locus of control and perceived competence is highly predictive of subsequent mortality. In fact, instability in control and competence was considerably more predictive of mortality than were the average levels of control and competence.

The more general answer to the question of whether motion-picture panel studies of other than economic phenomena would revolutionize conceptions of these phenomena is, of course, that we do not know. Nor are we likely to find out soon, because duration and turbulence are understudied dimensions of the constructs that interest us. It makes sense to begin to investigate these issues with small, well-focused studies of the type undertaken by Eizenman and colleagues (1997) before thinking about more expensive large-scale studies.

Me, Without the PSID

In 1994 I left Michigan and the PSID and joined the faculties of the Human Development and Social Policy (HDSP) program and the Institute for Policy Research at Northwestern University. Although my attachment to both the PSID and the Survey Research Center caused me to agonize over the decision, it is now clear that the change was a good one.

My interests in interdisciplinary work involving human development, economics, and social policy meshed perfectly with the structure and philosophy of the HDSP. Fulfilling an ambition formed as a Grinnell undergraduate, I traded administrative duties running the PSID for the rewards of teaching and mentoring the remarkably motivated, capable, and mature HDSP graduate students. The Institute for Policy Research has provided a fertile environment for sustaining my research program. I surprised myself with the extent of my comfort with only an interdisciplinary affiliation, requesting neither a joint nor even a courtesy appointment in Northwestern's prestigious economics department.

My experiences have reinforced my excitement over the synergistic possibilities of incorporating economic and policy insights into studies of human development. Developmentalists, in general, are strong on theory and measurement but relatively weak in thinking critically about the fact that people's contexts are, in large part, chosen (endogenous) and in thinking systematically about the policy implications of their research.

The endogeneity problem is especially important. Does a positive association between a high-quality child-care setting and a child's subsequent school readiness tell us that the quality of child care promotes school readiness or that school readiness is caused by the same, often unmeasured parental characteristics that lead to the choice of high-quality child care? The psychologist's and sociologist's first instinct is to assume the former; the economist's the latter. It is tempting to minimize the choices available to some, especially low-income, families. In fact, however, the child-care options for even low-income families are quite diverse, even if they do not include the highest-quality options. If most resilient children are found to have had an adult mentor, does this indicate that adult mentors would help less resilient children or merely that a manifestation of resilience is the seeking out of mentors? The policy implications depend fundamentally on the answers to these questions.

Economists are strong on the policy side, pose some interesting theoretical questions, and have developed a useful tool kit of techniques and approaches for the endogeneity problem. The gulf in vocabulary, methods, and instinct is wide but by no means insurmountable.

Some of my research still uses data from the PSID. What I find especially intriguing in this work are results indicating that some of the social psychological measures included in the PSID's early waves are much more predictive of long-run and intergenerational success than of short-run outcomes. Early analyses of the short-run (that is, five-year) effects on labor market earnings of measures such as personal control and achievement motivation fail to show robust and important connections (Duncan and Morgan 1981; Augustyniak, Duncan, and Liker 1985). However, when Rachel Dunifon and I (Dunifon and Duncan 1998) related levels of labor market success in the early 1990s to the early-wave measures of personal control and components of achievement motivation, we found linkages that are much more powerful. In fact, the collection of twenty-five-year-old social psychological measures account for as much of the variation in current earnings as does completed schooling.

Moreover, recent work on the intergenerational effects of these early-wave measures (Yeung, Duncan, and Hill 2000) shows the power for boys' future success of some behavioral traits of their fathers. In particular, having a risk-averse father (that is, one who reports fastening his seat belt, having automobile or medical insurance, and the like) is highly predictive of the son's completed schooling and early career attainments. Perhaps having a father who dampens rather than reinforces the excesses of youth is beneficial for boys. At any rate, these two sets of long-run results suggest the value for attainment research of taking a very long view.

For the most part, though, I have also been surprised at the speed with which other data have replaced the PSID in my research. My work with the MacArthur Middle Childhood Network has led John Modell, postdoctoral fellow Lori Kowaleski-Jones, and me to apply some of the methods developed for understanding the dynamics of income trajectories to children's achievement and behavior-problem trajectories.[21] Data on behavior problems and achievement collected every other year by the National Longitudinal Surveys of Youth's Child Survey display developmental trajectories that bounce around almost as much as does family income. Surprisingly, the seemingly chaotic developmental trajectories share many of the characteristics of income trajectories: heterogeneous levels and slopes and a substantial random component. In the case of the developmental trajectories, once thrown off course girls tend to return more slowly than boys to their individual "permanent" trajectories (Kowaleski-Jones and Duncan, 1999).

More ambitious are my projects involving randomized experiments, which offer much greater power than population surveys for addressing endogeneity problems. Such problems became painfully clear as Jeanne Brooks-Gunn, other members of the SSRC committee, and I worked with the PSID and other data to understand how neighborhood conditions affect children's development. Families are not assigned randomly to their neighborhoods, raising the question of whether the apparent neighborhood effects emerging from our regressions merely reflect unmeasured family factors that affected both choice of neighborhood and child well-being (Duncan and Raudenbush 1999).

Few developmental studies of contextual effects recognize, much less solve, the problem of bias caused by unmeasured selection factors. Jens Ludwig and I tackle these problems by taking advantage of Ludwig's involvement with the Department of Housing and Urban Development's Moving to Opportunity project. In this experiment, poor families from public housing projects in five of our nation's largest cities are offered a chance to enter a program that facilitates moves to low-poverty neighborhoods. Because families are randomly assigned to one of three "treatments," one of which provides no additional help at all, the problem of omitted-variable bias is eliminated. Early results indicate large beneficial effects on the criminal behavior of adolescent boys whose families moved to lower-poverty neighborhoods. These effects held for violent crimes but not for property crimes (Ludwig, Duncan, and Hirschfield 2001).

A second project that has added a developmental component to a randomized antipoverty experiment is called New Hope. Beginning in the early 1990s, New Hope offered low-income families in two poor areas of Milwaukee the chance of a "contingent social contract"—work thirty hours a week and receive a generous set of supports (a wage subsidy, child care, health insurance, and if needed, a temporary community service job). Interested families were randomly assigned to a group eligible to receive these supports and a control group that was eligible to receive only the supports available to all low-income families from the city and state.

Understanding how this program affects family functioning and child development is the goal of our eclectic subgroup (Aletha Huston, Robert Granger, Vonnie McLoyd, and Tom Weisner) of MacArthur Network members. Our methods include surveys two and five years into the program as well as qualitative interviews with a randomly chosen subset of both program and control families.

Because Milwaukee is only a ninety-minute drive from Evanston, Illinois, we have been able to involve four HDSP graduate students in both the qualitative and quantitative work, three of whom are using both methods simultaneously. Working with these talented students and fellow members of the MacArthur Network to make sense out of results from both ethnographic and survey data from a randomized experiment is my working definition of research nirvana. Although this work is still in progress, already the interaction between the qualitative and quantitative methods has proved most interesting and rewarding (Gibson and Duncan 2000). We simply would not have been able to nail down the story of the experimental effects without the insights gathered by the students over the course of their many hours of conversations in the living rooms of New Hope families.

With data from many other welfare experiments and new developmental surveys coming on-line in the next few years, we will have the opportunity to learn much more about the nature and policy implications of welfare reforms for family process and children's development. Two ambitious child development supplements, one compiled in 1997 and the other planned for 2001, will keep the PSID in the forefront of this work. I do not yet know whether I will become one of the analysts of these new sets of PSID data. Whatever my future may bring, the PSID's marks on my own development will remain indelible.

Notes

1. Morgan also feared OEO micromanagement; but micromanagement proved impossible for overburdened OEO staff, and the Panel Study of Income Dynamics enjoyed its own form of benign neglect.

2. Throughout his career, Morgan has responded to requests to perform proposed surveys with details on creative study designs that, in his often firmly stated opinion, the sponsors should have adopted. It worked in the case of the Panel Study of Income Dynamics but rarely afterward.

3. In personal communication, Larry Orr provided the following story of his behind-the-scenes maneuvering at the ASPE office: "At some point in the mid-1970s, it looked like the Contracts Office was finally losing patience with our annual noncompetitive extensions of the contract and was going to make us complete it. We were also starting to get some flak from the other parts of ASPE, who were asking whether this thing was worth the large chunk of the Policy Research budget that it was consuming. So I convened a blue-ribbon panel of folks I knew would be sympathetic to the project (and to Michigan's continued stewardship of it) and got a report saying that this should be just behind the Washington monument on the government's list of national treasures. It worked, and from that point on, the continuation of the survey was, as I recall, pretty much a nonissue." (E-mail correspondence with the author, 15 April 1999.)

4. Mary Corcoran, Martha Hill, and Karen Mason spearheaded the effort to establish comparability between the labor market information collected from men and women.

5. As National Science Foundation funding increased, the PSID Advisory Board became the PSID Board of Overseers. One prominent member sent us a letter shortly after the change, making sure we understood that the change was more than semantic.

6. Our typical situation had us preparing to release data gathered two years earlier, cleaning data collected one year earlier, attending to response rates and costs of the current round of data collection, pretesting questions for the following year, and writing proposals for possible question supplements two and three years hence. The highlight of these burdens for me was spending an Easter weekend in the late 1980s writing a proposal to the National Science Foundation that justified why the PSID was the quintessential study for understanding the economic and social consequence of global warming. It seems that a National Science Foundation global-warming initiative provided the social science divisions with an opportunity to substitute that initiative's funds for others.

7. One exception is U.S. families newly formed through immigration, which have no chance of entering a study like the PSID. Immigrant samples were added to the PSID in 1990 and 1997.

8. These publication data come from the PSID's 1996 proposal to the National Science Foundation.

9. An extension of this analysis by Richard Burkhauser and I (Burkhauser and Duncan 1994) shows that the basic patterns changed little between the 1970s and the late 1980s.

10. After a sequence of other questions about household income, respondents were asked, "What about the next few years, do you think you will be better off, or worse off, or what?"

11. In 1997 welfare reform replaced the AFDC program with Temporary Assistance for Needy Families (TANF).

12. Control variables include age of individual, calendar year, race, and the average size of the given person's household over the first five years of the window.

13. The coauthors—James Morgan, Richard Coe, Martha Hill, Saul Hoffman, Mary Corcoran—were cherished collaborators in my first years with the PSID.

14. Sixty percent was used, rather than 50 percent, to avoid classifying instances of small income changes as transitions out of poverty.

15. The instability measure used here is the median absolute percentage change in annual income among families in the bottom decile of the income distribution. Note that because data from the Scandinavian countries are based on administrative records, not subject to interview response errors, and do not show consistently different patterns, measurement error is not likely to be an overwhelming factor in these relative rankings.

16. Tom Cook was the initial head of the group. Other members included Larry Aber, Jeanne Brooks-Gunn, Linda Burton, Lindsay Chase-Lansdale, Jim Connell, Warren Critchlow, Ron Ferguson, Frank Furstenberg, Robin Jarrett, Vilma Ortiz, Tim Smeeding, Margaret Spencer, and Mercer Sullivan.

17. Economists and sociologists are, of course, just as insular in their separate ways.

18. The regression models also control for mother's schooling, family structure, race, gender, age of the mother at the birth of the child, total number of siblings, whether ever lived in South, number of geographic moves, and number of years mother worked for more than one thousand hours. Parental income is inflated to 1993 price levels.

19. As shown in table 6.5, we did find that high parental income during adolescence had a strong positive effect on completed schooling. Additional analyses produced the unsurprising result that having affluent parents as a teenager increases one's chances of attending college.

20. The 1997 meetings of the Society for Research on Child Development featured a wonderful lecture by Mark Applebaum, who nominated cutting-edge methodologies for inclusion in developmentalists' methodological tool kits. I was shocked when he included event-history methods, because I had presumed that they were widely known and used. But then I reflected on my limited reading of the developmental literature and realized

that there were virtually no examples in which developmental processes and stages were analyzed with duration-based methods.

21.   John Modell's proper insistence on a historical element to our research has led him to conduct a parallel analysis of life-course patterns of communion attendance in nineteenth-century Sweden.

References

Alwin, Duane F. 1994. "Aging, Personality, and Social Change: The Stability of Individual Differences over the Adult Life Span." In *Life-Span Development and Behavior*, edited by David L. Featherman, Richard M. Lerner, and Marion Perlmutter. Hillsdale, N.J.: Lawrence Erlbaum Associates.

Augustyniak, Sue, Greg J. Duncan, and Jeffrey Liker. 1985. "Panel Data and Models of Change: A Comparison of First Difference and Conventional Two-Wave Models." *Social Science Research* 14(1): 80–101.

Bane, Mary Jo, and David T. Ellwood. 1986. "Slipping In and Out of Poverty: The Dynamics of Spells." *Journal of Human Resources* 21(1): 1–23.

———. 1994. *Welfare Realities*. Cambridge, Mass.: Harvard University Press.

Boisjoly, Johanne, Greg Duncan, and Timothy Smeeding. 1998. "The Shifting Incidence of Involuntary Job Losses from 1968 to 1992." *Industrial Relations* 37(2): 207–31.

Brooks-Gunn, Jeanne, and Greg J. Duncan. 1997. "The Effects of Poverty on Children." *Future of Children* 7(2): 55–71.

Burkhauser, Richard, and Greg J. Duncan. 1994. "Sharing Prosperity Across the Age Distribution: A Comparison of the United States and Germany in the 1980s." *Gerontologist* 34(2): 150–60.

Children's Defense Fund. 1994. *Wasting America's Future*. Boston: Beacon Press.

Costa, Paul T., and Robert R. McCrae. 1980. "Still Stable After All These Years: Personality as a Key to Some Issues in Adulthood and Old Age." In *Life-Span Development and Behavior*, edited by Paul Baltes and Orville G. Brim. New York: Academic Press.

Duncan, Greg J. 1988. "The Volatility of Family Income over the Life Course." In *Life-Span Development and Behavior*, edited by Paul Baltes, David Featherman, and Richard M. Lerner. Hillsdale, N.J.: Lawrence Erlbaum Associates.

Duncan, Greg J., and Jeanne Brooks-Gunn, eds. 1997. *The Consequences of Growing Up Poor*. New York: Russell Sage Foundation.

Duncan, Greg J., Richard Coe, Mary Corcoran, Martha Hill, Saul Hoffman, and James N. Morgan. 1984. *Years of Poverty, Years of Plenty: The Changing Economic Fortunes of American Workers and Families*. Ann Arbor, Mich.: Institute for Social Research.

Duncan, Greg J., Bjorn Gustafsson, Richard Hauser, Guenther Schmaus, Stephen Jenkins, Hans Messinger, Ruud Muffels, Brian Nolan, Jean-Claude Ray, and Wolfgang Voges. 1995. "Poverty and Social-Assistance Dynamics in the United States, Canada, and Western Europe." In *Poverty, Inequality, and the Future of Social Policy: Western States in the New World Order*, edited by Katherine McFate, Roger Lawson, and William J. Wilson. New York: Russell Sage Foundation.

Duncan, Greg J., and James N. Morgan. 1981. "Sense of Efficacy and Changes in Economic Status: A Replication." *Journal of Human Resources* 16(4): 649–57.

Duncan, Greg J., and Stephen Raudenbush. 1999. "Assessing the Effects of Context in Studies of Child and Youth Development." *Educational Psychologist* 34(1): 29–41.

Duncan, Greg J., Wei-Jun Yeung, Jeanne Brooks-Gunn, and Judith Smith. 1998. "How Much Does Childhood Poverty Affect the Life Chances of Children?" *American Sociological Review* 63(3): 406–23.

Dunifon, Rachel, and Greg J. Duncan. 1998. "Long-Run Effects of Motivation on Labor Market Success." *Social Psychology Quarterly* 61(1): 33–48.

Eizenman, Dara R., John R. Nesselroade, David L. Featherman, and John W. Rowe. 1997. "Intra-Individual Variability in Perceived Control: The MacArthur Successful Aging Studies." *Psychology and Aging* 12(13): 489–502.

Elder, Glen H. 1974. *Children of the Great Depression.* Chicago: University of Chicago Press.

———, ed. 1985. *Life Course Dynamics from 1968 to 1980.* Ithaca: Cornell University Press.

Ellwood, David. 1988. *Poor Support: Poverty and the American Family.* New York: Basic Books.

Fitzgerald, John, Peter Gottschalk, and Robert Moffitt. 1998. "An Analysis of Sample Attrition in Panel Data: The Michigan Panel Study of Income Dynamics." *Journal of Human Resources* 33(2): 251–99.

Gibson, Christina, and Greg Duncan. 2000. "Qualitative/Quantitative Synergies in a Random-Assignment Program Evaluation." Northwestern University. Unpublished paper.

Hill, Martha. 1992. *The Panel Study of Income Dynamics.* Beverly Hills, Calif.: Sage Publications.

Kowaleski-Jones, Lori, and Greg J. Duncan. 1999. "The Structure of Achievement and Behavior Across Middle Childhood." *Child Development* 70(4): 930–43.

Ludwig, Jens, Greg J. Duncan, and Paul Hirschfield. 2001. "Urban Poverty and Juvenile Crime: Evidence from a Randomized Housing-Mobility Experiment." *Quarterly Journal of Economics* 116(2): 665–79.

Mayer, Susan. 1997. *What Money Can't Buy.* Cambridge, Mass.: Harvard University Press.

McDonough, Peggy, Greg J. Duncan, David Williams, and James House. 1997. "Income Dynamics and Adult Mortality in the United States, 1972–1989." *American Journal of Public Health* 87(9): 1476–83.

Morgan, James, Katherine Dickinson, Jonathan Dickinson, Jacob Benus, and Greg J. Duncan. 1974. *Five Thousand American Families: Patterns of Economic Progress.* Vol. I. Ann Arbor, Mich.: Institute for Social Research.

Murray, Charles. 1986. "According to Age: Longitudinal Profiles of AFDC Recipients and the Poor, by Age Group." Paper presented to the Working Seminar on the Family and American Welfare Policy, Washington, D.C.

Nesselroade, John R., and David. L. Featherman 1997. "Establishing a Reference Frame Against Which to Chart Age-Related Changes." In *Studying Aging and Social Change: Conceptual and Methodological Issues,* edited by Melissa A. Hardy. Newbury Park, Calif.: Sage Publications.

Newman, Katherine. 1988. *Falling from Grace: The Experience of Downward Mobility in the American Middle Class.* New York: Free Press.

Smeeding, Timothy. Luxembourg Income Study Project. Centre for Population, Poverty and Policy Studies (CEPS). Available at: *www.lis.ceps.lu.*

Tuma, Nancy B., and Lyle D. Groeneveld. 1979. "Dynamic Analysis of Event Histories." *American Journal of Sociology* 84(4): 820–54.

U.S. Department of Health and Human Services. 2001. "Indicators of Welfare Dependence." Annual report to Congress (March).

Weitzman, Lenore. 1985. *The Divorce Revolution.* New York: Free Press.

Yeung, Wei-Jun J., Greg J. Duncan., and Martha S. Hill. 2000. "Putting Fathers Back in the Picture: Parental Activities and Children's Attainment." *Marriage and Family Review* 29(4): 97–113.

PART III

THE IMPORTANCE OF TIMING
IN LIVES AND IN STUDIES OF LIVES

Chapter 7

Baltimore Beginning School Study in Perspective

DORIS R. ENTWISLE, KARL L. ALEXANDER,
AND LINDA STEFFEL OLSON

THE BALTIMORE Beginning School Study (BSS) crystallized around 1980. In contrast with most of the other studies described in this volume, the BSS began closer to the end of Doris Entwisle's career than to its beginning. For a number of years, Entwisle's research had been circling around a vexing question: What is schooling? This question was especially perplexing because at that time, variables related to school organization, such as promotion policies, class size, racial mix, or types of curriculum, to name a few, did not explain much variance in children's achievement. As Entwisle became convinced of these seemingly negligible effects of school organization, Congress commissioned a study of inequality in educational opportunity, headed by James Coleman, in the belief that differences in school quality would explain the gap in test scores between white and African American children. The hypothesis was that poor-quality (segregated) schools were mainly responsible for the gap.

The educational establishment was shocked by the finding of the Coleman Report (Coleman et al. 1966) that differences across schools hardly mattered compared with differences in background. This conclusion was so counterintuitive that it prompted a meticulous review of the report and its methodology (see Mosteller and Moynihan 1972). A shower of other large-scale studies (for example, Jencks et al. 1972) were undertaken mainly to challenge this conclusion.

Seasoned investigators just could not let go of the problem. Why did schools themselves explain so little of the variance? It was hard to believe that Exeter or Andover, or Boston Latin, had not prompted more cognitive growth over students' high school careers than other schools. Entwisle could not let go of the problem either. Her hypothesis at that time was twofold: First, by the time children reached secondary school, their educational trajectories had been determined, so the place to look for school differences was in the elementary years. Second, differences in language or dialect that separated ethnic and cultural groups would create static at the beginning of a child's schooling by interfering with his or her learning to read, the crucible skill for later success in school. After spending more than a decade bird-dogging this hypothesis, Entwisle heard of Wallace Lambert's longitudinal research in Montreal that placed middle-class Anglophone children in kindergartens and then in grade school classes in which French was the only language used (Lambert and Macnamara 1969; Lambert, Just, and Segalowitz 1970; Lambert and Tucker 1972). By fourth grade, having had exclusively French instruction, these children had English vocabularies almost as large as their counterparts who had been schooled only in English, and they had equally good standardized test scores in math and other school subjects. In addition, their French vocabularies rivaled their English vocabularies in size.

Lambert's demonstration made it clear that small differences in dialects or other features of the spoken languages children knew when they started school were unlikely to explain the lower achievement scores of disadvantaged or minority youth in U.S. schools. Furthermore, because teachers could accurately label children's social class origins from hearing ten to fifteen seconds of recorded speech (Harms 1961), Entwisle decided that the place to look for variables that explained success or failure in schooling was in the social context of the school. Other work of Coleman's (1961) strengthened this view.

When research on teacher expectations made the social genesis of school effects even clearer (an example, perhaps, of Pygmalion in the classroom), Entwisle persuaded Murray Webster, a colleague at Johns Hopkins University, to join in some field experiments on children's expectations. Entwisle and Webster (1974) found they could raise children's expectations, and the smaller the social distance between adults (teachers) and children, the better this raising of expectations worked.[1]

The next project, a set of case studies in collaboration with Leslie Hayduk (Entwisle and Hayduk 1978, 1982) begun in the early 1970s, examined children's and parents' expectations in three schools, studying about fifteen hundred children. These studies set the stage for the Beginning School Study, which began in 1982. They showed that children's and parents' performance expectations had a considerable influence on young children's achievement in reading and math over the first three grades and also that children's and parents' expectations in middle-class families were much closer than were those of working-class parents and children.

At this point, Entwisle was obsessed with going further in the search for the social determinants of schooling, using the three-school project as a pilot study. By then, Karl Alexander had joined the Department of Social Relations at Johns Hopkins University. With a doctorate from North Carolina and experience as Glen Elder's research advise for about a year, Alexander, whose main research interest was secondary school attainment, was no stranger to large-scale studies and ways to make sense of them. Alexander did not yet have tenure in 1981 but had published extensively. Most of his research to that point had focused on issues of educational equity in relation to variations in school organization and the ways in which family background affects school performance in the upper grades. It had become apparent to him that scrutinizing near-term, proximal causes could go only so far in explaining outcomes at the secondary level and beyond. He too had become convinced that to comprehend the dynamic of schooling, a long time frame was needed. When the opportunity arose to refocus his work on the early primary grades, he was eager to pursue the project.

In experience and interest, then, Entwisle and Alexander were a good match and complement to each other. The Beginning School Study was about to be launched. Their idea was to watch carefully how a group of typical urban schoolchildren negotiated the beginning school transition and, by monitoring the same youngsters over time, to explore links to later trajectories of personal and academic development. The original plan was to follow the panel from the fall of first grade until the end of second grade and then spend a year or so analyzing the data before moving on to other business. So much for plans—the BSS is still in the field some twenty years later.

In 1981, Entwisle and Alexander applied for support to study a stratified sample of about eight hundred public school students in Baltimore, Maryland. One after another, several private foundations and public agencies rejected their proposal. With each rejection they strengthened the proposal, and early in 1982 the William T. Grant Foundation approved their request. Soon afterward, the National Institute for Child Health and Development provided additional support. The BSS was not only launched but given a good push along the way.

This tale would not be complete without a description of what it was like to conduct individual interviews with close to eight hundred six-year-olds in a six-week period in both the fall and the spring and for one of the pair to supervise every interviewing team (of four to six interviewers) that entered a school. Data collection of parents' expectations had to precede receipt of their children's report cards (issued around Thanksgiving and at the end of the school year) to exclude the likelihood of feedback from report cards shaping parental expectations. This necessitated gathering data from at least eight hundred parents in each interviewing round. All work on the BSS—sampling, interview prepa-ration, interviewing, and data processing—was done in-house; none of it was subcontracted. With this workload, especially added to the ordi-nary demands on college faculty, it is not surprising that the first BSS publication was five years in gestation. (Fortunately, Alexander's earlier work was sufficient to support his promotion to tenure in 1984.) In the late 1980s, Linda Olson joined the BSS team as a research assistant. With a master's degree in history, Olson assumed more and more responsi-bility over the years, from planning analyses to collaborating on many of the publications emanating from the project. She now collaborates on most BSS research. A number of talented graduate students who shared the work have gone on to establish successful careers. Among them are Aaron Pallas, Doris Cadigan, Patricia Gucer, and Susan Dauber.

The Study

To return to the question "What is schooling?" we decided to observe a panel of children—to look carefully at them and their parents, teachers, and schools, beginning as early as possible in their formal school careers. Like Frank Furstenberg, who has also worked with economically dis-advantaged African Americans in Baltimore, we wanted to find out what helped the children do well. Despite the odds, almost 40 percent of our sample has attended some college, and more than half of these were in bachelor's degree programs.

At the time the BSS began, the transition into first grade had been overlooked as a developmental event, but we suspected it had enormous impact. One way for adults to imagine its impact is to recall their own reactions to being institutionalized—for example, how they felt upon their first hospitalization. First-graders, like hospital patients, are sepa-rated from friends and family. In the same way that patients lose control over life's small daily routines of eating or elimination, first-graders have little control over when they can get a drink of water or use the bath-room; first-graders, like patients, cannot leave the room without getting permission. They take a prescribed curriculum (course of treatment), move through a preordained daily schedule (wake up when nursing shifts change), and are evaluated (poked or questioned) according to cri-teria they do not understand.

We decided on a careful observational study of the first-grade tran-sition rather than an intervention type of study because it seemed to us then, and still seems true today, that among the changes made in schools—curriculum, classroom organization, the composition of stu-dent bodies, teachers' qualifications—almost none is based on solid sci-entific evidence. Also in 1982, very little sociological research centered on youth below the secondary level. Sociologists were paying little attention to young children or to young children nested in families. We suspected, however, that by the time youth reached high school, their educational trajectories were well determined and that these trajectories depended on their schooling at lower levels. We therefore decided to observe the way children made the transition into full-time schooling—how the trajectory began.

Our original goal was to follow a stratified sample of children through the first two years of school. Some key features of the research design were as follows: first, we limited the study to the city of Baltimore to reduce heterogeneity. All children would be attending schools with the same basic curriculum, taught by teachers on the same salary scale. Their records would be kept in the same manner, and they would have similar standardized tests or other evaluations at the same points in time. We also selected a two-stage random sample. This selection was undertaken not only so we could generalize back to the city as a whole but also because the parents who were most invested in their children would be most likely to volunteer for a study of this kind, and we wanted to keep this type of selectivity to a minimum. The blocked design crossed the racial composition (African American and white) of the school with family socioeconomic level and then focused on twenty schools selected randomly from the matrix formed by crossing race with socioeconomic status. After randomly selecting about forty students entering first grade in each of the twenty schools, we visited their homes and persuaded all but 3 percent of the families to take part in the study. We then interviewed these parents on the spot.

Because so little was known then about the schooling of children at this age, we measured a broad spectrum of outcomes: school achievement (based on standardized test scores and grades given by teachers), students' own expectations, self-esteem, locus of control, and other noncognitive characteristics. We also gathered contextual data from families and schools. School and neighborhood data included racial mix, classroom grouping practices, socioeconomic level, and so on. Directly from teachers every year, we ascertained grading standards, feelings about their jobs and schools, their expectations for the performance of individual children in their classes, ratings of children's personal traits (for example, aggressiveness), grouping practices, and so on. Parents told us about family structure, their occupations, education, and the like as well as expectations for their child's schooling and school performance, their feelings about the school, and their understanding of its evaluation procedures.

A fundamental decision was made to collect data as early as possible in first grade (that is, before the first report card was issued). With the splendid cooperation of the Baltimore school system, all BSS students took the California Achievement Test battery early in October of first grade, and every teacher provided information about individual students. This initial baseline from which to assess later progress has proved enormously important. Students were later tested at the end of the first year and then every fall and spring up through the end of elementary school; we thereby secured five years' data related to seasonal learning (gains on standardized tests when school was open, in the winter months, and gains on tests in summer months, when school was closed). Students were interviewed on many occasions, a total of nineteen times over thirteen years, with interviews most frequent in the early years (see table 7.1). The twentieth round of interviewing (the Young Adult Survey) was completed by the end of 1999. To interview a student on school time requires permission of the superintendent, principal, teacher, parent, and, of course, the student, and considerable coordination within this group.

How This Work Affected Us

This research affected our own lives in two major ways. First, we derived a wealth of personal experience and pleasure from interacting with so many young children, though our work schedules were greatly complicated for a very long time. Second, it enlarged our intellectual horizons in ways that could not have been foreseen.

Work Pressures

Interviewing six-year-old children provided many joys—one little girl, asked how good she was at being honest, replied, "Sometimes I'm very good, sometimes I'm very bad." It also provided challenges—such as how to score such a reply. We tried to be gentle and to devote as much time as each child required. The children were by turns thoughtful, quizzical, flattered, and surprisingly articulate. The interviews made them feel important.

As we have said, the levels of permission required to work with young children were daunting. We started with the parent, then the teacher and principal, and worked our way up through the school bureaucracy. Parental permission had to be renewed every two years, but permission by school personnel lasted at most one year. When principals or teachers changed, we had to reintroduce the project.

When we led small teams of interviewers into a school, we had to brief teachers before the school day started; we then set up interview stations in spare classrooms, the cafeteria, the school library, or even the nurse's office and escorted children from classrooms to interviewing stations. Because cafeteria schedules were not the same at each school and children in grade school sometimes start lunch at half past ten in the morning, we were often pressed for time. We grew to hate school holidays or "teacher

Table 7.1 Timeline for BSS Fieldwork and Coverage of Primary Data Sources

Fieldwork and Data Sources	Year One (1982 to 1983)		Year Two (1983 to 1984)		Year Three (1984 to 1985)		Year Four (1985 to 1986)		Year Five (1986 to 1987)		Year Six (1987 to 1988)		Year Seven (1988 to 1989)[a]	
	Fall	Spring	Fall	Spring	Fall	Spring	Fall	Spring	Fall	Spring	Fall	Spring	Fall	Spring
Student interviews[c]	788	784	638	605	No data		575	563	No data		490	486	250	175
Parent questionnaires[c]		756	627	477		327		471	No data			451		219
Teacher questionnaires	52	49	44	44	No data			140	No data			203	87	
Number of students covered	0	684	0	531	No data			398	No data			381		161
BCPS records[d]	725		644		622		567		551		517		475	
CAT scores[d]	705	742	670	651	607	565	561	545	602	568	502	497	No data	448

(Table continued on p. 174.)

Table 7.1 *Continued*

Fieldwork and Data Sources	Year Eight (1989 to 1990)		Year Nine (1990 to 1991)		Year Ten (1991 to 1992)	Year Eleven (1992 to 1993)	Year Twelve (1993 to 1994)	Year Thirteen (1994 to 1995)[b]	Year Seventeen (1998 to 1999)
	Fall	Spring	Fall	Spring					
Student interviews[c]	609	407	640	637	635	625	597	309	632
Parent questionnaires[c]		504		463	651	618	No data	No data	No data
Teacher questionnaires		158		400	No data	No data	No data	No data	No data
Number of students covered		336		478	No data	No data	No data	No data	No data
BCPS records[d]		498		486	465	394	250	Pending[e]	No data
CAT scores[d]	No data	410		No data	604[f]	No data	No data	No data	No data

Source: Authors' compilation.

Note: $N = 790$ Beginning School Study panel members.

[a] Figures in year seven are low because only youngsters who were making the transition to middle school that year were interviewed.

[b] In year thirteen, only youngsters still in high school and dropouts were interviewed.

[c] Through year seven, only students (and their parents) attending Baltimore City Public Schools (BCPS) were interviewed. Beginning in year eight, coverage extends to all members of the original cohort.

[d] Diminishing coverage over time reflects transfer out of the BCPS system (and, in the upper grades, dropout). School record information and testing data are now available for more than 150 youth who left the BCPS system at some point.

[e] These data are presently being processed.

[f] The BCPS system discontinued CAT testing after year eight. The BSS administered CAT tests during the spring 1991 through fall 1992 period.

workdays" and especially dreaded systemwide testing days, fire pre-vention week, and rainy days.[2]

By their fourth year of school, the BSS panel members, originally in twenty schools, were scattered across over a hundred schools through-out Baltimore, not counting those who had moved across the city line. As each new school was added, we were required to visit the principal to explain the research and to schedule spaces and times in which to do it. In the early days we were not allowed to use a copier to gather data from school records, but about six years into the project that restriction was, fortunately, no longer in place. Hand-copying thirty grades from each report card for eight hundred youngsters takes long enough in it-self, but tracking transfers and the like took even longer. We came to re-alize that schools have a strategic interest in keeping students on their rolls because appropriations are based on total enrollment.

The domination of BSS fieldwork over every other activity was a major career challenge. In October and November and again in May and June, almost every day there were field interviews, backtracking to get absentees, and sometimes filling in parent data. When we finally began to publish BSS findings, we faced another kind of pressure: to move ahead on several fronts at once. The responses of children to their early schooling was the major focus of the project, so achievement tests and teachers' grades were often at the top of the list of dependent variables. The possible independent variables were many, however, and except for single-answer questions, the psychometric burdens were heavy—deciding which questions to keep, matching scales from one year to the next, and so on. We could not fall behind in processing any of the infor-mation, because missing data had to be retrieved while the trail was still hot. Fortunately, with two major investigators, one person could spell the other when the inevitable personal or family crises erupted.

We decided at the beginning that both investigators' names, along with those of colleagues who participated, would appear on each pub-lication, even though in each case a single person took primary respon-sibility for organizing reports. Within the Department of Sociology at Johns Hopkins, a BSS group has emerged that celebrates Halloween, grant awards, major holidays, and the coming of summer. Business is often conducted at irregularly scheduled brown-bag project lunches with all the part-time and temporary members of the team. The staff nec-essarily swells when we are in the field and then shrinks back again when we return to recording and collating duties.

Intellectual Capital

Although the BSS was conceived as a two-year data collection effort fol-lowed by a year of analysis and write-up, before the second year had passed we were making plans to continue. By then we had also come to realize the need for much more comprehensive data about family structure and family changes than was usually collected in school research in those days. This need forced us to scramble to review the growing literature on parents' psychological, economic, and social capital in relation to elementary schooling—in other words, to enlighten ourselves on topics such as family structure and sibling effects. This kind of significant enlargement of our own thinking has continued to the present—lately we have been cramming on substance use, dating behavior, vocational planning, and many other adolescence topics. As BSS children have left middle childhood, moved through early and later adolescence, and entered young adulthood, we have had to broaden our intellectual horizons in ways we never foresaw.

The boundaries of the project's workload have always been fluid. Among Karl Alexander's major interests have been tracking, teacher variables, retention and dropout, and how patterns in the early grades play out over the longer term. Doris Entwisle has looked more at development in the early years, especially the way seasonal patterns, family structure, and work outside school affect progress in elementary and middle school.

The study was often in search of a sponsor. The William T. Grant Foundation not only placed an initial bet on the project but helped later on as well. The National Institute of Child Health and Human Development, the National Science Foundation, the Office of Educational Research and Improvement of the U.S. Department of Education, the Spencer Foundation, and the Foundation for Child Development have also picked up the ball.

What would we do differently? Realistically speaking, there is not much we could do differently, because of the huge workload imposed by personal interviews of young children. Had we had the necessary funds and the energy, however, we would have started earlier doing the kinds of unstructured qualitative interviews we began with BSS dropouts about five years ago. We know the whereabouts of the cohort, now in their mid-twenties, and are saddened that twenty of them are presently incarcerated, eight have died, and many others have had brushes with the law or other serious problems. The good news is that close to 40 percent of the sample started study at some kind of college, schools such as Swarthmore or Stanford among them. We take seriously Greg Duncan's admonition to "beware of the mean" and Elder's ideas about personal agency. We are now planning in-depth interviews with four groups: dropouts who stayed dropped out to the age of twenty, dropouts who were temporary because they returned to school to get either a conventional diploma or a certificate of General Educational Development (GED), nondropouts who ended their schooling upon receipt of a high school diploma, and nondropouts who attended college.

Some Thoughts on Times of Sampling

Repeated data collection—sampling the same units over time—is the major distinguishing feature of longitudinal research. Much of the power of the life-course perspective in developmental research stems from its central concepts, which emphasize time. For an obvious example, "transition" incorporates notions of time because it implies that something begins at one point, ends at another point, and changes between the two points. When we employ this concept, we naturally take observations at specific points in time.

Despite the obvious importance of timing of data collection in longitudinal studies, the issue has yet to receive the attention it deserves. Most texts on methodology do not even include "time" as an entry in the index, and although texts in experimental design happily discuss the number of subjects required to achieve a desired level of power, they say nothing about the optimal time at which to start a study or the optimal number of repeat observations.[3] Even economics, the source of most nonexperimental modeling techniques now in use, takes "time series" to mean "measurements at equal intervals of time." Longitudinal studies, however, begin with the notion that time, or timing, is critical, and time intervals are generally not the same. Timing of observations is thus not arbitrary, because it is highly relevant for resolving causal ambiguity.

Time Sampling

A basic issue in any longitudinal study is the timing of measurements. One would think that the more rapidly the dependent variable is changing, the more frequently we would want to sample. If readings are taken in synchrony with the rate of development, we might get a reasonable idea of the functional form of a developmental relationship by stringing together the short linear segments that connect successive readings. A more important reason for frequent sampling is that the variance across individuals is usually greater when growth is rapid than when growth is slower. In general, we would like to take measurements at the points at which variance in growth is greatest.

Putting aside all the complicated issues involved in the scaling of tests, we note that children's rates of growth on most standardized measures are not uniform—not linear in chronological time. In fact, Christopher Jencks (1985) estimates that the rate of cognitive growth in first grade is ten times the rate of cognitive growth in high school; cognitive growth rates, to the extent they are reflected in the metrics used by standardized tests, decelerate markedly over childhood and adolescence. If this is the case, then the number of observations we collect over the early life cycle should exceed the number of later observations. So far, however, sociologists have much more data collected from older than from younger children—just the reverse of what we might wish.

We also know that periods of transition are strategically advantageous to study because they are points of maximum continuity and discontinuity (that is, change) in individual lives. If we think in terms of a bicycle race, it is hard to make distinctions among people when all are pedaling ahead on the straightaway and bunched closely together. When a hill is encountered, however, the cyclists spread out, making it easier to see who is ahead and who behind. Transitions are like hills in that they widen the differences among people. Expanding the range along which people can be measured (that is, spreading them out) is a technical advantage for two reasons. First, when people are more spread out, we can more accurately (and therefore more reliably) estimate their positions relative to one another: for example, it is difficult to judge the success of two children who score within a point or two of each other on an achievement test, because the random error in the test is greater than the one or two points that separate them. Second, a transition hill also produces "wanted variance." Over life transitions, the variance across a set of individuals increases; and with more variance to explain, we often can do better at identifying predictors. These two statistical reasons for focusing on transitions in life-course studies add to the substantive reasons for focusing on transitions, the topic to which we now turn.

Concepts of Time

Life-course theorists employ many different concepts of time. Dennis Hogan's (1981) study of the adult transition relates social time to calendar time because calendar time is scaled in years, but on some socially normative scales—for example, being an unmarried adult—social time is scaled in units related to the length of role incumbency: adults experience a life event when they change from being single to being married. Notions of being "off time" or "on time" imply that roles like that of spouse can be assumed "too early" or "too late" on a social time scale.

Taking up or shedding a role, however, is often not an event. Youths' movement out of the student role is an extended process these days, because some students who drop out later return to high school and other students who graduate may work several years before going on to college. In the last couple of decades, most high school students have been moving between school and paid work on a daily basis, and many young workers either go to school part-time or get on-the-job training. It is no longer the case that school departure is one event and the beginning of work another. Thus it seems more reasonable to think of the length of the adult transition not as the length of time between two events but as the average number of months or years that individuals split their time between the student and worker roles.

Social time sometimes maps onto institutional time. Students in eighth grade can get there by attending school for seven or more years, but some arrive there by attending school for six or more years and others by attending for eight or more years. Eighth-graders who have attended more or less than seven years are labeled "off-time" because their chronological age is out of synchrony with their institutional age. Institutionally they are out of phase.

In the examples just noted, choice of scale has substantive implications. Whether we measure height in inches, feet, or meters does not matter as long as we know how to convert from one scale to another. When we convert height to a percentile (or normative) scale and judge children to be tall or short, however, the distribution to which we are comparing children matters. This judgment is shaded by whether we are considering boys or girls, for example. A tall girl may be the same height as a short boy. Similarly, a child who is a year ahead of chronological age in a highly selective school is likely to be quite different from an accelerated student of the same age in an inner-city school.

It goes without saying that scales of social time often have units that differ across societies or across social groups in the same society. For example, a young working-class woman is classified as an "old maid" at an earlier age than is her middle-class counterpart. Normative scales that are loosely derived from social parameters can have a biological component as well. Premature babies, for instance, are born "too soon" on a social scale. The use of social scales is often helpful in understanding social interaction, that is, for explaining why premature children are more often the targets of child abuse than are children born at term (see Klein and Stern 1971; Lynch and Roberts 1977; Elmer and Gregg 1967.)

Capitalizing on Time Overlaps

Some research strategies capitalize on the overlap between different kinds of time scales. By far the most extensive and ingenious use of such strategies are Elder's (1974, 1978) cohort studies that examine historical time in conjunction with ontological time. As is now so well known, Elder finds that the same level of family economic deprivation can have positive effects for some youth and negative effects for others, depending on the life stage of the individual. As he has shown, the effects of serving in the armed forces also vary by life stage. The technical difficulty of carrying out such studies is exceeded only by their importance in influencing the whole field of life-course research. In a way that is not contrived or artificial, these studies force us to integrate history, psychology, economics, sociology, and human development to create more adequate models than we would do otherwise.

Roberta Simmons and her colleagues (Simmons et al. 1979; Simmons and Blyth 1987) have pioneered other kinds of studies with an ingenious use of time in their research on students' self-esteem. Until that point, puberty had been seen as the culprit in the lowering of self-esteem, but Simmons suspected that the drop was triggered less by hormones than by the transition from elementary school to junior high school. To test this hypothesis, she compared seventh-grade youth who had gone through puberty in sixth grade with other youth who went through puberty in seventh grade. She found a drop in self-esteem for all seventh-graders, including the nonpubertal seventh-graders, but no drop for pubertal sixth-graders. Pairing an event scaled in institutional time (the school transition) with an event scaled in biological time (puberty) achieved a logical separation of the two influences.

The transition into formal schooling is another period during which biological and institutional time can be pitted against each other. In the United States, typically all children born within one twelve-month period are placed in one grade school cohort. In Baltimore, for example, BSS children who had turned six by December 31, 1982, were enrolled in first grade in September 1982, while those born after that date had to wait until September 1983 to enroll. This age rule determined that children up to six years and eight months of age began first grade with others as young as five years and eight months. When "young" first-graders (those with birth dates in November and December, just before the cutoff) in the Beginning School Study were compared with "old" first-graders (those with birth dates in January and February, eleven or twelve months before the cutoff), the gains on achievement tests in both reading and math over first grade made by the older and younger students were almost equivalent. The test scores of younger first-graders in the study at the end of the school year were still lower than the test scores of the older first-graders because the younger children had lower scores to start with, but children in both age groups gained the same number of points on standardized tests over that school year. This pattern strongly suggests that attending school, and not maturational factors, prompted children's growth over first grade.

Further evidence of the same kind comes from an Israeli study of fourth-, fifth-, and sixth-grade students (Cahan and Cohen 1989) and from other studies of first-graders employing the grade school cutoff strategy (Morrison, Smith, and Dow-Ehrensberger 1995). The Israeli study compares the scores predicted for the youngest children in fourth grade with scores predicted for the oldest children in third grade. If age matters, then the oldest children in third grade should have about the same scores as the youngest children in fourth grade because their ages are very close. However, a gap separated the scores of third-grade and fourth-grade children of the same age in the Jerusalem study. Again, the amount of time spent in school, rather than age, was the key factor explaining the children's growth.[4]

Barbara Heyns (1978) capitalized on institutional time in a different way. Following up on earlier leads (Hayes and Grether 1969; Murnane 1975), she compared achievement growth in summer (time out of school) with achievement growth in winter (time spent in school). As she suspected, growth was greater in winter, when children were in school, than during the summer vacation. By comparing students' progress when school was and was not in session, she separated growth attributable to schooling from growth attributable to other sources. She found, as we did, that children who came from homes with higher socioeconomic status gained much more over summer periods than did those from less advantaged families. A mismatch between institutional time and maturational time allowed isolation of one institutional influence from another.

The BSS elaborated Heyns's design by following children over the first five years of school. This strategy led to perhaps the most important finding from the BSS so far: growth varies by family socioeconomic status when school is closed but not when school is in session (see Entwisle, Alexander, and Olson 1997; Entwisle and Alexander 1992, 1994). Taken at face value, this finding suggests that models of schooling that use testing measurements at twelve-month intervals are misspecified, because growth attributable to school is confounded with growth attributable to other sources, like home or neighborhood.

Before continuing, we must mention a related strategy that imposes a randomized experiment over a transition period. In an ingenious study, Robert Felner and Angela Adan (1988) randomly allocated students about to enter high school into one group whose current peers accompanied them into high school and another group of students who were separated from their peers. The first group was "peer supported," the second, "peer deprived." Over the transition into high school, not only did the peer-supported group exhibit greater academic success, better adjustment, and fewer psychological problems in the short-term, but in a four-year follow-up they were found to be less than half as likely to drop out as the peer-deprived group. Separating out one of the variables known to affect transitions and using it as the fulcrum of a randomized experiment was a clever strategy.

Major Findings: Seasonal Learning

According to the BSS findings, background affects the schooling of young children in a number of ways. First, family economic status is strongly correlated with children's schooling success. Study after study links income and other measures of family economic status to the amount of schooling children complete (for example, Garfinkel and McLanahan 1986; Haveman and Wolfe 1994; Elder 1974, 1998; McLoyd 1989, 1990); those living in poverty for at least one year are 6 percent less likely than those with no experience of poverty to graduate from high school (Haveman and Wolfe 1994). Longitudinal research on young children's school achievement is not extensive, but research increasingly indicates that family background probably matters more for their test scores than it does for those of older children (Duncan et al. 1998; Alwin and Thornton 1984; Marjoribanks 1979). Children from impoverished backgrounds also do not do as well on achievement tests as their better-off classmates and, in fact, arrive at first grade with verbal and math skills at a lower level than those of children from advantaged homes (Smith 1972; Huston 1994; Entwisle, Alexander, and Olson 1997). The strong relationship between family economic background and children's schooling thus begins early (see, for example, Murnane 1975; Marjoribanks 1979; Alexander and Entwisle 1996), and this fact was a major reason we decided to study the first-grade transition.

Many hypotheses could explain the correlation between parents' economic status and children's cognitive growth, the most common one being that better-off families have more resources with which to buy books, games, computers, and other tools that help children learn more in school. We have come to believe that the learning that goes on in school is not directly affected by economic conditions in the home, however, at least in the early grades. We think instead that the process of schooling is not the same for economically disadvantaged children and those who are better off—the main difference being that poor children's cognitive growth is more episodic than that of their more advantaged peers. The growth of advantaged children is continuous over the entire year because their families and neighborhoods can supply the resources needed to support their growth when schools are not in session, whereas the families and neighborhoods of poorer children cannot provide the necessary resources (see Heyns 1978; Entwisle and Alexander 1992, 1994.) Over the summer, when school is closed, or before first grade, when children start their formal schooling, poor children lack sufficient resources to promote their full development. The idea that home resources affect learning over the summer is not new (see Heyns 1978, 1987; Murnane 1975), but the idea that these resources matter mainly (or only) in summer is.

Individual Gains

In the United States, schools are organized around an agricultural calendar. They are open in winter (about nine months) but closed in summer (about three months). This episodic nature of schooling creates a strategic advantage for studying the process of children's cognitive growth because the opening and closing of schools produces a natural experiment. Schools can provide resources to promote children's cognitive development in winter but not in summer. In summer, resources come only from home or neighborhood.

Poor children in the BSS, on average, did as well as their better-off classmates during the winter, when schools were open (Entwisle, Alexander, and Olson 1997). Children of all family backgrounds gained equal amounts on achievement tests given in winter over the first five years of school. Only in summer did poor children fall behind.

However, when the BSS children started first grade, the children from families with higher socioeconomic status had an initial advantage. We think that small differences present when the children started school depended mainly on the family resources they had up to that point. Some families could provide more resources than others. These initial differences then increased because though the poor children kept pace in winter, the better-off children pulled further ahead of the poor children each summer, when school was closed. The better-off children had the resources to continue learning outside school during the summer, but poor children did not. By the end of elementary school, the average achievement gaps between the better-off and poor children in the BSS had increased noticeably because of these differential summer gains, even though children of all socioeconomic levels learned equivalent amounts when schools were open. Because all children's academic growth decelerates markedly as they progress through elementary school, the gains or losses made by the BSS children grew smaller year by year, but the seasonal patterns relative to family background continued through the five-year period.

School-Level Gains

So far we have reviewed the seasonal patterns of children's school achievement by family socioeconomic status. These seasonal patterns in test scores also relate to the average socioeconomic level of the schools they attended. We divided the twenty Beginning School Study schools into two groups, so that students in the ten schools with the highest percentage of students on meal subsidy could be compared with students in the ten schools with the lowest percentage of students on meal subsidy. Children in both sets of schools made virtually the same gains over the winter (Entwisle, Alexander, and Olson 1997). A significant difference between gains made over the winters in the two sets of schools appears only in the second year of the study, and in that year students in the low-socioeconomic status schools did better. When we pooled gains over the five winters, students in the two sets of schools gained almost exactly the same amount on standardized tests. All of the differences between high- and low-socioeconomic-status schools accrued in summer periods, when schools were closed.

The Faucet Theory

We propose a "faucet theory" to make sense of these seasonal patterns: When school is in session, the resource faucet is turned on for all children, and with resources equally available to everyone, all children gain. When school is not in session, poor children stop gaining because the faucet is turned off. The resources available to them in summer (mainly family resources) are not sufficient to underwrite their continued growth.

The sawtooth pattern of seasonal test gains made by low-income children—moving smartly ahead in winter but stopping or regressing in summers—is far different from the pattern seen when data are pooled over winter and summer seasons. Because tests given once a year do not distinguish between children's progress in winter and summer, yearly test scores give the distinct impression that high-socioeconomic-status children are gaining at a more rapid rate than low-socioeconomic-status children over the entire year. When seasonal differences in growth rates are ignored, the differences in children's summer environments that favor the better-off children are hidden, but so is the equality of their achievement in winters.

The seasonal data in Baltimore agree with similar data for children in Atlanta (Heyns 1978), New Haven (Murnane 1975), and many other localities (see Hayes and Grether 1969; David 1974; Hayes and King 1974; Pelavin and David 1977; David and Pelavin 1978; Hammond and Frechtling 1979). These data strongly suggest that the process of schooling has been misconceptualized, at least for young children. Home resources do not "add on" to school resources in winter, because in winter poor children do as well as those who are well off. Home resources come into play mainly in summer. When children's cognitive gains are measured yearly by using test scores procured once every twelve months, however, researchers "see" relatively slower progress among the poorer children all year and then conclude that poorer youngsters derive less from school than do their better-off classmates.

Most models of school learning thus imply that there is a constant relationship over time (that is, the slope is constant) between the level of home resources and children's school achievement, and this implication leads to the erroneous conclusion that a family's higher socioeconomic status boosts school performance by helping these children do better in school. The conclusion that home resources facilitate school learning is not warranted if we credit BSS data, because during the months that school is in session the socioeconomic status of the family does not appear to matter. The conclusion instead, we think, should be that the process of achievement changes from winter to summer. Resources in families do not enhance regular schooling, at least at the elementary level and for students like those in the BSS; rather, they keep the resources faucet open when school shuts down for the summer. When the faucet is turned off, family resources are critical. Home resources provide the better-off students the opportunity to continue their learning outside school over summer periods when schools are closed.

Lack of resources in neighborhoods is another dimension of poverty interwoven in this picture (see Wilson 1987; Sampson 1992) that could affect children more in summer. The faucet theory would predict that neighborhood resources also matter more in summer than in winter, because when children are not in school, resources in high-socioeconomic-status neighborhoods could supplant the resources furnished by the school, whereas resources in ghetto neighborhoods could not.

The twenty original BSS schools were located in neighborhoods that ranged from very low socioeconomic status (close to 40 percent of families in poverty, the average parent a school dropout, and only 5 percent of workers in professional or managerial jobs) to relatively high socioeconomic status (2 percent of families in poverty, the average parent nearly a college graduate, and 64 percent of workers in professional or managerial jobs). To see whether children's growth on achievement tests would respond to neighborhood resources in summer, we computed partial correlations between children's test score gains in summer and several measures of neighborhood quality. Over the first three years of school, after removing effects of both poverty measured at the household level and parents' education, children's achievement gains in summer were related to both the percentage of families in their neighborhoods living above the poverty line and to poverty rates by school. Median family income of the neighborhood was also positively correlated with the extent of children's summer gains.

The other half of this demonstration is that during the winters, neighborhood resources had either negligible or even inverse effects on children's school progress. While schools were in session, and controlling for individual-level resources, children who lived in poorer neighborhoods gained more than their counterparts in better neighborhoods. The schools were thus to some extent making up in winter for the dearth of neighborhood resources—just the opposite of the pattern seen in summer.

Policy Implications:
Schooling and Human Development

The extremely rapid rate of children's cognitive and social development from four to eight years of age is a powerful reason to focus on elementary schooling. In these years they are launched into achievement trajectories, they start to construct their academic self-images, and they necessarily build school dossiers that then shadow them through the rest of school and beyond. Still, the organizational imperatives that so effectively track students over this early period get little notice. These include limited access to preschools or kindergarten for three- to five-year-old children, the wide differences in social class from one elementary school to another, and the triagelike sorting of students in the first and second grades by grade retention, ability grouping, and special education (Entwisle and Alexander 1993).

The boundaries of U.S. neighborhoods and school catchment areas faithfully mirror the fault lines in the larger society. Children who live in good neighborhoods effectively land on academic fast tracks in first grade because their parents and teachers perceive them and treat them as high-ability children, whereas children who live in poor neighborhoods land on academic slow tracks because they are perceived and treated as low-ability children. The myth that elementary schools share the same curriculum is false. Even when schools use the same lesson plans and textbooks, as in Baltimore, the socioeconomic status of the neighborhood determines the way instruction proceeds and the quality of life children experience in their classrooms. Space here does not permit an elaboration of the details, but the grading levels, expectations of teachers and parents, and much else strongly favors the better-off children.

The good news is that despite widespread poverty and family disruption, young children's ability to learn in elementary school seems little affected. The transition to first grade has to be a bumpy ride for children at the low end of the socioeconomic scale, however, because their seasonal growth rates are markedly uneven, and society confuses their uneven growth trajectories with a reduced ability to grow. The Beginning School Study children of all socioeconomic levels advanced at the same rate while school was in session, but parents and teachers of children in low-socioeconomic-status schools had lower expectations for those children, and the grades awarded those children were much lower than those awarded their counterparts in higher-socioeconomic-status schools. Many more of the poorer children were also held back.

Some Contradictions Resolved

After many years, we have finally come to understand the schooling process better than we did in 1982. In particular, findings from the Baltimore Beginning School Study, and the faucet theory of schooling, make sense out of a number of well-established facts that seemed paradoxical.

1. Studies, starting with the Coleman Report in 1966, have consistently found much less variance in children's achievement across than

within schools. Data for elementary schools (the Beginning School Study) and middle schools (Heyns 1978) show that winter gains are much the same for children from various family backgrounds and, furthermore, that disadvantaged children gain at the same rate as the advantaged ones do while school is in session. Differences between schools are small because schools induce substantial growth in all children. Poorer children appear to be behind other children at the end of first grade because they started school a little behind. The shortfall in the test scores of poorer children at the end of first grade compared with those of better-off children is not attributable to the school, however. Rather, it is attributable to a lack of home background resources before they begin first grade. The paradox of large within-school variance and small between-school variance is now explained.

2. The research also suggests that pouring resources into schools, altering their curriculums, or reducing class size makes little difference in children's achievement levels, because it is the times during which children are not in school when poorer children fall behind. Resources, then, need to be directed at families and neighborhoods.

3. Studies repeatedly demonstrate that attending summer school does not benefit disadvantaged students. So far summer school attendance or special summer programs have not boosted the achievement scores of disadvantaged children (see Heyns's 1987 review). Most of these programs have been short (six weeks or less), poorly designed academically, and aimed mainly at "problem" students. Even the largest effort to date, the national Sustaining Effects Study (Klibanoff and Haggart 1981; Carter 1983, 1984), despite its thoughtful design and careful execution, did not accomplish the desired goal of helping poorer students catch up in summer. In fact, Heyns's (1987, 1155) reanalysis of these data shows that in the Sustaining Effects Study the racial gap actually increased during the summer.

    Why has summer school proved ineffective in boosting scores of disadvantaged children? We suggest two possible answers. One is that summer programs have been inappropriately timed. Most concentrate on the later elementary grades, after children are already on a trajectory of failure. If reading achievement moves up twice as fast in the first year of schooling as in the third, as is true for BSS children, then the optimum time to intervene would be in the summer after (or before) first grade. Correcting "failures" is harder than preventing them in the first place. The other reason is the nature of the program provided. Summer activities should afford children different learning experiences from those provided in the school year, experiences similar to those provided for middle-class children in summer.

4. Schools that enroll better-off children whose scores are somewhat above average when they start first grade credit themselves with producing children who excel, and society takes this view as well. The starting point of children depends on their access to resources outside school in the preschool years, not on what the school provides. The BSS children from resource-poor home environments, if anything, gained relatively more from school than did children from resource-rich home environments. Schools are thus unjustly blamed for the lower achievement levels of poor children, when in fact they are making up to some extent for the dearth of resources in poorer homes.

Timing Is Everything

Recent work by Greg Duncan and colleagues (1998) shows that family economic resources have the greatest impact on achievement in early childhood, especially for children in low-income families. Marshall Smith (1972, 265) notes that the relationship between background variables and achievement is initially strong in first grade—because the early years of life prepare the child for school and because the selection and assignment practices carried out by schools probably exacerbate the relationship between social class and achievement in the early grades. Characteristics of home and school are usually most closely matched at the elementary level, so the gradient across schools follows the gradient across neighborhoods.

A key requisite for achieving equity in schooling is to bring poorer children up to speed before they start school. We already know that school readiness can be improved for less advantaged children (see, for example, the Head Start evaluations by Irving Lazar and Richard Darlington [1982] and the report of the Consortium of Longitudinal Studies [1983]; see also Steven Barnett's [1996] summary of findings from randomized experiments). Attending preschool away from home helps close the gap between rich and poor children's school performance before they start first grade. The original Head Start programs were exceedingly variable in content and even in the ages of the children they enrolled, but for these very reasons, the benefits children derived from Head Start are strong testimony to the importance of school attendance itself rather than the details of programs or settings. Less advantaged BSS children who spent full days rather than half days in Baltimore kindergartens also did better when they started first grade—again, attending school is the answer.

Future Plans

Developmental theorists have focused much more intently on changes within the child than on changes in the child's surroundings. Research on schooling helps redress this imbalance, because a child's achievement does not occur in a social vacuum. The seasonal action of neighborhood resources coupled with the seasonal action of family resources strengthens the argument that effects of the school context are relatively independent of other contextual effects on achievement growth in the elementary years. Still, it is important to examine how neighborhoods contribute to schooling, especially from the standpoint of how resources in the neighborhood could replace resources in the home. If resources in neighborhoods supplement family resources in summer, as we suspect, then providing neighborhood centers and community activities in summer could boost children's achievement independent of family status. We suspect that organized sports and games in neighborhoods are an important resource supporting children's math development (Entwisle, Alexander, and Olson 1994).

The BSS has begun the search for long-term effects of children's experiences as they make the transition to first grade. The panel members, born in 1976, are now young adults. By the time they reached the age of twenty-two or twenty-three, about 20 percent had dropped out of school and another 30 percent had obtained a high school diploma or a GED but had gone no further in school. Of the remaining members of the study, the majority attended two-year colleges or undertook certificate or license training (28 percent); 22 percent were in four-year college programs.

We are seeing the influences of first-grade performance (grades, classroom behavior, track placements) on the level of educational attainment in young adulthood net of test scores and family background. We also are beginning to see that those who drop out were more often absent in first grade and had poorer deportment than those who stayed in school through high school, even taking into account academic performance and family background. Investigation of the effects of first-grade experiences on labor market behavior in early adulthood is now beginning.

We hope to follow the BSS cohort into their late twenties because by that age work and family careers are more clearly established. An important task for our future research is to study BSS panel members who are the most successful despite the odds, especially those who achieved a high school education or less; the BSS project is pointed next in exactly that direction. A parallel effort aims at understanding the overall role of education at every level in fostering well-being in adulthood, family relationships, and psychological measures included along with employment outcomes.

Notes

1.   Around this time (1968), Entwisle finally got a tenure-track job. By then she had published three books and fourteen articles and felt empowered to follow her own research agenda even more closely.

2. A happy circumstance all along was having Karl's daughter, Karen Alexander, available to help us at every transition. The same age as members of the BSS cohort, on many occasions she graciously helped us phrase questions and time questionnaires. When she was old enough, she worked summers in the lab doing coding and the like. A recent Brown graduate, she is now a master's degree candidate at the University of North Carolina, Chapel Hill.

3. "Intensity" in pretest and post-test designs has recently surfaced as a topic in experimental design (see Maxwell 1994, 1998). "Intensity" in this context means several equally spaced interviews between the pretest and post-test.

4. Evidence from natural experiments also suggests that time spent in school rather than age explains how much children know. Stephen Ceci (1991) estimates that children's IQ scores drop between 0.25 and 6.00 points a year when schools are shut down. He notes that when the public schools in Prince Edward County, Virginia, were closed between 1959 and 1964 to avoid integration, most African American children received no formal education. On average, their dropped by about six points a year for every year they missed school; children of all ages were affected (Green et al. 1964). For another example, when World War II forced Holland's schools to close, the IQ scores of children whose schooling was delayed dropped by about seven points (deGroot 1951).

References

Alexander, Karl L., and Doris R. Entwisle. 1996. "Educational Tracking in the Early Years: First-Grade Placements and Middle-School Constraints." In *Generating Social Stratification: Toward a New Research Agenda*, edited by Alan C. Kerckhoff. New York: Westview Press.

Alwin, Duane F., and Arland Thornton. 1984. "Family Origins and the Schooling Process: Early Versus Late Influence of Parental Characteristics." *American Sociological Review* 49(6): 784–802.

Barnett, W. Steven. 1996. "Long-Term Effects of Early Childhood Care and Education on Disadvantaged Children's Cognitive Development and School Success." *Future of Children* 5(3): 25–50.

Cahan, Sorel, and Nora Cohen. 1989. "Age Versus Schooling Effects on Intelligence Development." *Child Development* 60(5): 1237–49.

Carter, Launor F. 1983. "A Study of Compensatory and Elementary Education: The Sustaining Effects Study." Paper prepared by the U.S. Department of Education for the System Development Corporation, Santa Monica, Calif.

———. 1984. "The Sustaining Effects Study of Compensatory and Elementary Education." *Educational Researcher* 13(7): 4–13.

Ceci, Stephen J. 1991. "How Much Does Schooling Influence General Intelligence and Its Cognitive Components? A Reassessment of the Evidence." *Developmental Psychology* 27(5): 703–22.

Coleman, James S. 1961. *The Adolescent Society*. Glencoe, Ill.: Free Press.

Coleman, James S., Ernest O. Campbell, Carol J. Hobson, James McPartland, Alexander Mood, Frederic D. Weinfeld, and Robert L. York. 1966. *Equality of Educational Opportunity*. Washington: U.S. Government Printing Office.

Consortium of Longitudinal Studies. 1983. *As the Twig Is Bent: Lasting Effect of Preschool Programs*. Hillsdale, N.J.: Lawrence Erlbaum Associates.

David, Jane. 1974. "Follow Through Summer Study: A Two-Part Investigation of the Impact of Exposure to Schooling on Achievement Growth." Ph.D. diss., Harvard Graduate School of Education.

David, Jane, and Sol H. Pelavin. 1978. "Secondary Analysis in Compensatory Education Programs." *New Directions for Program Evaluation* 4: 31–44.

deGroot, A. D. 1951. "Short Articles and Notes: War and the Intelligence of Youth." *Journal of Abnormal and Social Psychology* 46: 596–97.

Duncan, Greg J., W. Jean Yeung, Jeanne Brooks-Gunn, and Judith K. Smith. 1998. "How Much Does Childhood Poverty Affect the Life Chances of Children?" *American Sociological Review* 63(June): 406–23.

Elder, Glen H., Jr. 1974. *Children of the Great Depression: Social Change in Life Experience*. Chicago: University of Chicago Press.

———. 1998. "The Life Course and Human Development." In *Theoretical Models of Human Development*, edited by Richard M. Lerner, vol. 1 of *Handbook of Child Psychology*, edited by William Damon. New York: Wiley.

Elmer, Elizabeth, and Gary S. Gregg. 1967. "Developmental Characteristics of Abused Children." *Pediatrics* 40: 596–602.

Entwisle, Doris R., and Karl L. Alexander. 1992. "Summer Setback: Race, Poverty, School Composition, and Mathematics Achievement in the First Two Years of School." *American Sociological Review* 57(February): 72–84.

———. 1993. "Entry into School: The Beginning School Transition and Educational Stratification in the United States." *Annual Review of Sociology* 19: 401–23.

———. 1994. "Winter Setback: School Racial Composition and Learning to Read." *American Sociological Review* 59(June): 446–60.

Entwisle, Doris R., Karl L. Alexander, and Linda Steffel Olson. 1994. "The Gender Gap in Math: Its Possible Origins in Neighborhood Effects." *American Sociological Review* 59(December): 822–38.

———. 1997. *Children, Schools, and Inequality*. New York: Westview Press.

Entwisle, Doris R., and Leslie A. Hayduk. 1978. *Too Great Expectations: The Academic Outlook of Young Children*. Baltimore: Johns Hopkins University Press.

———. 1982. *Early Schooling: Cognitive and Affective Outcomes*. Baltimore: Johns Hopkins University Press.

Entwisle, Doris R., and Murray Webster. 1974. "Expectations in Mixed Racial Groups." *Sociology of Education* 47(3): 301–18.

Felner, Robert D., and Angela M. Adan. 1988. "The School Transitional Environment Project: An Ecological Intervention and Evaluation." In *Fourteen Ounces of Prevention: A Casebook for Practitioners*, edited by Richard H. Price, Emory L. Cowen, Raymond P. Lorion, and Julia Ramos-McKay. Washington, D.C.: American Psychological Association.

Garfinkel, Irwin, and Sara S. McLanahan. 1986. *Single Mothers and Their Children: A New American Dilemma*. Washington, D.C.: Urban Institute Press.

Green, Robert Lee, Louis J. Hofman, Richard J. Morse, Marilyn E. Hayes, Robert F. Morgan. 1964. *The Educational Status of Children in a District Without Public Schools*. Cooperative Research Project, vol. 2321. East Lansing: Michigan State University, Bureau of Educational Research.

Hammond, Pierce A., and Joy A. Frechtling. 1979. "Twelve-, Nine-, and Three-Month Achievement Gains of Low- and Average-Achieving Elementary School Students." Paper presented at the annual meeting of the American Educational Research Association, San Francisco, Calif. (April 8).

Harms, Leroy. S. 1961. "Listener Judgements of Status Cues in Speech." *Quarterly Journal of Speech* 47: 164–68.

Haveman, Robert, and Barbara Wolfe. 1994. *Succeeding Generations*. New York: Russell Sage Foundation.

Hayes, Donald P., and Judith Grether. 1969. "The School Year and Vacations: When Do Students Learn?" *Cornell Journal of Social Relations* 17(1983): 56–71.

Hayes, Donald P., and John P. King. 1974. "The Development of Reading Achievement Differentials During the School Year and Vacations." Cornell University. Unpublished paper.

Heyns, Barbara. 1978. *Summer Learning and the Effects of Schooling*. New York: Academic Press.

———. 1987. "Schooling and Cognitive Development: Is There a Season for Learning?" *Child Development* 58(October): 1151–60.

Hogan, Dennis P. 1981. *Transitions and Social Change*. New York: Academic Press.

Huston, Aletha C. 1994. "Children in Poverty: Designing Research to Affect Policy." *Social Policy Report* (of the Society for Research in Child Development) 8(2): 1–15.

Jencks, Christopher. 1985. "How Much Do High School Students Learn?" *Sociology of Education* 58(2): 128–53.

Jencks, Christopher, Marshall Smith, Henry Ackland, Mary Jo Bane, David Cohen, Herbert Gintis, Barbara Heyns, and Stephan Michelson. 1972. *Inequality: A Reassessment of the Effect of Failure and Schooling in America*. New York: Basic Books.

Klein, Michael, and Leo Stern. 1971. "Low Birthweight and the Battered Child Syndrome." *American Journal of Diseases of Children* 122: 15–18.

Klibanoff, Leonard S., and Sue A. Haggart. 1981. "Summer Growth and the Effectiveness of Summer School." Technical Report to the Office of Program Evaluation. U.S. Department of Education, report 8. Mountain View, Calif.: RMC Research Corporation (February).

Lambert, Wallace E., M. Just, and N. Segalowitz. 1970. "Some Cognitive Consequences of Following the Curricula of the Early School Grades in a Foreign Language." In *21st Annual Roundtable*, edited by J. Alatis. Washington, D.C.: Georgetown University Press.

Lambert, Wallace E., and J. Macnamara. 1969. "Some Cognitive Consequences of Following a First Grade Curriculum in a Second Language." *Journal of Educational Psychology* 60(2): 86–96.

Lambert, Wallace E., and G. R. Tucker. 1972. *The St. Lambert Program of Home-School Language Switch, Grades K Through Five*. Mimeo. Montreal: McGill University.

Lazar, Irving, and Richard Darlington. 1982. "Lasting Effects of Early Education: A Report from the Consortium for Longitudinal Studies." *Monographs of the Society for Research in Child Development* 47(2–3): ix–151.

Lynch, Margaret A., and Jacqueline Roberts. 1977. "Predicting Child Abuse: Signs of Bonding Failure in the Maternity Hospital." *British Medical Journal* 1: 624–26.

Marjoribanks, Kevin. 1979. *Families and Their Learning Environments.* London: Routledge.

Maxwell, Scott E. 1994. "Optimal Allocation of Assessment Time in Randomized Pretest-Posttest Designs." *Psychological Bulletin* 115(January): 142–52.

———. 1998. "Longitudinal Designs in Randomized Group Comparisons: When Will Intermediate Observations Increase Statistical Power?" *Psychological Methods* 3: 275–90.

McLoyd, Vonnie. 1989. "Socialization and Development in a Changing Economy: The Effects of Paternal Income and Job Loss on Children." *American Psychologist* 44(February): 293–302.

———. 1990. "The Impact of Economic Hardship on Black Families and Children: Psychological Distress, Parenting, and Socioemotional Development." *Child Development* 61(2): 311–46.

Morrison, Fredrick J., Lisa Smith, and Maureen Dow-Ehrensberger. 1995. "Education and Cognitive Development: A Natural Experiment." *Developmental Psychology* 31(5): 789–99.

Mosteller, Frederick, and Daniel P. Moynihan. 1972. *On Equality of Educational Opportunity.* New York: Vintage Books.

Murnane, Richard J. 1975. *The Impact of School Resources on the Learning of Inner-City Children.* Cambridge, Mass.: Ballinger.

Pelavin, S. H., and Jane L. David. 1977. "Evaluating Long-Term Achievement: An Analysis of Longitudinal Data from Compensatory Educational Programs." Report 4537-15. Report prepared for the Office of the Assistant Secretary for Education, U.S. Department of Health, Education and Welfare. Washington, D.C.: SRI International Educational Policy Research Center.

Sampson, Robert J. 1992. "Family Management and Child Development: Insights from Social Disorganization Theory." In *Advances in Criminology Theory,* vol. 3, *Fact, Frameworks, and Forecasts,* edited by Joan McCord. New Brunswick, N.J.: Transaction Books.

Simmons, Roberta G., and Dale A. Blyth. 1987. *Moving into Adolescence: The Impact of Pubertal Change and School Context.* Hawthorne, N.Y.: Aldine de Gruyter.

Simmons, Roberta G., Dale A. Blyth, Edward F. Van Cleave, and Diane Bush. 1979. "Entry into Early Adolescence: The Impact of School Structure, Puberty, and Early Dating on Self-Esteem." *American Sociological Review* 44(6): 948–67.

Smith, Marshall S. 1972. "Equality of Educational Opportunity: The Basic Findings Reconsidered." In *On Equality of Educational Opportunity,* edited by Frederick Mosteller and Daniel P. Moynihan. New York: Vintage Books.

Wilson, William J. 1987. *The Truly Disadvantaged.* Chicago: University of Chicago Press.

Chapter 8

Historical Times and Lives: A Journey Through Time and Space

GLEN H. ELDER JR.

> Historical transformations carry meanings not only for individual ways
> of life, but for the very . . . limits and possibilities of the human being.
> —C. Wright Mills

RESEARCH ADVANCES of some note often stem from modest beginnings. This observation applies to empirical studies of historical
times in people's lives, a central theme of my research career and
of this chapter. The stimulus for this line of work owes much to psychologists who launched a series of longitudinal studies of child development more than seventy years ago at Stanford University and the
University of California, Berkeley (Elder 1998b). In sociology, W. I.
Thomas provided support in the 1920s with the claim that priority
should be given to the "longitudinal approach to life history," and that
studies should investigate "many types of individuals with regard to
their experiences and various past periods of life in different situations"
(quoted in Thomas and Volkart 1951, 593). Thomas envisioned a study
that followed children from their earliest years to young adulthood. The
first half of life, he assumed, would lay the foundation for the pathways
of later life.

Four decades passed before prospective longitudinal studies became
widespread in the social and behavioral sciences, both in the United States
and abroad. Today, there are literally hundreds of such longitudinal

studies (in which data are collected from an individual study member over multiple waves), and many of them extend from childhood into the middle years and beyond (for example, Young, Savola, and Phelps 1991) or from the middle years to old age. An important example of this revolution is the Panel Study of Income Dynamics at the University of Michigan. Launched in 1968, this national study soon became a model for socioeconomic panels in Canada and western European countries (see chapter 6, this volume).

Also noteworthy are three national birth cohort studies in Great Britain. The first began in 1946, right after World War II; the second and third longitudinal cohort studies were launched in 1958 and in 1970, respectively. A new millennial cohort was launched in the spring of 2001. When prospective longitudinal studies were not possible or were not available on the time period in question, investigators have turned to retrospective life-history techniques to collect biographical data on past lives and times. The German Life History Study (Brückner and Mayer 1998) is a prominent example of this approach.

In studies of people across the years, changing times should be seen as a potential source of life variations. However, the early investigators of the 1920s were largely oblivious to such influences. At the same time, it should be noted that they intended to establish only short-term longitudinal studies of children. This goal changed as new questions were posed by the ongoing projects. Before long the original panel members of the Berkeley and Stanford studies had moved through adolescence and young adulthood into middle age. Most of the men eventually married, had children, and pursued careers, often interrupted by wartime service in the early 1940s. By the 1950s, they were well established in their own careers and families. The study of adult development was becoming a significant field of research.

The investigators' neglect of historical times could not erase the cumulating records at the Berkeley Institute of Human Development and their portrait of the study members amid Depression hardships and World War II (Elder 1999). At war's end, new levels of prosperity came to many parts of the United States, as well as new questions for the institute's investigators. How did some men and women manage to overcome troubled childhoods and achieve rewarding lives in adulthood? How did the changing times influence their lives and who they eventually became? Fortunately, the study members had been followed well into the middle years, and this effort has been continued.

I first encountered the rich Berkeley data in the early 1960s upon my arrival for a new position—half-time in the Institute of Human Development at the University of California, Berkeley, under the direction of sociologist John A. Clausen and half-time in the university's Department of Sociology. I had completed doctoral studies in sociology, with a minor in psychology, under Charles Bowerman at the University of North Carolina, Chapel Hill, and a one-year postdoctoral fellowship funded by the National Institute of Mental Health. The psychology minor gave me a deeper understanding of the theories and methods of developmental studies, preparing me for the psychological world of the institute.

Unbeknownst to me at the time, both Bowerman and Clausen had been educated in the Ernest Burgess and W. I. Thomas tradition of family and life-history research during their prewar doctoral studies at the University of Chicago. I brought this Chicago perspective to my work at the institute, along with training in social psychology and a long-standing appreciation for social history, but I possessed no prior knowledge of, or expertise in, longitudinal studies. My dissertation had focused on parent-peer influences, using a large survey of adolescents in North Carolina and the Midwest.

In retrospect, my transition from sociology at Chapel Hill to the Berkeley Institute of Human Development, with its wealth of longitudinal data, marks a truly life-shaping event. This chapter tells the story of this journey from my early days in Berkeley to the 1990s, with emphasis on the formative influence of my archival research.

Archival work led to a series of challenges and new questions, including the construction of methods for working with archival data and with life-course studies in general. Methods and measurement strategies appropriate to this line of inquiry were not available in the 1960s. Another challenge centered on a way of thinking about lives and human development in a changing world—now called a theoretical orientation on the life course (Elder 1998a, 1998b; Elder and Kirkpatrick Johnson 2002). This theoretical orientation is a product of many individual contributions and disciplines, though its contextual inspiration is rooted in sociology. I have been fortunate to be part of its development. A third challenge has been the exploration of issues of life-course continuity and change through turning points.

Working with Archival Data

A quarter century after my childhood in the Great Depression, I returned to the 1930s to investigate the life experience of Californians from the Oakland Growth Study. This project was one of three longitudinal studies that were launched in the 1920s and 1930s at the Institute of Human Development (then called the Institute for Child Welfare).[1] My assignment involved the large task of coding both childhood and adult interviews of members of the Oakland study and their parents. A planned collaboration with John Clausen did not materialize at the time, owing to his administrative duties, and I used this opportunity to develop my own projects.

The coding project became the first stage in building a method for making archival data more responsive to new research questions (Elder, Pavalko, and Clipp 1993). In any long-term longitudinal study, data are collected along the way for different purposes. To make good use of such data for new objectives, it must be "recast" or recoded. The relationship between research questions and archival data takes the form of a model-fitting enterprise. Questions are refined in the process, and the data are recoded with such concerns in mind.

In the Oakland Growth Study, the primary topic of physical growth and development had nothing to do with the family hardship I assessed and studied in the lives of men and women who grew up in the 1930s. As I later discovered, this disparity between data collected for old questions and the posing of a new question is typical of encounters with longitudinal studies. The disparity may be only partial, however. The Oakland project provided information on income loss during the early 1930s, which was essential to my objectives.

The task of recoding longitudinal data proved tedious and demanding, as one might expect. On the other hand, the enterprise often produced new insights that prompted questions about old ways of perceiving reality as well as different perspectives. The Oakland mothers were interviewed at three points from 1932 to 1936, and annual ratings across the adolescent years were based on observations of the children by staff and classmates. During this time period, the adolescents completed annual surveys on physical growth, interests, attitudes, and social relationships. In the adult years, the study members were contacted for comprehensive follow-up interviews on multiple occasions from 1954 to 1986. When I arrived at the Institute of Human Development in the fall of 1962, I found cartons of such data stacked in storage rooms, waiting to be coded, keypunched, and filed.

Over a three-year period, archival research led me to a broader vision of lives and revealed the dramatic instability of families under changing economic conditions during the Great Depression. A good many study members could say that they were once "well off" and then "quite poor." Institute records note frequent changes of residence and jobs. Case examples include the family of an unemployed lawyer who had to settle for a series of low-rent apartments as his job search moved him from one temporary position to another.

In view of such change, conventional ways of thinking about social class or family status at any point seemed futile. With such concerns in mind, I began to think of the family economy, its division of labor and resource allocation, as a dynamic enterprise in which parents, children, and even relatives play different roles, depending on the circumstances. I also began to think of children's lives as embedded in a changing family pattern. Any parental responses or adaptations to income loss altered their family environment and possibly the way hardship changed their lives and development.

From Berkeley institute records, I could see a child from an economically deprived family who seemed "old beyond his time" and then later appeared to recover his youthful exuberance when family income improved. I wondered whether the change reflected the better economic conditions or the adaptations of the family to hard-times. Some families seemed to be more resilient than others. Because institute staff had followed the Oakland study's "children of the Great Depression" well into the middle years, I could see that some of the adults did well despite the great hardships they had experienced. Childhood disadvantage did not always lead to continuing disadvantage in adult life. For the most part, the children managed to bounce back and succeed beyond any expectations set in the 1930s.

To understand such turning points, I began to make comparisons with a younger cohort, the Berkeley Guidance Study members, born just before the Great Depression. A comparative study of the two cohorts would indicate whether the life experience of the Oakland men and women paralleled that of the younger Berkeley group. The latter were of preschool age when the economy collapsed and thus were subject to family disruption and strain at a vulnerable time in their lives. The Oakland youth, on the other hand, were old enough when the Depression began to understand the changes taking place, having passed the most vulnerable stage of life.

The data archive was not organized to answer questions about the experiences of study members, however. Life histories on the parents and children had not been collected systematically. No data file was available on key events of the life course—birth year of parents and children, the parents' education, first job and work life, war service, and so on. This limitation owed in part to uncoded interviews with parents and children up to the 1960s and to a lack of machine-readable data files with such information. Most of the longitudinal analyses up to the early 1960s had used test score and personality inventory data, without attention to the social pathways of the study members.

In the absence of any tested guidelines for working with archival data, I followed a four-phase approach:

• I took a thorough inventory of the archive, one that extended beyond listed materials. This occurred while I supervised the coding of interviews for the institute. The resulting knowledge led to the Depression study.

• I constructed life records of all study members, including family, work, and household socioeconomic events. The development of chronological life records serve an important function in studies of lives when data come from archives that have been developed for other purposes. These records also enabled me to address missing data by drawing upon the full range of information.

• I developed a codebook on key variables and coded study members on them. Preliminary life-course ideas, such as the use of constructs that capture change, informed this codebook. Examples include fluctuations and progress in subjects' working lives. By structuring each life record in terms of common categories for coding, I retained the option of moving back and forth between quantitative analyses and case studies.

• I refined the steps in this approach in an effort to "recast" the Berkeley Guidance data for the purposes of making comparisons between the Oakland and Berkeley cohorts. I devoted an entire year (1972 to 1973) with a small research team at the Institute of Human Development to this recasting project.

At the time, I wrote that "life history analysts encounter many archival challenges, but few are more demanding than the redesign of data sets or a study archive in order to achieve a better fit between question and answer. . . . The Oakland Growth and Berkeley Guidance archives posed a challenge to me because neither represented a complete life course framework when I first reviewed them" (Elder 1973, 13; 1984). Of course, I did not know the full scope of preparatory work that would be required to make good use of these data archives. As I noted some years ago, "limited vision" can be merciful.

Our methods of archival research have become more refined and articulated over the years. The most important stage of development occurred when, beginning in 1986, we explored the archives of Lewis Terman's Life Cycle Study of Children with High Ability for an investigation of wartime conditions and military service in the lives of men. The Terman men were approximately thirty years old when World War II began, and thus we had a chance to explore the lifetime implications of age at mobilization for men who came to war at what is generally considered a late age. Terman data were collected in 1922 for the first time and then again in 1928 and about every five years up to 1960. Data collections were initiated again in 1972 and continued in 1977, 1982, 1986, and 1992.

To understand the effects of military service, we needed good measures of health, but the study was never designed for this purpose. By conceiving of health as a trajectory over time rather than as a particular state, we discovered that excellent measures of health could be constructed from the data at hand. To obtain needed medical expertise, I developed a collaborative project with Elizabeth Clipp of the Durham (North

Carolina) Veterans Administration Hospital, who had been a student of mine at Cornell University. Eliza Pavalko, a postdoctoral fellow in the program, also joined the research team.

At the time, we contributed to a sequence of Henry A. Murray Center conferences on archival data (in 1989 and 1991), and our preparations led to the development of a small monograph detailing all stages of the research process in "recasting" data sets (Elder, Pavalko, and Clipp 1993). The first step assessed the potential of the Terman data in addressing the questions we posed. In the second step we faced a decision on whether or not to recode. We decided to proceed despite the work involved because the potential was so great. The third step brought us back to our questions and to the need for more refined questions. From this point on, the process involved the construction of new codes and preparation of a codebook, the coding process itself, and the calculation of reliabilities and validities.

As the children of the Berkeley institute studies became young adults and then entered middle age, they required theory that made sense of the social organization and change of individual lives and provided a way of connecting lives to the times in which they lived. Life-course theory emerged to fill this void, and one of the early efforts to move in this direction can be seen in Children of the Great Depression (Elder 1999). Longitudinal studies over the life span and life-course theory called for new questions and statistical models, from structural equation and event-history analysis to multilevel modeling.

Lives, Observations, and Theory

During graduate studies, I had encountered a little book with an inspiring title that had something compelling to say about the study of lives. In *The Sociological Imagination,* C. Wright Mills (1959, 149) proposes "the study of biography, of history, and of the problems of their intersection within social structure" as an orienting concept in the behavioral sciences. Mills had few empirical examples to draw upon at the time, and he did not provide a method or analytic model that could be applied to questions of this kind. Human lives and development were an uncommon subject of study in their historical context, and research had not investigated the interplay of changing lives in changing times. Concepts of the life course were not available in the scholarly literature at the time, and no graduate seminars were taught on the subject. I left graduate school with neither exposure to nor an understanding of the life course as theory, concept, and field of inquiry.

I did, however, have an appreciation for life-history studies in the old Chicago tradition, and this proved useful as I made the transition from cross-sectional surveys at Chapel Hill to forty years of longitudinal data at the Institute of Human Development. Two tasks, in particular, accelerated movement toward a framework on what is now recognized as the life course (Elder 1998a, 1998b): to think about the social organization of human lives over the life span and across the generations and to relate human lives to an ever changing society, with emphasis on the developmental effects of changing circumstances. At the time, we had two common ways of thinking about social pathways—career and life cycle—and neither placed individuals in history. Typically career referred to an evolving activity (work life, criminal enterprises) and thus tended to oversimplify the lives of people with multiple roles at the same time. The large-scale entry of mothers into the labor force produced circumstances that favored a new concept of multiple interlocking trajectories that varied in synchronization. Career perspectives also failed to incorporate notions of age-graded expectations in a systematic way, and they did not orient analyses to the historical context of lives across the generations.

The life-cycle concept usefully knits together the full array of life stages and generations, providing insight into the context of individual lives through relationships. Life-cycle processes of socialization and social control link developing individuals to one another, their careers, and their communities. However, the life-cycle focus on birth and parenting lessened its value as a way of viewing lives, especially in an age of growing diversity. For example, it does not apply to those who never married, to those who never had children, and to those who have been divorced more than once. Also important is the concept's inability to represent the interlocking roles of family, work, and civic and leisure activities. Each person typically occupies multiple roles at the same time, whether parent, spouse, or employee. Yet concurrent roles are not part of the life-cycle concept (but see Wilensky 1961). Consequently, the life-cycle concept fails to address the management of concurrent activities or roles and their synchrony.

The life cycle, as a sequence of parenting roles, is also insensitive to matters of the timing and historical location of life events (see Hill and Foote 1970). Social roles are not linked to age, and so we do not know when transitions occur, whether early or late. Stages of parenting can occur across a wide span of the life course, from twelve to forty-five years of age or older. The notion of generation, as a conceptual element of the life-cycle model, also shares a certain blindness to historical time. Each member of a three-generation family does not have a precise historical location. People with young children may vary in historical time by as many as thirty years, a time frame that could include eras of economic depression, a world war, resurgent prosperity, and peace in the twentieth century.

Both career and life-cycle distinctions contributed initially to a Depression study of the 167 Oakland Growth Study children that eventually became *Children of the Great Depression* (Elder 1974). The study members were born in the early 1920s, experienced adolescence in the depressed 1930s, and were subject to the manpower demands of World War II. Families in the middle and working classes of 1929 were classified as deprived (having experienced an income loss of 35 percent or more between 1929 and 1933, during which time the cost of living dropped by 25 percent) or nondeprived (having suffered a lower income loss). For this project, data were obtained from subjects across their thirties and at multiple times up to their midsixties. Within each social class, I linked economic hardship to children's lives through observed household changes toward labor-intensive activity, new forms of relationships, and greater emotional and social stresses.

The fast-changing world of the 1930s raised questions for this study of Depression children that could not be addressed by the life-cycle and career perspectives. For example, the impact of economic losses depended on many factors that called for a different perspective, including the differential exposure of family members to the income loss and resulting adaptations as well as the age or life stage of both children and parents. I also wondered about the generality of any findings. Was a drastic income loss in the thirties comparable in meaning to prior economic declines? Would the effects be similar? These questions made the age-based distinctions of life stage, birth cohort, and timing of life events especially relevant. Thus, the age of the Oakland children located them in the 1930s as adolescents, whereas an older birth cohort would have experienced adolescence during the prosperous 1920s.

These contrasting social worlds and their developmental implications affirmed a principle of historical time and place: *The life course of individuals is embedded in and shaped by the historical times and places they experience over their lifetimes.* Historical context has much to do with the experiences of a young person's significant others, including parents, siblings, and friends. Hardships in the 1930s influenced the lives of youth through the economic and job losses of their parents and also through the Depression's effects on grandparents, who often had to move in with them. For young people during World War II, the distinctive features of adolescence included the war-related employment of parents, the military service and war trauma of older brothers, and the mobilization of schoolchildren for civil defense and the war effort.

To understand the human impact of such historical forces, one needs an approach that begins with the transforming environment, not with the individual. This is a defining feature of *Children of the Great Depression.* The study is framed around the task of linking historical change to developmental outcomes. Other points of entry in the project center on interpersonal relationships and social networks. *Children of the Great*

Depression investigates these relationships and their effects as well, but the analytical frame remains the effect of historical change.

In the 1970s, the Oakland and Berkeley cohort design enabled me to compare children who experienced the Depression at different times in their lives—who occupied different life stages. The two groups followed different timetables. The Oakland children were too old to be heavily dependent on distressed families during the 1930s and too young to be forced into an unwelcoming labor market. By contrast, the Berkeley children experienced family hardship when they were still very dependent on their parents. We found that the Berkeley children were more adversely influenced by the economic collapse in terms of psychological health, social competence, and academic success than the Oakland adolescents, especially the boys (Elder 1999).

Such life-stage implications led to another principle: *The developmental impact of a life transition or event is contingent on when it occurs in a person's life.* The life-course impact of a historical event, this principle in other words, is contingent on the cohort's life stage. Norman Ryder (1965, 846), for example, stresses this "life-stage" contingency by noting that as each cohort encounters a historical event, whether depression or prosperity, it "is distinctively marked by the career stage it occupies." However, the risk of exposure to hardship in the 1930s and its impact were not uniform in any cohort. Not all of the Oakland and Berkeley families were economically deprived, and the youngest boys in the Berkeley study were at particular risk. The youngest girls received more support and nurturance from their mothers.

These differences emerged from a comparison of the two birth cohorts (Elder 1979, 1999). The Oakland boys from deprived families followed a more positive course on psychological health through adolescence when compared with the deprived Berkeley boys, who ranked at the bottom in this respect among both boys and girls. The cohort differences were reversed among girls. The Berkeley girls from deprived families showed more psychological health through adolescence and young adulthood; the older Oakland girls in such families experienced greater social costs in adolescence from inadequate clothes and limited resources.

Economically deprived men in both cohorts encountered educational barriers, such as the lack of financial resources for higher education, but their work-life achievements tended to make up for such limitations. The latter were more pronounced for the deprived Berkeley males and had more to do with their lack of self-confidence, ambition, and goals. Their vulnerability to family deprivation conforms to findings that show such hardships to be especially pathogenic for boys in early childhood (Rutter and Madge 1976).

Among women in both cohorts, the deprived Berkeley group fared remarkably well on emotional stability and self-perceptions of adequacy

compared with women from nondeprived homes. Despite the unques-
tioned trials of their family experience, most of these women emerged
from their Depression years as competent, resourceful adults. This advantage persisted into the middle years of life, even though family hardship had limited their education, as it had for the Oakland women.

Why did the Oakland boys fare as well as they did? Part of the explanation centers on their family roles and social status at the time. They
were more likely to take on jobs outside the home to assist their economically troubled families. Change of this sort strengthened their social
independence and reduced their exposure to family stress. The Oakland
girls were more exposed to such stress through household activities. In
the Berkeley cohort, girls were more insulated than their male peers in
deprived families by their mothers' protectiveness. These girls became
closer to their mothers as they entered adolescence, whereas the boys
became more distant.

These historical variations show that life-course timing in the Great
Depression varied significantly by gender. Another example of this
contingency appears in the timing of marriage and work roles among
women in both cohorts. Some of the women married before their twentieth birthdays, while others were still unmarried eight years later. With
early marriage came an accumulation of life disadvantages, from economic hardship to the loss of education and occupational advancement
(Elder, Downey, and Cross 1986). The timing of births had similar implications. The timing of marriage and parenting presented no consequences of this kind for men in both cohorts, though timing became an
important distinction in their work lives.

Historical events and their timing are connected to the developmental experiences of individuals through the family and the "linked" fates
of its members. The misfortune of one member is shared through relationships over time. Hard times in the 1930s placed greater strain on
marriages, sometimes by accentuating depressed feelings, resentment,
and frustration. Among the Oakland families, this strain increased the
central role of the mother and diminished the parenting significance of
the father. These men frequently became problem drinkers and problematic figures for children. A similar effect appears with some clarity
in the Berkeley families. Economic stress increased the irritability and
explosiveness of fathers, which in turn undermined their marriages and
fueled a more punitive, erratic approach to parenting.

These observations support the principle of linked lives: *Lives are
lived interdependently, and social historical influences are expressed through
this network of shared relationships.* This life-course principle represents
the oldest tradition in life studies, that of relationship theories—of
role theory, social networks, and the life cycle of successive generations. Lives are linked within and across the generations. We found

unstable personalities (explosive, volatile) and unstable family relations (marital and between parent and child) to be mutually reinforcing dynamics across the life course (Elder, Caspi, and Downey 1986). These relationships persisted from one generation to the next through behavioral continuity among individuals and intergenerational transmission.

The four generations in this analysis come from the Berkeley Guidance Study: grandparents (G1), who were born around the 1870s; parents (G2) of Depression children, who were born between 1890 and 1910; study members (G3), the children of the Great Depression (born between 1927 and 1930); and their postwar children (G4). As observed by sons and daughters (G2), emotionally unstable and irritable parents (G1) were usually involved in discordant marriages and expressed hostile feelings toward offspring. A comparable dynamic appears in the Depression experience of the second generation (G2). Because of difficult, ill-tempered behaviors of the G3 generation (as measured in childhood and in adulthood), they were likely to be seen by their own children (G4) as out of control and unaffectionate.

Negative family dynamics tended to accentuate the influence of unstable parents on children, and they were carried forward in the next generation through the development of children who were least able to sustain and nurture enduring relationships. Examples include members of the G2 and G3 generations who reproduced the marital discord of their upbringing in their own families. We also identified notable "turning points and breaks" in the generational cycle, however. For example, the developmental risk of drastic income loss during the 1930s was much less for children of resourceful fathers who were relatively calm under stress than for the offspring of irritable, explosive fathers (Elder, Nguyen, and Caspi 1985). Protective factors that shielded children from harsh parenting included the child's physical attractiveness and a nurturant mother.

Although family stress is an important part of Depression life, there is another side of the picture in which families often worked out successful responses under trying circumstances. Mothers entered the labor force to supplement family income, and families cut back on expenditures. In some cases, families sought residential alternatives to the unmanageable cost of a rented house by moving in with friends or parents.

When hard-pressed families moved their residence to cheaper quarters and sought other forms of income, they were constructing a new life course in accord with the principle of human agency: *Individuals construct their own life course through the choices and actions they take within the opportunities and constraints of history and social circumstances.* In deprived families, the Oakland boys who managed paid jobs in the 1930s were judged by staff observers to be more efficacious than youth who lacked such work experience. This work was appealing to the industrious and became a source of enhanced beliefs in personal efficacy.

One working boy was described by his mother as having "one driving interest after another, usually a practical one" (Elder 1974, 145). Those who worked became more socially independent in adolescence when compared with other boys, according to staff observers, and were considered by their mothers to be more responsible on economic matters. With more chores to do in the household, employed adolescents experienced something like adult commitments. Indeed, they appeared to observers to be more adult oriented in values and activities when compared with other youth.

Social transitions across the life course are marked by choice points and thus provide a strategic place for observing the initiative of individuals in making and interpreting their life course and identity. Consider military service: For the Oakland men, military service was an obligation and not simply an option; virtually all able-bodied men participated in World War II. The decision to volunteer was more of an option for the younger Berkeley men when they reached the age of eighteen, typically after 1945, and 73 percent eventually ended up in the military for two years or more. Men from hard-pressed families had more reason than other men to join up as soon as possible, especially in view of the educational benefits of the GI bill, and they did so.

Expectations from the Depression era focused on the imagery of "a lost generation" when thoughts turned to the children who had grown up in poverty and broken families. I expected that hard times would take the form of a legacy of social disadvantage. However, the lives of Depression children proved me wrong. A substantial number managed to rise above the limitations of their childhoods. They followed trajectories of resilience into adulthood and the middle years. Owing partly to military service, their lives were turned around toward greater life opportunity.

Turning Lives Around

The principal story of *Children of the Great Depression* is achievement despite adversity. To an unexpected degree, we found little evidence of impaired health and accomplishments among men and women who had grown up in hard-pressed families when compared with the nondeprived. This conclusion applies to the Berkeley cohort as well as to men and women from the Oakland Growth Study. As a group, these children of the Great Depression, with backgrounds of family deprivation, were doing better than expected, following a trajectory of resilience into the middle years of life. In Michael Rutter's words (1985, 608), "The quality of resilience resides in how people deal with life changes and what they do about their situations."

No turnaround was more surprising than that of the Berkeley men who grew up in deprived families. They lacked self-confidence, a sense of emotional well-being, and achievement goals in adolescence, but at midlife they were almost equal to the nondeprived on health and work-life accomplishments. Perhaps the mastery of adversity has relevance to this turning point. The longtime director of the Berkeley Guidance Study, Jean Macfarlane (1963, 338), comes to this conclusion from anecdotal materials when she speculates about the positive changes observed in the lives of a number of boys who had very difficult childhoods.

Macfarlane claims that some of the Berkeley boys had become more stable and effective adults than any of the research team had predicted. Especially noteworthy are the men whose poor academic records, in Macfarlane's account, "completely belie the creative intelligence demands of their present position." A large proportion of the "most outstandingly mature adults in our entire group . . . are recruited from those who were confronted with very difficult situations and whose characteristic responses during childhood and adolescence seemed to us to compound their problems" (Macfarlane 1971, 413). These reflections are not scientific observations by any means, but they do correspond with the results presented here.

Macfarlane seeks explanations for the disparity between early experiences and adult life by stressing the common failure of psychology to recognize the maturing potential of hardship experiences, particularly when they are not overwhelming. As she observes, "We have learned that no one becomes mature without living through the pains and confusions of maturing experiences." She also addresses the developmental significance of late adolescence and early adult experiences, including the potential of later events for altering life trajectories. In her view, a number of the boys did not achieve a sense of ego identity and strength until later transitions "forced them or presented an opportunity to them to fulfill a role that gave them a sense of worth." Developmental gains, she surmises, may be associated with a departure from home and community, changes that promote both the need and the opportunity to "work through the early confusions and inhibitions" (Macfarlane 1971, 341).

As a clinical psychologist with developmental interests, Macfarlane did not concern herself with larger processes of historical change such as the economic collapse of the 1930s, mass migration, or war mobilization. More than 70 percent of the boys in her study were recruited into the military from the end of World War II to the Korean War. The Berkeley boys were young teenagers when many eighteen- and nineteen-year-olds were entering the armed forces in World War II. However, Macfarlane never mentions this often traumatic passage into adulthood.

In 1985 we surveyed all men from the Oakland and Berkeley studies who had served in the military on the benefits of service (Elder and Clipp 1989). Between 60 and 70 percent of the men selected "a broader perspective," "greater independence," "self-discipline," and "learned to cope

with adversity." Half of the men selected the benefits of "learned cooperation," followed by a third or less who chose "education benefits,"
"valuing life more," "positive feelings about self," "lifelong friends," and
"job skills" at the very bottom. Self-confidence in leadership and managerial competence is not mentioned in this survey, though "command
experiences" placed a great many young men in positions of leadership,
often with little preparation.

Confidence in one's capacity to lead was nurtured by bonds of comradeship. From interviews with Chicago veterans, Alan Ehrenhalt (1995,
219) concludes that "common experience" in World War II was a "confidence builder unlike anything that any generation of American political
leaders had experienced. It led them to the conclusion that they were the
natural wellspring of leadership and authority in the community, no matter how young they might be, and that the citizens would accept them."

For children of the Great Depression, higher education, a good marriage, and military service offered plausible exits from disadvantage. In
the state of California, access to higher education was available at relatively low cost, and educational benefits from the GI bill made this option more attractive. A good marriage provided social support for men
and a means for women to escape the limitations of family misfortune.
Military service has long been viewed as a bridge to greater opportunity
for disadvantaged populations, and it became the centerpiece of our
work because it often led to both college and marriage. Entry into the
armed forces established social independence from family influences,
provided a time-out from age-graded pressures, and offered a broad
range of developmental experiences that come with overseas duty.

By pulling young men from diverse and insular communities and plac-
ing them on large training bases, military mobilization favored dramatic
life changes, breaking the hold of family hardship. Induction "knifed
off" the recruit's past experience, however disadvantaged or privileged,
and basic training fostered peer equality and comradeship. In addition
to independence, the military provided a legitimate time-out from educational, work, and family pressures in a structured environment. This
break from age expectations enabled youth to think about their futures
in terms of the present and past. The third feature of mobilization entailed a broader range of experiences. Fortunately, war casualties were
very light in the Berkeley and Oakland cohorts.

Berkeley youth from deprived families responded to the military option as if it provided a path to greater opportunity. They observed the respect accorded men in uniform during World War II, and this prestige
became a popular goal. Boys from deprived families were more likely
than other youth to enter the service before the age of twenty-one (Elder
1986). In this context, military service could reduce the persistence of disadvantage by enabling these young men to use their personal resources

to maximum effect in education, work, and family. Motivation is part of the explanation, along with personal qualities that veterans ascribe to their service experience—such as self-discipline, effective coping with adversity, and skill in managing people.

With these distinctions in mind, we assumed that military service would be more predictive of occupational achievement among Berkeley men from hard-pressed families than among the nondeprived. Furthermore, we expected this effect to be expressed through higher education. The results conform to these expectations (Elder 1999, 315): military service had a significant effect only among the economically deprived, whereas IQ was generally predictive in both groups. In addition, the military effect occurred primarily through higher education. Judging from these results, we concluded that some children of the Depression broke the cycle of disadvantage by entering the service. The more privileged men, from nondeprived homes, made their way in adulthood largely in terms of their own abilities. Military service was not a factor.

Military service altered men's life course and enhanced their developmental change up to midlife. The effects appeared most clearly when we compared two groups of Berkeley men who were similar in background—the early entrants into military service and the men who were not mobilized (Elder 1986). Four identical measures of psychological functioning in adolescence and at the age of forty were compared—goal orientation, social competence, submissiveness, and self-perceptions of adequacy. The veterans ranked well below the nonveterans on these measures in adolescence, but by midlife, this difference had faded to insignificance. Developmental gains turned out to be significantly greater among men who entered the service at an early age than the men who remained civilians. Moreover, the men became more positive about self, more socially competent, and more assertive by the age of forty.

These constructive life changes are linked to early entry, a timing that minimizes the disruption of mobilization and maximizes the benefits, such as skill training and later education through the GI bill. Early entry occurs before marriage, children, and even a stable career. Similar life-course benefits were observed among the Oakland men (Elder 1987), but what about a more disadvantaged population? Does early timing also matter for young men who are not likely to go on to college?

Using a panel of approximately one thousand Boston men from low-income families, Robert Sampson and John Laub (1996) found comparable results on early entry into the military. All of the men in their study were born between the mid-1920s and mid-1930s. They were originally members of Sheldon and Eleanor Glueck's (1968) matched sample of delinquents and controls. As expected, there were more dishonorable discharges and other forms of misconduct among the delinquents, but they were also more likely to benefit from the service over their life course when compared with the controls. This was especially the case for men who entered the service early. The benefits show up in terms of occupational status, job stability, and economic well-being in the middle years.

If military service provided a bridge to opportunity for men (born before 1935) who entered the military at an early age, the negative consequences may be concentrated in the lives of men who were mobilized much later, after marriage, children, and the beginnings of their careers. Late-entry veterans from the Oakland and Berkeley cohorts frequently cited career and family disruptions and separations as the most important costs of their service experience (Elder 1986, 1987). To address these issues, we focused on the Terman men who entered the service at an average age of twenty-nine.

Men in the older cohort (born before 1911) hit both the Depression and the war years at an "untimely point" in their lives compared with men who were born later (Elder and Chan 1999). They completed their higher education just as the economy collapsed, whereas the younger men continued their schooling through much of the Depression decade. More than a third of the older men were recruited for military duty. They experienced more divorce, greater work-life instability, and poorer health in comparison with the younger veterans. They also tended to retire at a younger age, regardless of health, and were less active in retirement than other men. Timeliness, then, represents an important correlate of enduring military influences from the 1930s to the postwar years.

A number of new research directions emerged from the Berkeley and Terman research on pathways of resilience and vulnerability. The first is the persistence of disadvantage and the extent to which it is countered by the diverse ways in which young people rise above the limitations of their environments. Second, empirical evidence documents the role of social agencies, personal relationships, and institutional supports in charting a resilient pathway out of disadvantage. Military service, higher education, and supportive marital relations were all important in this respect in the Berkeley studies. More research is needed on how military service changes the course and substance of lives, with an eye toward providing alternative transitional experiences. The influence of significant others beyond the family, such as teachers and coaches in school and ministers and youth workers in religious communities, is not well understood (see Furstenberg et al. 1999). Effective social interventions would benefit from a greater understanding of the pathways by which many young people escape the disadvantages of their social context.

Another research direction also has important policy implications: the strategic benefits of studying human development and aging from the early years to late life across the life course. Aging is a lifelong process, and the pioneering longitudinal studies at the Institute of Human Development at Berkeley have enabled me to study human development and aging across the life span. Most important from a policy standpoint, they have enabled me to investigate the formative experiences and pathways that account for the kinds of older adults young people become. Some young people follow a life course of resilience, whereas others end up in a downward spiral of increasing vulnerability.

Studies that follow children into adulthood and the later years make possible research on the link between changing times and lives. By contrast, none of the nationwide longitudinal studies that begin with older adults (for example, the Health and Retirement Survey and the older cohorts of the National Longitudinal Survey) have traced the impact of changing times (such as the Great Depression and wars) on lives and patterns of aging. Substantial attrition of study members severely limits such work in samples that begin with older adults. More generally, these samples rule out systematic study of the formative years of life and their developmental trajectories. In the field of aging, it is time that research funds be applied more proactively to opportunities for extending longitudinal studies of the first half of the life course.

Up to this point I have described the evolution of my studies of lives and times, with emphasis on the Berkeley studies, the interplay of research question and longitudinal data, and efforts to meet the need for appropriate theory and methods. The pathways followed may seem logical in retrospective accounts. The "accidental" feature of lives and the serendipity of key events can be lost in the attempt to make sense of paths taken. A life review that looks back across countless choice points, on the other hand, might note that I could have chosen a different path and become, most likely, a social scientist with a different mission and career. In closing, I reflect on the course I have followed, the paths not chosen, and some markers along the way.

Learning About Lives:
Markers Along the Way

Academic careers generally consist of a history of interactive relations between person and project. Changes in life trajectory are likely to influence the project, usually in ways unrecognized at the time; and changes in the project have implications for the investigator's knowledge, learning experience, and identity. Some careers are marked by a sequence of different careers and projects. Others may be linked to a lifelong project. Both can have enduring themes.

No theme better defines the work I have done over the years than the relationship between changing times and lives. It is easier to see and appreciate such a theme after several decades of work. Indeed, I did not think of myself in terms of this theme during the first decade of my postdoctoral research. Nevertheless, social change in lives was prominent throughout the research I completed in graduate school. Even my master's thesis examined change, the reference group orientations of students in the transition to college from small and large communities. My doctoral dissertation included a chapter on the changing family in the United States and its consequences for children. However, neither project was longitudinal or informed by knowledge of how to think about and study changing times and lives.

What event launched me on the road to such knowledge? Frequent early changes in residence may have been a factor, including a move from Cleveland to a Pennsylvania farm during my high school years. In large part, however, I believe the most significant factor was the transition from doctoral studies on a large cross-sectional study of adolescents to research with a longitudinal data archive that extended over thirty years, the Oakland Growth Study at the Institute of Human Development. The Oakland study forced me to address multiple changes over many years and their relations to one another—change in the economy and community across the 1930s, in families as they adapted to their context, and in the individual study members. The early challenges to life-course thinking are plain to see in this exploration. How to think about the changing lives of children and parents, their social patterning by events, social roles, and their sequences? How to connect social change to individual development?

With data on men and women from late childhood to the age of forty, as of 1962, the Oakland study also challenged me to think about human development beyond childhood and adolescence. My exposure to these challenges in longitudinal records clearly represented a decisive marker in my scientific development. Doctoral studies did not equip me to address these issues, but the Berkeley institute's community of colleagues, staff, and students offered assistance in coming up with effective ways of proceeding.

Another important marker consisted of a supportive but demanding environment in which to develop versions of *Children of the Great Depression*. During the summer of 1965, I produced a lengthy manuscript that described the effect of the Great Depression on the Oakland families, parents, and children. I remember showing this manuscript to John Clausen, then director of the institute. He was interested in it and actually cited the manuscript in a chapter he was writing, but he did not believe that I would carry on with the project. However, the puzzle of times and lives kept me going. I wanted to know how the depressed 1930s had made a difference in lives. The puzzle remained unresolved until the 1970s when I completed the final draft. Between this draft and the earlier version, I strengthened the book's conceptual structure. This intervening time provided a developmental experience in learning to think in life-course ways.

During the last months of working on the book (in 1971), I realized the need for a comparative birth cohort, the sample from the Berkeley Guidance Study, who were born between 1927 and 1930. A sabbatical year in Berkeley (from the summer of 1972 until the fall of 1973) to work up the Berkeley data represents another important marker in my scientific development because it enabled me to elaborate and generalize the original study and its archival methods. I remember the glaring contrast between the life histories and data files I prepared for *Children of the Great Depression* and the more sophisticated life histories and files I worked up on the Berkeley Guidance Study members. This method largely remained an oral tradition for another twenty years until I prepared with colleagues a methodology primer, *Working with Archival Data* (Elder, Pavalko, and Clipp 1993). An account of life-course methods emerged in the late 1990s (Giele and Elder 1998) through collaboration with colleagues on modes of data collection, file construction, and data storage and retrieval.

Just as the Oakland Growth Study moved me toward life-course studies, *Children of the Great Depression* produced readers that challenged me to clarify the theory and improve the methods. I most fully recognized this career marker when I sat down to prepare another chapter for the twenty-fifth anniversary edition of the book (Elder 1999). A new chapter 11 tells the story of advances in life-course theory and methods over the past twenty-five years and reveals some of the limitations of the original work. Most important, *Children of the Great Depression* failed to address the effects of World War II. This omission led to a program of research on war and military service in the lives of men, including studies in other countries (see Elder and Meguro 1987).

The book crosses the boundaries of sociology, psychology, and history, and I learned much from readers in each field. Interactions with historians while writing the book deepened my understanding of social history and led to collaborative efforts in 1975 to study the life course in 1880s Massachusetts (Hareven 1978). A weeklong conference in Williamstown, Massachusetts, provided the integrating exchange. Developmental psychologists tend to focus attention on the need for greater understanding of mechanisms that account for behavioral change and continuity. In the mid-1980s, these dialogues led to a book project that involved both developmentalists and historians, entitled *Children in Time and Place* (Elder, Modell, and Parke 1993). My colleagues and I believed at the time that developmentalists could benefit from the work of historians, by bringing social contexts to lives, and that historians had much to gain from knowledge of developmental theories and studies.

In the use of any approach or method, questions arise as to its applicability to other types of phenomena. Studies of wartime experience represent one application beyond the Great Depression, and an ongoing study of change in the rural Midwest represents another (Elder and Conger 2000). A massive economic downturn in the rural Midwest around 1980 led to my collaboration with a research team at Iowa State University in planning a multiyear study of economic stress in families and its effects on children. The basic model for this project came from the Depression study, with its focus on the family as a bridge between the declining economy and the lives of children. Unlike the Depression study and research on World War II, the Iowa project involved the construction of a longitudinal data archive. A total of 451 rural families were selected from eight north-central counties of the state; each family included a seventh-grade child and a sibling near in age. Data were collected by interview, survey form, and video tapes from 1989 through 1992 from both parents and children. The study has continued through data collections in 1994, 1995, 1997, and 2000. The original children are now in their midtwenties.

This research extension to rural America marked a new career stage and expanded the expertise I had gained from two decades of life-course studies. In this project I returned to the richness of data and perspectives that was characteristic of the Berkeley longitudinal studies. Although quantitative and qualitative data have often been assigned to different projects, the Berkeley and Iowa studies have made me more aware of the advantages of bringing both sets of data to the investigation of questions.

In the first stage of the Iowa project, Rand D. Conger and I traced the effects on children of economic hardship and pressure through family relations and the behavior of parents (Conger and Elder 1994). The impact of the economic decline, we learned, tended to fade over time. After four years, even the most distressed families and children had recovered to a remarkable degree. This finding led me to focus on pathways of resilience, a recurring theme in my prior studies of historical change, decline, and discontinuity. As reported by *Children of the Land* (Elder and Conger 2000), resilience among families and the young has much to do with community ties to social institutions, such as the local church and schools. Today we find that families on the land are more involved in these institutions, and their involvement is reflected in the school and community activities of their children. This culture of farm life also fostered work and academic disciplines in the young. All of these factors, along with the emotional support of parents, account for why children with farming ties to the land tended to outperform other students on academics and social leadership through the high school years.

In the years that lie ahead, the Iowa study is likely to become another landmark study in a region that has been much neglected by the social and behavioral sciences. There is literally no other study like it on rural society. With the addition of children from single-parent families in 1991, the panel study should reflect the imprint of rural change in the coming decade. The twenty-first century will find the study members in their twenties, the parents in their fifties and sixties, and most of the grand-parents in their seventies and eighties. Data collection will undoubtedly continue in the years ahead.

As a whole, these studies of changing times and lives have under-scored one important lesson for me and, I hope, for others. The lives people live and their developmental pathways are inextricably bound to particular social contexts and their social relationships. They reflect changing times and places—from the proximal worlds of local commu-nities to regions and the larger society. Change is expressed in the pop-ulation and cultural diversity, in social structures and institutions. What is most challenging is the fact that such change occurs across people's lives, not simply in restricted periods. This observation calls for study of the continual influence of social contexts across the life course, as social advantages and disadvantages cumulate. This demanding task remains unfinished though increasingly feasible.

A related lesson stems from the consequences of studying lives out of context. The early pioneers in longitudinal studies typically ignored the social context of lives, and consequently they risked misinterpreting the changes observed in the lives of their study members. They also were bound to ignore the social processes that constitute human development and the important explanatory mechanisms. Thus, for example, military service among the Berkeley panel members played an important role in turning men's lives away from the hardships of poverty to a better life through education, work, and marriage. It was not, however, recognized as such as a turning point. Other explanations were proposed instead.

Finally, the phenomenal growth of prospective and retrospective lon-gitudinal studies has made possible studies that can be used to address the issues posed in this chapter. These studies have also made possible remarkable advances in investigating human development and aging across the life span. Considering where we are today, it is still difficult for me to realize that my career began at a time when the empirical study of lives depended on access to a handful of longitudinal studies. The merit of such data was not generally appreciated, and great effort was expended in trying to fund panel studies. Now we are endowed with a wide array of longitudinal studies, both here and abroad; and we have the questions, theory, and methods to make the best of them. We have indeed come a long way in the study of lives.

Note

1. My project covered members of two different studies at the Institute of Human Development. The Oakland Growth Study includes up to two hun-dred people who attended public elementary schools in the northeastern cen-

ter of Oakland, California. Born between 1919 and 1922, their story of growing up in the 1930s is told in *Children of the Great Depression: Social Change in
Life Experience* (Elder 1974, reissued in expanded form 1999); additional research on this Depression experience is reported in Elder, Nguyen, and Caspi
1985. The Berkeley Guidance Study covers more than two hundred children
who were born at the end of the 1920s, between 1927 and 1930. Their Depression experience into adulthood is told in a number of publications, including
Elder 1979; Elder and Liker 1982; Elder, Liker, and Jaworski 1984; Elder, Liker,
and Cross 1984; Elder, Caspi, and Nguyen 1986; Elder, Caspi, and Downey
1986; and Elder, Downey, and Cross 1986. The Oakland and Berkeley birth cohorts were compared in a 1979 publication, and the results are reported in the
twenty-fifth anniversary edition of *Children of the Great Depression* (Elder 1999).

References

Brückner, Erica, and Karl U. Mayer. 1998. "Collecting Life History Data: Experiences from the German Life History Study." In *Methods of Life Course Research: Qualitative and Quantitative Approaches,* edited by J. Z. Giele and G. H.
Elder Jr. Thousand Oaks, Calif.: Sage Publications.

Conger, Rand D., and G. H. Elder Jr. 1994. *Families in Troubled Times: Adapting to
Change in Rural America.* Hawthorne, N.Y.: Aldine de Gruyter.

Ehrenhalt, Alan. 1995. *The Lost City: The Forgotten Virtues of Community in America.* New York: Basic Books.

Elder, Glen H., Jr. 1973. "Economic Deprivation in the Life Course." Unpublished report to National Science Foundation. First Year. Prepared at the University of California, Berkeley (July).

———. 1974. *Children of the Great Depression: Social Change in Life Experience.*
Chicago: University of Chicago Press.

———. 1979. "Historical Change in Life Patterns and Personality." In *Life-Span
Development and Behavior,* edited by P. B. Baltes and Orville G. Brim Jr. Vol. 2.
New York: Academic Press.

———. 1984. "Families, Kin, and the Life Course: A Sociological Perspective."
In *Review of Child Development Research: The Family,* edited by R. D. Parke.
Chicago: University of Chicago Press.

———. 1986. "Military Times and Turning Points in Men's Lives." *Developmental Psychology* 22(2): 233–45.

———. 1987. "War Mobilization and the Life Course: A Cohort of World War II
Veterans." *Sociological Forum* 2(3): 449–72.

———. 1998a. "The Life Course and Human Development." In *Theoretical Models of Human Development,* edited by R. M. Lerner, vol. 1 of *Handbook of Child
Psychology,* edited by William Damon. 5th ed. New York: Wiley.

———. 1998b. "The Life Course as Developmental Theory." *Child Development*
69(1): 1–12.

———. 1999. *Children of the Great Depression: Social Change in Life Experience.*
Twenty-fifth anniversary edition. Boulder, Colo.: Westview Press.

Elder, Glen H., Jr., Avshalom Caspi, and Geraldine Downey. 1986. "Problem Behavior and Family Relationships: Life Course and Intergenerational Themes."

In *Human Development and the Life Course: Multidisciplinary Perspectives,* edited by Aage B. Sørensen, Franz E. Weinert, and Lonnie R. Sherrod. Hillsdale, N.J.: Lawrence Erlbaum Associates.

Elder, Glen H., Jr., Avshalom Caspi, and Tri Van Nguyen. 1986. "Resourceful and Vulnerable Children: Family Influences in Hard Times." In *Development as Action in Context,* edited by R. K. Silbereisen, K. Eyferth, and G. Rudinger. Berlin: Springer-Verlag.

Elder, Glen H., Jr., and Christopher Chan. 1999. "War's Legacy in Men's Lives." In *A Nation Divided: Diversity, Inequality, and Community in American Society,* edited by P. Moen, D. Dempster-McClain, and H. A. Walker. Ithaca: Cornell University Press.

Elder, Glen H., Jr., and Elizabeth Colerick Clipp. 1989. "Combat Experience and Emotional Health: Impairment and Resilience in Later Life." *Journal of Personality* 57(2): 311–41.

Elder, Glen H., Jr., and Rand D. Conger. 2000. *Children of the Land: Adversity and Success in Rural America.* Chicago: University of Chicago Press.

Elder, Glen H., Jr., Geraldine Downey, and Catherine E. Cross. 1986. "Family Ties and Life Chances: Hard Times and Hard Choices in Women's Lives Since the Great Depression." In *Life-Span Developmental Psychology: International Relations,* edited by Nancy Datan, Anita L. Green, and Hayne W. Reece. Hillsdale, N.J.: Lawrence Erlbaum Associates.

Elder, Glen H., Jr., and Monica Kirkpatrick Johnson. 2002. "The Life Course and Aging: Challenges, Lessons, and New Directions." In *Invitation to the Life Course: Toward New Understandings of Later Life,* edited by Richard A. Settersten, Jr. Amityville, N.Y.: Baywood Publishing Company.

Elder, Glen H.,Jr., and Jeffrey K. Liker. 1982. "Hard Times in Women's Lives: Historical Influences Across 430 Years." *American Journal of Sociology* 88(2): 241–69.

Elder, Glen H., Jr., Jeffrey K. Liker, and Catherine E. Cross. 1984. "Parent-Child Behavior in the Great Depression: Life Course and Intergeneration Influences." In *Life-Span Development and Behavior,* edited by Paul B. Baltes and Orville G. Brim, Jr. Vol. 6. New York: Academic Press.

Elder, Glen H., Jr., Jeffrey K. Liker, and Bernard J. Jaworski. 1984. "Hardship in Lives: Depression Influences from the 1930s to Old Age in Postwar America." In *Life-Span Developmental Psychology: Historical and Generational Effects,* edited by Kathleen McClurskey and Hayne Reese. New York: Academic Press.

Elder, Glen H., Jr., and Yoriko Meguro. 1987. "Wartime in Men's Lives: A Comparative Study of American and Japanese Cohorts." *International Journal of Behavioral Development* 10: 439–66.

Elder, Glen H., Jr., John Modell, and Ross D. Parke, eds. 1993. *Children in Time and Place: Developmental and Historical Insights.* New York: Cambridge University Press.

Elder, Glen H., Jr., Tri Van Nguyen, and Avshalom Caspi. 1985. "Linking Family Hardship to Children's Lives." *Child Development* 56: 361–75.

Elder, Glen H., Jr., Eliza K. Pavalko, and Elizabeth C. Clipp. 1993. *Working with Archival Data: Studying Lives.* Newbury Park, Calif.: Sage Publications.

218   *Looking at Lives*

Furstenberg, Frank F., Thomas Cook, Jacquelynne Eccles, Glen H. Elder, and Arnold Sameroff. 1999. *Managing to Make It: Urban Families in High-Risk Neighborhoods*. Chicago: University of Chicago Press.

Giele, Janet A., and Glen H. Elder Jr., eds. 1998. *Methods of Life Course Research: Qualitative and Quantitative Approaches*. Thousand Oaks, Calif.: Sage Publications.

Glueck, Sheldon, and Eleanor Glueck. 1968. *Delinquents and Nondelinquents in Perspective*. Cambridge, Mass.: Harvard University Press.

Hareven, Tamara K. 1978. *Transitions: The Family and the Life Course in Historical Perspective*. New York: Academic Press.

Hill, Reuben, and Nelson N. Foote. 1970. *Family Development in Three Generations: A Longitudinal Study of Changing Family Patterns of Planning and Achievement*. Cambridge, Mass.: Schenkman.

Macfarlane, Jean W. 1963. "From Infancy to Adulthood." *Childhood Education* 39(7): 336–42.

———. 1971. "Perspectives on Personality Consistency and Change from the Guidance Study." In *The Course of Human Development: Selected Papers from the Longitudinal Studies, Institute of Human Development, the University of California, Berkeley*, edited by Mary C. Jones, Nancy Bayley, Jean W. Macfarlane, and Margery P. Honzik. Waltham, Mass.: Xerox College Publishing.

Mills, C. Wright. 1959. *The Sociological Imagination*. New York: Oxford University Press.

Rutter, Michael. 1985. "Resilience in the Face of Adversity: Protective Factors and Resistance to Psychiatric Disorder." *British Journal of Psychiatry* 147(b): 598–611.

Rutter, Michael, and Nicola Madge. 1976. *Cycles of Disadvantage: A Review of Research*. London: Heinemann.

Ryder, Norman B. 1965. "The Cohort as a Concept in the Study of Social Change." *American Sociological Review* 30(6): 843–61.

Sampson, Robert J., and John H. Laub. 1996. "Socioeconomic Achievement in the Life Course of Disadvantaged Men: Military Service as a Turning Point, Circa 1940–1965." *American Sociological Review* 61(3): 347–67.

Thomas, William I., and Edmund H. Volkart. 1951. *Social Behavior and Personality: Contributions of W. I. Thomas to Theory and Social Research*. New York: Social Science Research Council.

Wilensky, Harold L. 1961. "Orderly Careers and Social Participation in the Middle Mass." *American Sociological Review* 26(4): 521–39.

Young, Copeland H., Kristen L. Savola, and Erin Phelps. 1991. *Inventory of Longitudinal Studies in the Social Sciences*. Newbury Park, Calif.: Sage Publications.

Chapter 9

Phenomenological Perspectives on Natural History Research: The Longitudinal Harlem Adolescent Cohort Study

ANN F. BRUNSWICK

WHAT A CHALLENGE, to recapitulate—as the editors of this book of papers from the Landmark Conference on longitudinal studies requested—experiences from a thirty-year broadly scoped life-history study of an African American cohort and compress them into a single chapter in a book. The editors' charge was to move beyond particular findings and search out their personal meaning and impact on both my professional and personal life; to consider their social policy implications and their implications for the conduct of longitudinal research. This required a shift away from the neutral, objective stance to which the scientist usually aspires to a contemplative, experiential one, a shift not easily achieved. If there is any lesson learned from a thirty-year study with a single community cohort, however, it is that no challenge is so great that an attempt to meet it cannot be made. The first word of this paper's title is intended to capture this attempt.

Adopting this phenomenological perspective, I realized, first, that a subtle effect of conducting a longitudinal study with a socially marginalized or minority group is that, through immersion in the cohort's experiences, reports of both current events and the research of others are appraised by how well they agree with what I have observed in my study group. That this identification is a particular and unintended by-product of engagement in a long-term prospective study brings to mind a special note of appreciation for the book's editors in their reference to "participants," not "human subjects." This conveys what too often is either overlooked or left unsaid: that any human research, even more so when it is longitudinal, must be a two-way collaboration between the investigator and the participants.

On the following pages, the experiences, lessons learned, and professional and personal impact of the Longitudinal Harlem Adolescent Cohort Study have been organized around a tripartite view of research: conceptualizing the problem (theory, hypotheses, study questions), conducting the research (procedures and methodology), and administration and management (the necessary though unrewarding chores associated with conducting research—staffing, budgeting, reporting, and other bureaucratic obligations and hassles). Within each of these areas special challenges and compensations arise when the research is longitudinal. Because life-history studies follow developing lives in changing contexts (be they changing historic events, secular trends, changing economic opportunities and political climates, changing social norms and values, or changing personal networks), these contextual factors are intricately and indissolubly linked to the particular ethnoracial identity of my study cohort of urban African Americans born in the 1950s (between 1951 and 1958). It is a group characterized by different strengths of ties to the existing social opportunity structure, both within the group and between the group and the dominant white culture.

My Lost Youth: History of the Longitudinal Harlem Adolescent Health Survey

What is now a life-course or natural history study of health, substance use, and human immunodeficiency virus (HIV) infection began more than thirty years ago as a cross-sectional survey of a community-representative sample of adolescents drawn from a single inner-city hospital district, central Harlem, in New York City. Birth pains, as well as a near abortion, attended this beginning. In 1968, Columbia University was not the place from which to launch a study in Harlem, a largely ghetto community contiguous to the university. The Harlem community recently had been antagonized by the university's proposal for a new gymnasium with a separate entrance for community access (Josephson 1970). Protests against this particular study were mounted, including a community march down Broadway to the university's main campus, and leaflets distributed at subway entrances and on the street proclaimed, "Don't tell nobody your business. What white cops couldn't do they're now sending black interviewers to do." The study directors were called down to the university provost's office and asked to cancel the research. Fortunately, we did not acquiesce to the request. Instead, a community advisory committee was activated through whose good graces and guidance we were able to proceed with our planned study. As a concession to community concerns, we deleted direct questioning of the adolescents about their substance use, other than alcohol and cigarettes, a concession that even the community advisory group regretted before two years had passed. Collecting systematic histories of drug use, as a consequence, began in the second study wave.[1]

In April 1968 the Harlem Adolescent Health Survey was successfully launched, with a starting staff of approximately twenty trained field interviewers. According to the survey design, over the course of the next two years the staff would conduct interviews with 668 African American adolescents, who were ages twelve through seventeen at the start of the survey. The sample was similarly drawn over two years from a stratified area probability sample of central Harlem residences, using a sampling ratio of 4 percent (one in twenty-five households) each year. With funding from the U.S. Department of Maternal and Child Health Services (formerly the Children's Bureau), the objective was to provide a comprehensive description of health problems and needs for health care, including recommendations for meeting those needs in what was then a medically underserved adolescent population. Study procedures and content benefited from the guidance of the community advisory committee throughout what became a longitudinal survey. (Unfortunately, death has claimed many of the original committee members— another problem peculiar to longitudinal research but seemingly exacerbated when the community represented is one, such as this, with lower life expectancy than the general population.)

A brief introductory personal interview with a parent—usually the mother—preceded the detailed one-and-a-half-hour structured personal interview, which included both precoded and open-ended questions, with the adolescent. Interviews were conducted in the adolescent's home by the specially recruited, gender- and race-matched young adult interviewers, who were given their assignments only after they had completed an intensive weeklong training session and demonstrated their ability on at least two practice interviews. Half or more of well-screened applicants dropped out of interviewer training, an experience repeated in subsequent study waves. This self-selection process was a fortunate by-product of the rigorous training procedures, leaving the better motivated and more capable interviewers to handle the assignments. One trainee lasted until the fifth day, during which time his attire had graduated from grey flannel suit to dashiki. He announced his withdrawal, based on ideological principles, explaining that he could not lend himself to a study that would reveal so much about African American adolescents' thoughts and feelings to a white researcher. I respected his decision in the context of the black zeitgeist of the late 1960s. His was not the usual reaction. For a number of other interviewers, work on the study has led to ongoing careers in interviewing and related fields. This is an example of another reward of longitudinal research, staff development.

The 668 adolescent interviews constituted a completion rate of 83 percent of the listed sample. To supplement information from the personal interviews, adolescents were invited to a free two-hour medical examination arranged by the study's medical team and conducted at the local municipal Harlem Hospital. Seventy-five percent of those interviewed showed up for the exam. Additionally, school data (academic grades, achievement test scores, health histories) were abstracted from school records. Detailed procedures and findings from the adolescent study were published in a special *American Journal of Public Health* supplement (Brunswick and Josephson 1972).

Activities were undertaken to disseminate major study findings. A daylong community conference was held at the local hospital, attended by primary health-care providers, health educators, parents, and the adolescents themselves. Adolescents cochaired each of ten workshop groups along with a health professional. Local political and newspaper representatives also attended. Finally, on the basis of findings from the study and the recommendations from the community conference, the investigator joined the study's community advisory committee in its efforts to establish an adolescent service at Harlem Hospital, where none had previously existed. The adolescent unit continues in service today. These activities are noted here because "context" refers not only to an important dimension in longitudinal research but also to a locus of research activity, a part of the requisite two-way collaboration between researcher and community. Longitudinal study brings the community into the research (which occurs ipso facto when a community representative sample is the data source) and brings the research into the community.

On a personal note, the timing of this research on adolescence intersected with my personal life history: my daughters, who were twelve and fifteen years old at the time, served as guinea pigs for testing questions I was developing for the adolescent interview. Their manifest interest in being asked about health and healthful activities, self-esteem, personal efficacy, time orientation, aspirations, and expectations was subsequently echoed in the reaction of the adolescents in the Harlem sample.

My summative conclusion from the adolescent phase of this research related to the high degree of interest that "ghetto" adolescents showed in their own health, along with their willingness and ability to talk about it. (The significance of this finding is that, even thirty years later, health information still is often sought from the parent rather than directly from the adolescent.) My conclusion was echoed in the reaction of the study's examining physicians, who had not anticipated the adolescents' willing participation. In poststudy debriefings, they admitted that experience in this study had changed their attitudes about working with adolescents: initially fearful, they had grown to enjoy them as responsive "patients."

The study became longitudinal in 1975 and 1976 with second interviews conducted when cohort members were between the ages of eighteen and twenty-three, inclusive. The second wave (funded by the National Institute on Drug Abuse, as were all subsequent study waves) was designed to use the adolescent health information as a baseline for analyzing health consequences of substance use, licit and illicit. Reinterviews were completed in 1975 and 1976 with 536 Harlem adolescents—89 percent of the original sample who were still alive and not identified with residences beyond sixty miles from New York City. (This geographic limitation was imposed in all restudy waves for both budgetary and methodological reasons, specifically, to limit variance that would come from geographic heterogeneity.)

Reflecting the effect of historical context on the conduct of research, in the first two study waves the sponsoring agencies doubted that the proposed surveys could be successfully completed, given their locus in the minority community. For this reason funding in both the first and second study waves was released in two stages: partial funding was disbursed for a feasibility study with a limited part of the sample and then, upon demonstration of results, full funding was granted to complete the research.

The third study wave was conducted in 1983, seven to eight years after the second, when panel members were aged twenty-six through thirty-two and approximately fifteen years had elapsed since the study began. The response rate was 86 percent of the surviving second-wave sample (net of those located with addresses beyond the sixty-mile limit of New York City). Combined with fifteen respondents who had not been available for their second interviews, a total of 426 interviews were completed in the third wave.

The fourth and fifth study waves were conducted, respectively, in 1989 and 1990, when participants were aged thirty-two through thirty-seven, and in 1993, with participants at ages thirty-six through forty-one. The prospective natural history study of HIV and AIDS (acquired immunodeficiency syndrome) infection in the cohort became a central concern in these waves. Interviews included questions directed at perceptions, attitudes, and behaviors associated with HIV transmission and infection risk in addition to the ongoing health, substance use, and psychosocial histories that were collected in every study wave. Immediately following these interviews in the home, respondents were asked to provide a blood sample (fourth wave, with 79 percent participation) or saliva sample (fifth wave, with 90 percent cooperation) for HIV-1 antigen assay. With the approval of the Columbia University Health Sciences Institutional Review Board, these assays were performed "for research purposes only" so that participation necessary for obtaining population representative results might be maximized. (Phlebotomists and interviewers encouraged participants to obtain a personal HIV test. The study arranged the appointments and offered a stipend plus carfare for keeping their personal test appointments.)

Characteristics of the full interviewed sample were compared with those participating in the HIV assay; no differential loss appeared on any of the sex or drug-injecting risk behaviors, assuring external validity of the relationships between HIV risk behaviors, other predictors, and infection that were observed in the tested sample. Comparison of the subsample of tested respondents with those of the full interviewed cohort calls to mind an important advantage (as well as one of the obligations) of longitudinal studies generally: continued testing for potential selection bias from sample attrition. The latter is to some degree unavoidable in longitudinal research, no matter how arduous the efforts at sample retention.

Parenthetically, not all sample loss denotes bias. That from mortality, for example, reflected the actual experiences of the cohort and its composition as members aged. By the time participants reached the ages of approximately thirty-six to forty-one, 17 percent of the men and 5 percent of the women in the cohort had died. Homicide accounted for 29 percent of all male deaths in the cohort by these ages, nearly one quarter (23 percent) resulted from HIV-AIDS infection, and 7 percent was otherwise attributable to substance misuse. Among females, HIV-AIDS accounted for 41 percent and substance misuse for 24 percent of deaths (half of this related to alcohol).

Cohort Retention

The homogeneous African American study panel is of predominantly southern U.S., not Caribbean, descent. Fortunately the study cohort was recruited during adolescence, before the critical early adult ages when the most socially estranged African American males become undercounted in the census and in adult household samples. This advantage of sample listing at earlier ages can be seen when comparing the sample composition at our most recent interview wave (in 1993), twenty-five years after the original adolescent survey. Males still constituted 48 percent of study participants (compared with 52 percent representation in adolescence, a gender-biased attrition substantially linked to the elevated male mortality risk of 17 percent compared with 5 percent for females). In the 1990 New York City census, in contrast, males constituted only 41 percent of the non-Hispanic black population at equivalent ages. The fifth wave of the study retained 74 percent of the entire initial adolescent cohort, net of deaths and of those residing outside the sixty-mile radius of New York City.

Among all the procedural concerns in longitudinal research, none is more important than maximizing cohort retention, a necessity for maintaining both the external and internal validity of findings otherwise threatened by biased sample attrition. Sample replenishment or replacement is not an option in prospective longitudinal research, in which each sample member or participant is his or her own control and for whom, accordingly, no substitution is possible. Furthermore, as I have discussed elsewhere (Brunswick 1998b), weighting for missing cases on the basis of demographic matches only (age, race, gender) to the completed cases may be a biased solution because it assumes that those lost to study did not differ on behavioral variables that are likely to be critical to the study.

Maximizing retention of a sample drawn to be representative of a predominantly low-income minority population requires strategic and tactical planning as arduous as any other phase of study. This is particularly the case when confronted with increasing numbers of transients or floaters, those with multiple domiciles, and those without any domicile at all. In all, about a quarter of this sample lacked telephone access. Increasing suspicion of authorities and the increasing difficulty for strangers (that is, interviewers) to gain access to buildings and homes similarly added to the complexity of sample follow-up.

The general strategy used in locating the cohort in each restudy begins with procedures that can simultaneously reach the greatest number (in the case of our study, two mailings enclosing stamped and addressed return envelopes for response letters), followed by telephone contacts (including telephone and reverse address directories) and individually tailored location steps using prior study-wave information (for example, contact with last place of employment, the usual source of medical care [hospital, clinic, or doctor], welfare and housing authorities, corrections department, and even homeless shelter lists). About a year is set aside before fieldwork begins for this address-tracking process. Other procedures that the study has used to maximize sample retention include sending annual Christmas cards, providing medical referrals, presenting honoraria for participation, emphasizing interviewer-respondent rapport (such as matching interviewers with respondents by gender and race and stressing courtesy and confidentiality in interviewer training), pilot interviews and pretesting of interview procedures as well as interview schedules, and repeated callbacks to participants, as necessary, to complete the interview (as many as twenty-five in the fifth wave).

In longitudinal studies, the researcher needs to move into the habitat of the study participant. Locating members of this cohort has required interviewers' visits to relatives, to superintendents and neighbors in the building where the respondent last resided, and to neighborhood streets, stores, churches, and homeless shelters. Identifying and activating linkages to community organizations and involvement in community interests are, therefore, an integral part of maintaining longitudinal studies, perhaps even more so when a geographically defined area is involved such as was the case here. Ties to community organizations help in locating mobile study members who require multiple tracking strategies. Community collaboration and linkages play an obvious role in cohort retention.

Research Model

The research model guiding this project from the outset has posited health as a biopsychosocial complex. Influences affecting health outcomes have been studied within an ecological or contextual perspective—that is, the view that interaction both with the immediate social and physical environment and with more distal societal institutions and the broader social opportunity structure have an impact on a person's health and health-related behaviors. I have discussed these latter influences elsewhere as structural or social strain (Brunswick 1999). Simply put, as the threads that bind a person to the social structure vary in number and strength, his or her health accordingly varies with the resultant stress.

An ecological approach is particularly appropriate for studying health in a minority population. The study's ecological model follows Uri Bronfenbrenner's (1979) theory of "nested contexts" (see table 9.1). It outlines the multiple domains that influence individual behavior and therefore need to be included in causal analyses. Each of the domains is subject to and modified by the societal position of the particular group under study vis-à-vis dominant white middle-class norms and expectations, as well as in relation to the individual's status within the group (Brunswick 1999).

The ecological biopsychosocial framework has been applied to the Harlem study data set with the inclusion of variables on somatic and affective health status; the utilization of medical and dental care; personal health practices; cognitive dispositions (self-perceptions [that is, self-esteem, efficacy, time orientation, hopelessness], general life outlooks, and attainment expectations); substance use histories (cigarettes, alcohol, and nine drugs that are either illegal or used for nonmedical purposes) that measure substance type, age at onset, frequency, recency, and duration of use, mode of administration, and problems arising from their use; substance-misuse treatment histories; role attainment (education, work, fertility, marital, and partnering histories); household composition; residential mobility; and census-tract poverty level. Complete histories are kept also of mortality, by cause based on death certificates. Beginning with the fourth wave, natural histories were expanded to include sexual orientation, number of and relationship to sex partners, cognitive orientations regarding HIV risk and risk behaviors, HIV prevalence, exposure routes, and immunoassay for infection status (see appendix).

Table 9.1 Ecological "Nested Contexts" Paradigm of Influences on Drug Involvement

Level One: Macrosystem (Structural: values, norms, and social expectancies governing behavior)	Level Two: Exosystem (Legal and institutional: situational and institutional arrangements; spatial and temporal factors)	Level Three: Microsystem (Interpersonal: Interpersonal settings, social networks; interpersonal relationships and social bonds)	Level Four: Ontogenic System (Intrapersonal: biopsychosocial attributes and life histories)
General economic and political climate	Drug arrest and interception laws and policies	Familial (spousal, parental, children)	Values, attitudes, beliefs, self-image
Loss of unskilled jobs, migration	Availability and quality of drugs	Peer	Health, biological factors
Gender defined roles and expectations	Ease of access to drug supply	Educational	
Ethnicity and race	Treatment availability	Neighborhood group memberships	
Birth cohort, age	Neighborhood violence	Organizational affiliations	
Geographic location	Churches and church-centered activities	Personal networks within and outside own neighborhood	
Income and wealth	Community drug prevention programs		
	Proximity to educational and recreational facilities		

Source: Brunswick 1999.

Challenges of Longitudinal Research

Considerable agreement probably exists among the investigators whose studies are assembled in this volume about the complexities of conducting longitudinal research. Reflecting on my own experiences over five waves and thirty years of an ongoing study, the least troublesome lie in the theoretical-conceptual domain (see the tripartite research scheme suggested at the beginning of this chapter). The structural-strain ecological theory outlined earlier is adaptive to emerging diseases, changing life situations, and changing patterns of drug use. Following the tripartite research scheme, complexities peculiar to the longitudinal design arise in executing the research and in the administrative domains. A list of these, by no means exhaustive, would include modifications of the interview schedule and data collected necessitated by changing life stage, changing cultural phenomena, or both, along with probing serendipitous findings observed in a prior study wave. The Harlem study provides an example of the latter: during the fourth-wave interviews, four out of five HIV-infected individuals were found to be unaware of their infection (Brunswick 1998a; Brunswick et al. 1993). This prompted the addition of a short battery of questions in the next wave about trajectories to awareness of infection.

Modifications that are required in a key variable that is being tracked for change over time have more far-reaching effects. This was the case with the reported number of health problems, a continuous measure of health status that we use because of its psychometric properties—that is, strong criterion validity when compared with several functional and global health measures and its scalability. The number of particular health conditions initially asked about increased from forty-six at the first wave to sixty-seven at the third and eighty-nine at the fourth and fifth waves. A variety of methods can be and have been applied to adjust for these differences when estimating cross-life-stage change—for example, collapsing individual health problems into a broader body-system classification and using regressed change scores that represent the individual's deviation from the mean number reported by all individuals at that study wave.

Other analysis problems are encountered when a cohort member has missed one or two interviews and returns to the panel in a subsequent study wave. Life-history information, including dates, is collected at every study wave (for example, first and most recent use of a reported substance). This can be helpful in reconstructing missing information by using data from an earlier interview or from retrospective reports on a more recent one (after checking for consistency among the multiple measures). Repeated measures in a longitudinal data set also are useful for estimating bias when comparing procedures that alternately may include or exclude certain individuals or certain values from a study wave. This is but one example of the painstaking care and added time that longitudinal research requires. (Note here, also, the earlier discussion of sample retention and the criticality of each participant when sample replenishment and substitution are not available as alternatives.)

Other difficulties present themselves in relation to storing and merging data from multiple study waves. Changing technology requires updating and changing data processing procedures, both hardware and software. In this study, data from the first wave were stored on punch cards.[2] Mainframe data tapes requiring cold storage were the prevailing technology in the third wave, and analyses were performed through modem connections to the university computer center. The fourth wave still required mainframe tapes (because the data set was too extensive for archives to be stored on personal computers). Variables, therefore, were downloaded from the mainframe as needed for analysis. Enhanced storage capacity allowed all fifth-wave data archives to be stored on individual desktop computers.

Longitudinal data analysis, quite obviously, is more time consuming than data analysis in one-shot studies. More time and, arguably, different skills are entailed that range from painstaking checking for errors when reconstructing the new cross-wave (that is, longitudinal) variables to the increased complexity of the statistical models, procedures, and replications for testing the data.

Perhaps the greatest headache of all in a longitudinal study is that the only constant staff member is the principal investigator, who is then solely responsible for knowing not only what exists (in terms of documentation, variables, reports, publications, and references for each wave) but also where each item is kept, in order to orient succeeding generations of staff. Staffing needs must—and do—change with the timing of each wave's funding.

The consolations and rewards of longitudinal research obviously outweigh the burdens, or we would not continue to engage in it. These derive in large measure from immersion in a single cohort's ongoing life experiences. Two particular areas of satisfaction lie in discerning repeated patterns or regularities in the data over time (for example, gender-specific relationships) and discerning new patterns that correct, if not refute, past assumptions—in the case of the Harlem study, past assumptions about developmental trajectories in this minority-community-representative cohort. These assumptions have been generalized either from studies of other ethnoracial groups (usually white) or from select samples of the population such as prisoners, drug addicts, and welfare or other benefits recipients. Even successfully locating and interviewing a hard-to-reach participant becomes a source of gratification. One example of such satisfaction is presented in figure 9.1, a letter of appreciation from a

Figure 9.1   Letter from a Participant

Dear Ann F Brunswick.

I would like to thank you and Mr. Tony Scott the projects interviewer for going through all the trouble of comming to my place of incarceration to continue to be part of your project. Mr. Scott was an easy gentlman to open up to. He made it very easy for me to relax and put my memory to work. Besides jail, this survey gives one a chance to reevaluate there life, to see where we've been and possibly where were heading. Again I just want to thank you for allowing me to be part of something that is important to us all. P.S. Mr. Scott mentioned a fee for my participation $35.00 I would like that to be sent to my wife and son please. Her name is

---

study participant for his interview in prison. Another participant found his way to my office through a labyrinth of corridors, guided only by the stationery letterhead, because he wanted to be sure that we had his new address for the next interview.

As much as we attempt to avoid them in our study procedures, selection factors undoubtedly operate in the characteristics of researchers who pursue longitudinal studies. From my vantage point, these would include strong motivation (for example, undertaking work in a relatively unexplored area of study, as was adolescence when this study began, especially given the focus on a representative cross section of black adolescents who had seldom been studied from other than a "deviance" perspective); persistence, stubbornness, or both; an appreciation of the challenge of testing changing theories and methodologies in data from a single-study cohort transiting through time; and a capacity for attention to detail that the methodological complexities of sample retention, data processing, and longitudinal analysis require. This last quality is indispensable in researchers: in natural history studies, no error is so small that it can be allowed to remain uncorrected, because future observations will be linked to it.

An anecdote from the second study wave is illustrative here. Interviewers are instructed always to record respondents' full comments verbatim in the margins of the interview schedule, and coders are instructed to check these comments to ensure that the proper precode has been assigned to the response. Consequently this one was brought to the principal investigator for interpretation: a respondent, asked if we had ever used cocaine, replied, "Yes," with the further comment, "The doctor gave it to me for the pilots in my nose." Realizing that whatever it was the doctor had said had been mediated by both the respondent and the interviewer's verbatim recording, the comment was translated as meaning that the doctor had given the young man novocaine for the polyps in his nose. This was consistent with the absence of any other reported drug use by the participant.

Engaging in longitudinal research had, for me, two more generalized and far-reaching advantages. First, it afforded me an opportunity to refine the theoretical base of the research and enhance its procedural and analytic methods. Second, it has brought increased focus and a concomitant sense of purpose that extends from my professional to my personal life.

Older and Wiser: Lessons from a Longitudinal Study

Notwithstanding our best hopes and wildest expectations, longitudinal research is not a quick fix on causality, in the ontological sense. What it does—and this is no mean contribution—is identify the temporal ordering of observations and permit us to move beyond the purely correlational connections that cross-sectional data, in essence, reveal. The complexity of causality, which has been referred to elsewhere as the "complex web of causality" (Brunswick and Rier 1995, 225), is thrown into sharper relief with longitudinal data. Analyzing changing health, drug use, and life situations in this cohort enabled us to hone in on a number of strands of the complex causal web—the timing of life events and its effects, maturational and secular influences, gender effects, and the social nexus in causal processes—that may well resonate with the experience of other longitudinal investigators.

Timing of Key Life Roles

Data from this cohort dispel any doubts that position in the social structure has an impact on group norms and expectations for the timing of adult roles, as well as for their ultimate fulfillment. As an example, our introduction to differential subgroup norms came in the first study wave, conducted in 1968 and 1969. When adolescent girls were asked the age at which they wanted to marry and the age at which they wanted to have their first child, the reported desired age for childbearing preceded that for marriage (Brunswick 1971).

Except for marital and partnering status (a logical exception), role attainment in the cohort conformed to the model of divergent gender trajectories. By the age of thirty-six to forty-one (the fifth wave), 10 percent of the men in our study, compared with 16 percent of the women, had earned the Bachelor of Arts degree. Scarcely more than a third of the men (39 percent) and women (35 percent) were living with a partner or spouse between the ages of twenty-five and thirty-two; even ten years later, when participants were thirty-six to forty-one years old, this proportion still remained less than half (46 percent of the men and 48 percent of the women were living with a spouse or partner). Indeed, by approximately the age of forty, 49 percent of men and 51 percent of women in the cohort had never been married (consistent with difficulties among African Americans, as described by others, in finding suitable marriage partners). As to the myth of high fertility rates among urban African American females, although one in five had a baby by the age of seventeen (as had 9 percent of the men), by the age of thirty-six to forty-one about the same proportion (19 percent) had borne no children, half (51 percent) had one or two children only, and a minority of 29 percent reported having borne as many as three or more children as they entered midlife.

Clearly reflective of their marginalized position in the social structure, a third of men (34 percent) but slightly more women (37 percent) were unemployed; 15 percent of the men and 27 percent of the women were dependent on public assistance when interviewed in 1993, at the age of thirty-six to forty-one. (Note that this was before the new work mandates were imposed on public assistance recipients.)

To date, most of our studies have modeled role attainment variables as predictors of drug use and health outcomes. One exception was a study of women's life outcomes at the age of twenty-six to thirty-one (the third study wave), using a typology created by cross-classifying age at first birth and heroin use. Analysis shows that education, employment, fertility, and health deficits were restricted to those women who combined early childbearing (before the age of eighteen) with heroin use. Either condition without the other, particularly early childbearing without heroin use, showed no deleterious consequences for life outcomes (Brunswick and Aidala 1995). This interactive or conditional relationship is strong demonstration of the critical role of multivariate analysis in avoiding spurious attribution of causality and in arriving at valid interpretations. As is demonstrated later in this chapter, this interactive relationship conditioned other results as well.

Disentangling Maturational and Secular Influences

A chief contribution of longitudinal research, one that falls well within the purview of the ecological or contextual perspective, is the need to distinguish the often confounded effects of maturation and secular time. A dramatic example of this potential confounding occurred early in this study. Although the study group encompasses only six single-year birth cohorts (1952, 1953, 1954, 1955, 1956, and 1957), the participants manifested a dramatic shift in heroin use within the confines of these six birth years. Non-experimental heroin use rates declined monotonically, from a prevalence of 28 percent in the oldest cohort, born in 1952, to 3 percent among the youngest, born in 1957 (Boyle and Brunswick 1980; Brunswick and Boyle 1979). This secular shift was subsequently confirmed both in New York City and in national data on entry into treatment. When a more extended analysis of conjoint effects on drug use of maturation (age), cohort (general socialization influences), and situational availability was performed with prevalence and incidence rates for four major drugs (marijuana, cocaine, heroin, and psychedelics), prevalence of use of particular drugs varied by age cohort, but age at initiation did not. Onset of drug use was concluded to be a maturational phenomenon, whereas the choice of particular substances was subject to situational or period influences (Brunswick and Boyle 1979).

In another study (Messeri and Brunswick 1987), chronological concurrence of decline in heroin use reported in the sample was analyzed against annual fluctuations in drug price and purity (taken as indicators of direct government intervention to control drug supply). No close association was found. Additional data from the personal interviews (such as reasons given for not using drugs) were analyzed. These data supported the hypothesis that broader social changes had differential effects on successive birth cohorts as they entered the adolescent period of risk for heroin initiation (which in this sample began at the age of thirteen), reducing the attractiveness of initiating and, to a lesser extent, of continuing heroin use. This was postulated to explain the dramatic drop in rates of heroin use from the sample's oldest (28 percent) to youngest (3 percent) of the six-year annual birth cohorts.

Both these analyses, performed initially with data from the second wave (in 1975 and 1976, when participants were between the ages of eighteen through twenty-three), were replicated using third-wave data (collected in 1983 and 1984, when participants were twenty-six through thirty-one), when observations were extended through the age of twenty-five for all panel members. This follow-up seven to eight years after the initial observation confirmed that the decrease in heroin use had not resulted from a change in timing or onset of heroin use but was rather a true secular decline in recruitment to heroin. Thus the major substantive finding of the earlier study, in which drug experiences were analyzed only through the age of eighteen, remained intact: age at initiation was constant, and the observed decline in heroin had not resulted from delayed initiation (Brunswick, Merzel, and Messeri 1985).

Divergent Gender Trajectories

A simple example of differences in gender trajectories is provided by a second-wave analysis (cohort aged eighteen to twenty-three) that tested for gender differences in the influence of age, frequency, and duration of heroin use at the time of entry into a drug-treatment program. Analysis reveals a strong and significant difference between the young men and women of the study cohort in their timing of first treatment relative to the length of exposure to heroin. Men tended to enter treatment at an earlier stage of their heroin careers than women, a finding that ran counter to the thinking at that time about treatment entry (Brunswick and Messeri 1985).

The same study was subsequently replicated with data from the third wave and extended to include social support and social attainment variables. Analysis returns the same finding, that men entered treatment earlier, and women later, in their drug (heroin) careers. Other analyses indicate that, once they had entered, women remained in treatment longer, and men were more likely to have briefer but repeated episodes (Brunswick and Messeri 1986b).

Findings from another study of drug use continuing into adulthood (Brunswick, Messeri, and Titus 1992) demonstrate sharp gender differences in the nature and timing of social integration effects. Analysis of adolescent (aged twelve to seventeen) and postadolescent (age eighteen to twenty-three) predictors shows that for women, all effects from adolescence were processed through postadolescent role attainment. Specifically, being unmarried and unemployed each increased young women's likelihood of continuing heavy drug use. (This is in sharp contrast with the most successful equivalently aged women from this predominantly low-income urban area who, in the early 1980s, were single and employed.) For men, to the contrary, influences on the avoidance of heavy adult drug use derived directly from adolescence—notably, the social bond and social support denoted by religious involvement in adolescence. No significant postadolescent life-stage effects appeared: that is, young African American men's trajectory to heavy drug use in adulthood was set in adolescence. Studies that have analyzed HIV infection rates and exposure modalities similarly demonstrate sharp gender-differentiated trajectories (Brunswick et al. 1993; Brunswick and Flory 1998).

Complex Timing Effects in Studies of Health Change

As indicated earlier, the raison d'être for the longitudinal dimension of the Harlem adolescent cohort study was the perceived need to investigate health effects of drug use in a predominantly disadvantaged inner-city African American population sample. The first of these studies, performed with second-wave data, tested two different somatic health formulations—psychophysical and a more inclusive general somatic scale—against nonexperimental use of seven substances (computed for each substance as the base-10 log transformation of number of uses of that substance up to the second wave), including interaction terms as appropriate and lagged terms for individual substances used before the baseline measurement was taken.

A set of lifestyle indicators, measured concurrently with second-wave health data, were added to control for spuriously attributing health change to drugs. Controls were also included for age and baseline health. In effect, the outcome investigated was health change between baseline adolescence and postadolescence. Controlling for other factors, drug use was observed to have a significant adverse health effect. For males, the use of inhalants was associated with the strongest adverse change. For females, increased reports of health symptoms were identified for methadone in the presence of heavy alcohol use, cigarette smoking, and a delayed effect from earlier heroin use. For both males and females, the introduction of lifestyle variables (social networks and role attainment) did little to diminish the direct impact of drugs on health. They did, however, show an independent additive contribution to diminished health that varied by gender. The critical variable for men was social support, whereas for women it was unemployment (Brunswick and Messeri 1986a).

The study was repeated at the third wave (cohort aged twenty-six to thirty-one), extending the earlier study through the next life stage and bridging a similar intervening period of approximately seven years between measurements. This study had the added objective of investigating the drug effects of differences in maturational stage (see Brunswick and Messeri 1999). The individual and collective impact of eight licit and illicit substances on change in self-reported health problems was examined over this seven-year period, when the cohort passed from postadolescence (age eighteen through twenty-three) to adulthood (age twenty-six through thirty-one). As in the previous study, concomitant lifestyle measures were included to test the extent to which those variables might explain or reduce the observed association between drug use and change in somatic health and to guard against spurious attribution. The study was also aimed at the broader research question of gender differences in the etiology of physical morbidity—specifically, gender differences in the role of drug use and certain lifestyle indicators in health prediction. To this end, two separate but parallel gender analyses of the impact of continued drug use were performed.

Analysis of adult drug use explained significant portions of health variance among both men and women but accounted for more of the variance in men's health (almost 17 percent) than in women's (9 percent). When drug use from the earlier time period was added to the model, the total contribution of recent and earlier drug use to health decline was 21 percent for men and 15 percent for women.

For men, the most powerful drug contributors were heavy alcohol use combined with methadone use, phencyclidine (PCP) use, and earlier inhalants use. Drug effects were dispersed over a wider range of substances for women than for men, with significant effects from heavy alcohol use, cigarette and marijuana use, and earlier heroin use when left untreated. Effects from earlier (lagged) heroin use were stronger than those from more recent use.

The timing and pattern of these gender-differentiated drug effects can only be noted, they cannot be explained. Differences in norms of tolerance or acceptability for women's as against men's drug use—the norms tend to be more stringent for women than for men—with resulting differences in the lifestyles of the users are likely to play a role. Heroin use shows a delayed or lagged effect on women's health. For men, earlier inhalant use exerted a strong continuing—rather than lagged—effect, even in the absence of recent use. This shows that deleterious effects from use of inhalants in early adolescence continued into adulthood, after use of the substance had subsided. Overall, substance use made a larger contribution in absolute terms to women's health decline, notwithstanding its accounting for a larger proportion of the more limited variance in men's health.

Because the longitudinal data set allowed both adult and lagged drug use measures to be entered in a single model, a phenomenon appeared that has received little prior documentation. Health effects of certain drugs appear to be conditioned on life stage. In some cases, effects from earlier substance use were ameliorated with cessation of use of that substance—for example, women's health when cigarette smoking, marijuana smoking, or both ceased. This was not true of other substances, however; the effects of males' use of inhalants, for example, continued even after usage stopped. Still another timing effect associated with marijuana use—negative health effects—did not appear until adulthood, with the observation of significant effects from continued use restricted to women.

The addition of lifestyle variables to the model merely confirmed the pattern of direct health effects from substance use. Although the lifestyle variables had been entered chiefly to control against spurious causal attribution to drugs, the results were of particular interest, both because they pointed to a considerably weaker unique lifestyle effect on somatic health than that experienced from substance use, and also because, unexpectedly, limited overlap (collinearity) appeared between drug use and other lifestyle factors. Among the latter, the gender-differentiated finding that unemployment added to women's health decline, but not to men's, was consistent with findings from subsequent studies of vulnerability factors in HIV infection in this cohort.[3]

Complexities of Causal Processes Linked to Social Disadvantage

A study was undertaken to disentangle two opposing functions attributed to drug use—as causal of stress and as buffer or coping mechanism (mediator) for stress. Longitudinal gender-specific models controlled for baseline measures of distress. The first series of tests posited acute life events as predictors of distress; the second series tested enduring unemployment as the predictor (chronic) stressor. Results show, first, that acute negative life events did not increase levels of distress in the African American cohort. In contrast, the chronic stressor—unemployment—did have a significant impact on distress. Subsequent tests were performed introducing drug use into the model to test for its causal as against buffering or mediating role. By now, not surprisingly, different processes were observed for men and women. For men, moderate to heavy (weekly to daily) drug use exacerbated the stressful effects of unemployment; drug use was not stressful if men were employed (suggesting an interaction or multiplicative relationship between drug use and unemployment). For women, unemployment stress was ameliorated modestly by light (less than weekly) use of an illicit drug. Heavier use (weekly or more) added to increased distress for women, independent of unemployment. These differences again appear to reflect stricter antidrug norms for African American women and more relaxed ones for men.

Further complexities in timing the effects of social disadvantage are illustrated in findings from parallel longitudinal investigations performed to examine vulnerability factors in HIV infection. Predictors were drawn from the second and third waves, and thus all preceded infection by at least seven years. Logistic models were based on the 168 women assayed for HIV antigen in the fourth or fifth wave (or both) who also participated in both the second and third waves. Results identified social disadvantage at the second wave (an index of having dropped out of high school and months unemployed in the two years preceding that interview), which was thirteen to fifteen years before the outcome measure, as a significant source of stress-enhanced infection risk. It significantly increased the likelihood of HIV infection over and above the significant contribution of use of injected drugs and multiple sex partners. Furthermore, results reveal a strong HIV risk from the interaction (or conditional relationship) between injecting drug use and having had a baby before the age of eighteen. Risk for HIV was confined entirely to the latter condition; no injecting woman was infected unless she had also had a baby before the age of eighteen. A series of alternative health and lifestyle variables were interposed and tested to see if they might account for this observed interaction. None did.

Perhaps the most unanticipated complexity in the timing of effects appeared when both the second- and third-wave values (seven years later) were entered simultaneously as predictors. In every test, the earlier, second-wave values were stronger and significant, not only overriding but in some cases even modifying the direction of the observed third-wave effects. (Remember that in this analysis even the third wave preceded HIV infection by seven years).

A parallel logistic analysis of antecedent influences on men's HIV infection again demonstrates the stronger predictiveness of the earlier postadolescent life stage (second wave) compared with the more proximal adult ages of twenty-six to thirty-one (third wave). For men, demoralization (depressed affect, low self-esteem, worry, feeling that nothing is worthwhile, and feeling alone) in postadolescence added significantly to their risk of HIV infection thirteen to fifteen years later, independent of the effects of male-male sex but conditioning the risk from injecting drug use exposure.

These studies are cited to demonstrate the utility of multiwave longitudinal data that incorporate an extended time period for identifying effects of maturational stage and the opportunity they provide to identify alternative timing processes that might be linked to them. Much remains to be learned about nonlinearity and variability in the timing of the causal sequence.

Implications for Policy and Research

In the eyes of this investigator, who is more accustomed to the scientist's than the policy maker's role, the policy and research implications prompted by this research show considerable overlap. Accordingly, they are discussed within a single rubric. For example, the model of the complex biopsychosocial web of causality reflected in this study of health and health behaviors is appropriate, similarly, for guiding policy formulations directed at intervening in those behaviors. So too the ecological model that incorporates increasingly broader realms of social influences on health and health behavior can inform particular intervention strategies. In so doing, intervention strategies would move beyond individual knowledge, motivation, and volition and even beyond the parent and peer network approaches that are today in programmatic and research vogue. They would increasingly encompass other influences in the social environment: neighborhood (community organizations and outreach, support groups), institutions (churches, medical services), and the opportunity structure (jobs and job training, educational opportunity). The examples given are intended as illustrative, not exhaustive.

Some of the more specific implications for African American health-related policy that flow from this research include the following:

1. Based on the study's findings of long-term detrimental effects of stressful conditions and poor health in adolescence, health and social services targeted at childhood and early adolescence need to be increased and improved in low-income minority communities.

2. Specifically, there is a need to develop more community programs and institutions sensitive to the needs of young African American men for affiliation, value structuring, achievement, and mastery.

This need was demonstrated by the important role that was observed in this research of adolescent church affiliation in diverting drug careers and improving life outcomes in this generational unit of young African American men.

3. Policy makers should move away from the dualistic approach to physical and mental health in intervention and therapeutic programs. Research has found them largely inseparable as antecedents to later poor health and other life outcomes.

4. When developing and executing policy, more than lip service needs to be given to the truism that behavior occurs in contexts or settings. What we call undesirable "unintended consequences" can be reduced by incorporating interpersonal and institutional linkages (see appendix) in intervention policies and programs.

5. Supporting a need for population-specific programs and interventions that are cognizant of particular population settings, the dire and lasting ill effects from early use of inhalants by the cohort's young men may have been compounded by their high rates of respiratory symptoms.[4]

6. Related to the foregoing, note that few single or individual behaviors have deleterious consequences. When undesirable behaviors occur in combination, however, they betoken poorer life outcomes. A recurring case in point is the combination of heavy substance use (for example, heroin) and adolescent childbearing for young women's later diminished health and life attainment, including risk of HIV infection. The two behaviors together signal reduced within-group attainment and access to the opportunity structure.

7. Unemployment plays a critical role in life outcomes for young African American women. Job competency training should be incorporated into elementary, junior high school, and high school curricula or other community programs.

8. Finally, social contexts and their effects change with time. Policy makers need to update their databases with more than census figures by using carefully sampled (population-representative) cohorts such as the one reported on here.

Certain research policy recommendations follow from this paradigm:

1. Capturing changing sociocultural contexts and maturational trajectories requires tracking with a broad spectrum of variables.

2. Research issues and data collected also need to be conceptualized broadly so that they can be applicable when new health and behavioral issues emerge.

3. To explicate more clearly the effects of culture and societal position, comparative longitudinal cohort studies need to be planned and coordinated that use a common core of measures, adjusting them as necessary for cultural sensitivity and specificity.

4. Because ethnoracial and geographic groups differ in the degree and distribution of their heterogeneity (socioeconomic status and other attributes), this heterogeneity, unless accounted for, will undermine the accuracy and validity of intergroup comparisons, whether made across different studies or within an individual longitudinal study.

5. The increased external validity (generalizability) of the findings are well worth the added cost in time, money, and effort of developing and maintaining an area-representative cohort.

6. In planning and funding, the time and manpower resources needed for maintaining longitudinal data archives and other records must be included.

7. Mechanisms should be developed for continuity in funding, contingent on meeting quality controls and other performance criteria. This would reduce the inefficiency and potential for error in the management and analysis of a longitudinal data set that are linked to staff turnover.

8. Funding consideration should be given to coordinated comparative (cross-study) analyses with longitudinal data from different ethnoracial groups to better identify commonalities and variability in life-course development.

It is no news to longitudinal researchers (and others) that lives develop within and intersect with their contexts at multiple levels of complexity. The task of longitudinal research is to disentangle these complex strands. Do the theory and methods in our research accurately and adequately capture this needed contextual grounding of developmental trajectories and human behavior? That has been the ongoing challenge in this study of a homogeneously urban African American cohort born in the 1950s. By virtue of having come of age in the late 1960s and the early 1970s, they have been part of the historic change wrought by the black civil rights movement, and as the data show, cohort members have been differentially impacted by it. Simply put, this study directs attention to contextual factors, broadly scoped, that should be in place in our research; sensitivity to changing contexts that can be captured by including multiple age cohorts within study groups; and studying different ethnoracial groups to learn more about heterogeneity in developmental trajectories.

Appendix: Variables Used in the Longitudinal Harlem Adolescent Cohort Study

Drug Use and Drug Treatment

1. Patterns of drug use (cigarettes, alcohol, marijuana, cocaine, heroin, methadone, other opiates, phencyclidine (PCP), other psychedelics, amphetamines, barbiturates, glue or other inhalants)

   —Ever use

   —Frequency of use

   —Recency of use

   —Onset of use

   —Duration of use

   —Amount used (tobacco, alcohol, marijuana)

   —Attitude toward own tobacco and alcohol use

   —Mode of administration

   —Continuous or interrupted use

   —Trouble experienced as a result of use

   —Drug combinations (simultaneous use)

   —Use of multiple drugs

2. Drug treatment experience

   —Perceptions of treatment

   —Exposure

   —Sources of influence on entry

   —Treatment environment

   —Motivations for entering treatment

   —Treatment modality

   —Treatment preferences

   —Treatment effects

   —Treatment barriers

3. Perceptions of and attitudes toward drug use

   —Salience of drug problems

   —Tolerance of drug use

   —Health consequences attributed to drug use

Predictor Variables
(Arranged by Ecological Model)

1. Social structure
   —Current life role or activity
   —Household composition
   —Economic status (source, level, and adequacy of income)
   —Mobility
   —Age, cohort
   —Gender

2. Spacial and temporal contexts
   —Census tract and address of residence
   —Wave (timing) of interview

3. Social contexts
   —Living arrangements
   —Support networks
   —Network size and diversity
   —Kin networks
   —Friend networks
   —Drug and alcohol use in friend networks
   —Alternative network norms and exposure
   —Network strain
   —Stability of networks
   —Community participation
   —Life stress events

4. Ontogenic system: personal resources (self-perceptions and outlooks on life) and coping strategies
   —Mood, depression
   —Anxiety, worry, fears
   —Hostility, anger
   —Self-esteem
   —Sense of personal efficacy, control, mastery
   —Alienation, hopelessness

—Time orientation

—Perceptions of parents

—Values orientation

—Coping strategies: adaptive or nonadaptive

—Perceived strains: general, economic, health, education, parenting, conjugal, and job

—health

Notes

1. The staff recruited to conduct pretest interviews included graduate students from nearby Rutgers University, a tactical mistake on our part considering the militancy of college students in the late 1960s. The protest, thus, was engineered by outsiders. We persevered because we felt the protest reflected neither the true sentiments of the community nor a recognition of the potential medical service benefits to be derived for adolescent health in Harlem.

2. I do not have clear recall of the storage mode in the second wave—it was possibly a primitive form of data tape.

3. These findings are reported later in this chapter.

4. Respiratory risk was reflected in the 18 percent of adolescent boys who reported frequent colds, 13 percent who reported a long-lasting cough or bronchitis, and 10 percent who reported asthma or wheezing.

References

Boyle, John, and Ann F. Brunswick. 1980. "What Happened in Harlem? Analysis of a Decline in Heroin Use Among a Generation Unit of Urban Black Youth." *Journal of Drug Issues* 10(1): 109–30.

Bronfenbrenner, Uri. 1979. *The Ecology of Human Development.* Cambridge, Mass.: Harvard University Press.

Brunswick, Ann F. 1971. "Adolescent Health, Sex, and Fertility." *American Journal of Public Health* 61(4): 711–29.

———. 1998a. "Needed: A Relevant Public Policy for HIV Infection Among African Americans." In *AIDS Research/AIDS Policy: Competing Paradigms of Science and Public Policy,* edited by Eric Margolis. Greenwich, Conn.: JAI Press.

———. 1998b. "Racial Differences in Surveys of Drug Prevalence: More than Measurement Error?" *1997 American Statistical Association Joint Proceedings on Survey Research Methods.* Washington, D.C.

———. 1999. "Structural Strain: An Ecological Paradigm for Studying African American Drug Use." In *Conducting Drug Abuse Research with Minority Populations: Advances and Issues,* edited by Mario R. De La Rosa, Bernard Siegal, and Richard Lopez. Binghamton, N.Y.: Haworth Press.

Brunswick, Ann F., and Angela Aidala. 1995. "Adult Consequences of Adolescent Childbearing: The Longitudinal Harlem Health Study." In *African American Youth: Their Social and Economic Status in the United States,* edited by R. L. Taylor. Westport, Conn.: Praeger.

Brunswick, Ann F., Angela Aidala, Jay Dobkin, Joyce Moon-Howard, Stephen P. Titus, and Jane Banaszak-Holl. 1993. "HIV-1 Seroprevalence and Risk Behaviors in an African American Community Cohort." *American Journal of Public Health* 83(10): 1390–94.

Brunswick, Ann F., and John Boyle. 1979. "Patterns of Drug Involvement: Developmental and Secular Influences on Age at Initiation." *Youth and Society* 11(2): 139–62.

Brunswick, Ann F., and Michael Flory. 1998. "Changing HIV Infection Rates and Risks in an African American Community Cohort." *Journal of AIDS Care* 10(3): 267–81.

Brunswick, Ann F., and Eric Josephson. 1972. "A Study of Adolescent Health in Harlem." Supplement to *American Journal of Public Health* (October).

Brunswick, Ann F., Cheryl Merzel, and Peter Messeri. 1985. "Drug Use Initiation Among Urban Black Youth: A Seven-Year Follow-up of Developmental and Secular Influences." *Youth and Society* 17(2): 189–216.

Brunswick, Ann F., and Peter Messeri. 1985. "Timing of First Drug Treatment: A Longitudinal Study of Urban Black Youth." *Contemporary Drug Problems* 2(3): 401–18.

———. 1986a. "Drugs, Life Style, and Health: A Longitudinal Study of Urban Black Youth." *American Journal of Public Health* 76(1): 52–57.

———. 1986b. "Pathways to Heroin Abstinence: A Longitudinal Study of Urban Black Youth." *Advances in Alcohol and Substance Abuse* 5(3): 103–22.

———. 1999. "Life Stage, Substance Use, and Health Decline in a Community Cohort of Urban African Americans." *Journal of Addictive Diseases* 18(1): 53–71.

Brunswick, Ann F., Peter Messeri, and Stephen P. Titus. 1992. "Predictive Factors in Adult Substance Abuse: A Prospective Study of African American Adolescents." In *Vulnerability to Drug Abuse,* edited by M. D. Glantz and R. W. Pickens. Washington, D.C.: American Psychological Association Press.

Brunswick, Ann F., and David A. Rier. 1995. "Structural Strain: Drug Use Among African American Youth." In *African American Youth: Their Social and Economic Status in the United States,* edited by R. L. Taylor. Westport, Conn.: Praeger.

Josephson, Eric. 1970. "Resistance to Community Surveys." *Social Problems* 18(1): 117–29.

Messeri, Peter, and Ann F. Brunswick. 1987. "Heroin Availability and Aggregate Levels of Use: Secular Trends in an Urban Black Cohort." *American Journal of Drug and Alcohol Abuse* 13(1–2): 105–29.

Chapter 10

The Origin and Development of Preschool Intervention Projects

DAVID P. WEIKART

W
HEN I BEGAN my professional career, I was not thinking of long-term studies and clearly defined goals. I was eager for professional challenges but ignorant, really, of where those challenges would eventually take me. A researcher does not wake up one morning and say, "Today I'll begin that forty-year study I've been thinking about!" Instead, such efforts emerge from a gradual accretion of ideas assembled and executed one experience at a time; at least that is the way it has been for me. When my first project idea, the High/Scope Perry Preschool Project, began to form in 1959, it was the result of my desire to meet a local need I had identified through my professional experience. Yet in retrospect I can see that none of the six long-term studies of ten to forty years' duration in which I am engaged could have happened without three key elements: a genuine set of debatable questions that demand factual answers so that policy, both educational and financial, can be established; a group of staff who care about the questions and who are willing to work creatively, diligently, and objectively to find the answers; and a commitment to the scientific method that results in a strong research design so that outcome data support recommendations for action.

A longitudinal study can develop without an initial grand research design. Long-term studies may develop from logical questions that lead from a first step to a second and then beyond. However, these early research steps must be sufficiently well organized to support the longitudinal structure that is eventually built on this foundation.

Throughout my professional career, I have been interested in changing the practice of education to enable children, especially disadvantaged children, to attain greater personal, social, and economic success. Thus my work has been characterized by intervention projects. I have wanted to know what would happen if a child's experiences were influenced by an educational intervention that enabled both the child and the family to become more personally involved in an educational program. This type of quest has required me to employ the classical research design, using experimental and control groups, whenever possible. Of course, the types of interventions I conducted were the products of the social and political times I lived through, and the theories I used to guide my work represented the thinking of the period. In addition, as with any longitudinal study spanning these particular forty years, the work began at the dawn of the computer age and has been expedited over the decades by the evolution of this technology.

These reflections are primarily based on the High/Scope Perry Preschool Project, the first longitudinal study I initiated. The study continues today with the support of a new five-year grant from the McCormick Tribune Foundation. The current phase will examine the impact of early education on the midlife events for this group of adults. What are the health issues? Is there any evidence of family generational transmission of personal success and social stability? I chose this project as the basis of my contribution to this volume because it is the most influential of my studies, both here in the United States and in a number of foreign countries, in terms of having an impact on public policy and changing local educational practice.

Genesis of the Study and Development of the Curriculum Framework

Throughout the struggle for civil rights in the 1960s and 1970s, African Americans and many whites have demanded an end to the racial injustice evident in both northern and southern states. In Ypsilanti, Michigan, in 1960, for example, all black children attended one elementary school because they all lived in a single, restricted neighborhood. This strict segregation broke down for later schooling—the community of Ypsilanti has only two middle schools and one high school. There were African American teachers at the elementary school but few at the other levels. These staffing and housing practices were the result of conventions permitted by social consensus, not by law.

As the civil rights movement gained force, impetus developed for changing these traditional practices. A new consensus was formed. As director of special services and school psychologist in the local Ypsilanti public schools, I was new on the scene. Indeed I was the first to hold those positions under new state funding. In my presentation to school principals on systemwide achievement testing during my first year on the job (1958), I displayed charts documenting what I saw as a serious problem: over the previous ten years of standardized achievement testing (from 1948 to 1957), no class in the school attended by African Americans had scored above the tenth percentile; yet in the elementary school across town, which served the college professors' children, no class ever scored below the ninetieth percentile. The reaction was electric. Several principals went to the window to have a smoke (it was the 1950s, and smoking at meetings was accepted); several left the room (without comment); one pulled back from the table (tightly crossing arms and legs); only my "reform" group of three principals out of the twelve present really focused on the topic. The discussion ended with the conclusion that everything possible was already being done; the test scores just represented the status quo. With reform of the school system out of the question, or at least beyond the professional reach of my first job, my attention turned to more feasible alternatives.

After a period of discussion and thought, the idea of intervention at the preschool level evolved. Such a step had much to commend it. First, the state did not require that children of this age attend school, and so the proposal represented no threat to the existing schools and asked no change of the school system as a whole. Second, the state had just passed laws allowing counties to fund special education services for three- and four-year-old children in local school districts; thus the funding to operate early education programs was available. Third, the support group of three reform-minded principals included the principal of the school the African American children attended, who was happy to support such an intervention and willing to permit "his" attendance district and school to be used for that purpose. Finally, I had a staff deeply committed to social change and the goals of the civil rights movement; thus I had the necessary internal departmental support to undertake the project.

From a theoretical view I was on more difficult ground. In a review of the literature, I found little support for such a novel undertaking with disadvantaged children in a public school—or indeed anywhere. My program idea predated J. McVicker Hunt's extraordinary 1961 book, *Intelligence and Experience*, by several years. At the time, most people felt that intelligence was a God-given trait that could not be improved on, that minority children with low IQs were just born that way. Yet my experience as a psychologist had convinced me that the accurate assignment of IQ was not so simple as that. Studies on low-IQ children, conducted by Beth Lucy Wellman, Howard Skeels, Marie Skodka, and others at the Iowa Child Welfare Station in the 1930s, offered some support for the belief that under special limiting circumstances (such as placement in a state facility for the retarded), major environmental changes (such as placement with a family) might have a dramatic effect on a child's IQ score. Finally, with a zoology minor in college, I was influenced by the 1960 studies on maze performance of cage-reared as against playground-reared rats by Stanford University researchers David Krech, Michael Rosenzweig, and Edward Bennett (1960). These studies strongly suggest that problems caused by limited environments can be ameliorated by stimulus-rich opportunities. Excited by these ideas, I was disappointed to discover that most of the available research on early childhood focused on higher-income children and was not relevant to the population my project planned to serve.

In developing a curriculum for the project, I was influenced by several studies on special education and by the writings of directors of university-based early childhood demonstration programs. Sam Kirk at the University of Illinois had completed a five-year study in 1958 in a preschool setting of special education children with a range of etiologies. His major finding was that the experience did not seem to help most of the youngsters, although those who had come from severely disadvantaged homes did show some improvement (Kirk 1958). I wrote Kirk to ask what curriculum he had used and if I might have access to the documentation. His response was illustrative of the field. He directed me to his book and to its single paragraph on curriculum. In general, the writings of the directors of early childhood demonstration centers gave similar advice. They recommended nonstructured play and training in a "curriculum" that focused on toilet training, hand washing, coat buttoning, and shoe tying. Pauline Sears and her colleague, Edith Dowley, listed the ten major concerns of their model preschool at Stanford University but included no information on areas such as children's language or general cognitive development (Sears and Dowley 1963).

The High/Scope curriculum was born, then, not out of what I found in the research of the time but rather of what I could not find. I forged ahead, following my hunches. During the first years of the project, I chose to draw from John Dewey's educational philosophy and from the experiences of the project's teachers; the result was a focus on active learning experiences for children, including much hands-on activity. To assist us, we invited the noted educators Robert Hess, of the University of Chicago, and Sara Smilanski, of the Hebrew University in Israel, to visit our preschool and to observe, discuss, and offer their advice. In addition, in 1963 I came upon Jean Piaget's theories on child development and discovered that his research spoke directly to our needs. From these influences, High/Scope curriculum developed its basic structure: an emphasis on active, hands-on learning; a comprehensive daily routine that includes a plan-do-review cycle; a learning setting stocked with appropriate materials and organized to appeal to young children; and the definition of the adult's role as careful observer and active supporter of children.

Seeds were sown for the later development of evaluation instruments to access children's progress through teacher observation and to assess the level of program implementation by judging the presence or absence of the program key elements, especially the quality of interaction between teacher and child and the richness of the setting. Finally, the curriculum was strengthened by the grouping of important theoretical aspects from child development into "key experience" areas such as language and literacy, creative representation, movement, music, classification, number, and time. This organization gave the adults an intellectual basis for working with children, observing their play activity, and making program decisions.

Operating the High/Scope Perry Preschool Project

The development of the High/Scope Perry Preschool Project began in response to my frustration at my inability to effect some small reform in a small school system. The political and social events of the times demanded change. I was fairly young (twenty-nine years old) at the time and impatient to make things happen. Three things occurred at this point to shape the program. First, with the backing of the three principals and the promise of a place to hold the program, the Ypsilanti School Board gave me permission to begin, provided I could locate the funds to cover direct expenses. Second, state government officials began to understand what I had in mind: a classroom-based program supplemented by weekly home visits. Officials in special education from the Michigan Board of Education were alarmed by this strategy, though it was neither encouraged nor discouraged in the legislation. When the officials had shaped the regulations to permit spending state funds on three- and four-year-olds, they had envisioned a parent advisory service providing referrals for medical services, primarily to physically or emotionally handicapped children. Serving socially and economically disadvantaged children who superficially met mentally handicapped regulations was not their idea of effective use of funds.

After extensive review of our plans and evidence from individual pilot testing I had provided, they nevertheless accepted our application for classroom funds. They insisted, however, that I employ only teachers who were certified by the state in three areas: preschool education, elementary education, and the education of the mentally handicapped. With that requirement satisfied, they felt, I would be able to operate a sound program. (Or perhaps they thought I would never be able to find such teachers in a period of severe teacher shortage, and thus the issue of funding would be rendered moot.) Third, a series of meetings occurred with university professors I had recruited as advisers on the program. After reviewing our plans, several of these experts decided not to support the program: in their opinion, only children with a mental age of at least six (as determined by the Stanford-Binet Intelligence Test) had the maturity required to attend a school-based program. They concluded that three- and four-year-olds, especially from disadvantaged backgrounds, would be unable to handle the program I hoped to offer.

These three events all influenced the program development, but none was as important as the last. It seemed unethical to continue in disregard of such startling advice. The advisers had asked a legitimate question: "Does participation by disadvantaged children in an early education program improve their intellectual and academic abilities?" After several weeks of discussion within the special service staff and with the three principals, however, we decided to continue, and the High/Scope Perry Preschool Study as a research undertaking was born, with this as the overarching question.

The study officially began in October 1962. Until the spring of 1967, it operated as both a limited research project and a service project, working with both program and nonprogram groups (randomly assigned). Since that time, the project has operated as a longitudinal study assessing participants' progress annually from ages three to ten and then again at ages fourteen or fifteen, nineteen, and twenty-seven.

The study's capacity to answer this basic question, "Does preschool work?," rests on four pillars. The first of these is the random assignment of samples (as difficult as that was to accomplish). Second, no family, once selected, failed to participate. It took the intervention of the school principal and members of several neighborhood service clubs to reach this goal, but I was determined that the study would not be flawed by having only those who wished to participate involved. Once screened for the study criteria and randomly assigned to either the program or no-program group, all families agreed to be involved. Third, group assignment was random: no one entered the study because they had requested the service (and after a few years of operation, there were always requests) or because staff or service agencies perceived a special need for a particular child. Fourth, throughout the study there has been little loss of sample or missing data. By the age of twenty-seven, only 5 percent of the data were missing. High retention of participants and complete data are necessities for a long-term, small-sample study such as this one. With this attention to the integrity of the sample, its random assignment, and the location of all participants for follow-up, the High/Scope Perry Preschool Study was robust enough to support its extensive longitudinal structure and its astonishing conclusions.

When the study first began, the research question was related to early education effects on IQ development and the resulting benefits on elementary school performance; it was not conceived as an extended longitudinal study. However, as part of my duties as a school system director of special services, I found myself assembling the data from the groups each year and establishing a sequential wave design for the small groups entering the program each year. That is, after all, what schools do: they enroll children each year.

The outcome of the project was an extraordinary increase of fifteen points, on average, in children's assessed performance on the Stanford-Binet IQ test. My staff and I were exhilarated at the results and vindicated in our faith that we could provide an effective intervention in the lives of poor children at risk of school failure. The improvement on test scores moved many of these disadvantaged children out of the "mildly retarded" IQ level and into the normal range. Our program's contribution to the improvement of the nation was the stuff of the social and civil change going on around us. We had something that we, as individuals, could do and that the schools, as institutions, should do. I could not change the schools, but I could prepare the children: poor children could come to the uncompromising elementary schools better prepared to engage in traditional education.

The one nasty problem we found, however, was that in early elementary grades the measured achievement in the program group was not significantly different from that of the control group, the children who were not part of the program. This second finding put a damper on our enthusiasm. By third grade, however, things changed again. Although the measured IQ of the program group returned to the level of the control group, significant gains were seen in the achievement test scores and teacher ratings of classroom behavior of the program group. This pattern has remained steady throughout the study. Critics pointed to the washout of the IQ gains, reformers pointed to the achievement gains. I declared a victory, and in 1967 and 1968 I started three new, but related, projects.

New Studies

The fundamental finding from the High/Scope Perry Preschool Study was that early education for disadvantaged three- and four-year-olds could result in their improved school achievement—if not to middle-class levels, at least significantly beyond the level of their nonprogram peers. Three new questions now interested me: First, if programs begun when children were three years of age had positive results, wouldn't earlier intervention—as early, even, as infancy—bring about more dramatic results? The answer from our study (Lambie, Bond, and Weikart 1974; Epstein and Weikart 1979) proved to be no. In a carefully designed study with random assignment of sample, we followed children for two years, beginning at three, seven, or eleven months of age; at the age of four, and again at seven, we found that the intervention through weekly home visits that promoted infant stimulation and improved parenting did not produce any long-term educational gains for the child. This outcome was in spite of significant differences between program and non-program groups at the end of the two-year treatment period.

Second, if early education programs were followed with improved elementary school programs, could the preschool gains be maintained? The answer proved to be complicated. Specially designed programs in the national Project Follow Through for various model curriculum methods were implemented by various model sponsors (see Weikart, Hohmann, and Rhine 1981), and those that focused on drill-and-practice teaching methods (teaching information similar to the standardized tests used in the national assessment) showed some modest and immediate results. The Follow Through Project, however, operated in the real world, with little capacity for the niceties of controlled studies, and our federal funding was discontinued. We do not know, then, what might have been possible; but it did seem unlikely that without major changes in the schools themselves, we could make enough of a difference to sustain children's improved performance produced by early childhood education.

I moved on to my third question: Do high-quality early childhood programs work regardless of the theoretical method employed? That is, are gains possible with any early education program, or do some curriculum models work better than others? The answer, I found, is that different models of early childhood education do indeed work differently (Schweinhart and Weikart 1997). Teacher-directed preschool instruction based on drill and practice in "the basics" appears to provide no academic advantage as the disadvantaged child progresses through school, nor does it appear to improve social and behavioral outcomes. In fact, children in such programs behave as though they had never had the benefit of attending a preschool education program. On the other hand, children who attend programs using model curriculums, such as High/Scope's, that are based on active learning and other self-initiated activities do substantially better both socially and behaviorally. The story here, however, is my experience in the development and operation of the High/Scope Perry Preschool Study.

Staffing

With the blessing of the state, the staffing requirements for the preschool itself created an almost impossible employment situation. Required to hire only fully certified teachers within three areas of endorsement (regular elementary, early childhood education, and special education for the mentally handicapped), I almost abandoned the project. In the early 1960s, few teachers with even temporary certificates were available for any position whatsoever. The Ypsilanti public school system was as desperate to hire teachers as any system in Michigan, even though the High/Scope program offered salaries that were 10 percent above schedule compensation for any teacher with certification in special education. Persistence paid off, however, and in the spring of 1962, I identified four candidates with at least two of the required certificates. I supported their return to summer school to obtain temporary certification in the third area, and we opened in the fall with four staff members—the only four I could cajole into taking a risk on such an unusual project.

Building a research staff was less of a problem. I was still a graduate student at the University of Michigan and had contact with fellow students whom I could hire for short-term assignments. As director of special services, I had a regular staff of several school diagnosticians and social workers who were anxious to take part in the work. The assignments were pieced together, both to meet state standards for program reimbursement and to assure the quality needed to operate the study.

More complicated was the task of integrating research and teaching staff. With the identification of Piagetian theory in 1963 as a theoretical base for guiding our classroom practice, several research staff members began to move into the (self-appointed) role of giving teachers specific directions for the daily activities. As researchers, they understood the theory and what was required, but they felt that the teachers were not similarly prepared. It was almost impossible to breach the lines drawn between theory, in which the researchers held expertise, and daily program operation, in which the teachers had extensive experience.

This issue was complex on another level. I did not want to slip into an eclectic style of curriculum—I wanted to be firmly guided by theory—and I feared that the conflict would result in the departure of either my research staff or my teaching staff. I decided to accept the less formal view of Piagetian theory favored by the teachers rather than the stricter interpretation of my research staff. In my view, the use of theory, even well-documented theory, must be tempered by real-world advice from experienced practitioners. Thus today, the High/Scope curriculum is an amalgam of related developmental theories hammered into usefulness by decades of classroom and home-visit experiences of dedicated teachers. I have not regretted this decision nor questioned the results. When I see our approach currently being used throughout the United States, and in more than twenty countries, by a wide range of ethnic, religious, and language groups, I feel the accessibility supports the decision.

Financing

Obtaining money for any project is always difficult when one has to depend upon the kindness of strangers; obtaining money for an innovative study for an extended period of time is even more so. The initial funding for the High/Scope Perry Preschool Project came from four sources. The funds that paid for daily project services to children and families came from the State of Michigan, which permitted expenditure of state funds for handicapped children as young as three years of age. These funds were supplemented by the Washtenaw County Intermediate School District and the Ypsilanti Public Schools, which provided administrative services and space. The fourth source supported the direct research cost. These were funds from a Cooperative Education Research Grant from the U.S. Office of Education, which was then part of the Department of Health, Education, and Welfare. This four-year grant of $120,000, a princely sum in those days, was first disbursed in January 1964, eighteen months after the launch of the project. I later talked with Robert Thorndike, a member of the five-person review committee, who said that it had been the program's first grant to a public school. Committee members believed that such research at the preschool level, though little risky and odd, was innovative and full of promise.

The end of the project, in 1967, was also the end of the research grant. From then until 1970 I relied on regularly hired special services staff and small-scale Washtenaw County Intermediate School District assistance for data collection and coding. In 1970 I wrote Tom James, of the newly established Spencer Foundation, to locate assistance with follow-up. He suggested I visit his office in Chicago, in the John Hancock building, and I, of course, agreed. During the meeting we talked about many things— the weather, conditions of living and working in such a tall, modern structure, and the future direction of education in America—but only superficially discussed the study. I was disappointed with this failed opportunity to obtain funding for this work to which I had committed a decade of my life. Thus it came as a great and welcome surprise to receive approval a month later for a three-year grant of $300,000. Tom James's endorsement of our work enabled the High/Scope Perry Preschool Study to continue. I was so naive that I had not recognized the meeting for what it was: a relaxed session during which James was able to assess the individual behind the project.[1] Later study funding came from the Ford Foundation, the Carnegie Corporation of New York, and the U.S. Office of Special Education, among others.

I discovered a critical funding problem in that monies are not easily acquired for studies like ours. One-time funding to start the service component and initial research was obtained in 1963, only after a U.S. Office of Education grant review board accepted the notion that a public school staff could actually conduct a research study on this topic. (Granted, the concept of early childhood education was novel at the time and would have been considered a risky venture for anyone to undertake and to fund.) Over time, however, I managed to fund the study both by soliciting contracts and grants and by reassigning my own staff. The McCormick Tribune Foundation has now extended complete funding for the required five-year period to complete the current phase of the study—follow-up of participants at the age of forty. At no point since the 1962 initiation of this study have I been able to plan activities with such certainty.

Personal Implications

Longitudinal studies have an impact on the researcher in a number of ways. Undertaking decades-long longitudinal research studies requires an extensive commitment on the part of the principal investigator—not just a commitment of time but also a recognition that one's professional life will be shaped by the study. I have worked with children at other age levels—indeed, given a choice, I would work with adolescents—but other issues and opportunities conspired to create the High/Scope Perry Preschool Project. Once it had been formulated and launched, my commitment to the study required that I turn down other professional job opportunities—not always an easy choice. In my case, the sample was geographically based, and I felt I needed to continue to work for the public schools while executing the follow-up phase of the study. (Obviously, the decision also determined where my wife and I raised our children.) Given the extraordinary permission, coordination, and financing issues, it would have been difficult, if not impossible, for an outside researcher to operate the study.

Engagement in a project like mine also requires a certain flexibility on the part of a researcher's employer. I was fortunate that local school district officials and the building principal recognized the work's value to the children and families in the community, as well as to the public interest, and they seldom questioned my commitment to it.

Finally, the theoretical position selected to define the project represents a major professional decision and commitment that must stand up over time. The trend of moving from theory to theory or fad to fad is common in education; the newest answer, it seems, lasts for about twenty years. Either a study must be completed within that time frame or one must be ready to defend the right to stay with the old. For example, I have been asked why I used Piaget's theory, rather than Lev Vygotsky's, as a curriculum framework. Vygotsky's concept of a zone of proximal development seems, to some observers, to describe my recommendations for teacher-child interaction so much better than Piaget's. The questioner, however, had overlooked the timing of accessibility of these two theorists to an American audience. Clearly, useful longitudinal research results from a well-designed and well-executed study. If properly constructed, a study will stand on its own merits over time.

How to solve these problems without letting them dominate and close off the research? In my case, I adopted two basic strategies. First, I established an independent corporate home for the project (and related work) to avoid the lack of control I might have experienced working for the public schools, a university, or an established research institution. Second, I searched for high-quality staff to operate the organization, to develop its projects, and to invent its future.

Creating an organization to house the longitudinal study was a multistep process. The first inkling that I had an institutional problem beyond the usual came in the fall of 1969, when the school superintendent, who was sympathetic to my work, informed me that I could continue working for the public schools only if I dropped all my outside research and consulting work. I was stunned: My special services, project, and research staff totaled sixty persons out of about three hundred staff in the entire system. We were located in a separate, rented office building. Our department's travel budget was larger than that of all the rest of the school system combined, and we were operating innovative training programs and research projects with school systems all over the nation. Yet we were being blocked in Ypsilanti. Consulting with a group of outside advisers, I reviewed my options: I could stay with the public schools and abandon outside projects; I could leave my job with the Ypsilanti public schools and accept the invitation to move all operations to the local university; or I could create an independent agency, if the schools would let me move accounts, contracts, grants, and my staff—if *they* were willing to move. This was not an easy option for staff with retirement plans, guaranteed employment, and good salary schedules if they stayed with the schools but would face uncertainties on all counts if they followed me to an independent agency.

I elected the third option. On July 1, 1970, I officially established the High/Scope Educational Research Foundation in Ypsilanti, Michigan. All of my staff transferred to the new organization. ("Why not," they said. "You've always raised the money that paid our salaries, and besides, the work is interesting.") The superintendent went out of his way to facilitate the transfer of staff and equipment, writing off the paper debts of the department and overlooking ownership of some equipment. ("You are my pain-in-the-side, but who will get things done now?" was his parting comment.) All the granter and contractor organizations accepted the change and reassigned the work. The six outside advisers I had brought together to assist me in evaluating my options agreed to support their recommendation by forming the initial High/Scope Board of Directors for the newly created nonprofit (501[c]3) organization. The name "High/Scope" was drawn from the summer camping program for talented teenagers from the United States and abroad that my wife and I had operated since 1963. "High" signified our aspiration level, and "Scope" the breadth of vision we hoped to reach. An Austrian graphic artist placed the slash in the name to, as he put it, "join the two little words into one big whole."

Why the High/Scope Perry Preschool Project Happened

Looking back over forty years to understand why the study occurred brings forth a series of reasons—some deeply personal, some richly professional, and all only a part of the whole picture. The High/Scope Perry Preschool Project was fundamentally the result of my family upbringing. My parents were community social workers. My father ran settlement houses in Youngstown, Ohio, until his death at the age of forty-five, when I was fifteen years old. My mother left social work at that time and switched to elementary school teaching, which gave her the regular schedule necessary for raising four youngsters. Throughout my childhood, all kinds of people visited our home—from newly arrived immigrants struggling to adjust to life in a strange country to professionals discussing issues the community faced. I remember sitting for hours, at the dinner table or in the living room, listening to the adults discuss these issues. These experiences gave me an enduring respect for all individuals, regardless of race, creed, or ethnicity.

It was the result of my education. While attending elementary school and high school in Youngstown, I had the opportunity to associate with people from many different backgrounds. I cannot say I was aware of the differences during my elementary school years, but by high school I certainly was. The tensions and issues I experienced as a teenager in such a mix in the late 1940s reinforced my enduring sense of hope. The war was over, and great change was predicted (though for the adolescent, the most important change was that cars were being produced again). College was important for all the acknowledged reasons that still hold true today: new ideas, exacting academic standards, new friends, challenging freedoms, and the responsibility to blend all these into advantage and action. Using money earned from years delivering newspapers, part-time work, and scholarships, I entered Oberlin College, in Ohio, with the enthusiasm (and fear) only a freshman can muster. The first college in the United States to admit women (1841) and the first to admit African Americans (1935), Oberlin had a proud heritage of a commitment to learning and to applying that knowledge gained in socially responsible ways.

It was the result of my experience in the U.S. Marine Corps at the end of the Korean War. All the lofty goals of a liberal arts education were knocked about by the practical demands of learning to be hard, to be unsympathetic except to one's buddies, to accept the transformation of the Fifth Commandment—the "Thou shalt not kill" of my Methodist boyhood—into the military service equivalent, "Thou shalt not commit murder." The military shaped me into an adult with personal directives: to be in charge at least of myself and to set goals that must be reached. While I treasured the central influences of my childhood and family and carried them into adulthood, experiences from the military threw my life into sharp relief. I later discovered that if I could meet those demands, if I could adjust and survive in the military, then surely as a young professional I could meet with a school superintendent—such a meeting was nothing compared with facing my battalion commander.

It was the result of the times. In December 1955, in Montgomery, Alabama, Rosa Parks had refused to relinquish her bus seat to a white passenger, thereby marking the beginning of the end of segregation in the United States. Parks also liberated many of the rest of us to ask why things were as they were. Why do people have to live where they do? Why do inequitable educational practices exist? Why do we accept persistent differences caused by conditions and events that can be changed—or at least influenced? In such a bubbling cauldron of social questioning it was easy to believe that new approaches would produce different and better outcomes.

It was the result of being in graduate school at the time. Advanced study is the opportunity to maximize one's engagement with new ideas, to "think big," to imagine various futures. Thus when several members of the advisory committee argued that disadvantaged children of preschool age would be harmed by the program, it was an obvious step for me to convert that opinion into a hypothesis and to structure the service program as a research study. The university lectures on research design, especially sample selection, were easily applied. No one mentioned that our study designs would be rarely implemented because field studies present too many difficulties and force too many compromises.

It was the result of holding a job with genuine service responsibility. The school system management staff competently performed their jobs as they saw them. With the exception of the three reform-minded principals, they felt they were doing all that could be done—indeed all that was required. They were not concerned with what I did within the special services department, as long as I established programs for the children they could not manage in regular classrooms. The central administration was not concerned with what I did, as long as the direct expenses were covered by county, state, or other sources. Although there was little support for invention and initiative, so too was there little professional constraint.

Finally, it was the result of a change in state regulations. The State of Michigan had opened up the opportunity to counties to establish intermediate school districts, funded by county taxes, to expand special services to disabled youth between the ages of two and twenty-six. Because of these funds, I arrived on the scene in Ypsilanti as a part-time psychological examiner in the fall of 1957 to help identify elementary school children for assignment in several new classes. When the immediate work had been completed I stayed on, moving into the director's position when that post was made official in late 1958. Funds for special education programs could be procured by simply filling out the forms and meeting diagnostic standards. With few current programs in operation and extraordinary needs for countywide programs in most disability categories, the only requirement was to create effective ideas.

Study Implications

The High/Scope Perry Preschool Study has unfolded in a consistent fashion, documenting the power of intervention to improve the life chances of African American children. The advantages of attendance are evident from kindergarten onward. At no point do the children of the control group surpass the program group members. At the last study point, the program's young adults (both male and female), at the age of twenty-seven, demonstrated significantly less crime, lower welfare use, more employment with higher wages, fewer out-of-wedlock births, more car and home ownership, and higher rates of high school graduation than the no-program group (Schweinhart, Barnes, and Weikart 1993). Specific findings at the age of twenty-seven were as follows:

• Social responsibility: Only one-fifth as many program group members as no-program group members were arrested five or more times (7 percent as against 35 percent), and only one-third as many were ever arrested for dealing drugs (7 percent as against 25 percent).

• Earnings and economic status: Four times as many program group members as no-program group members earned $2,000 (1992 dollars) or more a month (29 percent as against 7 percent). Almost three times as many program group members as no-program group members owned their own homes (36 percent as against 13 percent), and more than twice as many owned second cars (30 percent as against 13 percent). Three-fourths as many program group members as no-program group members received welfare assistance or other social services at some time as adults (59 percent as against 80 percent).

• Educational performance: One-third again as many program group members as no-program group members graduated from regular or adult high school or received General Educational Development (GED) certification (71 percent as against 54 percent). Earlier in the study, the program group had significantly higher average achievement scores at the age of fourteen and higher literacy scores at the age of nineteen than the no-program group.

• Commitment to marriage: Although the same percentages of program males and no-program males were married (26 percent), the married program males were married nearly twice as long as the married no-program males (on average, 6.2 years as against 3.3 years). Five times as many program females as no-program females were currently married at the time of the follow-up interviews at the age of twenty-seven (40 percent as against 8 percent). Program females had only about two-thirds as many out-of-wedlock births as did no-program females (57 percent, as against 83 percent, of births).

• Return on investment: A benefit-cost analysis was conducted by estimating the monetary value of the program and its effects, in constant 1992 dollars discounted annually at 32 percent. Dividing the $88,433 in average benefits achieved for each participant by the $12,356 in average cost for each participant results in a benefit-cost ratio of $7.16 returned to the public for every dollar invested in the High/Scope Perry program, substantially exceeding earlier estimates. The program was an extremely good economic investment, better than most other public and private uses of society's resources (Barnett 1996). By increasing class size slightly, increasing the number of children for each adult from five to eight, the program's average annual cost for each child could be reduced to $5,500 with virtually no loss in quality or benefits.

The carefully prepared benefit-cost study using standard economic analytic procedures was undertaken to give a better basis for discussions with the corporate and public policy worlds. The findings, developed under these rigid constraints, were that for each $1.00 spent on program children, society can expect to spend $7.16 on no-program children. Investment in high-quality early childhood programs for African American disadvantaged children is clearly both a social and an economic necessity. (Data from other studies find this statement generally to be true for other groups of disadvantaged children, as well.)

What does this mean? Simply put, the ages of three and four represent a developmental period of physical, mental, and social transition that establishes the child's growth trajectory for life. We await evidence that intervention at any other point in time with any other method can be as effective. Intervention programs at other ages and developmental stages may be equally effective, or even more so, but well-designed research studies establishing their value are not available.

Public Policy

The High/Scope Perry Preschool Study has drawn great interest from public policy groups well beyond the early childhood field. During the period of this study (though certainly not as a result of this study), the national Head Start program was initiated in 1965 as part of President Lyndon Johnson's War on Poverty. During the 1970s, my basic public presentation focused on the value of early childhood education and the need for financial support for both child-care and Head Start programs. As these reports became known and melded with other social and economic factors such as the movement of women into the paid workforce, early childhood programs expanded. Federal funding growth slowed in the 1980s, but interest continued to expand at the state and local levels.

In the 1990s, Head Start appeared headed for full funding, and states such as Georgia offered an educational experience for any four-year-old child, in a mix of public and private programs financed with funds raised by a state lottery. Other states are considering similar programs. Early childhood care and education programs are undergoing major expansion in a number of states—California, Colorado, New Jersey, Michigan, and New York, to name only a few. Overseas, the High/Scope Perry study has been the basis for recommendations from Great Britain's Chief Constable Association, one of the groups urging early childhood education throughout the United Kingdom. Other countries such as the Netherlands, Norway, Finland, and Singapore have used these data in developing national policy on early childhood care and education services. The World Bank and the Inter-American Development Bank have also based new initiatives on High/Scope findings. In these efforts, the High/Scope Perry Preschool Study is frequently cited as the research base for expansion.

I would be remiss, however, if I did not point out a major problem that policy makers fail to consider. The study has been used to justify programs and procedures wildly different from the actual High/Scope program. It has even been used as a basis for programs that are at odds with the findings. For example, the High/Scope Perry Preschool Study has been mistakenly said to support the delivery of full-day kindergartens. As so often happens in public policy debates, general statements are derived from specific findings, and these general descriptions are then transferred to a very different concept. Although the study has been used inappropriately at times, it more often has been applied correctly. However, the issue is complicated. A number of studies are reporting, as we have in the High/Scope Curriculum Comparison Study (Schweinhart and Weikart 1997), that the content of the program, not simply participation in any program, is the deciding factor in its success. There is little reason to believe that spending a few hours a day with a strange adult would have any positive impact on a child's development. One task for education policy makers in the first decade of the twenty-first century will be to bring all programs up to at least the benchmark quality documented in the High/Scope Perry Preschool Study. This issue needs dedicated research both within the United States and in other countries.

The most important conclusion from the High/Scope study is the central importance of this developmental period for the child. Although the study focused on disadvantaged African Americans, it must be assumed that opportunities for active learning and for key play experiences are important for all three- and four-year-olds, regardless of race, ethnic origin, or the economic circumstances of their families. Studies in Norway, the Netherlands, Portugal, and the United Kingdom have replicated aspects of these studies on their own children with parallel results. The specific approach employed, the High/Scope curriculum approach—designed to enable children to plan, think, and work from their own understanding and interests—certainly played a major part in the success of the children studied. The High/Scope Perry Preschool Study finds that early childhood education presents a major opportunity for public investment to improve the life chances of disadvantaged children, to increase the quality of life for society, and to reduce the general public tax burden. Other studies, though not as strong, point to these same conclusions. We need to act on these findings.

Going to Scale

A number of steps are required to take an idea to wide-scale implementation and dissemination. I suggest seven criteria that are essential to a model curriculum approach. They track the work I have done over the past forty years. I did not have the benefit of these criteria when I began; rather, I recognized the needs at different points and developed responses as required.

1. A model curriculum approach must represent a coherent system based on a developmentally valid theory or belief system.

2. A model curriculum approach must be documented so that it can be understood and used by a wide range of individuals from different educational and social backgrounds.

3. A model curriculum approach needs to be validated by significant research to demonstrate that, when well implemented, it is effective.

4. A model curriculum approach needs a documented training system so that it can be transferred successfully from the model developers to a wide range of classroom or child-care settings.

5. A model curriculum approach needs to be implemented in a wide range of settings to be certain that the system actually works.

6. A model curriculum approach requires the availability of a well-developed and validated monitoring system to ensure that the curriculum is actually in operation when it is said to be employed.

7.   Finally, a model curriculum approach needs a well-developed and validated assessment system indicating the extent of growth achieved by the child.

Taking program ideas that meet these standards to scale is a major challenge. Careful studies need to be undertaken to understand this process of application.

Plans for the Future

My plans for the future are many and varied. My personal plans include retirement. From an "at-will" employer I plan to become an "at-my-will" consultant, which includes my dismal attempts to grow orchids and my better efforts at establishing summer flower beds, more time with children and grandchildren, trips with my wife, and catching up on delayed canoeing and camping expeditions.

My professional plans include supporting work to take the High/Scope curriculum approach to scale. We have the documented curriculum and staff-training methods, the validation for their use, and the instruments for assessing child growth and program implementation. We have the organizational capacity to train more than four thousand leaders in early childhood education who, in turn, will train others to implement the High/Scope approach over the next five years. In an ever widening circle, they can train and supervise a hundred thousand teachers serving a million children each year. Such a program, if tightly monitored, has the capacity to change the social and educational face of the nation within the next fifteen years. Ah, but I have learned one other thing. It probably takes more than the life span of one career to accomplish the task from invention through research to "at-scale" application. If only educational change were simpler: if only people would just do what we know works.

Note

1.   It was only the third grant I had received; the second was from the Carnegie Corporation of New York, after a site visit by Barbara Finberg in 1967.

References

Barnett, W. Steven. 1996. "Lives in the Balance: Age-27 Benefit-Cost Analysis of the High/Scope Perry Preschool Program." *Monographs of the High/Scope Educational Research Foundation.* No. 11. Ypsilanti, Mich.: High/Scope Press.

Epstein, Ann, and David P. Weikart. 1979. "The Ypsilanti-Carnegie Infant Education Project: Longitudinal Follow-Up." *Monographs of the High/Scope Educational Research Foundation.* No. 6. Ypsilanti, Mich.: High/Scope Press.

Hunt, J. McVicker. 1961. *Intelligence and Experience.* New York: Ronald Press.

Kirk, Samuel A. 1958. *Early Education of the Mentally Retarded.* Urbana: University of Illinois Press.

Krech, David, M. R. Rozenzweig, and Edward L. Bennett. 1960. "Effects of Environmental Complexity and Training on Brain Chemistry." *Journal of Comparative Physiological Psychology* 53: 509–19.

Lambie, Dolores, James Bond, and David P. Weikart. 1974. "Home Teaching with Mothers and Infants: The Ypsilanti-Carnegie Infant Education Project—An Experiment." *Monographs of the High/Scope Educational Research Foundation.* No. 2. Ypsilanti, Mich.: High/Scope Press.

Schweinhart, Lawrence, Helen Barnes, and David P. Weikart. 1993. "Significant Benefits: The High/Scope Perry Preschool Study Through Age 27." *Monographs of the High/Scope Educational Research Foundation.* No. 10. Ypsilanti, Mich.: High/Scope Press.

Schweinhart, Lawrence, and David P. Weikart. 1997. "Lasting Differences: The High Scope Preschool Curriculum Comparison Study Through Age 23." *Monographs of the High/Scope Educational Research Foundation.* No. 12. Ypsilanti, Mich.: High/Scope Press.

Sears, Pauline S., and Edith M. Dowley. 1963. "Research on Teaching in the Nursery School." In *Handbook of Research on Teaching,* edited by Nathaniel L. Gage. Chicago: Rand McNally.

Skeels, Howard M. 1966. "Adult Status of Children with Contrasting Early Life Experiences: A Follow-Up Study." *Monographs of the Society for Research in Child Development* 32.

Weikart, David P., Charles Hohmann, and W. Ray Rhine. 1981. "High/Scope Cognitively Oriented Curriculum Model." In *Making Schools More Effective: New Directions from Follow Through,* edited by W. Ray Rhine. New York: Academic Press.

PART IV

CONNECTING LIVES

Chapter 11

Plotting Developmental Pathways: Methods, Measures, Models, and Madness

ROBERT B. CAIRNS AND BEVERLEY D. CAIRNS

"How did you find me here?" Marylou blurted out, when we located her for the annual assessment at fourteen years of age. "I just can't believe you found me. I know you said you would, but I didn't really believe you. Will you find me again next year.... Promise?"

Marylou was crying as she spoke. She had just lived through a miserable year. She and her sister had been abandoned by their mother, placed in a foster home, removed from it to return to their mother, rejected anew by the mother after three weeks, placed in an emergency home care center for sixty days, and then placed in an orphanage. In the course of these moves, she had been assigned a different surname from the one she had in the seventh grade and had moved to a different part of the country. She was puzzled as to how we had located her. We found her over the next several years as well. When she married and had children, we videotaped Marylou's interactions with her children, and when the children entered school, we assessed them with the same procedures we had used with their mother when she herself had been in school.

Marylou had another distinction that our research associates and colleagues were unaware of: before entering the study, she had been identified as being in the top 5 percent of the girls judged to be at high risk for aggression and future problems of living. She had initially been nominated by school administrators, but the classification was confirmed by direct observations, peer nominations, self-reports of conflicts, and teacher ratings. She clearly qualified. When asked at the age of thirteen about a conflict with another girl, Marylou told us about a recent fight she had had with her sister. "She got hurt. I threw a board at her. I was throwing at her feet and it hit her in the head, busted her head, and she had to get stitches, four of them. Me and her just fight all the time, sometimes I even forget, forget what we're fighting over."

We also asked about a conflict Marylou had had with a boy the same year. Our field notes record the following dialogue:

Marylou: Herman was the one behind me, he was the one that popped my bra. I was doing my work and he just popped me and I got up and slapped him, I don't know how it started.
Interviewer: What did he do?
M.: He just stopped after about five hits.
I.: What happened?
M.: Nothing. He stopped, I guess he learned a lesson. I guess he got tired of me popping him.
I.: Did anything else come of it?
M.: No, Mr. Green never did tell him [not to].
I.: How did you feel about that?
M.: Embarrassed.
I.: How did Herman feel?
M.: I don't know, he probably felt hurt because I hit him.

In the reports of conflicts among children and adolescents, we find that more than 95 percent of the time the "other person" started it. By the time Marylou was in the tenth grade, her life had changed for the better, owing in large measure to the acceptance and support of her original foster parents, who reentered her life when she was sixteen. When Marylou decided to marry her boyfriend shortly after graduation from high school, however, her mother moved back into her life, temporarily, to serve as her bridesmaid. Marylou, the abandoned, angry teenager, became the mother of two children in a stable and happy marriage. Last year, twenty-seven-year-old Marylou and her husband bought their own property and located a new home for themselves and their son and daughter. Her younger sister is a welcome and frequent visitor to their home.

Marylou is one of the 695 young people who were panel members in the Carolina Longitudinal Study. She and her cohort have been followed the past nineteen years, from childhood through adolescence and into adulthood. She was initially seen in school, along with 694 of her peers. Participants shared their thoughts about themselves annually as they were growing up. We also obtained independent assessments from teachers and peers about their behaviors and social networks. Along the way, we interviewed participants' spouses, parents, and grandparents. After Marylou and her fellow participants had formed families, we saw their children in a linked longitudinal investigation.

Marylou's life illustrates some important lessons learned in our longitudinal work.

1. Lives are dynamic, and change inevitably occurs across ontogeny and generations. The processes that lead to stability and those that lead to change are equally important.

2. There is a need for renewed attention to measurement to preserve fidelity and accuracy in the description of concrete phenomena in the context of lives and groups.

3. Social influences—family and network—continuously reshape and redirect lives, and these phenomena presuppose new levels of analysis directed toward understanding social networks and social relations.

4. Predicting across generations is a hazardous but informative business. The initial returns from animal and human studies explode myths on inevitable intergenerational cycles that obscure the dynamics of change, as seen in Marylou's life.

5. There are covert hazards in longitudinal study, including phenomena lost through multivariate statistical methodologies that treat individual patterns as error variance.

Virtually all of the participants in this two-cohort longitudinal study—one begun with 220 participants in the fourth grade, the other with 475 participants in the seventh grade—continue to be involved with this study. At the end of high school, more than 98 percent of the living original participants were interviewed, regardless of whether they were enrolled in or had dropped out of school. At that time, the participants lived throughout, and a few outside, the continental United States. The Carolina Longitudinal Study is an ongoing investigation; it continues to interview participants, who are now in their twenties and thirties, along with their children, who range in age from one to fourteen years of age.

Descriptions of procedures used in longitudinal studies are usually presented in fine print, on the apparent assumption that lives speak for themselves. That belief is an illusion. The techniques adopted in longitudinal research are the heart and soul of the science. If the methods and measures are weak, misapplied, or inappropriate, the advanced statistical analyses are likely to be in error. Even behavioral observations are not "mere records." Filters exist at several levels, from the lens of behavioral observers to the syntax of the recording scheme and the statistical manipulation of data.

Antecedents

Our reason for getting into the business of studying lives over time was modestly linked to our academic experiences. We were both graduate students in the 1950s at Stanford University—Beverley in education and Bob in psychology—when modern social learning theory was undergoing a fresh evolution under the direction of Robert Sears, Albert Bandura, and Richard Walters. Although we played a role in that evolution, our early commitment to individual pathways and longitudinal study was more directly linked to what we did for a living at that time. Beverley was an elementary school teacher and administrator in a poor urban area south of San Francisco, while Bob worked as a clinician in an Alameda County, California, residential facility for delinquents.

Bonnie, Beth, and Zorrie

In her job, Beverley had responsibility for the care and teaching of a large class of fifth-grade students in a San Francisco–area school. About half of the students qualified for placement in special education classrooms, and 80 percent of the class were economically deprived. A thirteen-year-old girl named Bonnie was the class leader, and she controlled much of the rest of the school. Bonnie had been retained for three years: she was the largest, the oldest, and the lowest-achieving student in the class. She lived in a nearby house of prostitution in the care of a friend of her mother. Though she was feared, Bonnie was not without friends. Together with a couple of other girls, Beth and Zorrie, she controlled students and teachers. J. L. Moreno's (1934, 8) question—"Who shall survive?"—had special meaning here. The class's two previous teachers had left teaching in midyear rather than contend with these sullen and aggressive youth.

In the course of a year, a remarkable transformation occurred in Bonnie and in the class as a whole. For the class, a new policy had been instituted whereby every student was required to perform perfectly on selected academic assignments before the end of each week. New focus was given to how students could learn and create rather than why they had earlier failed. Individual and whole-class achievements were recognized and celebrated by field trips, class visits, and other rewards that were at once fun and educationally enriching, and a supportive structure was provided to ensure that all students met or exceeded the requirements. The performance goals were realized for all the students, including Beth, Bonnie, and Zorrie. Expectations were scaled according to ability, but the standards were unbending.

In the years that followed we kept in contact with Bonnie, whose life and prospects became increasingly dismal. After three years of failure in junior high school, she left school and conventional society. A similar trajectory held for Beth. After dropping out of school and then out of society, Beth was convicted of homicide and sentenced to life imprisonment for a death that occurred during a robbery. The lives of both girls had been genuinely shifted in their early adolescence, but the shifts did not square with the constraints they faced the next years. The goal in our own longitudinal work has been to better understand how tragedies like those of Bonnie and Beth can be understood and prevented.

At the same time Beverley was teaching, Bob worked in the clinic of a county prison for teenagers. His experiences in changing developmental trajectories were also successful, for a time. The deviant behaviors and hostile attitudes of most of the youth in the program changed remarkably—as long as they remained in custody. The most successful kids graduated and were returned home. What followed illustrates a darker meaning of the word "resilience." Regardless of level of success in the training school or therapy, virtually all of the kids reverted to some form of delinquency when they were returned to the desperate constraints of inner-city Oakland, from whence they had come. For most, graduation meant recidivism.

We both believed a fresh view was required on the methods and constructs of social development and how this information should be used in applications. We faced large obstacles, however, in translating these beliefs into research and action. The basic issues seemed so formidable and the cost so great that we felt we first had to get an overall map of the landscape of development. While social learning was clearly involved, the conceptual framework was flawed by the omission of significant developmental changes within and social forces without. Neither biological nor social ecology was included. Moreover, the seemingly robust behavioral concepts of the theory—including social reinforcement, acquired drive, and modeling—failed to fulfill their original promise. Under empirical examination, they were reduced from general behavioral learning constructs to childhood beliefs and expectations. A more inclusive developmental model was clearly required, one that focused on individuals rather than variables. We also believed that the model should explicitly integrate biological, social learning, and social ecological forces.

Comparative Investigations

To get a fresh perspective on the issues of development, Bob temporarily abandoned the conventional methods of his training. His research experiences were extended in work with J. L. Fuller, a founder of modern behavioral genetics and developmental psychobiology, at the Jackson Laboratory in Bar Harbor, Maine. If the issues of development were truly general and fundamental, they should be informed by the formulation of animal models, following the conventions adopted in sister biological sciences. Accordingly, Bob began our longitudinal intergenerational work by conducting developmental studies in assorted mammals, from sheep and dogs to rabbits and mice. Coming at animal behavior from the perspective of human development, he manipulated new genetic lines of mice and their developmental trajectories of social behavior. The comparative research proceeded rapidly and productively, in part, because animals have shorter life spans and fewer constraints in measures and design, and they carry less theoretical baggage than human beings. That work is now in its third decade and its thirty-sixth generation, having won a life of its own in basic studies of developmental genetics, neurobiology, and social change over ontogeny (Cairns 1973; Cairns, MacCombie, and Hood 1983; Cairns, Gariepy, and Hood 1990; Gariepy, Lewis, and Cairns 1996).

The design and measurement strategies of the Carolina Longitudinal Study reflect lessons in social development and intergenerational change first discovered in animal studies. The same holds for theory. In the study of ontogeny and evolution, we found that social development is a dynamic, continuing, and accommodating process in animals, as it is in humans. Methods and measures at both levels must be sensitive to change and novelty and to individual variation across development and over generations.

Methods

When we began the longitudinal study of humans more than two decades ago, we felt that progress in social development had become stalled by severe methodological and theoretical shortcomings. In methodology, there was widespread reliance upon short-term, time-limited designs and statistical procedures, which obscured individual dynamics and variability over time. In theory, there was a preference for constructs biased toward finding stability despite pervasive changes in development. In addition, reified psychopathology constructs, including attachment, aggression, and anxiety, became the primary vehicles for understanding human social development. In contrast, we have assumed that social development reflects the operation of productive, adaptive processes for individuals and the social units of which they are a part. A corollary proposition is that genetic, learning, and cognitive processes are necessarily interwoven for accommodation across ontogeny and across generations.

Longitudinal designs are not without pitfalls. Some of them have been summarized by William Kessen (1960) and more recently by David Magnusson and Lars Bergman (1990a). The difficult areas range from the issue of data quality and confounding to the problems of biased sampling in selective attrition. Time and age are also factors. It is usually the case that the effective lifetime of the investigation extends beyond the effective lifetime of the investigator. The persons who had the foresight to initiate the project and design the measures are often not the ones to complete the major analyses and interpretations. There is the possible problem that persons being studied might get to know the assessments and researchers too well, allowing them to anticipate questions and tests and also to cover up critical information that might be embarrassing. When there is slippage between the aims, the measures, and the secondary analyses and interpretations, the likelihood of error increases. There is also the special problem of mistaking temporal sequence for causality. This is the error of assuming that events that occur before a given outcome can be seen as causing the event.

At the outset, we recognized that subject loss and lack of cooperation loom as special problems in longitudinal studies of aggressive and antisocial behavior. The persons who are most likely to be lost are those who are at greatest risk for dropping out of school and other deviant outcomes (Farrington 1986; Cairns and Cairns 1994). One important factor is the social network in which subjects are embedded. The network can function as a catalyst for continued involvement and cooperation. The maintenance of the sample also interacts with the issue of data quality, in that the instruments used should take into account the cost to participants (both perceived and real) as well as the information that the procedures will yield. Quantity of information should not be equated with quality. Subjects may be overwhelmed by the number of questions and the level of their intrusiveness. Furthermore, researchers may be tyrannized by the amount of data that are yielded. On this count, nothing can substitute for thoughtful a priori analysis of instruments. Moreover, repeating exactly the same lengthy battery of inventories over multiple assessments is likely to diminish, not enhance, the value of the study. If behavioral novelty and developmental changes are anticipated, the procedures should be age appropriate and relevant to the person's motives and interests. In brief, some of the limitations included the following:

• Forgotten girls: Girls have often been underrepresented in modern longitudinal investigation. Gender bias has been particularly strong in studies of conduct disorder and violent behavior in which, until recently, females were omitted completely as participants. This underrepresentation of females persisted even in the face of strong evidence implicating females as a primary cross-generational link.

• Slippery scales: Different criteria have been employed in arriving at judgments of altruism, aggression, and social isolation, among other personality patterns, across ages, investigations, and societies. Accordingly, attempts to generalize across investigations require careful attention to the operations of measurement and analysis to determine the ways in which compatibility may be established.

• Attrition and missing persons: The loss of participants (for example, through a failure to find them in follow-up or their failure to cooperate) is a continuing concern for longitudinal researchers, with some studies reporting greater than 50 percent attrition. Failure to keep track of participants occurs easily within an open society, and it is often the most important participants who cannot be found or who refuse to cooperate. Times are shifting, and recent reports indicate much higher rates of successful tracking than were typical even ten years ago.

• Phenomena lost: Psychological measures have often demonstrated an insensitivity to developmental change because true novelties in behavior and morphology arise in adolescence and early maturity. Phenomena are "lost" by measures and statistical techniques that obscure these ontogenetic changes, either by virtue of static categories or by standard score transformations and nondevelopmental metrics and analyses.

• Safe risks: Sampling is also a large problem in the study of children and families at risk. The greater the risk, the less likely it is that children and parents will agree to participate in a longitudinal study and the more likely it is that they will drop out of it. One solution is to establish samples of convenience in poor neighborhoods and assume that the entire population is at risk, including whoever shows up. This strategy permits the researcher to get on with research, but it carries large hazards. An alternative is to create truly representative samples and invest whatever effort and time is called for to promote initial agreement and continued involvement.

• Illusionary families: Postmodern families in America and Europe show considerable diversity in structure. Only a minority of young families fits the stereotype of two natural parents who are married and living with two or more children. For example, most women in Sweden under the age of twenty-five who bear children are not married. A similar trend holds for young women in the United States, with African American women leading the way. If the research is restricted to children at home with intact families, most children will be left out of the sample.

• Lost signs: Because of the expense of longitudinal research, intervals between observations often range from two to five years, and that is responsible for a loss of information about critical events in the past (that is, "lost signs" from the past). Significant changes may occur in a life trajectory over short intervals, and it seems reasonable to expect that observations of and interviews with adolescents should take place at least annually.

• Replication: The most powerful evidence for the reliability of a phenomenon is its independent replication. On this score, many of the classic longitudinal studies are one-dimensional investigations, because no attempt was made to select independent cohorts (cohorts are separate longitudinal samples of persons within the framework of the same investigation). Generalizations from the study must be limited to that sample, and the sample has already matured.

Preparation and Preliminary Study

In the three years preceding the initiation of the Carolina Longitudinal Study (from 1977 to 1980), we completed several preliminary studies and a full-scale investigation that served as a dress rehearsal for the measures and the methods. This dress rehearsal was conducted over a one-year period in a nearby city of 135,000 persons. It involved a brief, one-year longitudinal investigation of children in three grades. In the course of that work, we revised the basic participant interview and scoring standards, refined the Interpersonal Competence Scale, developed the Social Cognitive Map social network assessment, and sharpened our procedures for assessment and evaluation (Cairns, Perrin, and Cairns 1985).

The importance of this preliminary work cannot be overstated. It helped establish a workable and efficient methodology attractive to children as well as schools and teachers. Among other issues, preliminary studies were conducted with several hundred younger children to establish the measurement properties of the instruments. These include, for example, investigations of the short-term stability and cohesiveness of social networks and friendships and the cross-national replication of our findings on social organization of peer groups.

Research Design

The Carolina Longitudinal Study is a multiple-cohort, multiple-method, multiple-level longitudinal investigation of 695 youth. The cohorts were studied separately but simultaneously in successive years on an annual basis through the end of high school. After three years, the two groups overlapped in coverage because annual assessments had begun in fourth grade for one group and in seventh grade for the other. Multiple measures were used to define each significant variable. We felt that an investigation of this magnitude requires the assurance, or measurement protection, provided by the use of several different measures of presumably the same characteristic. By design, the research is conducted at multiple levels because it seemed important to be able to zoom in, to study individuals and homogeneous subgroups, and to zoom out, to study social networks and the entire sample, in any given year. Within each cohort, subgroups of the most aggressive boys and girls were identified at the beginning of the study, along with control groups of individually matched nonaggressive children (matched with respect to classroom attended, age, sex, race, physical size, and neighborhood).

That, at least, is the official design line we provide in grant applications, books, and articles. Although it is an accurate description, it omits information about how the design was actually created. Owing to budget limits, we originally proposed to study only eighty children in two cohorts—a high-risk group and a matched control group—over three years. After the National Institute of Child Health and Human Development site visitors, and schools approved the design, we took a second and more critical look at the research design. On review, we deemed it hazardous to children, especially those most vulnerable to exposure and labeling. No matter how carefully we concealed the risk and control designations, the disguise would be transparent and only effective temporarily, if at all. Parents, teachers, schools, and the kids themselves would quickly figure out which children had been deemed "highly aggressive." To prevent this exposure, participation in the research should be inclusive and universal, we decided, regardless of a child's risk status. We revised the research design to include all children in the designated school grades, a plan that was reapproved by the schools and agencies. Risk-control comparisons were kept, but they were embedded in the total sample. Only the two principal investigators knew which children were in the hidden subgroups.

This design decision increased the workload almost ninefold. However, the revision not only protected children, it also changed the entire character of the investigation, from a limited longitudinal study of developmental psychopathology to a general longitudinal study of social development. We now had a rare opportunity to track a reasonably large representative sample of children without imposing artificial constraints related to variations in family composition, ethnicity, or presumed psychopathology. The saturated sampling procedure also had the advantage of permitting us to identify social networks in schools and the roles they play in development for all children.

The moral of this story is that what makes for good ethics also makes for good science. This lesson has been validated throughout the life of this project and its offspring programs.

When the participants were of school age, we saw each one every year, wherever they lived and whether or not they were in school. Longitudinal analyses are essential to clarify issues of individual continuity, growth trajectories, and changes over development. The design also permits a person-oriented analysis of individual ontogeny. Given the possible cultural dependency and the certain generational dependency of longitudinal findings, it seemed especially important to determine the stability and generality of the present results.

This work may also be described as 695 experiments. In this regard, each of our participants—along with families, friends, schools, spouses or live-ins, and children—constituted a separate study in progress. Each person who had been originally enrolled was considered important to the investigation. We were unwilling to write off any individual as dispensable or lost. Given the goals of our work, we rejected the assumption that attrition in some portion of the sample was normal and permissible. Persons who "disappear" in the course of longitudinal research may well be those whose lives have undergone the most radical or distinctive changes. To the extent that they remained the same or changed in outlook, they may provide the data that outlines the limits of malleability. Moreover, idiographic sources of control can be extraordinarily powerful in the lives of individuals. If it is required that all dimensions must be shared by the entire population, the most important influences in the construction of a particular life may be ignored.

The Sample

For the Carolina Longitudinal Study, 220 fourth-grade children were selected from four different public elementary schools (cohort 1), and 475 adolescents were selected from the seventh-grade classes of four public middle schools (cohort 2). The average age at midyear of cohort 1 was 10.2 years, that of cohort 2 was 13.4 years.

Overall, the sample was representative in race and socioeconomic factors. Twenty-five percent of the participants were minority status. The proportion of African American participants in the study was virtually identical to the proportion of the African American population in the communities selected for study. The mean family socioeconomic status of the sample was near the center of the Duncan-Featherman scale. The parents or guardians of our participants represented the full range of occupations. They included the chairman of a medical school department in a major university, attorneys, regional sales managers, small-business owners, truck drivers, domestics, farmworkers, and the chronically unemployed. Following the Duncan-Featherman scale, a numerical score from 11 to 87 was assigned to each family based on the highest job level in the family (that of the primary wage earner). The average was 30.2 in cohort 1 and 31.6 in cohort 2—close to the national mean of 34.5.

All children in the designated classrooms were invited to join without regard to selection factors (such as intact families or age or number of siblings). A signed letter of permission was required, indicating informed consent from parents and children. Parents and grandparents were also interviewed, but only with the consent and support of the original participants. In the schools, we attempted to identify the social network in which the children were embedded. This required that we obtain information about the friends and peers of each of the original participants.

The idea behind such extensive data collection was that each person was embedded in a context of influences. Given that assumption, it was not sufficient to measure only the individual; we had to assess the effective social context of which the individual was a part. The effects of parents and grandparents are not just historical. Parents and grandparents are also contemporaneous agents who contribute to the quality and direction of the individual's behaviors and attitudes. As circumstances change, so too must some features of the individual. Peer influences are not merely a phenomenon of adolescence, so it was necessary to identify social groups preceding and following puberty.

The Context

A brief look at the character and demographic properties of the rural and suburban communities made us realize that the "community" is not so easily identified. In any longitudinal study that extends beyond a decade, the place where the observations begin cannot be assumed to be the same as the place where the observations continue. This is the case even when children remain in the same house from infancy through adolescence. Over time, changes in the environment may occur owing to shifts in family residence or age-related changes in mobility and personal definition of the environment, alone or combined with secular changes in the character of the communities themselves. Over the period from childhood to adulthood, children may move from one house to another, from one community to another, or from one state or country to another. In this regard, change itself may be less important than the reasons for change. Is the move the result of a shift in parental employment, family breakup because of death or divorce, or a pattern of chronic migration and instability? Does the change in the character of the community reflect a national recession or expanding growth and local economic opportunities? The reasons for environmental change are doubtless important.

For children and adolescents, the definition of community was age dependent. Once adolescents in this region reached the age of sixteen, they qualified for driver's licenses, and cars were available for most of them. On Friday and Saturday nights it was commonplace for some teenagers in Georgetown[1] to drive to nearby cities. Change in the boundaries of "the community" at this stage reflected an age-related expansion that had been in process since early childhood and would accelerate throughout the transition years.

Each of the communities themselves underwent changes, some major and some minor, over the decade. All of the communities suffered from the deep recession that occurred in 1982 and 1983, and the dominant manufacturing facilities in the region became depressed. This economic downturn translated into a major loss of income for a significant number of families whose children were involved in our observations. There were also periods of economic growth, however, during which some sectors of the community prospered.

Community settings can constrain individual pathways in life. Depending on where they live and the circumstances of their families, children can be affected by events as broad as perturbations in the national interest rate, and its effect on the closing of the only manufacturing plant in town, or as local as the widening of a two-lane road into a highway. Not only do children and families develop and change, so too do the communities in which they live and the social networks of which they are a part. In the course of growing up, many participants and their families moved. By the age of nineteen, only half of the individuals lived in the county in which they resided at the beginning of our study. In the first year, a significant portion of the participants dispersed to distant points—north to Alaska and south to Ecuador—as well as other rural and urban areas of the United States. It was sometimes a major task to find these young people and their families, especially those who sought deliberately to lose the past and create new lives. Any effort to identify the person in context must recognize that the contexts are likely to change over time, along with the person.

Cooperation and Trust

We typically found cooperation, helpfulness, and a genuine desire to assist from everyone whose life our study touched. We discovered that most persons in most schools across the country were extremely helpful, as were most parents and guardians. Perhaps the most important element in maintaining individual cooperation was to secure support from the community at large and the effective social unit of which the participant was a part. The levels of participation increased in the schools as the community became better acquainted with us. Participation rates of seventh-graders (as determined by the proportion of children and parents who signed and returned informed consent permission forms) rose from 50 percent in the first middle school to 89 percent in the last.

Beyond the home and school, public and state agencies provided assistance to the project as well. These included the courts, residential psychiatric facilities, social service agencies, probation departments, and other locations for the treatment of deviant or disturbed adolescents. None could be taken for granted, and every new contact was a challenge. All required patience and persistence. Virtually every school had at least one ill-tempered, suspicious, or neurotic person on staff. In each case, critical issues had to be dealt with sensitively and rapidly. At each stage of the research it was necessary for investigators to balance their responsibility to participants, schools, and parents, on the one hand, and their responsibility to the research program, on the other. Ordinarily, these two commitments were not in conflict. In the present case, it helped that one of us was experienced in school administration and acquainted with the multiple problems that confront teachers, parents, and participants.

The cooperation of the participants themselves also could never be taken for granted. Each year they received small gifts, and smaller children got smaller gifts. For participants in the fourth grade, we began with paper stickers and pencils featuring the logo of neighboring universities. These school-related gifts to participants escalated each year until the twelfth grade, when each received a see-through solar calculator. High school seniors were also given a T-shirt specially designed for them by a nationally syndicated cartoonist.

We were committed to the proposition that no one would be hurt by his or her participation. In the course of this investigation, we sometimes were informed of incidents that were illegal, embarrassing, and harmful to the participants; we always honored their trust. Many of the participants, after years of receiving gifts, reciprocated in later adolescence and gave us gifts to express their affection and respect. We now have a collection of ceramic dishes, T-shirts, photographs, pictures, pens, and so on.

Although we tried to keep a low profile in day-to-day activities in the schools, we felt it important to keep students and teachers fully informed about the investigation. We helped student reporters prepare stories about the project for school newspapers, conducted workshops for teachers and counselors, and met with the administrative boards of school districts. An attractive pamphlet, answering the ten most frequently asked questions about the project, was printed and distributed to members of school boards, parents, participants, and teachers. As the work progressed, we were invited to meet with the leaders of the state General Assembly regarding recommendations on the prevention of school dropout. These activities reduced misunderstanding about our work, and they provided a protective buffer when potential problems arose.

Lost and Found: The Problem of Attrition

All longitudinal studies are vulnerable to sample attrition, and our research was no exception. Loss of participants means that the information obtained may be biased toward the most stable and conventional members of the community. It is not safe to assume that participants will be lost at random. Reasons for sample attrition are multiple: participants become "lost," for example, because of family breakup, because parents or guardians move to unknown destinations, because child custody arrangements change, because an adolescent runs away from home or joins the military. Other participants are not lost at all; they simply no longer wish to participate, or their parents withdraw permission.

In 1990, at the end of the tenth year of the study, all 695 participants in our original research sample were relocated. A small proportion (0.6 percent) were no longer living, and some (1.3 percent) declined to be interviewed. In mid-1990, the sample became national in scope. The participants lived throughout the United States, from Alaska to Florida and from California to Massachusetts. Locating most of the participants was routine; the task was not a major issue for six out of ten participants. The remainder were found with increasing difficulty.

Participants who dropped out of school before graduation were a special challenge to locate, even when they did not leave the community. The problems were multiplied when they migrated across the country. Finding these "lost" participants required ingenuity and stubbornness. No simple recipe could be followed because new problems continued to present themselves. The job was made easier when close relationships were established with persons in key positions in the school system and the community. They could then be relied upon for directions and clues as to the current whereabouts of the individual, and they sometimes provided invaluable assistance in gaining the participant's cooperation and confidence.

Are the returns of tracking worth the costs? No simple answer can be given without detailed information about the actual characteristics of the individual participant. One may argue, on the one hand, that the individuals who become lost are more likely than those who are easily found to have experienced further difficulties in living. Hence the lost participants may be seen as a special risk sample, according to Leonard Eron and Rowell Huesmann (1987). On the other hand, the participants who are "lost" may experience such a sharp shift in living circumstances as to lead to enduring changes in their lives and subsequent behavior. In our experience, some of the more serious problems and dramatic changes took place in the lives of individuals who would have been entirely lost from standard longitudinal tracking. What to one child is a risk may be a lifeline to another. Given the goals of this investigation—to identify naturalistic shifts in circumstances that could bring a turnabout in a life trajectory—it was imperative that we attempt to relocate all participants.

The children and adolescents who were difficult to find year after year were the ones who were at greatest risk for problems in school and in the community. We found, for instance, that there was a greater likelihood of early school dropout if the child or adolescent moved from one residence to another. This effect held for both males and females, and it held in both groups of participants. The risk for dropout was consistently three to four times as great if moves had occurred, regardless of gender or sample. Further analysis indicates that dropping out was not merely an effect of moving itself: even before moving, individuals who would later change residence differed from those who would not, on those behavioral dimensions predictive of dropout—namely, aggression and academic incompetence (as measured by grades failed or ratings of academic performance). They did not differ on socioeconomic status, and they differed only marginally on measures of popularity and peer acceptance. The last effect suggests that, although there may be quite different reasons for moving depending upon socioeconomic status, those participants whose families did change residence tended to differ from peers in terms of behaviors that are generally associated with school failure and interpersonal difficulties.

The lesson is clear. Participants who are most likely to be lost from longitudinal studies are not random cases. To the contrary, they are likely to be those persons who are at greatest risk for problems of living and health.

Measures

The heart of any investigation lies in the objectivity, replicability, and validity of the measures it employs. The public transduction of empirical phenomena into theoretical constructs distinguishes this enterprise from common sense and clinical intuition. In the study of social patterns, validity is hard won, and slippage may occur at any step of the design-measurement-generalization process. In the absence of a standard for longitudinal assessment, we proceeded cautiously in the selection and refinement of measurement instruments. For this reason, we spent two years in preliminary study to ensure that the procedures were sensitive to the phenomena we wanted to focus upon.

We have proposed the idea that the puzzles of human development require researchers to study each life as a whole (Cairns and Cairns 1994). This general proposition goes beyond a vague commitment to individuality, integration, and holism. It has strong implications for how the business of science should proceed. Among other things, it implies that multiple levels of measurement are required rather than a focus upon single variables, single tests, or single contexts. One of the reasons is that the momentary features of relationships and contexts, for the most part, limit behaviors.

Behavioral actions and cognitions, the stuff of psychology, have a special status for biological adaptation and integration. In the accommodations of human development—particularly social patterns—the actions and counteractions of other persons constitute major extra-organismic sources of behavioral organization. These actions are at the interface between the internal constraints of the individual and the external constraints of the setting. Some actions and cognitions, including one's self-concept, are tailored for specific functions, such as providing reasons for getting out of bed in the morning. Other actions, such as those dictated by social etiquette and styles, are more strongly constrained by the immediate context. Several domains of activity are organized within the individual and provide mutual constraints; but synchrony does not mean substitutability. Each system is organized on its own terms, and one's self-reflections may be poorly associated with the judgments that others make.

The practical implication is that we had better be careful about how and what we measure. Self-reports, such as survey interviews or tests, are necessary but not sufficient. Also needed are objective observations of behavior taken by independent researchers, which can provide information about unconscious actions that are beyond the individual's own awareness. Other informants outside the self and outside the extended self of the family are important as well. These include information from peers and teachers. Other individual measures include contemporaneous records—from schools, the courts, the state. These have clear limitations, but they help transcend context and permit us to bridge the gap between individual measures and epidemiological statistics.

Then there are measures of the world beyond the individual. In life, the "environment" is not a single thing; nor is it a stable, unchanging entity. To the contrary, at any one stage, a person's life has multiple contexts, including different individuals and groups that are important to the person. In these contexts, each of us potentially has different selves. This means that the longitudinal measurement of individual actions must identify the multiple social contexts of a person's life: the family, best friends, peers, social groups and networks, spouse, and children. It is also critical to identify the several physical contexts afforded by the home, the school, and the community. The behavioral phenomena we observe in individuals over time represents a complex equation that incorporates all of these.

In recognition of the fallibility of single information sources, we employed multiple measures of each quality or characteristic. We thought it essential to understand the source of variance that each measure captured before we attempted to combine the components. That was no small trick when the sources for our information extended from teachers, peers, parents, social networks, the courts, and probation departments to school records, school yearbooks and newspapers, and interviews from the individuals themselves. In addition, parents and grandparents participated in semistructured interviews when subjects were in their late adolescence.

Data tyranny is a special hazard in longitudinal work. To have sufficient statistical power to conduct multivariate analyses, a reasonably large number of participants must be studied on repeated occasions. More participants and more measures inevitably lead to more data. The problems are compounded by the accumulation of data year by year. Computers help, but nothing can substitute in the analysis for a clear statement of aims of the research and the establishment of priorities.

We adopted a minimalistic strategy in data collection (see appendix 11.A). Two of the points that led to that decision are especially worthy of note because they are opposite to the assumption that more is better. Greater depth of understanding is not always associated with greater coverage or length of assessments, in that the costs of extensive subject participation can outweigh the returns. There are special needs in longitudinal assessment for data quality, subject retention, and community support. Attention should be given to minimizing the demands of the assessment upon individual children and parents. Wherever possible, the assessments should be subject friendly or take advantage of involvement in other normal functions (for example, preschool and school activities, health checkups). In general, priority was given in all measurement to brevity consistent with clarity and reliability. The backbone of our yearly contact was a semistructured face-to-face interview conducted annually with each subject. The interviews were tape-recorded and solicited information about social networks, friendships, conflicts, perceived parental attitudes, and other domains. Our interview procedures differed from those employed in many other contemporary research settings, and a comment is required to clarify the nature of the information obtained. Our semistructured procedures were modeled after those pioneered by Robert Sears and his colleagues (Sears, Maccoby, and Levin 1957) in studies of child rearing and development and extended by Albert Bandura and Richard Walters (1963) in studies of delinquency and Michael Rutter in longitudinal investigation. The interviewers were extensively trained to follow an interview protocol. It was semistructured along two axes: (1) the interviewers permitted the subjects to give extended answers (as opposed to multiple choice) and to express their concerns in their own words as opposed to responses to items and constructs defined by the interviewer, and (2) an explicit interview protocol was followed, along with standard probes to gain additional information. On the one hand, this method differs significantly from survey methods whereby subjects are given explicitly defined categories of response from which they must select, and it differs from clinical interviews, which provide modest or loose structure.

Data Quality

The question of data quality refers to the reliability and validity of the raw information and the research measures. Confidence in the information obtained on a specific issue can be no stronger than the weakest link in the process of sampling, measure design, data collection, transcription, transduction, and analysis. Accordingly, we felt that it would be misguided to assign the primary data collection to the least informed or most naive members of a research team. Exactly the opposite research strategy should be followed, if history is a reliable guide to the achievement of future progress. The essential contributions of Alfred Binet, Wilhelm Preyer, Sigmund Freud, Jean Piaget, J. M. Baldwin, Zing-Yang Kuo, T. C. Schneirla, and Arnold Gesell may be traced, in large measure, to instances in which the investigators themselves participated in the data collection.

Twenty-one persons were involved in the primary data collection at some time over the several years of this study. At least two persons served as interviewers in each of the years, and typically four individuals were involved. However, one of us (Beverley) was always one of the interviewers in the first several years of the study. This ensured continuity in contact with parents, schools, and subjects. Interviewers were rotated to different participants from year to year so that potential biases could be eliminated; this rule was modified only in unusual circumstances. In addition, appropriate safeguards were instituted to ensure that the observers, interviewers, raters, and coders were blind with respect to the participant's standing on the relevant variables and information gathered from other sources. Each year, different teachers acted as raters. When appropriate, fresh investigators were introduced into the study to safeguard the objectivity of the measures and the coding.

One issue of data quality should be emphasized, namely, the decision to rely upon concrete measures of adaptation and outcome rather than on standardized survey instruments and inventories. This is the most serious criticism that might be offered of the methodology in this investigation. We believe that the criticism is misguided on five counts.

1. Self-report measures (whether called tests, surveys, or interviews) are seriously constrained by the perceptions of the persons who are providing the information. Hence lengthy assessments by overlapping inventories that purport to measure a given quality tend to provide correlated information. On this score, they provide an overload for the subjects without a redeeming increase in information.

2. Longitudinal assessments that are conducted on an annual basis yield information about stability and change and thereby enhance the reliability of any given measure. For example, brief assessments can become robust by permitting the investigator to contrast, construct, or combine data over adjacent years.

3. It is an illusion to view measures with constrained response categories for subjects as more "objective" than measures that permit

individual response variation. The objectivity arises in the scoring and interpretation process, not in the way information is recorded at the first stage.

4. This investigation gave priority to the concrete realities of the individual's life and his or her perceptions rather than to the tracking of psychological constructs as defined by tests currently in vogue. We felt that the more concrete measures we obtained could, at any generation, be translated by cross-validation into the results of comparable tests and surveys.

5. Perhaps most important, we felt that currently available procedures tended to obscure real developmental changes by focusing upon between-individual differences rather than the concrete adaptations of individuals. On the other hand, currently available standardized techniques focus upon individual differences at the expense of the analysis of systematic developmental change. We hoped to preserve information about both phenomena in our measurement strategy. This meant that we needed to conduct additional assessments to ensure that our procedures showed an expected network of relationships with other commonly employed measures, in addition to our demonstration of their ability to predict real-life outcomes (see appendix 11.B).

Models

In a prescient essay that appeared in the first *Handbook of Child Psychology*, Kurt Lewin (1933) outlines the need to study the dynamic relations between the individual and the environment in the concrete particularity of the total situation. Lewin challenges the dominant methodology of psychological inquiry of his time on two counts; namely, its reliance on aggregation for description and statistical analysis to describe the mythical "average child" or "average family" and its focus on psychological "variables" independent of the context in which they occurred. On the first matter, Lewin argues that the "average child" is a statistical invention. It is more than a benign illusion; it is a productive mischief. For Lewin, clumping together children who are similar with respect to salient extrinsic or demographic characteristics—but different with respect to psychological dynamics—is guaranteed to mislead.

More than a half century has passed since Lewin's seminal contributions. Some of his ideas on the need to establish ecological validity have been incorporated into the mainstream of the field, and they are no longer identified as distinctively Lewinian. One nuclear issue—namely, the need to understand the behavior of specific individuals in specific settings—remains to be resolved by developmental psychologists. At first blush, the problem of when or whether to group participants may seem to be an important though technical issue, one that should be decided by statistical and methodological journeymen. However, the choice of the unit of analysis—whether the person, the variable, or the group—is the cornerstone upon which all subsequent decisions of research strategy necessarily rest. An issue so central to understanding science is too important to leave to the experts.

In a cogent analysis of the issues, David Magnusson has outlined a framework for developmental research that has radical implications for how the scientific enterprise should proceed. In brief, Magnusson (1988) argues that the field should make a commitment to understand the processes of human behavior and that technological goals (that is, prediction and control) should be secondary. The configuration of factors that operate in each individual's life requires that attention be given to the behavior of each person as an "integrated totality." The action patterns of every person represent a unique mosaic of biological, interactional, and situational factors. To the extent that these configurations are distinctive and individual over time, the person's status on a single variable (or set of variables, independent of context) is a fallible guide for understanding.

Developmental researchers are usually confronted with networks of relationships, not single linkages between antecedent and consequent. This state of affairs has yielded a cornucopia of positive findings and interpretations. The abundance of "significant" findings in contemporary developmental research has also had a negative side in that it shifts responsibility for understanding phenomena away from the data themselves. The findings have often become projective tests for the field, and the burden for interpretation shifted thereby from data to a priori beliefs.

It has been widely assumed that because social phenomena are multi-determined and complex, the statistical analyses employed to study them should be equally complex. We believe that this assumption is misguided. When the complexity within the phenomenon is permitted to breed complexity in the analysis and interpretation, it often means that there has been a failure in theory or a lack of creativity in design. To clarify complicated issues, the simpler the statistic, the better. Parsimony in analysis may be permitted because the major analytic problems have been solved earlier—namely, in the design created, in the methods adopted, and in the precision of the hypotheses.

Beyond the usual challenges that face social science investigators who are confronted with complex data sets, developmental researchers have special problems. Virtually all life-course and developmental hypotheses presuppose that fresh influences and new opportunities arise from within the individual or in the social context. Most theoretical statistical models assume, however, that there is nothing new under the sun.

How might categories and dimensions that permit novelty be introduced, without presupposing that the same pattern of latent variables is expressed at all developmental stages or in all persons? The factor or dimensional stability question has been investigated in our research by employing concrete categories at the first level of data collection. Whenever feasible, the initial coding distinctions are qualitative rather than quantitative. We adopted measures that preserved the concrete characteristics, functions, and features of the behaviors of participants. This technique of data recording was followed in direct behavioral observations, in interview reports, and in community reports. The use of qualitative categorical classifications permitted us to determine whether some concrete behaviors would rise and others would fall across time and still others would emerge anew or disappear. In addition, the information has permitted the use of multivariate statistical techniques to determine whether new dimensions appeared over time. This strategy permitted us to conclude, for example, that a new dimension of social aggression appeared in girls in early adolescence that coexisted with confrontational aggression (Cairns et al. 1989).

A second issue concerns the appropriate unit or dimension of analysis. Magnusson and Bergman (1990a, b) observe that most analyses of behavior are "variable oriented" rather than "person oriented." One alternative to multivariate analysis is a multiperson analysis, the task of which is to identify the patterns of problem behaviors that occur across individuals—the "packages" of deviance. The second step in this strategy is to determine the reason for covariance of delinquent characteristics in particular combinations. Such a "person-oriented" analytic strategy would support investigations that are addressed to the processes and dynamics of deviant behavior rather than to their dissection in populations. The proposal may be subsumed by the more radical proposition that certain developmental phenomena are sufficiently unique as to require analysis at the individual, configurational level rather than at the sample, population level. Generalizations may then be reached on the basis of the lawfulness of processes within persons over time as opposed to the lawfulness of associations within populations (see Allport 1937). The unit of study becomes the individual, not populations. One enduring problem in behavioral study concerns the issue of how to translate ephemeral processes about individual adaptation—actions and interactions—into quantifiable patterns without a loss of essential information.

One strategy we have adopted has been to identify configurations of boys and girls who had common behavioral and demographic profiles in childhood. Such a configurational strategy is based on the assumption that developmental trajectories of aggressive behavior reflect the operation of both personal and social factors over time. Hence the simultaneous employment of internal and external characteristics should be key to isolating commonalities in developmental pathways. Such a strategy directs as much attention to the "failures" of prediction as to its "successes." The hazard with conventional models has been that developmental phenomena may themselves become distorted by the very operations designed to make them accessible to empirical analysis. The problem is magnified when standard multivariate analyses treat distinctive trajectories of individual development as error variance.

The pitfalls in understanding are more often logical than mathematical. On this score, it is a minor irony that many of the statistical procedures introduced to study children of different ages have served to reduce or eliminate the impact of maturation and developmental change. For example, the workhorse of longitudinal research, the familiar correlation coefficient, eliminates real differences in performance associated with maturation as it is typically employed. Similarly, statistical transformations that underlie the IQ ratio get rid of age-related differences in cognitive functioning. Modern refinements of scaling have achieved the same outcome through standardization of scores, in which same-age peers provide the reference group. These scaling techniques are not limited to the study of intelligence. They have become the strategies of choice for measures of aggressiveness, deviance, and unconventional behavior.

To sum up, methods and measures reflect both the art of design and the objectivity of science. Systematic theory, when combined with appropriate methods and analyses, is a necessary springboard to extend our understanding beyond common sense as well as to understand common sense. Precise methods and advanced analyses, however, do not guarantee progress. To the contrary, misleading findings may arise when there is a gap between the ideas that gave rise to the work and the empirical operations adopted to define and analyze those ideas.

Madness

"Understanding the integrity of the life course," Richard Jessor writes, "tracing its continuity over large segments of time, distinguishing what is ephemeral from what is lasting, grasping the role that the past plays in shaping the future—all these, and more, are issues that yield only to research that is longitudinal and developmental in design" (Jessor, Donovan, and Costa 1991, 3). The necessity for longitudinal study seems compelling and the research priorities seem clear. Beneath the surface, however, there are elements of madness in longitudinal efforts that deserve attention, if not awe. These include the following:

1. Theory-method schizophrenia: Developmental change is easily recognized but difficult to capture. Change and development are abstract and ephemeral ideas, while stability seems concrete and lasting.

Maybe that is why psychology has tried to get rid of developmental change in measures, statistics, and constructs. Indeed, many longitudinal studies themselves reduce developmental changes by z-score transformations or by standardization of the results. Developmental changes are further obscured in longitudinal study by stability correlations and regression coefficients or the use of aggregated measures that do not shift over time. One of the primary criteria for selecting measures reflects the bias. Requiring high test-retest reliabilities in measures helps ensure that short-term changes will not be detected; they are treated as error variance. Once eliminated empirically, developmental change is then removed in theory by assuming latent constructs that do not change over time. Intelligence, attachment, and aggression refer to dynamic processes that have been reified and transformed into stable psychological structures. The pervasive bias toward minimizing change defeats a primary attribute of longitudinal research and qualifies as a special form of schizophrenia. A related schizophrenic subtype is the adoption of a social ecological model of the development of persons in context without the adoption of explicit measures of proximal social influences such as close friendships, social network membership, and neighborhoods.

2. Dissociation in basic and action research: This phenomenon is not easily diagnosed, but it has had a crippling impact on prevention research. It seems reasonable to expect that, after a half-century investment in the dynamics of human lives over the life course, we would have identified a set of principles that could be transmitted to practitioners and others involved in applied settings, including prevention researchers. Although some instances of such integration may be cited, it seems to be more often the case that there is a dissociation between "basic" longitudinal research and "applied" prevention and action studies. To be sure, the two types of research seem to require different talents, and they have distinctive goals. The individuals being studied provide a common denominator, however, and this fundamental commonality should transcend disciplinary and methodological differences. In our experience, applied research can be guided by longitudinal findings. Conversely, action studies provide opportunities to gain experimental confirmation of correlational longitudinal findings. The dissociation in research in action can be overcome, but only with explicit attention to the problem.

3. Generation gaps: One of the common ideas in the popular media, and in some scientific circles, is that there are inevitable intergenerational cycles of behavior, attitude, and thought. A prime example is the purported "cycle of violence"; another is the "bell curve" assumption of innate determinants of intelligence. The most compelling informa-

tion on hypothesized intergenerational cycles is provided when two linked generations are studied prospectively and longitudinally, from the childhood of the parents, in their own time, to the childhood of the parents' offspring. To complete the intergenerational cycle, the same measures should be employed in longitudinal studies of the two generations. The early returns from using this intergenerational methodology are highly provocative, indicating that predictions from the childhood of generation X to generation Y are surprisingly modest for aggressive behavior (Cairns and Cairns 1994). Given the level of investment in longitudinal study, extensions to studies that follow two generations seem imperative. This kind of study can be promoted by a system of shared professional identities.

4. Lost identities: Who of sound mind would invest his or her most productive years in a study that could not possibly be finished in one scientific lifetime? If not mad, those who knowingly spend their lives and talents in the design and conduct of a long-term longitudinal investigation must represent a high form of scientific altruism. Accordingly, they deserve headline or byline recognition in all publications that report the harvest of their labors. Unless this ethical imperative holds even when the original investigators are dead or forgotten, it seems madness, as well.

5. Egocentrism, narcissism, and chauvinism in longitudinal research: This scientific pathology refers to the errors of interpretation that are invited when researchers fail to view longitudinal findings in international and comparative contexts. Independent replication is called for. In this regard, the investigative team itself may attempt to extend the longitudinal work to other settings or to use multiple settings in the first iteration. For example, we did not have a large inner-city sample in the original Carolina Longitudinal Study design, so we have spent an additional five years in an accelerated longitudinal study of inner-city youth in four age cohorts, covering the span from the first through the twelfth grades. This within-laboratory investigation cannot, however, substitute for close collaboration with other ongoing investigations in this country and elsewhere. Moreover, if biobehavioral principles are truly general—including those of behavioral genetics and developmental psychobiology—they can be explored and confirmed in coordinated longitudinal-intergenerational comparisons of selected mammalian species and cross-national studies.

In conclusion, the conduct of longitudinal-intergenerational research is far from mad. What we have called madness is the tendency to treat longitudinal study as business as usual. We believe that Richard Jessor, along with some other of our colleagues, provides a sane vision of the potential of longitudinal and intergenerational research. We are collectively engaged in an activity—the interdisciplinary study of human beings over time and generations—that requires a new way of thinking and conducting research. The concepts and procedures that have evolved extend beyond the disciplines from which the studies originally emerged. There is something new under the sun, and developmental science is an appropriate label for this emerging discipline.

Appendix 11.A: Criteria for the Selection of Longitudinal Measures

1. Multilevel, multimethod measures are required to establish the course and maintenance of behaviors across development.

2. There are special needs in longitudinal assessment for data quality, subject retention, and community support. Attention should be given to minimize the demands of the assessment on individual children and parents. Wherever possible, the assessments should be "subject friendly" and take advantage of involvement in other normal functions (for example, preschool and school activities, health checkups). In general, priority should be given in all measurement to brevity consistent with reliability.

3. Assessments should include but not be limited to standardized procedure (for example, tests, structured interviews); they should include procedures that capture the concrete details of lives in context.

4. In the study of social development, there is a special need to assess units beyond individuals. This includes the need to include measures of dyads, social networks, and neighborhoods.

5. Social and physical contexts change over time along with individuals. Developmental analysis presupposes precise measures of contextual events beyond the individual, including shifts in social networks, family structures, neighborhoods, and societal events.

6. The stages of individual and social development should be explicitly defined, and the task of assessment should be organized in ways that are sensitive to these stages.

7. Decisions on the frequency of assessment and intervals between assessment should respect the individual's stage of development and the nature of the phenomena. In individual assessment, there will be a need to impose different calendars according to the developmental stage of the individual and the phenomenon.

8. Greater depth of understanding is not always associated with greater coverage or length of assessments, in that the costs of extensive subject participation can outweigh the returns.

9. Continued involvement in the study should be independent of the completion of any given instrument or assessment period. Suitable techniques are available for the estimation of missing data; it is more problematic to estimate the effects of missing subjects.

10. Rigid replication of the total assessment procedure each year is not only unnecessary, it can diminish the data quality by failure to attend to the special properties of repeated assessment demanded by longitudinal involvement.

Appendix 11.B: Summary of Primary Carolina Longitudinal Study Measures

The subjects and their teachers annually completed a brief test (the Interpersonal Competence Test), which originally consisted of a series of fifteen items for the teacher and eighteen items for subjects (including three "filler" or distracter items). Consistent with the minimalist bias, we attempted to keep the interview and related test procedures brief. This succeeded for the initial years of measurement (interviews were approximately twenty to thirty minutes in length), but in later years they grew longer (forty-five to sixty minutes in length).

Beyond these annual measures directly from participants and teachers, information was gathered from the school yearbooks, newspapers, and reports from schools on school dropout. In brief, the fourteen domains of information in the school period include the following:

1. Social networks: Composite cognitive maps of the social network and social organization of the classes and schools were developed on the basis of information provided by participants and peers. The networks yielded information about the persons with whom each participant was affiliated, if they had an affiliative group. Information on networks and friendships was collected annually.

2. At-risk and nonrisk control: Identification of children who were at high aggressive risk, along with matched nonrisk control subjects, were obtained before the beginning of the study from teachers and principals when children were in the fourth grade (cohort 1) or seventh grade (cohort 2). (The "risk" definition is discussed more fully in Cairns and Cairns 1994, chapter 4.)

3. Social cognitive interview: Self-reports and self-cognitions, derived from individual interviews that cover the self, family, and peers, along with perceptions of friendships, recent conflicts, and goals for the future, were recorded. The interview was age graded and circumstance sensitive. The semistructured interviews were conducted annually and tape-recorded.

4. Direct behavioral observations: Extensive, weeklong observations were made that employed synchronized, multilevel observational procedures in school classrooms and physical education classes. These observations were made for all subjects in the high-risk and matched control groups upon entry. This process occupied much of the research assessment time in the first three years of the investigation. Additional observations were made after three years.

5. Interpersonal Competence Scale (ICS): Ratings by teachers, counselors, and parents on social acceptance, peer conflicts, academic performance, and social relations yielded assessments of behavior in the school or the home on popularity, aggressiveness, academic competence, affiliation, and a summary dimension, social competence. In addition, subscales of the ICS tapped appearance, athletics, and emotionality as well as withdrawn and shy behaviors. These ratings are available annually as long as participants remained in school.

6. Interpersonal Competence Scale self-reports (ICS-S): Participants rated themselves annually on the same scales employed by teachers, permitting the longitudinal plotting of self-attributions and comparisons with sources outside the self. This information is available annually for all years of the investigation.

7. Peer nominations: Each year, participants and peers provided a "cognitive map" of the social network, nominating best friends, boyfriend or girlfriend, and persons with whom they have had recent conflicts, thereby allowing peer assessments of each participant's behaviors. This information is available annually.

8. Maturation: Each year observers rated participants on dimensions of morphological maturation and, for girls, the age of menarche. In addition to the self-reports and observations on maturation, yearly photographs were obtained of the participants and, when possible, their infants and children, along with ratings of physical attractiveness. The morphological development and attractiveness ratings from researchers (along with ratings by self and teachers) are available annually.

9. Academic progress: School performance and failure was determined from counselors, teachers, and the participants themselves. The information from the school included school grade placement, graduation, school dropout, and serious problems of attendance. This information was available annually.

10. Delinquency and crime: These measures were obtained from court records, reports from probation officers, self-reports, Department of Motor Vehicle records, visits to detention facilities and prisons,

and published records of arrests and court actions. This information was available after subjects were old enough to drive.

11. Marriage and births: Information was obtained from county records, self-reports, and direct interactions with the spouse and infants, or both, in year-to-year assessments. This information was collected on a continuing basis from newspaper reports.

12. Family status and runaway: Changes in family composition, incidents of runaway, and familial attitudes were determined in the annual interviews with participants, late-adolescent interviews with parents, and visits to the locations where the participants lived.

13. Employment: Various economic data, including teenage jobs and automobile operation and ownership, were obtained from the participants themselves and, in some instances, visits to the workplace. This information was collected annually from midadolescence.

14. Health, accidents, and mortality: Information was obtained from participants, school personnel, newspaper reports, the Department of Motor Vehicles, and, in the case of death, the Office of the State Medical Examiner.

These procedures are described in greater detail in several technical reports on research for the Carolina Longitudinal Study.

Note

1. Georgetown is a fictitious town name.

References

Allport, Gordon W. 1937. *Personality: A Psychological Interpretation.* New York: Holt, Rinehart and Winston.

Bandura, Albert, and Richard H. Walters. 1963. *Social Learning and Personality Development.* New York: Holt, Rinehart and Winston.

Cairns, Robert B. 1973. "Fighting and Punishment from a Developmental Perspective." In *Nebraska Symposium on Motivation,* edited by James K. Coles and Donald D. Jensen. Lincoln: University of Nebraska Press.

Cairns, Robert B., and Beverley D. Cairns. 1994. *Lifelines and Risks: Pathways of Youth in Our Time.* New York: Cambridge University Press.

Cairns, Robert B., Beverley D. Cairns, Holly J. Neckerman, Lynda L. Ferguson, and Jean-Louis Gariepy. 1989. "Growth and Aggression: I. Childhood to Early Adolescence." *Developmental Psychology* 25: 320–30.

Cairns, Robert B., Jean-Louis Gariepy, and Kathryn E. Hood. 1990. "Development, Microevolution, and Social Behavior." *Psychological Review* 97: 49–65.

Cairns, Robert B., Dennis J. MacCombie, and Kathryn E. Hood. 1983. "A Developmental-Genetic Analysis of Aggressive Behavior in Mice: I. Behavioral Outcomes." *Journal of Comparative Psychology* 97: 69–89.

Cairns, Robert B., Jane E. Perrin, and Beverley D. Cairns, 1985. "Social Structure and Social Cognition in Early Adolescence: Affiliative Patterns." *Journal of Early Adolescence* 5: 339–55.

Elliott, Delbert S., David Huizinga, and Scott Menard. 1989. *Multiple Problem Youth: Delinquency, Substance Use, and Mental Health Problems.* New York: Springer-Verlag.

Eron, Leonard, and L. Rowell Huesmann. 1987. "The Control of Aggressive Behavior by Changes in Attitudes, Values, and the Conditions of Learning." In *Advances in the Study of Aggression,* vol. 2, edited by Robert J. Blanchard and D. Caroline Blanchard. New York: Academic Press.

Farrington, David P. 1986. "Stepping Stones to Adult Criminal Careers." In *Development of Antisocial and Prosocial Behavior: Research, Theories, and Issues,* edited by Dan Olweus, Jack Block, and Marion Radke-Yarrow. New York: Academic Press.

Gariepy, Jean-Louis, Mark H. Lewis, and Robert B. Cairns. 1996. "Genes, Neurobiology, and Aggression: Time Frames and Functions of Social Behavior in Adaptation." In *Aggression and Violence: Neurobiological, Biosocial, and Genetic Perspectives,* edited by David M. Stoff and Robert B. Cairns. Hillsdale, N.J.: Lawrence Erlbaum Associates.

Jessor, Richard, John E. Donovan, and Frances M. Costa. 1991. *Beyond Adolescence: Problem Behavior and Young Adult Development.* New York: Cambridge University Press.

Kessen, William. 1960. "Research Design in the Study of Developmental Problems." In *Handbook of Research Methods in Child Development,* edited by Paul H. Mussen. New York: Wiley.

Lewin, Kurt. 1933. "Environmental Forces in Child Behavior and Development." In *A Handbook of Child Psychology,* edited by Carl Murchison. 2d ed. Worcester, Mass.: Clark University Press.

Loeber, Rolf, and Marc Le Blanc. 1990. "Toward a Developmental Criminology." In *Crime and Justice: A Review of Research,* vol. 12, edited by M. Tonry and N. Morris. Chicago: University of Chicago Press.

Magnusson, David. 1988. "Individual Development from an Interactional Perspective." In *Paths Through Life: A Longtitudinal Research Program,* edited by David Magnusson. Vol. 1. Hillsdale, N.J.: Lawrence Erlbaum Associates.

Magnusson, David, and Lars R. Bergman, eds. 1990a. *Data Quality in Longitudinal Research.* New York: Cambridge University Press.

———. 1990b. "A Pattern Approach to the Study of Pathways from Childhood to Adulthood." In *Straight and Devious Pathways from Childhood to Adulthood,* edited by Lee N. Robins and Michael Rutter. Cambridge: Cambridge University Press.

Moreno, J. L. 1934. *Who Shall Survive? A New Approach to the Problem of Human Interrelations.* Washington, D.C.: Nervous and Mental Disease Publishing Co.

Rutter, Michael, and George W. Brown. 1966. "The Reliability and Validity of Measures of Family Life and Relationships in Families Containing a Psychiatric Patient." *Social Psychiatry* 1: 38–53.

Sears, Robert R., Eleanor E. Maccoby, and Harry Levin. 1957. *Patterns of Child Rearing.* Evanston, Ill.: Row, Peterson, and Co.

Chapter 12

Looking for Trouble in Paradise: Some Lessons Learned from the Kauai Longitudinal Study

EMMY E. WERNER

I FIRST LEARNED about longitudinal studies in the spring of 1949, in an unlikely setting. My classroom was in the barracks that had remained intact amid the rubble of a bombed-out city on the Rhine—the core of what would become the Johannes-Gutenberg Universität in Mainz. I was in my second semester as a psychology student. My professors had come from the University of Leipzig, where Wilhelm Wundt had founded the science of psychology in the late 1800s. They had fled to West Germany to escape the Communist takeover in the eastern part of the country.

My instructor in developmental psychology had an unlikely name, Dr. Undeutsch, which means, literally, "un-German," and he behaved accordingly. He was relatively informal and did not insist that we call him "Herr Professor" (a custom that, alas, had survived World War II); most important, he was enthusiastic about the subject he taught. That spring he told us about the longitudinal studies that were being conducted halfway around the world, at the University of California at Berkeley. He held our rapt attention.

Five years later, I found myself, as a young graduate student in child development, in the offices of three women on the Berkeley campus of the University of California. These women became my first mentors: Nancy Bayley, the principal investigator of the Berkeley Growth Study, Jean W. Macfarlane, the director of the Berkeley Guidance Study, and Marjorie Honzik, who through the years became the repository of knowledge of everything one ever wanted to know about the large data files at Berkeley's Institute for Human Development (Jones et al. 1971).

The dedication of these three women and their passion for the lives of the children and families they studied were unique, especially at a time when women in academia could reap few tangible professional rewards. Neither Nancy Bayley nor Marjorie Honzik were given "ladder" positions leading to tenure, nor were they allowed to write grants under their own names, although they were pioneers in developmental psychology. Only Jean Macfarlane held a professorship at the time—in the university's psychology department. She is honored today by "Macfarlane Lane," an easily overlooked, tiny thoroughfare between two imposing science buildings on campus.

These three women cared deeply about the individuals who opened their lives to them and about the accuracy and quality of the data that became the basis of influential books such as Jack Block's (1971) *Lives Through Time,* John Clausen's (1993) *American Lives,* and Glen Elder's (1999) *Children of The Great Depression.* They also cared about the young graduate students with whom they generously shared their knowledge and experience. There were four other individuals whose examples of intellectual honesty and personal integrity sustained my budding interest in longitudinal research. John E. Anderson and Dale B. Harris, at the University of Minnesota's Institute of Child Development, encouraged my venture into field research on the adaptation of Midwestern adolescents in a rural county, a context quite different from that of the youngsters who had grown up in the metropolitan San Francisco Bay area. In Nobles County, I met my husband, Stanley Jacobsen, a quiet Dane who keeps me grounded, especially when I get carried away with path analyses as complex as my erratic driving record.

Jessie M. Bierman, a professor of maternal and child health at Berkeley, introduced me to the children of Kauai and to Ruth Smith, a clinical psychologist who lives on the island. Together we have had the opportunity to watch the multiethnic youngsters of Hawaii's Garden Island grow from childhood into midlife, and I have cherished the privilege of documenting the vulnerability and resiliency of "ordinary people." I have been lucky—I found my paradise—though it was occasionally troubled by economic hard times and hurricanes.

The Context of This Study

The cohort of 698 individuals, born in 1955, who participated in the Kauai Longitudinal Study, live, indeed, in a physical paradise. Kauai has great natural beauty and is regarded by many people, visitors and residents alike, as the loveliest of the Hawaiian Islands. However, the world-class hotels that the tourists see mask the presence of chronic poverty in this westernmost county of the United States. At the time of our last follow-up, the unemployment rate on Kauai exceeded 10 percent—more than double the national average.

The parents of the 1955 cohort grew up in families who had come from Southeast Asia to work on the sugar and pineapple plantations— the major agricultural industries in Hawaii in the mid-1950s. They brought to Kauai a mixture of tongues, from Cantonese and Hakka to Japanese and Korean, from Spanish and Portuguese to Ilocano and Tagalog. They belonged to a variety of religions, from Buddhism to Shintoism and from Catholicism to various Protestant denominations. They had experienced the hardships of the Great Depression, World War II, and the Korean War.

The children in this cohort were four years old when the Territory of Hawaii became the fiftieth state of the Union. They were in grade school when President John F. Kennedy, his brother Robert Kennedy, and Martin Luther King Jr. were assassinated and when the civil rights movement and the War on Poverty captured national attention. They grew up under the shadows of the war in Vietnam, and some of their fathers and older brothers served on the battlefields in Southeast Asia.

In the 1970s and early 1980s, hippies, surfers, and seekers from the mainland, notably California, brought the drug scene to the island. Kauai, like the other Hawaiian Islands, became famous for its high-quality marijuana crop. During that time the island's economy also shifted from agriculture to tourism. By the time the members of the 1955 birth cohort graduated from high school and were ready to enter the workforce, the energy crisis had brought the first of a series of economic recessions to Hawaii. When our cohort reached their late twenties, Hurricane Iwa hit Kauai and brought much destruction. Ten years later, in 1992, Hurricane Iniki caused even more devastation. The oldest of the sugar plantations on the island closed in 1995, when the "children of Kauai" were in their fortieth year. Thus their adult lives have been marked by a cycle of repeated economic hardships and natural disasters.

Important social changes, however, have also increased the options available for this cohort. The years of their adolescence witnessed a considerable expansion of educational and social services, from Head Start at the preschool level to the opening of the Kauai Community College, a branch of the University of Hawaii, in 1968. The repeal of Hawaii's abortion law in 1970, when the young women of this cohort were reaching childbearing age, marked a major turning point in the state's legal history. In 1973, the State of Hawaii passed a liberal no-fault divorce law, just as the men and women of this cohort were coming of age. Divorce is now granted in Hawaii on the basis of the affirmation of the partners that their marriage is irretrievably broken and becomes final no later than one month from the date of the decree. Thus the members of this birth cohort had options as marriage partners and parents that were quite different from those of earlier generations.

What has endured across these many social and economic changes on Kauai has been the island's spirit of "kokua"—the Hawaiian word for "cooperation." The world got a glimpse of it when the islanders rescued the film crew of *Jurassic Park* from the eye of Hurricane Iniki before tending to their neighbors' needs and, only then, to their own. Our study has been the beneficiary of that kokua for four decades now, and since, according to the demographers, people on Kauai have a longer life expectancy than "mainlanders," we have every expectation that this spirit will live well into the twenty-first century.

Thanks to the goodwill of the island community, we were able to carry out a long-term investigation that drew on the professional skills and commitment of individuals from several disciplines—pediatrics, psychology, psychiatry, public health, and social work; from several institutions—the University of California, Berkeley and Davis campuses, and the University of Hawaii; and the Departments of Education, Health, Mental Health, and Social Services of the State of Hawaii.

The Kauai Longitudinal Study has monitored, with relatively little attrition, the impact of a variety of biological and psychosocial risk factors, stressful life events, and protective factors on the development of the men and women of the 1955 birth cohort in infancy, early and middle childhood, late adolescence, young adulthood, and midlife. The study has tracked all 698 children born on Kauai in 1955 from the perinatal period, gathering data at the ages of one, two, ten, eighteen, thirty-two, and forty. The principal goals of our investigation were to document, in natural history fashion, the course of all pregnancies and their outcomes in an entire community from birth until the offspring had reached adulthood, and to assess the long-term consequences of perinatal complications, poverty, and adverse rearing conditions on the individuals' development and adaptation to life (Werner, Bierman, and French 1971; Werner and Smith 1977, 1982, 1992, 2001).

Major Findings in Childhood and Adolescence

Like the participants in many other landmark longitudinal studies, the men and women in the Kauai Longitudinal Study shared a unique ethnic heritage and a unique historical experience in a unique geographic setting. When we compare our findings with other longitudinal studies of individuals from different generations (Elder 1999; Vaillant 1977) and from different social and geographic contexts, we are encouraged by the fact that the protective factors and processes that acted as buffers against chronic sources of stress among the children of Kauai have also been found in cities on the shores of the Pacific as well as the Atlantic Ocean, today and in the past. These findings also are being replicated in longitudinal studies on the European continent, in Great Britain, Germany, and Sweden (Magnusson 1988), to name but a few. I suspect that cohort effects may influence the definition and prevalence of what one considers a developmental risk more than the process by which individuals manage to cope with their vulnerabilities.

When our study began, there was a strong interest, in part politically based, in documenting the negative outcomes of reproductive risk and perinatal complications. It was during this time that the family of President John F. Kennedy revealed the existence of a mentally retarded sister and Vice President Hubert H. Humphrey spoke publicly about his grandchild, who suffered from Down syndrome. We have a recurrence of such concerns today as thousands of HIV-infected children survive and enter American classrooms and as ever smaller low-birth weight babies leave the neonatal intensive care units of American hospitals.

There is, then, a lesson from our study that bears remembering: the impact of reproductive stress tends to diminish with time, and the developmental outcomes of virtually every biological risk condition become more and more dependent on the quality of the environment in which children are raised. Prenatal and perinatal complications in our longitudinal study were consistently related to serious impairment of physical and psychological development in childhood, adolescence, and adulthood only when they were combined with chronic poverty, parental psychopathology, or persistently poor rearing conditions—unless there had been serious damage to the central nervous system.

In short, overall rearing conditions were more powerful determinants of developmental outcome than perinatal trauma. The better the quality of the home environment in infancy, childhood, and adolescence, the more competence the children displayed. This was seen when the children of Kauai were only two years old. Toddlers who had experienced severe perinatal stress but lived in middle-class or stable family settings did nearly as well on developmental tests of sensorimotor and verbal skills as toddlers who had experienced no such stress. The most impaired toddlers were those who had been exposed to both severe perinatal stress and impoverished, unstable home environments.

A sizable minority among the children of Kauai—about 30 percent—had faced such a combination of biological and psychosocial risk factors by the age of two. They had experienced perinatal stress and had grown up in chronic poverty, were raised by parents who had not graduated from high school, and lived in family environments troubled by chronic discord, parental alcoholism, or mental illness. When we first published these findings, we thought these figures were unusually high, but we now know that they are fairly typical for children in poor communities all over the country—whether among poor white children in Denver, poor Hispanics in Los Angeles, or poor African American children in Harlem.

Not surprisingly, some two-thirds of the children (129 in all) who had experienced four or more of these risk factors by the age of 2 did develop serious learning or behavior problems by the age of ten or had delinquency records, mental health problems, or teenage pregnancies, or all of these, by the age of eighteen. Yet one out of three of the high-risk children—72 individuals (32 males and 40 females)—grew into competent, confident, and caring young adults. They developed no learning or behavior problems during childhood or adolescence. They succeeded in school, managed home and social lives well, set realistic educational and vocational goals and expectations for themselves, and expressed a strong desire to improve themselves.

Their very existence challenges the prevailing myth that a child who is a member of a high-risk group is fated to become one of life's losers. At the age of forty, at a time of serious economic recession and high unemployment on the island, not one of these individuals was unemployed, none had been in trouble with the law, and none had to rely on social services. Their divorce rates, mortality rates, and rates of serious health problems were significantly lower at midlife than those of their same-sex peers in the entire cohort. Interestingly enough, about half had moved from Kauai to the other islands in search of better opportunities—the majority to metropolitan Honolulu and the U.S. mainland. In adulthood, their educational and vocational accomplishments were equal to or exceeded those of the low-risk children (the majority in the cohort) who had grown up in more secure and stable home environments.

Three clusters of protective factors differentiated this resilient group, who successfully overcame the odds, from the other high-risk youths who developed serious and persistent coping problems in childhood or adolescence: (1) at least average intelligence and scholastic competence and temperamental attributes that elicited positive responses from family members, strangers, teachers, and peers, such as robustness, vigor, and an active, sociable, engaging temperament; (2) affectional ties with parent substitutes, such as grandparents, older siblings, teachers, and elder mentors, who encouraged trust, autonomy, and initiative; and (3) an external support system in church, youth groups (such as 4-H Clubs, the YMCA, and Big Brothers Big Sisters of America) or school that rewarded their competence and provided them with faith and hope in their futures.

Many of these protective factors have since been found to be significant in other studies of contemporary children in different geographic settings and ethnic groups. They also have been found in analyses of studies of the children of the Great Depression who succeeded against great odds. The lesson we learned from the Kauai Longitudinal Study, however, is that one needs a context larger than that of the middle-class white nuclear family, the favorite subject of past longitudinal studies, to understand the significance of members of the extended family, such as siblings and grandparents, as positive role models and buffers for at-risk children.

Studies of African American, Asian American, and Hispanic families in the United States allow for such a perspective. They broaden our understanding of the attachment process to a much wider network of "significant others" than was possible with previous research on child development. In many ways, "minority" families, though they may be poor, provide more opportunities for emotional support to children by kith and kin than the more affluent homes of Berkeley, Baltimore, or Boston.

The poor also seem more likely to call on religion and the church as important buffers in times of stress. For the children of Kauai and their families, especially teenagers and young adults, involvement in church activities and a strong faith provided meaning in their lives. Their faith was not tied exclusively to a specific denomination or religious affiliation; rather, it was a confidence in some center of value. It did not seem to matter whether they were nominally Buddhists, Catholic, mainstream Protestant, or a member of a minority religious group, such as Jehovah's Witnesses or the Latter-day Saints: the resilient individuals in our study used their faith to reinterpret the traumatic experiences of their childhood and youth constructively. It enabled them to successfully negotiate an abundance of emotionally hazardous experiences without losing a positive outlook on life. Is such faith mere "myth," or is it a constructive perspective on reality? I do not have the answer, but I think we need to look more closely at the role faith plays in shaping the quality of an individual's adaptation and sense of psychological well-being across the life span (Antonovsky 1987).

Major Findings in Early Adulthood and Midlife

One of the striking findings of our two follow-ups in adulthood, at ages thirty-two and forty, was that most of the high-risk youths who had developed serious coping problems in adolescence had staged a recovery by the time they reached midlife. This was true for the majority of the troubled teens but more so for high-risk females than for high-risk males.

We were able to obtain follow-up data in adulthood on some 90 percent of the individuals in this cohort who had been diagnosed with behavior disorders or who had delinquency records by the age of eighteen. Our criteria for evaluating the quality of their adult adaptation were based on two perspectives: first, the individuals' own account of success and satisfaction with work, family life, social life, and their state of well-being, and second, their records in the community. The latter included records from the courts, the state Departments of Health and Mental Health, social service and vocational rehabilitation agencies, and the U.S. Veterans Administration (for men and women who had served in the armed forces).

Overall, "troubled teenagers" had a slightly higher mortality rate by the age of forty (4.4 percent) than both the resilient high-risk participants (3.3 percent) and the low-risk members of the same birth cohort (2.8 percent). The majority of the survivors, however, had no serious adaptation problems by the time they reached midlife. They were in stable marriages and jobs, were satisfied with their relationships with their spouses and teenage children, and were responsible citizens in their community.

Some seventy high-risk youths were diagnosed as having serious mental health problems by the age of eighteen. Their diagnoses ranged from problems of sexual identity to neurotic symptoms, hysteria, severe depression (including two suicide attempts), obsessive compulsive behavior, and paranoid schizophrenic behavior. Thirty percent of this group also had records of juvenile offenses or teenage pregnancies. By the age of thirty-two, a significant positive shift in life trajectories had taken place in about half of these individuals, but a higher proportion of men than women in this group still had difficulties finding and keeping a steady job, had marriages that ended in divorce, or were delinquent in child support.

By the age of forty, only one-third of the males and one-fifth of the females with behavior disorders in childhood or adolescence had some continuing midlife problems, including financial problems, problems in marital or interpersonal relationships, and problems with substance abuse. The proportion of troubled youths who showed spontaneous recovery in adulthood in this Asian Pacific cohort are identical with those reported by Lee Robins and Michael Rutter (1990) in follow-up studies of African American and white children in St. Louis, Missouri, and by David Magnusson (1988) in his longitudinal study of a cohort of Swedish youngsters.

Contrary to prevailing myths, most of the 104 delinquent youths did not go on to adult criminal careers. By the age of thirty-two, only one in four male delinquents, and one in ten female delinquents, had criminal records. By the age of forty, only 4 percent of the former delinquents had committed additional crimes; these included narcotic drug offenses, theft, spouse or child abuse, and, in the case of a single mother, forgery of a welfare check. The majority of the adult crimes in this cohort were committed by a small group of individuals with an average of four or more arrests before the age of eighteen who had also had serious mental health problems in their teens. About 43 percent of the men and 25 percent of the women in this group still had serious coping problems at the age of forty, including domestic violence and substance abuse.

The vast majority of these chronic offenders had been in need of remedial education by the age of ten, before they began their delinquent careers, and had been considered "troublesome" in early grade school by their teachers in the classroom and by their parents at home. Both parents and teachers had independently observed that these children were "aggressive," "bullying," and "frequent liars."

Our findings are similar to those reported by Marvin Wolfgang, Terence Thornberry, and Robert Figlio (1987), from two cohorts of African American and white males born in Philadelphia, and by David Farrington (1989), from a cohort of London males born in the mid-1950s. All three studies find that the earlier offenders start their "careers" in crime, the more juvenile and criminal offenses they accumulate.

Factors Contributing to Adult Recovery of Troubled Teenagers

Looking back at the lives of the troubled teenagers who made successful adaptations by midlife, we note a number of factors that contributed to their recoveries. Among the men and women who overcame their adolescent mental health problems was a significantly higher proportion whose primary caregivers in infancy were characterized by predominantly positive characteristics. The mothers of the men whose lives had taken a positive turn in adulthood had higher levels of education than the mothers of the men whose problems persisted, and they had fewer children. The women whose lives took a positive turn had been more advanced in physical and mental development in infancy and had received more emotional support in early and middle childhood than the women whose mental health problems persisted into adulthood.

The men and women who made successful adaptations to adulthood despite the presence of serious mental health problems in their teens also had scored significantly higher on scholastic competence, reasoning, and reading tests than did those whose problems persisted into midlife. Troubled teenage males who made satisfactory adult adjustments had a more favorable attitude toward school by the time they reached their senior year in high school and more realistic educational and vocational plans beyond high school than did males whose problems persisted into midlife. They also rated themselves as more active in early adulthood and less fearful in midlife. Troubled teenage females who rebounded in adulthood rated themselves as more sociable and drew on a larger number of sources of emotional support than did females with chronic mental health problems.

Most of the troubled teenagers who recovered in adulthood grew up in homes where both parents were present. The majority had household chores to attend to, and their parents provided structures and rules for them. In early adulthood, a significant proportion (one out of three women, one out of five men) joined religious denominations, such as the Jehovah's Witnesses and the Church of Latter-day Saints, that assured them salvation, security, and a sense of mission. Voluntary military service proved to be a positive turning point in the adult lives of many "crime-resistant" juvenile offenders, as did attendance at a community college, marriage to a stable partner, and the support of longtime friends—especially for women who had successfully overcome their mental health problems. Some of the same protective buffers have also been observed by Glen Elder (1999) in the adult lives of the children of the Great Depression, and by Frank Furstenberg, Jeanne Brooks-Gunn, and Philip Morgan (1987), in the later lives of African American teenage mothers whose prospects improved in the third and fourth decades of their lives. Among those persons whose life trajectories shifted in a positive direction, from vulnerability to resilience, there were generally more women than men. Individuals of average or above-average intelligence who had also been rated as more affectionate and less anxious as children managed this shift more easily than those who had difficulties availing themselves of external sources of emotional support in adulthood.

Overall, the outlook in adulthood for individuals who had been shy or lacked confidence as children or teenagers was considerably better than for youths who displayed antisocial behavior or for youngsters whose parents had chronic mental health or substance abuse problems and who had also been exposed to serious perinatal complications. Similar findings have been reported from studies with other ethnic groups on the U.S. mainland and in Europe (Mednick, Parnas, and Schulsinger 1987; Patterson, DeBaryshe, and Ramsey 1989).

Links Between Protective Factors Within Individuals and Outside Sources of Support

One of the major objectives of our two follow-up studies in adulthood was to document the process by which a chain of protective factors, linked across time, afforded individuals who had been raised in poverty, and surrounded by family discord and parental psychopathology, an escape from adversity and contributed to positive outcomes in their adult lives. When we examined the links between protective factors within the individual and outside sources of support or stress, we discovered that the men and women on Kauai were not passively reacting to the constraints of the negative circumstances; rather, they sought out and attracted the people and the opportunities that led to positive turnarounds in their lives. Their individual dispositions led them to select or construct environments that reinforced and sustained their active, outgoing dispositions and rewarded their competencies. Elder (1999) has observed this same process in children of the Depression, a generation that grew up in a different sociocultural and historical context.

These protective processes were at work early in life. For example, there was a significant positive link between an easy, engaging infant temperament and the sources of emotional support available to the individual in early and middle childhood. Active and sociable babies without distressing eating and sleeping habits tended to elicit more positive responses from their caregivers—both mothers and substitute caregivers—at one and two years of age than did the "difficult" babies. In middle childhood, such children also tended to rely on a wider network of caring adults, both within and outside the family circle.

Positive interactions between parent and infant were associated with greater autonomy and social maturity in the child at the age of two and with greater scholastic competence at the age of ten. Scholastic competence, in turn, was positively linked with the number of sources of emotional support the teenager attracted, including support from teachers and peers as well as members of the extended family. It was also positively linked with a greater sense of self-efficacy (self-esteem and an internal locus of control) at the age of eighteen. A greater sense of self-efficacy and planning was, in turn, linked to less distress and emotionality at the ages of thirty-two and forty and a greater number of emotional supports in early adulthood and midlife, including support from a spouse or mate.

Individual dispositions and competencies were also strongly related to the number of stressful life events encountered and reported at each developmental stage. Children who had displayed a greater amount of autonomy and social maturity at the age of two reported fewer stressful life events by the age of ten. Individuals with higher scholastic competence at the age of ten reported fewer stressful life events in adolescence. Men and women who displayed a higher degree of self-efficacy and planning in their teens reported fewer stressful life events in their thirties and forties—even though they had grown up in poverty and under trying family circumstances.

The resilient individuals were in their late thirties when Hurricane Iniki hit the island. They heeded storm warnings and hence experienced less property damage than most of their peers. They were more likely to have financial savings and insurance and could avoid foreclosures, the fate of many of Iniki's victims. They also lost fewer jobs and reported a smaller percentage of post-traumatic stress symptoms among their children. In short, with few exceptions (two who were offspring of psychotic parents) the resilient men and women were planners and problem solvers who managed to surmount natural disasters as well as economic hardships.

Parental competence, as manifested in the educational level of the mother and father, proved to be a significant positive protective factor in the lives of the men and women on Kauai who grew up in chronic poverty. Parental education had a significant positive correlation with the quality of their offspring's adaptation in adulthood. The better-educated mothers had more positive interactions with their sons and daughters in early childhood and provided more emotional support for them in middle childhood—even when the family lived in poverty. Maternal education was also positively linked with the child's health and physical status, especially in the early years.

There was also a significant positive link between parental level of education and the child's scholastic competence at the age of ten; one path was direct, the other was mediated through the child's health and physical status. The better-educated parents had children with better problem-solving, reasoning, and reading skills, but they also had healthier children with fewer developmental disabilities and absences from school owing to repeated illnesses.

Although parental education and the sources of support available in childhood were positively linked with the quality of adult adaptation, these factors had a less direct impact in adulthood than the individual's competencies, sense of self-efficacy, and temperamental dispositions. Many resilient high-risk youths left the adverse conditions of their childhood homes (and their island community) after high school and sought environments they found more compatible. In short, they picked their own niches. However, protective factors within the individual (such as temperament, cognitive skills, self-esteem, and locus of control) tended to have a greater impact on the quality of adult adaptation for the high-risk females than for the high-risk males. In contrast, outside sources of support tended to make a greater difference for the high-risk men than for the high-risk women.

Implications for Policy and Future Research

What implications can be drawn from the results of our study? Most of all, they provide us with a more hopeful perspective than that implied by the literature on youngsters who succumb to the negative consequences of biological insults and caregiving deficits. Our findings give us a greater awareness of the self-righting tendencies that move most children toward normal development under all but the most persistent adverse circumstances—absent serious damage to the central nervous system.

Throughout this study we noted large individual differences among high-risk children and youths in their responses to both negative and positive circumstances in their lives. The very fact of individual variations among youngsters who live in adverse conditions suggests the need for greater assistance to some than to others. It also suggests that any program that fosters resiliency will have variable effects, depending on the internal dispositions and competencies of the recipients of such programs (Werner 1997).

Our findings alert us to the need for setting priorities and to the choices we must make in our investment of time and resources for high-risk children and youth. Intervention programs need to focus on those youngsters who appear most vulnerable because they lack some of the essential personal resources or social supports that buffer chronic adversity. Among these are the increasing number of preterm survivors of neonatal intensive care, the offspring of parents with severe psychopathology or substance abuse, and preadolescents with conduct disorders who have poor reading skills and are in danger of becoming "early onset" delinquents. From a longitudinal perspective, these youngsters appear most at risk for developing serious and persistent coping problems in adulthood, especially if they are boys.

Assessment and diagnosis—the initial steps of any intervention program—need to focus not only on the risk factors but also on the protective factors in the lives of these children. These include existing sources of informal support in the extended family, the neighborhood, and the community at large. Most children and their families prefer such informal and personal ties to kith, kin, and community to impersonal contacts with formal bureaucracies. These ties need to be encouraged and strengthened by legislative action and social programs.

A cooperative effort by competent professionals and concerned volunteers could generate a continuum of care and caring that cuts across narrow disciplinary boundaries and extends from early childhood to adulthood. It would involve parent educators and health-care providers who deliver follow-up care for children with disabilities; the extension of early childhood programs to high-risk infants and toddlers; peer tutors for children who have reading problems in the primary grades; counselors who assist high school youths with realistic educational and vocational plans; elder mentors for potential school dropouts or jail-bound juvenile offenders; foster grandparents who work with teenage mothers and their infants; community college instructors who encourage young adults motivated to return to school to upgrade their skills; and political leaders who advocate for the nation's children in the legislative and executive branches of local, state, and federal government.

Although our study was conducted far away from the center of political power in Washington, D.C., over the years it has made an impact on social policy—slowly, incrementally, and on a bipartisan basis. The first step was a set of changes in the delivery of services for children in the state of Hawaii. Thanks to the efforts of many concerned people—members of the Teamsters' Union, mental health professionals, and volunteers—several community action and educational programs for high-risk youngsters have been established on Kauai since our study began. The modest royalties from our books support their work. Partly as a result of our findings, the Hawaiian state legislature has funded special mental health teams to provide services for troubled children and youths. On Kauai, a gamut of services—remedial education, therapy, family counseling, respite help, and home-based services are now available for youngsters with developmental disabilities and special needs.

During the period of welfare-to-work reform in California, our findings were utilized by the California Department of Social Services and the governor's Bipartisan Advisory Committee to plan services for children that would buffer the negative impact of the repeal of Aid to Families with Dependent Children (AFDC) and assist in the transition to Temporary Assistance for Needy Families (TANF).

Some of my graduate students have obtained grants from the David and Lucille Packard Foundation to brief new legislators in the California Assembly and Senate on issues concerning children, including the risk and protective factors that have significant influences on their lives. Because we have term limits in our state, this gave our students an opportunity, during each legislative session, to educate the assembly members and senators who were newcomers to social policy making in California.

In March 1996, the Consortium of Social Sciences Associations arranged a congressional breakfast seminar in Washington, D.C., that focused on fostering resiliency in children. It drew interested participants from the nation's legislative body and generated interest in the (fiscal) support of grassroots programs, such as elder mentorships, Big Brothers Big Sisters of America, and the 4-H Club, whose positive impact on the lives of high-risk youth we had documented in our work (Werner, Randolph, and Masten 1996).

North of the border, in Ottawa, the federal government of Canada has initiated a National Longitudinal Survey that monitors the development of children and youth every two years in all provinces—both English and French speaking—from infancy to early adulthood and includes considerable fiscal investment for needed services for those at risk. The design of this, the most ambitious study of children and youth in North America, has been closely modeled after our own, warts and all.

There are drawbacks, however, to the uncritical acceptance of some of the concepts that have emerged from our work. "Resilience" has become a bandwagon phenomenon, spawning a new category of interveners who preach the gospel that "no one is at risk, but everyone is at promise," neglecting the issue of individual differences in development that we have documented. Despite the urgent need for such research, there are today few evaluation studies of the effectiveness of programs that have been designed to foster resilience.

The life stories of resilient individuals have taught us that competence, confidence, and caring can flourish even under adverse circumstances if youngsters encounter persons who provide them with a secure basis for the development of trust, autonomy, and initiative. But we also need to examine the price exacted from such children. Some protective factors (such as the ability to detach oneself from a dysfunctional home environment) may promote positive adaptation in one context at one time but have negative effects in another context at a later stage of development (such as difficulties in forming intimate relationships).

Only recently, perhaps with the aging of the baby boomers, has the focus of research on resilience and protective factors shifted to early and middle adulthood. Such efforts need to be expanded. Resilience in later life is still largely uncharted territory. We have seen examples of positive changes in later years among the Harvard graduates studied by George Vaillant (1977) and among the children of the Great Depression who were followed into their sixties and seventies (Clausen 1993; Elder 1999). Most of these individuals were well educated and had achieved a measure of financial security by the time they reached middle age. They also lived in a historical period in which educational and occupational opportunities were more accessible to men than to women. It remains to be seen how well the baby boomers will manage the losses that come with the aging process and the new opportunities that are available to them, for they can count on longer and healthier lives than could previous generations.

Future research on risk and resilience also needs to acquire a cross-cultural perspective that focuses on the children of the developing world, and on immigrant children from these countries, who have to contend with many biological and psychosocial risk factors that increase their vulnerability far beyond that of their peers born in affluent industrialized countries. We need to know more about individual dispositions and sources of support that transcend cultural boundaries and operate effectively in a variety of high-risk contexts.

Research on risk and resilience must pay more attention to the testing of hypotheses about causal relationships by making use of behavior genetic strategies. Many stressful experiences, such as parental discord, parental mental illness, parental substance abuse, and divorce, impinge differently on siblings in the same family. We need to look more carefully at the contributions of shared as against nonshared family environments to the vulnerability and resilience of high-risk children.

Ultimately, the most powerful tests of hypotheses about protective factors and individual resilience may come from two sources: intergenerational studies of siblings in high-risk families who differ in developmental outcomes and evaluation studies of early intervention programs whose objective is to change the course of development in children exposed to potent biological or psychosocial risk factors. These types of studies should have high priority for future longitudinal research (Werner 2000).

Training New Researchers in Human Development

I believe that all of us involved in longitudinal research are obliged to encourage our students to ask hard questions that require a look at stability and change in human behavior, if not across the entire life span then at least at some important transition points in human development. I also believe that graduate students interested in developmental research should get their feet wet by conducting their own field research, to teach them how to interact intelligently and sensitively with real people from different cultural contexts, not just with an impersonal mass of coded data.

Our longitudinal research with the multiethnic families and children on Kauai has made me keenly aware of the urgent need to train students in human development research who come from different contexts than that white middle-class Americans living in urban areas. Throughout this study I have taken great pains to work with graduate students and research assistants who come from the same backgrounds as our study population. This was not an easy task at first: in the mid-1960s only a few Japanese American graduate students worked with me; a generation later the pool of "minority" students has greatly expanded. Today, California, like Hawaii, has become a state in which the majority of school-age children are "people of color." Caucasians are the new minority.

I am proud to have mentored a "rainbow" of graduate students—Filipino, Japanese, Hawaiian, Hispanic, Portuguese, Chinese, and Caucasian—who represent the different ethnic groups of Kauai and of my home state of California. When I first met them, they were, like me, the first in their families to have graduated from a university. Today they are college teachers, researchers, and social policy makers. I salute them all.

The venues for publication of the results of their endeavors may change considerably in the future. Besides the standard professional journals, monographs, and university press books, there will be other options, including the Internet. Predictably, there will be changes in research methodology and in ways of analyzing and interpreting longitudinal data. Maybe there will be more paths and arrows, straight and crooked, and models of human development we have never dreamed of. I, for one, hope that there will be a synthesis of individual- and context-based approaches to the understanding of human development—with respect for the ultimate mystery that each individual presents.

Piet Hein, a Danish physicist, wrote the following admonition to cheer up his countrymen during World War II. It seems to me to apply equally well to life in general and, more specifically, to longitudinal research.

Put up in a place,
where it is easy to see,
the cryptic admonishment
T.T.T.

When you feel how depressingly
slowly you climb,
it's well to remember that
Things Take Time.
(Hein 1966, 5)

References

Antonovsky, Aaron. 1987. *Unraveling the Mystery of Health: How People Manage Stress and Stay Well.* San Francisco: Jossey-Bass.

Block, Jack. 1971. *Lives Through Time.* Berkeley, Calif.: Bancroft Books.

Clausen, John A. 1993. *American Lives.* New York: Free Press.

Elder, Glen H., Jr. 1999. *Children of the Great Depression.* Twenty-fifth anniversary edition. Boulder, Colo.: Westview Press. Original edition, Chicago: University of Chicago Press, 1974.

Farrington, David P. 1989. "Later Adult Life Outcomes of Offenders and Non-Offenders." In *Children at Risk: Assessment, Longitudinal Research and Intervention,* edited by Michael Brambring, Friedrich Lösel, and Helmut Skowronek. Berlin-New York: Walter de Gruyter.

Furstenberg, Frank F., Jeanne Brooks-Gunn, and S. Philip Morgan. 1987. *Adolescent Mothers in Later Life.* New York: Cambridge University Press.

Hein, Piet. 1966. *Grooks.* Garden City, N.Y.: Doubleday.

Jones, Mary C., Nancy Bayley, Jean W. Macfarlane, and Marjorie P. Honzik. 1971. *The Course of Human Development.* Waltham, Mass.: Xerox Publishing.

Magnusson, David. 1988. *Individual Development from an Interactional Perspective: A Longitudinal Study.* Hillsdale, N.J.: Lawrence Erlbaum Associates.

Mednick, S. A., Josef Parnas, and Fini Schulsinger. 1987. "The Copenhagen High Risk Project." *Schizophrenia* 16(3): 485–95.

Patterson, George R., Barbara DeBaryshe, and Elizabeth Ramsey. 1989. "A Developmental Perspective on Antisocial Behavior." *American Psychologist* 44(2): 329–35.

Robins, Lee N., and Michael Rutter. 1990. *Straight and Deviant Pathways from Childhood to Adulthood.* Cambridge: Cambridge University Press.

Vaillant, George E. 1977. *Adaptation to Life.* Boston: Little, Brown.

Werner, Emmy E. 1997. "The Value of Applied Research for Head Start: A Cross-Cultural and Longitudinal Perspective." *National Head Start Association Research Quarterly* 1(1): 15–24.

————. 2000. "Protective Factors and Individual Resilience." In *Handbook of Early Intervention*, edited by Jack P. Shonkoff and Samuel J. Meisels. 2d ed. New York: Cambridge University Press.

Werner, Emmy E., Jessie M. Bierman, and Fern E. French. 1971. *The Children of Kauai: A Longitudinal Study from the Prenatal Period to Age Ten*. Honolulu: University of Hawaii Press.

Werner, Emmy E., Susan M. Randolph, and Ann S. Masten. 1996. "Fostering Resiliency in Kids: Overcoming Adversity." Proceedings of the Consortium of Social Sciences Associations. Washington, D.C. (March).

Werner, Emmy E., and Ruth S. Smith. 1977. *Kauai's Children Come of Age*. Honolulu: University of Hawaii Press.

————. 1982. *Vulnerable but Invincible: A Longitudinal Study of Resilient Children and Youth*. New York: McGraw Hill.

————. 1992. *Overcoming the Odds: High-Risk Children from Birth to Adulthood*. Ithaca, N.Y.: Cornell University Press.

————. 2001. *Journeys from Childhood to Midlife: Risk, Resilience, and Recovery*. Ithaca: Cornell University Press.

Wolfgang, Marvin E., Terence P. Thornberry, and Robert M. Figlio. 1987. *From Boy to Man: From Delinquency to Crime*. Chicago: University of Chicago Press.

Chapter 13

Intergenerational Panel Study of Parents and Children

ARLAND THORNTON, RONALD FREEDMAN,
AND WILLIAM G. AXINN

I N 1962, David Goldberg and Ronald Freedman began a modest longitudinal study in the Detroit area with a probability sample of women
who had married or who had borne a first, second, or fourth child in
1961. The first interview wave was conducted early in 1962, just as the
baby boom was ending. The study sought to investigate the subsequent
fertility of these women and the stability and changes in their desired, expected, and realized family size. Ronald Freedman was principally responsible, with the considerable assistance of Lolagene Coombs, for the
first three waves of follow-up interviews, conducted in 1962, 1963, and
1966, and for the direction of the research using those data.[1]

Because of a heavy commitment to research in Taiwan during that period (Freedman 1998), Freedman and Coombs were unable to continue interviews after 1966. Realizing that they could not give the Detroit study the
attention it deserved, they asked Arland Thornton and Deborah Freedman
to take over the project. Thornton has been primarily responsible (with
the able collaboration of Deborah Freedman, William Axinn, and others)
for the study from 1975 to the present. After an eleven year hiatus the
women were interviewed again in 1977.

In 1980 the study became intergenerational when the women's children, born in 1961, were added to the study, at the age of eighteen. Henceforth, interviews were conducted with these children and with their
mothers. The inclusion of the children added to the power of longitudinal data the strength of interviews with two generations in each family.
Both the children and the mothers were interviewed again in 1985, when

315

the children were twenty-three, and in 1993, when the children were thirty-one. The study now has data from eight waves of interviews, the last three involving two generations.

In accordance with the study's emphasis on fertility, women of specific relevant parities were selected. The original study was also designed to examine the interrelationships of childbearing with the familial institutions in which it is rooted. We wanted to know how childbearing was influenced by the economic position and resources of the family, by the family's social mobility, by religious affiliation and commitment, by the internal structure of the family, and by the linkages between the family and other kinds of social relationships. From the beginning the study was designed to include a wide range of family information; and as the project developed it became clear that it provided a promising vehicle for the study of a wide range of family issues.

Interest in fertility expectations and preferences among scholars had increased in the 1950s as almost universal use of contraception made it possible (theoretically, at least) for women to control the number of children they bore. Furthermore, there was a substantial interest in using distributions of individual expectations of family size as a basis for improving population forecasts.

Collection of such data had been an integral part of the very first study (in 1955) of a national sample of women of childbearing age, which covered family-size values, contraception, and similar reproductive issues (Freedman, Whelpton, and Campbell 1959).[2] Interest in these issues grew further when distributions of family-size expectations from the 1955 study proved remarkably accurate in predicting the number of U.S. births during the subsequent five years (Whelpton, Campbell, and Patterson 1966). The national aggregate expectations distribution in 1960 was little different from that of 1955.

Expectation data missed the mark when the "baby boom" became the "baby bust." However, other reproductive and family issues motivated the continuation of such research. The result was a series of national studies modeled roughly on the 1955 study but with certain improvements. These became the U.S. National Surveys of Family Growth, which continue to this day.

In an earlier two-wave follow-up study in Detroit looking into the stability of expectations, Goldberg, Sharp, and Freedman (1959) had already found that social and economic change could modify what was normatively desired for fertility. They hoped that what would be learned about individual correlates of preference expectations through their new research project would help in understanding and possibly predicting aggregate changes when they occurred.

When the Intergenerational Panel Study began, few longitudinal studies of family issues existed. One that encouraged further work was a longitudinal study by Charles Westoff, Elliot Mishler, and Lowell Kelley (1957) of a panel of fecund, predominantly Protestant couples interviewed about fertility preferences at the time of their engagement and then, twenty years later, about their completed fertility. The average initial desired fertility of couples in the sample proved to be an accurate predictor of aggregate completed fertility twenty years later. However, as would be true in later studies, although this prediction was correct in the aggregate, it was produced by many compensating variations. The correlation between early preference and the later fertility of individuals was only .26.

The original sample consisted of 1,113 women selected on a probability basis from all birth records of married white women who had a first, second, or fourth birth in July 1961. Approximately equal numbers of women were selected from each of the parity groups. An additional sample of 191 recently married white women was also included, bringing the total sample to 1,304 respondents.[3] The initial response rate of those eligible was 92 percent. In each of the three reinterviews of the 1960s the response rates were between 98 and 99 percent of those who had not become ineligible through the death of either spouse, divorce, or separation (Coombs and Freedman 1970b). Response rates from 1977 to 1993 were comparable.

Telephone interviews for the relatively short callback interviews were used to minimize costs and because several colleagues had experienced success with such interviews.[4] We obtained telephone numbers from those who had them at the first interview. At the end of each interview we also obtained names, addresses, and telephone numbers of three friends or relatives who would know how to reach the respondents if they moved. We told the respondents that we were interested in interviewing them again about changes in their family situations. The overwhelming majority of respondents gladly gave us the information we needed to keep in touch with them.

In both the initial and follow-up interviews, many callbacks, including house calls, were made if necessary to obtain the interview. If the respondent moved to any place in the continental United States during the 1960s, she was followed by telephone and by a mailed questionnaire, if necessary. During the subsequent waves, respondents outside of the United States were also interviewed by telephone or by mail.

From the first reinterview forward, one measure we used to build and maintain rapport was a letter to respondents reminding them of the study and telling them they would be called soon. Brief reports, limited to some highlights of findings that would not prejudice responses in the next interview, were also sent. Beginning in the 1970s, we mailed the introductory letter to respondents before the interview, and following the interview we sent a brief report of findings from that wave of interviews.

Coombs and Freedman's discussion of the first reinterview wave of the study summarizes the reinterview success this project enjoyed:

> The respondents' reaction to the reinterviews was very favorable. Nearly all remembered the first interview, and many expressed pleasure at being contacted again. There appeared to be no objection to being interviewed by telephone. . . . The interviewers' reaction is not unrelated to the high response rate. . . . Without their persistence and ingenuity, the follow-up would have been less successful. . . . It is clear that it is possible to obtain apparently reasonable responses from substantially all respondents on all questions. . . . [R]efusal to answer particular questions was negligible, although many of the questions dealt with topics that might be considered sensitive. (Coombs and Freedman 1964, 116–7)

Although it is now clear to us that the Detroit sample for this study was nationally applicable and thus proved adequate for studying American family processes, the initial aims were more modest. Only white women were represented: we believed that the differences between whites and nonwhites were great enough to require separate analysis for each, yet our resources were inadequate to draw the inflated sample of nonwhites that would give adequate numbers for analyses of this group. For a similar reason we knew that we could not obtain large samples of women of all parities and chose to represent only the parities we thought were most useful for studying American reproductive values of that time. Initially, we saw analyzing a sample for a specific metropolitan area with these limitations as a first step that would ideally be followed by studies both of other metropolitan areas and of national samples. Even initially, however, there were some important advantages to our procedure, and over time the sample proved as useful as larger national samples for studying family processes.

An important initial reason for us to work in the Detroit metropolitan area was that we could use the excellent survey resources of the Detroit Area Study.[5] This contributed to our high initial response rate. It also enabled us to do the matching of marriage and birth records essential for classifying the first births of all respondents by their pregnancy status at marriage. These data proved to be invaluable in predicting other crucial aspects of family building.

Some of the substantive areas in which the research from the 1960s data made significant contributions included outcomes associated with premarital pregnancies and the development of a new measure of reproductive preferences. We found that premarital pregnancies were associated with persistent poor economic position of the mothers (Coombs and Freedman 1970a), a relationship that persisted well into the 1970s (Freedman and Thornton 1979). In the later phases of the study, we found that a premaritally conceived birth in 1961 was related to the attitudes and behavior of the mother's children decades later. For example, maternal premarital pregnancies predict children's own union formation behavior during their own transitions to adulthood (Thornton and Camburn 1987; Thornton 1991).

A useful psychometric measure of reproductive preferences, developed by Lolagene and Clyde Coombs, was tested in our study. The measure captured the range of preferences underlying a single number preference. Obtaining this measure in 1962 helped to predict completed fertility in 1977, net of the conventional preference measure (Coombs 1979). After this experience, it was also used in Turkey, Taiwan, Hungary, and Nepal.

Our efforts to use expectations and preferences to help to predict, or at least understand, future fertility were not as successful as initially expected. The study began just when a developing "baby bust" was succeeding the postwar "baby boom," and preferences and expectations in Detroit clearly fell along with the declining national fertility rates. However, little progress was made in finding the determinants of expectations and preferences that might help us understand and, possibly, predict the fertility decline.

The 1977 Data Collection

After a hiatus of nearly a decade, the study was renewed in 1975 under the direction of Arland Thornton and Deborah Freedman. That year, one of the main issues facing the new research team was feasibility: the mothers had last been interviewed in 1966, and we wondered if it would be possible to locate and reinterview them after a decade without contact. To establish feasibility, we conducted a pilot study in October 1975, randomly choosing the names of one hundred study participants for a brief interview. This pilot study obtained a response rate of 96 percent of the pretest sample members who were still alive. This gave us confidence that we could successfully continue the study. The response rates for the full study in 1977 matched the rate achieved in the pilot study. The National Institute of Child Health and Human Development funded the 1977 data collection, as well as all subsequent interviews.

The 1977 data collection maintained a strong interest in childbearing, consistent with the earlier purposes of the study. Having collected our first wave of interviews at the height of the baby boom, we were well positioned to evaluate the dynamics of the subsequent baby bust. Because these women had begun their childbearing during the central years of the fertility expansion and had completed their families during the fertility contraction of the late 1960s and 1970s, we could examine how their original plans and preferences had changed over time. We could also continue studying the influences on and consequences of childbearing during this period.

The goals of the 1977 study were also expanded to include several new avenues of research, the most important being gender roles and marital instability. It was clear by the time of the 1977 reinterview that a revolution in gender roles was under way. Mothers were entering the labor force in record numbers, attitudes toward the roles of women and men were changing, and a national movement devoted to increasing the opportunities and rewards for women had emerged. We were in an advantageous position to study the dynamics of changes in men's and women's roles between 1962 and 1977 because we had included considerable information in our earlier interviews (1962, 1963, and 1966) about the employment of husbands and wives, future employment plans, family household division of labor, decision making in the family, and attitudes toward gender roles. By collecting information about these phenomena again in 1977, we could document changes in work and family life and study how these were interconnected with other family factors, such as childbearing and financial well-being.

Another important new phenomenon of the 1960s and 1970s was the dramatic increase in divorce. This new trend had already captured the attention of Arland Thornton, who had just completed his dissertation on the interrelationships between childbearing and marital instability. He saw the 1977 data collection as an excellent opportunity to extend this line of research. The rising interest in marital stability had also motivated Lolagene Coombs and Zena Zumeta (1970) to use our 1960s interviews to study factors associated with marital dissolution. Although relatively few women in our study had divorced between the 1962 and 1966 interviews, the initial study by Coombs and Zumeta uncovered several interesting relationships and established the usefulness of our data for studies of marital dissolution. The extension of the study to 1977, along with the rising divorce rates, provided an adequate number of divorces for reliable statistical analysis. Marital dissolution and its intersection with other important social and economic factors became one focus of our new project.

The expansion of the study goals to include marital instability necessitated a change in study protocols. During the second, third, and fourth waves of the study, between 1962 and 1966, the women who had experienced a marital dissolution were excluded from follow-up. This approach seemed prudent at the time because marital dissolution is so intricately related to fertility that it must be taken into account in childbearing analyses. Yet the small number of divorced women in the sample between 1962 and 1966 prevented systematic use of their data for this purpose.

With the expansion of the study goals to include the causes and consequences of marital instability, in 1977 we changed the study protocols to reinterview all women who had been interviewed in 1966, even if they had experienced a marital dissolution. In addition, we decided to reintegrate into the study all women who had been dropped between the 1962 and 1966 interviews because of marital dissolution. These women were successfully reintegrated into the study, and their childbearing, marital, economic, and labor force histories were updated. The response rates and quality of data received from these women were high, and they were comparable to the data received from the continuously married.

Expansion to an Intergenerational Panel Study from 1980 through 1993

During the planning of the 1977 data collection, we realized that our study provided an excellent opportunity to address an important new set of issues: the influence of the parental family on the attitudes and behavior of children. Social scientists had long been interested in the ways in which children are influenced by the parental family, and growing concerns about the effects of parental poverty, marital instability, and female employment on children's well-being had increased interest in these questions.

At the same time, there was growing recognition about the severity of the data demands necessary to study the influence of the parental family on children, especially older children as they matured into their own adulthood. At the time we designed our 1980 study, we noted that most studies of these issues had concentrated on the family organization and child-rearing practices of parents or on the behavior and attitudes of the young. The result was primarily data sets that were tilted toward measures collected either from parents or from children. However, the essential component for studying familial influence on adolescent development—long-term panel data from both generations within the same family—was often missing.

Several features of our study made it possible to address these issues. One is that most of our original families were selected because the mother had given birth to a child in July 1961. This birth cohort of children could form the basis of a study in which age was precisely controlled, an advantage both for data collection and for data analysis. A second, and more important, element was the availability of a large body of demographic, social, economic, and attitudinal data about these children's families. These family data covered the entire first fifteen years of the children's lives. In addition, this information was collected not retrospectively but at important points in the lives of the families as the children matured. By designing a data collection that now included the children, we could collect extensive information about them that would permit us to study how multiple aspects of life in the second generation are influenced by parents.

These unique opportunities led us to plan and design the 1980 data collection immediately after the 1977 data were in hand. Although we already had a wealth of information about the parental families, several considerations caused us to include the mothers in the 1980 data collection. Of central importance was the need to update the information on the parental family through 1980, when the child was age eighteen. In addition, we wanted information from the mother specifically about the child, including the mother's relationship with and aspirations for the child. Furthermore, all of our previous contact had been with the mothers; they would be our entree to interviews with their children. We conducted the 1980 interviews with the mothers first, to solicit their assistance in locating and interviewing their children.

The shift of our project from a study of a single generation to an intergenerational study led to an important adjustment of the composition of our sample. Although most of the women in our original 1962 sample were selected because they had given birth to a child in 1961, another just-married group was selected from the marriage records of 1961. Most of these recently married women went on to have children, but these births were distributed over several years following 1961. Those children could not be integrated with the birth cohort of children from 1961, and we decided not to include these families in the interviews conducted in 1980, 1985, and 1993. We defined the eligible sample as those children whose mothers had been interviewed in 1977 or had died before the time of the 1977 interview.

The 1980 interviews with the children were designed with two goals in mind: First, we wanted to collect the information necessary to examine the influence of the parental family on its offspring's current behavior, attitudes, and plans. Second, in anticipation of follow-up interviews with the children, we wanted to collect baseline information from the children at the age of eighteen that would help us understand their subsequent transitions to adulthood.

Gathering these data required lengthy interviews with the children, which we believed would be most successful if conducted in face-to-face formats. However, we conducted telephone interviews with children who lived outside the range of our interviewers, those whose schedules prohibited a face-to-face interview, or those who preferred a telephone interview. As a last resort, in rare cases we obtained our information by mail. The use of mixed-mode interviewing has helped to minimize attrition, which threatens to undermine the validity of all panel studies.

Three interrelated forces guided the substantive goals of the study: scientific importance, our professional interests, and the existing database. These considerations led us to identify the marriage and child-bearing plans of the adolescents as the first goal of the new project. These dimensions of family life had changed dramatically during the 1960s and 1970s and had become the focus of intense scholarly interest. Furthermore, because our earlier interviews with the mothers had focused on marriage, childbearing, and gender roles, it was both natural and compelling to investigate the ways these dimensions of life in the first generation affected similar life domains in the second.

Our second goal centered on socioeconomic achievements and aspirations. A large body of research, including our own, demonstrates that marriage and childbearing are intricately interrelated with school, employment, and socioeconomic achievement. In addition, a large body of status attainment research has shown the importance of the parental family for children's educational, occupational, and financial aspirations and achievements, and we saw our study as an opportunity to contribute to this line of research.

Our third research goal for the 1980 study moved us into an additional area: the personal, familial, and social adjustments of young people. We had become interested in the well-being of the children as reflected in their individual self-esteem and in their relationships with their parents. We were also interested in the relationships of young adults with their friends and peers, with particular emphasis on their dating and sexual behavior and attitudes. The availability of comprehensive data for both parents and children would allow us to analyze how the characteristics, attitudes, and behaviors of the parental family influence adolescent well-being.

In many respects the 1985 and 1993 studies flowed naturally out of the 1980 study. These later data collections were motivated by the same fundamental questions about the influence of parents on their children. They permitted us to study how circumstances of the parental home, extending back to early childhood, influenced the lives of children into early adulthood—an opportunity available in few other data sets.

The 1985 and 1993 interviews also provided information for panel analysis of the second generation. Just as the multiple waves of information about the mothers permitted examination of the influence of early life-course circumstances on later behavior, the data collected between 1980 and 1993 permitted similar analyses for the children. Furthermore, whereas the panel data for the mothers began after they had begun childbearing, the panel data for most of the children began before they had married and begun childbearing, thereby permitting these important transitions to be studied in a prospective panel study.

Both the 1985 and 1993 data collections with the children focused on important family and household decisions they faced during their transitions to adulthood. The specific decisions motivating these two data collections included residential separation from the parental household; dating, premarital sex, and cohabitation; marriage; marital dissolution; and childbearing.

The protocols for the 1985 and 1993 interviews for both mothers and children closely paralleled those for the 1980 data collection. We also continued our general practice of interviewing the mothers first, because they were less mobile than their children and could help us locate hard-to-find offspring. However, in the 1993 interview our study procedures became more flexible in this regard, as the children themselves were entering the part of the life course in which geographic movements tend to be less frequent.

With the 1985 study, we introduced a life-history calendar into our data collection. Our use of the life-history calendar was motivated by the increasing interest of social science in the processes that underlie change in the lives of individuals. It had become increasingly clear by 1985 that studies of the dynamics of individual behavior are greatly facilitated by detailed information about the timing and sequencing of events over the life course. However, the imperfections of human memory make the collection of reliable event-history information difficult, and the life-history calendar facilitates the collection of such information. Our study was also an ideal place to use a life-history calendar because all of the children had been born in the same year and were only twenty-three years of age at the time of the 1985 interview. We also made improvements in calendar procedures that have contributed to life-history calendar methodologies for others (Freedman et al. 1988; Caspi et al. 1996; Belli 1998).

The life-history calendar is a graphical document that visually portrays the life-course domains and times of interest to the researcher (Freedman et al. 1988). In our 1985 data collection, our calendar ascertained monthly information for the children between the ages of fifteen and twenty-three for residence, marital transitions, cohabiting relationships, births, living arrangements, school enrollment, employment, and military service. This grid of time and substantive domains is designed to assist respondents in recalling and relating events in their lives, both within and across different life domains. The grid format also helps both the interviewer and the respondent observe inconsistencies of reporting and provides the interviewer with a format for easily recording extensive and complicated data.

Because our calendar in 1985 covered the period from 1976 through 1985, we were able to compare the 1985 retrospective answers with those given in the prior 1980 interview. This comparison shows exceptional correspondence of contemporary and retrospective reports for marital and birth events. Our 1985 retrospective reports of school enrollment and employment also correspond well with contemporary reports from 1980, although they are less accurate than the reports of marriage and child-bearing (Freedman et al. 1988). We used a similar life-history calendar in our 1993 data collection to update information about events occurring after the 1985 interview.

An innovation in our 1993 wave was the collection of data about important life transitions of the adult siblings of the children participating in our study. This addition was motivated by the growing recognition of the usefulness of sibling data in controlling the influence of unmeasured family attributes. We collected this information by asking the mothers to report important transitions for each of their children in the areas of cohabitation, marriage, marital dissolution, and childbearing. Because we had reports of these same events about our sample children from the children themselves, we could test the reliability of the mother's reports. Our tests revealed that the maternal data are exceptionally good for reports of marriage and childbearing; maternal reports of children's cohabitation and marital dissolution are also good but not as exemplary (Axinn et al., forthcoming).

Response Rates for the Study

One of the most serious difficulties in long-term panel studies is the retention of respondents. Attrition not only reduces the size of the sample for analysis but also introduces potential for substantial bias. Even modest rates of loss to follow-up in each interview can result in substantial cumulative attrition across many study waves.

We have been very successful in minimizing respondent attrition, and our retention rates across successive interviews have been high. We began the study in 1962 with a response rate of 92 percent for the mothers who had given birth in 1961. This rate, especially high for an initial cross-sectional survey, gave us an excellent start. In 1993, fully 79 percent of the initial sample of women were still participating in the study. If we delete the women who died or became seriously ill in the intervening years, the effective response rate was 84 percent.

We were similarly successful in obtaining the participation of the children born in 1961. By 1993, 81 percent of the children of the mothers interviewed in 1962 were still participating in the study. If we delete the children who died or were seriously ill, the response rate rises to 83 percent. Fully 97 percent of these children participating in 1993 had been interviewed at each of the three interviews between 1980 and 1993. Of the original sample families in which neither the mother nor the child was known to be dead or seriously ill, interviews were obtained in 1993 from both the mother and child in 80 percent of the families. Multiplying this retention rate by the original 92 percent response rate indicates that fully 74 percent of the original sample universe of families is represented by interviews from both mother and child in the study thirty-one years later.

Our research team has published three articles that discuss our response rates, the procedures used, and some possible reasons for our success (Coombs and Freedman 1970b; Freedman, Thornton, and Camburn 1980; Thornton, Freedman, and Camburn 1982). Among the central reasons for our success are the exceptional efforts of the study staff and interviewers. It is important to design study procedures that generate rapport and enthusiasm among interviewers, who then transmit these qualities to respondents. We also went to great lengths to design the study procedures to maximize the satisfactions and minimize the burdens of respondent participation. Also important, of course, is the ability to locate respondents. Finally, the intrinsic interest of women and children in their families is an essential element of our high response rates.

Although the advantages of high response rates for minimizing both random and systematic error are well known, there are undoubtedly opportunity costs associated with high response rates. Our research team has tried to operate on the principle that the maximization of interviewer and respondent interest and pleasure in an interview and the minimization of burden are central ingredients for retaining respondents in long-term panel studies, and because of this we decided to keep our interviews of modest length. The emphasis upon brevity was particularly evident in the first two follow-up surveys. However, by the third reinterview, having become more confident regarding both content and time tolerance in our respondents, the questionnaire was considerably expanded (Coombs and Freedman 1970b). Both our confidence and interview length also increased in subsequent years, but even then, the average length of our interviews has always been modest. Of course, the downside of this approach is that the amount of information obtained was restricted to some extent.

When we were designing the 1980 wave of interviews that included both mothers and children, we considered including fathers as well. We knew that adding the children was a risk for continuance of the study, and in the end we decided not to heighten that risk further by trying to incorporate fathers. However, our excellent results in adding the children—both sons and daughters—suggest that we may have been able to include the fathers as well. We have asked both mothers and children a number of questions about the fathers and family structure that permit analyses of issues involving fathers and their relationships with the mothers and children.

Special Issues in the Evolution of a Long-Term Panel Study

A central theme of this paper is the ubiquity of family change at both the individual and societal levels. These changes in society and in the lives of individuals and families have inevitably led to an evolution of the goals and purposes of the study: from its beginning as a panel study of childbearing in the early 1960s, to a panel study of fertility, women's roles, and marital dissolution in the 1970s, to a study of the effects of parents on children in the early 1980s, and, in the mid-1980s and the 1990s, to an intergenerational panel study of children's lives during the transition to adulthood. As the original women and families participating in the study have become geographically dispersed over three decades, the geographic scope of the study has evolved from a narrow concentration in the Detroit metropolitan area to include families scattered throughout the United States and even into some foreign countries. The composition of the study respondents has also changed, as divorced women were dropped from the study between 1962 and 1966 and then reintegrated into the study in 1977, women who were just married in 1961 were dropped from the study in 1980, and the children born in 1961 became part of the study in 1980.

The evolution of the study has had some important implications. One interesting implication has been the identification of the study—specifically, its name. Because the study began as a project about the fertility behavior of Detroit women in 1962, it was originally titled Family Growth in Detroit. With the widening geographic distribution of the sample and the expansion of the content in 1980, the project was renamed the Study of American Families. However, because the study is not representative of the larger national population we were not totally comfortable with this name, and more recently we have referred to the project as the Intergenerational Panel Study of Parents and Children.

However, just as the study has evolved in many ways over its three decades, there have also been important continuities in the goals and substantive themes of the study from the early 1960s through the 1990s. Childbearing, religion, socioeconomic position, and family organization have been constant themes in the research, even as new topics such as cohabitation, marriage, divorce, living arrangements, relationships between parents and children, and self-esteem have been introduced. However, in many ways the research centered on these new themes has been built around the old themes.

The early decisions of the principal investigators also determined the scope of the study universe. Most important here is the fact that the study was originally limited to white women who had just married or given birth to a first, second, or fourth child in the Detroit metropolitan area in 1961. This definition of the original universe of families in terms of place, time, race, and life-course position, of course, places limits on our abilities to generalize from our sample results to a larger universe—that is, strictly speaking, we can only generalize the results from our analysis to the universe from which the families were originally drawn.

We have, of course, committed nearly four decades of our professional lives to this project because we believe that its advantages far outweigh its limitations. As we have suggested throughout this paper, the study offers an outstanding study design, a richness of information, excellent response rates, and high-quality data. Although the limitations restrict the range of issues that can be addressed using the data, they do not detract from the excellent opportunities provided by the data.

The most serious limitations of the sample are its white and urban nature, which make it impossible to generalize to nonwhite and rural populations. Family structures and processes in the African American population have captured the attention of scientists and policy makers in recent years, and the limitation of our sample to whites prevents our contribution to these important conversations. Nevertheless, we believe that our data are highly relevant to the urban white Americans who constitute the majority of the population today.

We have not found the limitation of our study to a single birth cohort of specific parities in one urban area to be particularly problematic. Our use of a narrow birth cohort of children follows a well-established and productive practice in the social sciences. Scholars now recognize the great difficulties associated with having a wide range of respondent ages in studies of childhood, adolescence, and the transition to adulthood. Consequently, most studies of these issues now include rather narrow birth cohorts or age ranges, to minimize the substantial heterogeneity and measurement difficulties resulting from having respondents of substantially different ages and positions in the life course. Studies following this approach include the National Longitudinal Study, the National Longitudinal Study of Youth, the National Longitudinal Study of the High School Class of 1972, the High School and Beyond study, the National Educational Longitudinal Study, the Early Childhood Longitudinal Studies (both the kindergarten and birth cohorts), the Monitoring the Future study, and several British panel studies (which have focused on single-week birth cohorts). Although each of these studies is limited in its ability to generalize across different time periods, each provides a valuable approach to studying processes and relationships in its time period.

We also believe that the limitation of our sample of children to first, second, and fourth births is benign. Although we do not have children of all parities in the sample, we represent children from three of the most frequent birth orders. By limiting the sample of children to first, second, and fourth births, average family size in our sample in 1961 was somewhat lower than the average in 1961 (2.33 for our sample as compared with 2.78 in the Detroit metropolitan area, 2.73 in the state of Michigan, and 2.58 in the nation). Of course, 1961 was close to the baby-boom peak in period fertility in the United States, and in subsequent years family size declined dramatically. So although high-birth-order children are slightly underrepresented in the sample, there are also fewer of them in more recent cohorts in the general population.

Even more important for this issue is the fact that we have a range of parities in our study and consistently fail to find relationships with birth order in the analyses we have conducted. We have found that the total number of children born to a family (as measured at the end of child-bearing) is correlated with other measures but have failed to find any significant or interpretable correlations with birth order when controls for family size are included. In addition, we know of no theoretical reasoning or empirical findings suggesting that the family processes and causal mechanisms motivating our studies interact with birth order. All of these considerations make us confident that the stratification of the original sample by parity does not represent a significant obstacle to the generalizability of findings using the data set.

One reason that community and regional studies such as ours have made important contributions to our general understanding of behavior is that theoretical models within the social sciences do not posit variance of underlying family processes across different urban areas. Although it may sometimes be shown that local circumstances, such as the economy, may additively influence certain family processes such as marriage and fertility, these models do not suggest that the processes and substantive relationships themselves interact with the metropolitan area of residence (Lichter, LeClere, and McLaughlin 1991; Lichter et al. 1992). Thus, although researchers using national data sets could routinely allow their substantive models to depend upon an individual's geographic residence, they seldom, if ever, do. This understanding buttresses the value of local studies for correctly portraying processes and relationships that extend far beyond the geographic boundaries of the local area.

We have made several comparisons of data and findings from the Intergenerational Panel Study of Parents and Children to data from nationally representative data sets. Those comparisons have been quite reassuring: we have found that the attitudes and behaviors of participants in our study are quite similar to those of respondents to surveys of the national population (Thornton and Axinn 1996). The similarities between the findings from our data and those of national studies—when such comparisons are possible—provide strong reasons to believe that when our Detroit-based study is able to examine the many issues that cannot currently be studied in national samples, those results are likely to be reflective of general processes that extend far beyond the Detroit area.

One limitation of the study is the incorporation of the children into the study in 1980 when they were eighteen years old rather than at a younger age. Although we have learned substantial amounts from the study with first interviews of the children at the age of eighteen, earlier interviews with the children would have produced even more valuable data. Inclusion of the children at an earlier time, however, was not possible because the original study focused on childbearing, not child rearing, because of the break from 1966 to 1977, and because of the time needed to establish the feasibility of extending the study in 1977 and again in 1980.

This is an example of a weakness in a study that evolves in terms of its goals and structures across time.

Of course, our study is not the only one to decide later that interviews with children earlier in their life courses would be useful. In fact, the recognition that younger is better has been a regular theme in American social sciences. For example, the National Longitudinal Study evolved from a study of adult men and women to a study of older teenagers to a study of younger teenagers. Similarly, the national studies of education have evolved from using samples of high school seniors (the National Longitudinal Study of the High School Class of 1972), to samples of high school sophomores and seniors (the High School and Beyond study), to samples of junior high school students (the National Educational Longitudinal Studies), to birth cohort and kindergarten samples (the Early Childhood Longitudinal Studies). The Monitoring the Future study has evolved from sampling just high school seniors to including tenth-graders, and more recently it has included eighth-graders as well. Thus our regrets for not having interviewed the children at a younger age may be reflective as much of current understandings and the benefits of hindsight and experience as of any constraints of the study in the 1970s.

The Intertwining of Individual Careers with the Study

As expected in a study extending over nearly three decades, the trajectory of the Intergenerational Panel Study and the careers of its primary investigators have been interrelated in important ways. Although the principal investigators, of course, shape the study, it in turn influences the lives and careers of the investigators. Furthermore, as is true of families and populations, a study over decades must eventually deal with issues of renewal and intergenerational succession.

As discussed earlier in this paper, the principal investigators for the 1962 through 1966 interviews—Ronald Freedman, David Goldberg, and Lolagene Coombs—had invested their careers primarily in the study of fertility and its causes and consequences. These interests led them to design the first waves of interviews to examine a broad range of determinants of fertility.

The early 1960s also brought new opportunities for demographers with international interests in fertility and population growth. Numerous countries were experiencing rapid population growth because of dramatically falling mortality, accompanied by stable fertility. This population growth captured the interest of scholars and policy makers alike in the possibility of fertility decline in these countries. Consequently, in the early 1960s, at the same time they were conducting the early waves of the Detroit study, Freedman and Coombs became heavily involved in research and consultation about Taiwan's nascent family planning program.

When they began their work on Taiwan's demographic transition from high to low fertility and from poverty to relative affluence, Freedman and Coombs had no idea that this work would be their principal research commitment for the rest of their professional careers. In 1960 and 1961, Bernard Berelson and Ronald Freedman discussed helping a country with high fertility mount a major action-research demonstration study with a sound experimental design with four goals in mind: to determine whether considerable latent demand for family planning was responsive to a good service program, to test a variety of ways of providing appropriate family planning services, to establish the power of diffusion in such a program, and to help indigenous collaborators convince their country's leadership that a strong national program would be a political asset, not a liability.

The considerable success of that initial experimental study in the city of Taichung, Taiwan, exceeded expectations. The scientific and political success of the Taichung study assisted the Taiwan public health and political leadership to move rapidly to a national family planning program. Freedman and colleagues were invited to take an ongoing consulting role for the national program. In this consulting role they helped in the design and interpretation of a series of national sample surveys to measure the course of the demographic transition, evaluate the program, and provide a social scientific base for understanding the increase in contraceptive use and fertility decline. The Taiwanese quickly learned the mysteries of doing sample surveys, although they kindly gave Freedman and colleagues a role as collaborators.

The heavy involvement of Freedman and Coombs in research in Taiwan prevented them from conducting follow-up studies with the Detroit sample after 1966. It had become clear that the work in Taiwan and elsewhere in Asia was likely to require their research time for the indefinite future. Yet the value of the Detroit panel and the potential for useful research from a new round of interviews suggested the need for renewal of the research team and the extension of the study. By turning the Detroit study over to a new group of researchers, the study could be continued while Freedman and Coombs could serve as social-science-based observers of the whole course of the demographic transition in Taiwan, a country with a uniquely valuable set of demographic and survey data. Although the planning and implementation of the Detroit study was transferred to other investigators, both Freedman and Coombs analyzed data from the 1977 interviews, and Freedman has provided consultation on an occasional basis in subsequent years.

The continuation of the Detroit study was facilitated by the availability of Deborah Freedman and Arland Thornton to take over the study in 1975. Deborah Freedman had completed a dissertation in 1967 concerning economic factors in reproductive behavior in Taiwan, with additional subsequent research on the project. She had also conducted research on the relation between income and fertility in the United States and was interested in doing further analyses of fertility in America. The Intergenerational Panel Study became the central element of her career for the two decades from the mid-1970s through the mid-1990s. She served as the principal investigator of the 1977 data collection and was a coinvestigator in each of the subsequent follow-up interviews.

In 1975, Arland Thornton was just finishing his doctoral dissertation on marital instability and fertility and had accepted a position at the University of Michigan's Survey Research Center studying economic influences on fertility. At the time, Thornton had assumed that the Survey Research Center position would be a temporary interlude between his doctoral work and a permanent position elsewhere. The invitation from the Freedmans to become involved with the Detroit panel study was a defining moment in Thornton's career. He decided that this opportunity to work on the Intergenerational Panel Study was so attractive that he would accept the Freedmans' invitation and continue his career at the Survey Research Center while working on the study. He served as coprincipal investigator of the 1977 data collection and principal investigator of the data collections from 1980 to 1993 and the analyses flowing from them.

Thornton's decision to become involved in this study set the course of his career for the next quarter century. Just as he has played a central role in guiding the direction of the study, the study has substantially shaped his career. Although Thornton has conducted several other projects in his professional career, the Intergenerational Panel Study has been a constant component of his activities. He has organized much of his research agenda around those of his substantive interests that could take advantage of the strengths and potential of the study. During the course of his career he has given priority to the use of the panel study to investigate important research questions about family life in the United States.

In this examination of interdependent scholarly life courses, it is useful to note that another project that has received Thornton's attention is family change in Taiwan—a project that grew directly out of the Taiwan project initiated by Ronald Freedman in the early 1960s. Thornton's involvement in this project led to the completion of a major monograph documenting and explaining the dramatic changes occurring in Taiwanese family structures and processes during the twentieth century (Thornton and Lin 1994). Thornton achieved tenure at Michigan's Survey Research Center and subsequently in the Department of Sociology—attaining the regular academic position at the University of Michigan that he had assumed would be achieved elsewhere.

The renewal of study personnel continued when William Axinn became a co-principal investigator on the 1993 round of interviews. Axinn had come to the University of Michigan in the mid-1980s as a graduate student interested in fertility research in Nepal. This interest led to his involvement in a project in Nepal directed by Tom Fricke, of which Arland Thornton was one of the coinvestigators. Thornton served as chair of Axinn's dissertation committee, and Ronald Freedman as one of its members. After completing his dissertation on Nepal, Axinn became a collaborator in the analysis of the 1985 Detroit project data concerning marriage and cohabitation and was later invited to become co-principal investigator of the 1993 data collection and of subsequent analysis projects using the data.

Numerous other people have made important contributions to the study. These include research colleagues who contributed to data collection and analysis, research and administrative personnel who have assisted in data collection, processing, and administration, and the interviewing, coding, and computing staffs of the Survey Research Center.[6]

Some Findings from the Interviews from 1977 Forward

The Intergenerational Panel Study has provided the basis for a wide variety of research concerning American family life. In addition to the methodological contributions discussed earlier, the study has in recent years made contributions to three broad substantive areas: the changing nature of American family life, the influence of the parental family on children, and the determinants of attitudes and behaviors during the transition to adulthood. Although space constraints do not permit thorough examination of all the findings from the study, we highlight here some of its central contributions.

Changing American Families

One of the central concerns of our research agenda throughout the project has been the changing nature of family life in the United States. Our research team has used our Intergenerational Panel Study, in conjunction with other data sources, to document substantial changes between the 1960s and the 1990s in family attitudes, values, and behavior. One overarching conclusion has been the substantial "relaxation of the social prescriptions for family behavior and an expansion of the range of individual choice." We have demonstrated "a weakening of the normative imperative to marry, to stay married, to have children, and to maintain a strict division of labor between men and women" (Thornton 1989, 887). We have also documented important increases in the acceptability of sexual expression, cohabitation, and childbearing outside of marriage. We have concluded that the "norms and values concerning marriage and intimate relationships may have been restructured in important ways, with marriage becoming less relevant in structuring intimate relationships" (Thornton 1989, 889; also see Thornton 1995; Axinn and Thornton 2000). The families participating in our study lived through the baby boom and the baby bust, the divorce revolution, and the dramatic increase in the employment of mothers. Because of these important trends, the families in our study in the 1990s were very different from those who began the study in the early 1960s.

Just as our study has helped to document intracohort trends in attitudes and behavior from the 1960s into the 1990s, it has also contributed to an understanding of the differences between the generations. We have shown, for example, that although the mothers in our study participated in the trend toward more egalitarian attitudes about gender roles, in the 1980s and 1990s their daughters were even more egalitarian than the mothers at the same time (Thornton 1989; Thornton and Young-DeMarco 2001). The daughters in the 1980s were also somewhat more negative toward marriage and more accepting of childlessness than their mothers were at the same time (Thornton 1989; Thornton and Young-DeMarco 2001). The differences between mothers and children were large enough and consistent enough to be considered a generation gap in the areas of premarital sex and cohabitation, of which the young adults were much more accepting than their mothers. This difference in attitudes toward nonmarital sex and cohabitation is clearly understood by the children and is probably a source of intergenerational tension and conflict (Thornton 1992).

The study has been valuable in documenting the emergence of new behaviors in the 1980s and the 1990s, especially in new living arrangements, including nonmarital cohabitation. Our studies of the nest-leaving process among young adults, using our life-history calendar data, have demonstrated the complexity of the process of leaving home (Thornton, Young-DeMarco, and Goldscheider 1993; Goldscheider, Thornton, and Young-DeMarco 1993). Young adults leave home for the first time in great numbers during their late teenage years, but the rate of returning home is also high. In addition, young people fan out in many different directions, experiencing a substantial number of diverse living arrangements before their residential arrangements become settled.

Our study has also contributed to an understanding of new patterns of marriage and nonmarital cohabitation. Large proportions of women and men experience cohabitation fairly early in their lives. In addition, these cohabiting relationships are also fairly unstable. Many dissolve, and others turn into marriage relatively quickly. Although many young people experience cohabitation, as they mature into their later twenties and thirties most of them spend substantially more time in marriage than in cohabitation (Thornton 1988). Both cohabiting and marital unions frequently experience short periods of separation and reconciliation as well as time spent apart because of educational, occupational, and familial responsibilities (Binstock and Thornton 1999).

The Influence of Parents on Children

An important motivation for integrating the children into the study was to examine the influence of parents on their children. We have investigated the influence of numerous dimensions of the parental home on the behavior and attitudes of children. These have included religious identification and commitment; socioeconomic position; work experience of the mother; the number and timing of children; family organization; marital history, including age at marriage; whether the mother was pregnant at the time of her own marriage; and divorce and remarriage experience. Among the dimensions of children's lives that we have examined are premarital sex, nonmarital cohabitation, marriage, living arrangements, childbearing, geographic proximity to the mother, relationships with parents, and self-esteem. We have studied both the behavior and the values of both generations.

Transmission of Attitudes and Values

One of the questions in our agenda concerns the transmission of attitudes and values from parents to children. We estimated correlations between the attitudes of mothers and children while controlling measurement error and important structural characteristics of the parental family. Our analyses demonstrate considerable intergenerational transmission of attitudes and values concerning divorce, premarital sex, and appropriate roles for women and men, with intergenerational standardized regression coefficients being about .3 (Thornton, Alwin, and Camburn 1983; Thornton 1985; Thornton and Camburn 1987). These coefficients are somewhat higher between mothers and daughters than between mothers and sons, but the differences are relatively small (Thornton 1992). The stability of these attitudes across generations is similar to their stability in the parental generation between 1962 and 1977 (Thornton 1992).

As expected, we have also found evidence that the extent of the intergenerational transmission of attitudes is influenced by the relationship between parents and children. For example, "the observed impact of maternal attitudes on the premarital sexual attitudes and behaviors of children is stronger in families where children and mothers have a close communicative relationship" (Thornton 1992, 257; also see Weinstein and Thornton 1989; Moore, Peterson, and Furstenberg 1986). This suggests the importance of strong and supportive relationships between parents and children for the success of parents in socializing their children.

Parental Attitudes and Children's Behavior

We have extensive evidence that the attitudes and values of parents concerning such matters as gender roles, premarital sex, cohabitation, marriage, and childbearing are associated with the children's behavior in these same domains. For example, children's premarital sexual experience is related to maternal attitudes toward premarital sex (Thornton and Camburn 1987). Similarly, maternal attitudes toward cohabitation without marriage have substantial relationships to the children's later experience with cohabitation (Axinn and Thornton 1993). Parental orientations toward marriage also seem to influence how fast their children marry, and the fertility attitudes and preferences of parents are related to the childbearing behavior of children (Axinn and Thornton 1992a; Barber 2000).

Religious Affiliation and Commitment

Our study confirms the continuing, although changing, role of religious affiliation and commitment in the behavior and values of American families. Our data are consistent with a growing body of research demonstrating the declining uniqueness of Catholic family behavior. Catholics today are similar to mainline Protestants in their attitudes and values concerning gender roles, divorce, and premarital sex (Thornton 1985, 1992). At the same time, family patterns of fundamentalist Protestants have become more distinct. For example, the young people in our study who are fundamentalist Protestants have more negative attitudes toward divorce and premarital sex and report less premarital sex than other Protestants and Catholics (Thornton 1985; Thornton and Camburn 1987).

Our research consistently shows that maternal religiosity may have more influence on children than religious affiliation. The influence of maternal religiosity extends to many dimensions of the children's lives. For example, the quality of parent-child relationships is related to the religiosity of the parents (Pearce and Axinn 1998). Mothers who attend religious services frequently have children who are, on average, less accepting of divorce and more positively oriented toward the bearing and rearing of children (Thornton 1985; Pearce, forthcoming). Frequent maternal attendance at religious services, and viewing religion as personally important, are also associated with lower rates of premarital sex and cohabitation and higher rates of marriage in the second generation (Thornton and Camburn 1987; Thornton, Axinn, and Hill 1992). Furthermore, the religiosity of the children themselves is strongly correlated with their own premarital sexual and cohabitation experience, and much of the influence of parental religiosity on the children's experience of union formation works through the children's own religiosity (Thornton, Axinn, and Hill 1992).

Our work concerning the intersection of religiosity and young people's behavior has extended the theoretical and empirical literature to consider explicitly the reciprocal relations between religiosity and behavior. Whereas most previous research has posited one-way causal influence from religiosity to family behavior, our data suggest reciprocal causation between children's behavior and their religiosity. This research is consistent with the hypothesis that in addition to the influence of children's religiosity on their behavior, their experience with premarital sex and cohabitation influences their religious commitment (Thornton and Camburn 1987; Thornton, Axinn, and Hill 1992).

Parental Marital Experience

Several dimensions of parental marital experience are strongly related to the lives of children. Our data provide strong evidence of the intergenerational transmission of union formation experience. Young maternal age at marriage is associated with more accepting attitudes toward premarital sex and more premarital sexual experience on the part of children (Thornton and Camburn 1987). Young age at marriage in the first generation is also associated with much more rapid entry into both marital and cohabiting unions in the second generation (Thornton 1991). Similarly, children of mothers who became pregnant before marriage had more approving attitudes toward premarital sex, perceived their mothers as more permissive, were more sexually active themselves, and entered into both marital and cohabiting unions more rapidly.

Our research has corroborated and extended a growing body of research showing the effect of marital dissolution on the lives of children. We have shown the negative effects of marital dissatisfaction and disruption on the quality of parent-child relationships (Orbuch, Thornton, and Cancio 2000). Divorced parents also have children who are less positively oriented toward marriage and more positively disposed toward divorce and premarital sex (Thornton and Freedman 1982; Thornton 1985; Thornton and Camburn 1987). This effect of parental divorce on children's attitudes is partially explained by the fact that divorce modifies the attitudes of the parents, which, in turn, affects the children's attitudes (Axinn and Thornton 1996). Children of divorced parents are more likely to be sexually active, have more sexual partners, and enter into coresidential unions more rapidly (Thornton and Camburn 1987; Thornton 1991). In addition, divorce shifts union formation of children away from marriage and toward cohabitation (Thornton 1991). One particularly provocative finding is that maternal remarriage magnifies, rather than decreases, many of the effects of divorce (Thornton and Camburn 1987; Thornton 1991). Our research also suggests that marital dissolution negatively influences children's educational attainments but that this effect is not further exacerbated by maternal remarriage (Axinn,

Duncan, and Thornton 1997). However, we find no statistically significant influence of parental marital dissolution on children's self-esteem (Axinn, Duncan, and Thornton 1997).

Parental Socioeconomic Position

An extensive body of literature has shown that parental socioeconomic standing is strongly associated with the achievements of children. Our research has contributed to this literature by demonstrating the importance of parental socioeconomic standing early in life. We have shown that parental education and financial standing when the children are born are significantly related to children's educational and cognitive achievements many years later (Alwin and Thornton 1984; Axinn, Duncan, and Thornton 1997). Furthermore, although the high correlation of early and late parental characteristics makes it difficult to disentangle the effects of early and late parental positions, our research suggests that early parental socioeconomic standing may be more important than later socioeconomic standing with respect to children's educational and cognitive achievements (Alwin and Thornton 1984). We have also found that although parental education positively influences children's self-esteem, there is no additional influence of parental financial resources (Axinn, Duncan, and Thornton 1997).

Both Deborah Freedman and Arland Thornton came to the Intergenerational Panel Study with research interests in the intergenerational transmission of consumption aspirations. This interest was motivated by the work of Richard Easterlin (1966, 1969) suggesting that the postwar trends in marriage and childbearing in the United States could be explained by trends in consumption aspirations and economic achievement. A key element of the Easterlin model was the untested assumption that the consumption aspirations of children are determined by the standard of living in the parental family. Freedman and Thornton tested this assumption and found that the empirical correlation between children's consumption aspirations and parental standard of living is positive, as expected, but it is also surprisingly small. This led to the hypothesis that children's own personal consumption levels and the influences of peers may be more important influences on children's aspirations than the levels of income and consumption in the parental family (Freedman and Thornton 1990).

Our research has consistently found a correlation between maternal education and the family attitudes of mothers: mothers with higher levels of education report more egalitarian attitudes toward gender roles and more permissive attitudes toward premarital sex and divorce. Yet we have not found strong or consistent influence of parental education on children's attitudes and behavior. Probably the largest effect we have observed of parental socioeconomic standing on children's family behavior is in the area of marriage and cohabitation, where parental education and financial resources both appear to reduce the rapidity of entrance into intimate coresidential unions (Axinn and Thornton 1992a).

Parental Family Integration

A major motivation of the original data collection in 1962 centered on the idea that the shift of many activities and relationships from the family to nonfamilial organizations would have important implications for family members. Our research shows that young people who grow up in families in which many of the activities of life are conducted within the family have higher levels of self-esteem than others (Yabiku, Axinn, and Thornton 1999).

Maternal Employment

Interestingly enough, we have found that maternal employment, a dimension of family organization that has generated considerable scientific and policy controversy, has no substantial or consistent effect on the dimensions of family life that we have studied. These include attitudes toward gender roles, premarital sex, and divorce (Thornton 1985; Thornton and Camburn 1987; Thornton, Alwin, and Camburn 1983). They also include the cognitive and educational achievements of young adults as well as their premarital sexual experience (Alwin and Thornton 1984; Thornton and Camburn 1987). Our research findings, therefore, cast doubt on the importance of maternal employment for the kinds of children's outcomes we have examined.

Children's Transition to Adulthood

Although much of our research focuses on the influence of parents on children, we have also used the study to examine how various dimensions of children's lives are intertwined as they make the transition to adulthood. We have noted the influence of children's religious participation and commitment on their subsequent entrance into marital and cohabiting unions as well as the feedback loops from children's cohabitation experience to their subsequent religiosity.

We have contributed to the growing body of research showing the importance of attitudes and values in the lives of young people. We have, for example, shown the interconnections between the premarital sexual attitudes and behaviors of young adults (Thornton and Camburn 1987). We have also shown that prior positive attitudes toward cohabitation predict subsequent cohabiting behavior (Axinn and Thornton

1993). At the same time, cohabitation leads to more positive attitudes toward cohabitation (Axinn and Thornton 1993). The cohabitation experience of children also influences the attitudes of the mothers (Axinn and Thornton 1993). Similarly, positive attitudes toward divorce and negative attitudes toward marriage predict children's cohabitation experience, while cohabitation has feedback loops on these attitudes (Axinn and Thornton 1992b). In fact, our results suggest that cohabiting experience both increases tolerance of divorce and reduces desired family size (Axinn and Barber 1997).

Our research has also demonstrated some important interconnections between the family lives of children and educational achievements. The nest-leaving process is directly interrelated with the tempo of schooling, as many children leave and return to the parental home in rhythm with their educational trajectories (Goldscheider, Thornton, and Young-DeMarco 1993). Furthermore, school enrollment is a substantial barrier to the formation of marital and cohabiting unions, although the effect is greater on marriage than on cohabitation. However, as schooling is completed, high levels of educational achievement are associated with high rates of marriage and low rates of cohabitation (Thornton, Axinn, and Teachman 1995).

We have also investigated the ways in which early dating and going steady are related to the initiation of sexual activity. Young people who begin to date at an early age and who initiate steady relationships early are more likely to have sexual experience early. These young people also have had sex with more partners and are more sexually active as teenagers (Thornton 1990). Young people who begin dating early, go steady at a young age, and have their first sexual experience early enter into both cohabitation and marital unions much faster than others. They also tend to enter into cohabitation, rather than marital unions.

Notes

1. Two interviews were conducted with the women in 1962. The original interview was conducted in the winter and spring of 1962. The first follow-up was conducted in the fall of 1962.

2. When the 1955 study was being planned, there was great trepidation among professional colleagues, prospective interviewers, and funding agencies that the "sensitive" character of the questions (especially, it was thought, among Catholics and less educated women) would lead to many refusals. Careful pretests and other steps to minimize these problems and the intrinsic interest of the subject matter to women resulted in a response rate of 91 percent of those initially sampled. Refusals to answer occurred less often in response to questions on contraception than to those on income. The success of the study in all major strata of the sample unquestionably helped to decrease concerns about such studies.

3. To control for important but relatively rare circumstances in 1962, the sample of recent mothers was limited to women who were married at the time of both the 1961 birth and the 1962 interview. Also excluded were families in which the child of the 1961 birth had died or was seriously ill. The age range of mothers was restricted as follows: first parity, fifteen to thirty-four; second parity, fifteen to thirty-nine; and fourth parity, twenty to thirty-nine. Eligibility requirements for the recently married were that both husband and wife had married only once and were living together in 1962 (or only temporarily apart); that they had had no live births to date; and that the wife was between the ages of fifteen and thirty-four and the husband was not older than forty-five. Because of the low rates of marital dissolution and childbearing outside of marriage in the early 1960s, the marital status restrictions on the sample eliminated relatively few women from the universe of study.

4. David Goldberg had conducted follow-up interviews about family-size expectations in the Detroit area in 1957 (Goldberg, Sharp, and Freedman 1959). William Mooney, in a study designed for eleven successive telephone interviews in eight months, had obtained a response rate of 93 percent (Corsa and Mooney 1960).

5. The Detroit Area Study (DAS) of the University of Michigan conducts sample surveys in Detroit as part of the training in survey research for graduate students in the social sciences. It is at the same time a research facility for social science faculty. Our baseline survey was the subject of the DAS research in 1962. After that, the Survey Research Center field staff conducted the re-interviews. The research for our study was first based at the Population Studies Center and directed by Ronald Freedman, David Goldberg, and Lolagene Coombs. Since 1975 it has been based at the Survey Research Center and the Population Studies Center and directed by Arland Thornton. Deborah Freedman was his research associate from 1975 to 1995.

6. Among faculty contributors are Duane Alwin, Jennifer Barber, Frances Goldscheider, David Mann, Terri Orbuch, Paul Siegel, and Yu Xie. Judith Baughn, Donald Camburn, and Linda Young-DeMarco have provided extensive research and administrative support. Interviewers who have made invaluable contributions over multiple waves of the study include Elsie Bremen, Helen Flanagan, and Jackie Thorsby.

References

Alwin, Duane F., and Arland Thornton. 1984. "Family Origins and the Schooling Process: Early Versus Late Influence of Parental Characteristics." *American Sociological Review* 49(6): 784–802.

Axinn, William G., and Jennifer Barber. 1997. "Non-family Living and Family Formation Values in Early Adulthood." *Journal of Marriage and the Family* 59(3): 595–611.

Axinn, William G., Greg Duncan, and Arland Thornton. 1997. "The Effects of Parental Income, Wealth, and Attitudes on Children's Completed Schooling and Self-esteem." In *Growing Up Poor*, edited by Jeanne Brooks-Gunn and Greg Duncan. New York: Russell Sage Foundation.

Axinn, William G., and Arland Thornton. 1992a. "The Influence of Parental Resources on the Timing of the Transition to Marriage." *Social Science Research* 21(3): 261–85.

———. 1992b. "The Relationship Between Cohabitation and Divorce: Selectivity or Causal Influence?" *Demography* 29(3): 357–74.

———. 1993. "Mothers, Children, and Cohabitation: The Intergenerational Effects of Attitudes and Behavior." *American Sociological Review* 58(2): 233–46.

———. 1996. "The Influence of Parents' Marital Dissolutions on Children's Family Formation Attitudes." *Demography* 33(1): 66–81.

———. 2000. "The Transformation in the Meaning of Marriage." In *The Ties That Bind*, edited by Linda J. Waite, Christine Bachrach, Michelle Hindin, Elizabeth Thomson, and Arland Thornton. New York: Aldine de Gruyter.

Axinn, William G., Arland Thornton, LiShou Yang, Linda Young-DeMarco, and Yu Xie. Forthcoming. "Mothers' Reports of Children's Family Formation Behavior." *Social Science.*

Barber, Jennifer S. 2000. "Intergenerational Influences on the Entry into Parenthood: Mothers' Preferences for Family and Nonfamily Behavior." *Social Forces* 79(1): 319–48.

Belli, Robert F. 1998. "The Structure of Autobiographical Memory and the Event-History Calendar: Potential Improvements in the Quality of Retrospective Reports in Surveys." *Memory* 6(4): 383–406.

Binstock, Georgina P., and Arland Thornton. 1999. "Separations, Reconciliations, and Living Away in Marital and Cohabiting Unions." Paper presented at the annual meeting of the Population Association of America, New York (March 25–27).

Caspi, Avshalom, Terrie E. Moffitt, Arland Thornton, Deborah Freedman, James W. Amell, Honalee Harrington, Judith Smeijers, and Phillip A. Silva. 1996. "The Life-History Calendar: A Research and Clinical Assessment Method for Collecting Retrospective Event-History Data." *International Journal of Methods in Psychiatric Research* 6: 101–14.

Coombs, Lolagene C. 1979. "Reproductive Goals and Achieved Fertility: A Fifteen-Year Perspective." *Demography* 16(4): 523–34.

Coombs, Lolagene C., and Ronald Freedman. 1964. "Use of Telephone Interviews in a Longitudinal Fertility Study." *Public Opinion Quarterly* 28(1): 112–17.

———. 1970a. "Premarital Pregnancy, Childspacing, and Later Economic Achievement." *Population Studies* 24(3): 389–412.

———. 1970b. "Problems and Possibilities in Conducting Panel Fertility Studies." *Population et Famille* 20: 1–19.

Coombs, Lolagene C., and Zena Zumeta. 1970. "Correlates of Marital Dissolution in a Prospective Fertility Study." *Social Problems* 18(1): 92–102.

Corsa, Leslie, and William Mooney. 1960. "Epidemiological Study of Reproductive Wastage." Progress Report RG5331. Sacramento: California State Department of Public Health (May).

Easterlin, Richard A. 1966. "On the Relation of Economic Factors to Recent and Projected Fertility Changes." *Demography* 3(1): 131–53.

———. 1969. "Towards a Socioeconomic Theory of Fertility: Survey of Recent Research on Economic Factors in American Fertility." In *Fertility and Family*

Planning, edited by Samuel J. Behrman, Leslie L. Corsa Jr., and Ronald Freedman. Ann Arbor: University of Michigan Press.

Freedman, Deborah S., and Arland Thornton. 1979. "The Long-Term Impact of Pregnancy at Marriage on the Family's Economic Circumstances." *Family Planning Perspectives* 11(1): 6–21.

———. 1990. "The Consumption Aspirations of Adolescents: Determinants and Implications." *Youth and Society* 21(3): 259–81.

Freedman, Deborah S., Arland Thornton, and Donald Camburn. 1980. "Maintaining Response Rates in Longitudinal Studies." *Sociological Methods and Research* 9(1): 87–98.

Freedman, Deborah, Arland Thornton, Donald Camburn, Duane Alwin, and Linda Young-DeMarco. 1988. "The Life History Calendar: A Technique for Collecting Retrospective Data." In *Sociological Methodology,* edited by Clifford C. Clogg. Vol. 18. San Francisco: Jossey-Bass.

Freedman, Ronald. 1998. "Observing Taiwan's Demographic Transition: A Memoir." Research Report 98-426. Ann Arbor: University of Michigan, Population Studies Center.

Freedman, Ronald, Pascal K. Whelpton, and Arthur A. Campbell. 1959. *Family Planning, Sterility, and Population Growth.* New York: McGraw-Hill.

Goldberg, David, Harry Sharp, and Ronald Freedman. 1959. "The Stability and Reliability of Expected Family Size Data." *Milbank Memorial Fund Quarterly* 37(4): 369–85.

Goldscheider, Frances, Arland Thornton, and Linda Young-DeMarco. 1993. "A Portrait of the Nest-Leaving Process in Early Adulthood." *Demography* 30(4): 683–99.

Lichter, Daniel T., Felicia B. LeClere, and Diane K. McLaughlin. 1991. "Local Marriage Markets and the Marital Behavior of Black and White Women." *American Journal of Sociology* 96(4): 843–67.

Lichter, Daniel T., Diane K. McLaughlin, George Kephart, and David Landry. 1992. "Race and Retreat from Marriage: A Shortage of Marriageable Men?" *American Sociological Review* 57(6): 781–99.

Moore, Kristin A., James L. Peterson, and Frank F. Furstenberg Jr. 1986. "Parental Attitudes and the Occurrence of Early Sexual Activity." *Journal of Marriage and the Family* 48(4): 777–82.

Orbuch, Terri L., Arland Thornton, and Jennifer Cancio. 2000. "The Impact of Marital Quality, Divorce, and Remarriage on the Relationships Between Parents and Their Children." *Marriage and Family Review* 29(4): 221–46.

Pearce, Lisa D. Forthcoming. "The Influence of Early Life Course Religious Exposure on Young Adults' Disposition Toward Childbearing." *Journal for the Scientific Study of Religion.*

Pearce, Lisa, and William G. Axinn. 1998. "The Impact of Family Religious Life on the Quality of Parent-Child Relationships." *American Sociological Review* 63(6): 810–28.

Thornton, Arland. 1985. "Changing Attitudes Toward Separation and Divorce: Causes and Consequences." *American Journal of Sociology* 90(4): 856–72.

———. 1988. "Cohabitation and Marriage in the 1980s." *Demography* 25(4): 497–508.

———. 1989. "Changing Attitudes Toward Family Issues in the United States." *Journal of Marriage and the Family* 51(4): 873–93.

———. 1990. "The Courtship Process and Adolescent Sexuality." *Journal of Family Issues* 11(3): 239–73.

———. 1991. "Influence of the Marital History of Parents on the Marital and Cohabitational Experiences of Children." *American Journal of Sociology* 96(4): 868–94.

———. 1992. "The Influence of the Parental Family on the Attitudes and Behavior of Children." In *The Changing American Family: Sociological and Demographic Perspectives,* edited by Scott J. South and Stewart E. Tolnay. Boulder, Colo.: Westview Press.

———. 1995. "Attitudes, Values, and Norms Related to Nonmarital Fertility." In *Report to Congress on Out-of-Wedlock Childbearing.* DHHS Publication (PHS) 95-1257. Hyattsville, Md.: U.S. Department of Health and Human Services.

Thornton, Arland, Duane F. Alwin, and Donald Camburn. 1983. "Causes and Consequences of Sex-Role Attitudes and Attitude Change." *American Sociological Review* 48(2): 211–27.

Thornton, Arland, and William G. Axinn. 1996. "A Review of the Advantages and Limitations of the Intergenerational Panel Study of Parents and Children." University of Michigan. Unpublished paper.

Thornton, Arland, William G. Axinn, and Daniel H. Hill. 1992. "Reciprocal Effects of Religiosity, Cohabitation, and Marriage." *American Journal of Sociology* 98(3): 628–51.

Thornton, Arland, William G. Axinn, and Jay D. Teachman. 1995. "The Influence of School Enrollment and Accumulation on Cohabitation and Marriage in Early Adulthood." *American Sociological Review* 60(5): 762–74.

Thornton, Arland, and Donald Camburn. 1987. "The Influence of the Family on Premarital Sexual Attitudes and Behavior." *Demography* 24(3): 323–40.

Thornton, Arland, and Deborah S. Freedman. 1982. "Changing Attitudes Toward Marriage and Single Life." *Family Planning Perspectives* 14(6): 297–303.

Thornton, Arland, Deborah S. Freedman, and Donald Camburn. 1982. "Obtaining Respondent Cooperation in Family Panel Studies." *Sociological Methods and Research* 11(1): 33–51.

Thornton, Arland, and Hui-Sheng Lin. 1994. *Social Change and the Family in Taiwan.* Chicago: University of Chicago Press.

Thornton, Arland, and Linda Young-DeMarco. 2001. "Four Decades of Trends in Attitudes Toward Family Issues in the United States: The 1960s Through the 1990s." *Journal of Marriage and the Family* 63(4): 1009–1037.

Thornton, Arland, Linda Young-DeMarco, and Frances Goldscheider. 1993. "Leaving the Parental Nest: The Experience of a Young White Cohort in the 1980s." *Journal of Marriage and the Family* 55(1): 216–29.

Weinstein, Maxine, and Arland Thornton. 1989. "Mother-Child Relations and Adolescent Sexual Attitudes and Behavior." *Demography* 26(4): 563–77.

Westoff, Charles F., Elliot G. Mishler, and E. Lowell Kelley. 1957. "Preferences in Size of Family and Eventual Fertility Twenty Years After." *American Journal of Sociology* 62(5): 491–97.

Whelpton, Pascal K., Arthur A. Campbell, and John E. Patterson. 1966. *Fertility and Family Planning in the United States.* Princeton: Princeton University Press.

Yabiku, Scott, William G. Axinn, and Arland Thornton. 1999. "Family Integration and Children's Self-esteem." *American Journal of Sociology* 104(5): 1494–1524.

PART V

REFLECTIONS

Chapter 14

Generativity, Identity, and the Proclamation of Landmarks

John Modell

T HE CONFERENCE at which the antecedents of this volume's papers
were presented was titled "Landmark Studies," a compelling imagery, and one that led demonstrably to a set of papers and attendant discussion that sought fruitfully to place key longitudinal studies into an emergent historical-methodological framework. As I thought
about the notion of "landmark," I was struck by the choice of a geo-
graphical metaphor rather than a developmental one; a landmark is a
prominent element in an environment by which navigators, travelers,
and even (in a pleasing note included in my dictionary) surgeons can
orient themselves, so that they may move on in the direction they in-
tend. Such an intentional sense of making one's way, so fixed and objective the markers.

Had the conference been designated by a developmental metaphor,
we might have been more tempted to attend to the question of just where
in the "life" of longitudinal studies we imagine we are today. The accomplished scholars assembled at the conference all resonated with the
sound of generativity and the heady rejection of stagnation (to affirm
George Vaillant's penchant for Eriksonian notions). But I wish to propose that an earlier developmental stage, the struggle for identity, in
some modest ways also characterized our conference, and had we chosen resolutely to see ourselves in this light, we might have been led to a
somewhat less celebratory view of the history of longitudinal study. We
might then have directed our attention more to the sotto voce intellectual tensions present in our meeting.

Toward an Interdiscipline?

A repeated ellipsis in our group discussions was, for me, especially suggestive of the identity issue. Determinedly, I found, the participants asserted shared longitudinally oriented practices and perspectives, while overlooking considerable differences in what we do with longitudinal data and what longitudinal evidence does for us. In fact, as I read the papers and listened to the conversations I was persuaded that (although admitting of a good amount of within-group variation) many of the longitudinally inclined psychologists among us differ from many of their sociological colleagues in some important if conventional ways. (Muddying this distinction, of course, is the fact that prominent among the participants were scholars whose disciplinary label was neither of these, as well as one sociologist—Glen Elder—who "represented" in a sense a longitudinal study undertaken by psychologists, and a pair of sociological criminologists—John Laub and Robert Sampson—who "represented" the utterly eclectic Gluecks and their study.)

Despite these qualifications, let us reflect upon the implications of the disciplinary distinction made in passing at the conference by Ann Brunswick: that sociologists on the whole worry a lot about sampling and are casual about measurement, whereas psychologists worry about measurement but often let sampling take care of itself. Sociologists worry so much about sampling because near to their hearts they seek to understand populations and to discover what differentiates them by examining the correlates of the differences found therein. Psychologists, in the end, generally want to talk very carefully about individuals, as exemplars of the species. They do not seek to discover what differentiates a population, but instead how the several attributes of an individual work together to move that individual through life. Psychologists who study what they call "individual differences" usually do so as a means toward understanding the mechanisms that govern the way all members of their species live and develop; but for sociologists, most of what differentiates individuals is called "society," the central object of their inquiry.

This metatheoretical difference in disciplinary perspective has its methodological counterpart. Sociologists (who characteristically fetishize sampling) are baffled by exactly what to credit in psychologists' obviously conscientious accounts of the temporal organization of lives when these lives are those of members of samples governed by convenience. Those (psychologists) who, in contrast, fetishize precision of measurement often are uncertain about what to believe in sociologists' carefully conducted studies that intricately relate indicators whose reliability and validity are unsubstantiated, and thus rely heavily but implicitly on the randomization of measurement error.

Such matters of disciplinary focus and belief, in fact, seem to me to lie at the heart of the issue of our conference when it is seen as a quest for identity: just what do we have in common in our longitudinal inquiries that makes us instructive colleagues for one another? Once we are finished celebrating our shared longitudinal orientation, do we actually know how to incorporate the findings and arguments of one another's studies into a shared body of substantive knowledge? If so, does this knowledge cumulate in a principled fashion or in the form of aperçus that happen to strike our fancy?

Related but not identical to the disciplinary difference was a contrast, repeatedly visible, between those who by habit and preference analyze large samples and those who choose to get close up to a modest-sized special sample. The logic of the two approaches can be quite opposed, because they represent different attitudes toward what to do about the brute fact of variation. The large-scale representative study, as Greg Duncan pointed out, captures within it as many sources of variance as possible, so that their stepwise partialling out may offer a glimpse of the varied contextual influences on individuals and on processes of individual development. A closely examined small-scale sample, on the other hand, necessarily excludes many sources of variance but seeks to allow a detailed account of those individual-level processes that we commonly think of as "development." The affinity of this latter frame of mind to that which constructed the psychological laboratory ought to be clear, as ought the affinity of the large-n-sample-study orientation to the demographic accounting model from which much sociological study of the life course has grown.

Considerations of cost and convenience also matter and constitute a significant context to the search for identity of those committed to longitudinal study. Large-sample analysts are increasingly committed to (and adept at) the "communal" design and the opportunistic use of omnibus data sets that have considerable substantive range. Both Frank Mott and Greg Duncan describe with amusement and tightly constrained fury the divergences from the optimal seemingly always present in this kind of data set on account of political, bureaucratic, and other nonscholarly influences. Devotees of the small sample, by contrast, often finely control the content of their own data sets, gaining a kind of profound care that is arguably impossible in the analysis of data whose gathering one has not supervised but in a way limiting thereby the range of surprises and challenges that a highly complex sample can impose. As Elder, John Laub, and Rob Sampson argue as they extol archival data, nowhere do conceptual surprises and challenges abound more than when one must make sense of the evidence gathered under the research aegis of one's worthy but remote intellectual ancestors. George Vaillant takes this argument a step further, maintaining that a species of variability more powerful than that espoused by Mott and Duncan as a virtue of massive national samples is that available in bringing together from the archive multiple studies, each with its own conceptual and sampling quirks. (Think of how opposed Vaillant's perspective is to that of meta-analysis.)

At minimum, the question of criteria for mutual credibility—and thereby of the cumulation of scientific knowledge—is at the heart of our identity quest. The closest we came to a direct exploration of this issue were intriguing discussions of areas of possible common ground between the two outlooks that, as I maintain, divide our group. Most particularly, the logic of community-based samples was explored directly by Arland Thornton, Ronald Freedman, and William G. Axinn, by Laub and Sampson, by Emmy Werner, and a bit more tangentially by Doris Entwisle, Karl L. Alexander, and Linda Steffel Olson, and by Ann Brunswick. (Note the disciplinary mix of this cast of characters.) It will take another conference, however, to explore "community" as both a methodological and a substantive thread of common interest to our varied conferees. We should temper our inclination to triumphalism with the memory of earlier moments in "our" history.

A Little History

As the members of our "landmark" generation were gaining their first tastes of social science, the field of longitudinal study (if calling it that does not suggest too much cohesion) was in turbulent flux, as "longitudinal studies" in *Child Development Abstracts and Bibliography* proliferated, reaching a peak of thirty-nine in 1963, before retreating under a shower of potent critique. To that point, the heady optimism of an older tradition of casewise longitudinal developmental study was still very much alive. Orthodontists, thus, were told in 1958 to look at "the child as a whole" in their growth studies, for "the child grows in a lawful, orderly, and predictive way within himself, irrespective of how much his individual growth pattern may or may not conform to that of another child or group of children" (Hughes 1958).

An even more thoroughgoing linking of clinical understanding to longitudinal study informed the lesson that the director of a major longitudinal study of children's development sought to deliver to his fellow physicians. The longitudinal perspective, he told them, was a needed counterweight to the quick fix of the disease-specific antibiotics. The "young physician" who reaches first for the pill is "in danger of losing the very genuine satisfaction of really knowing thoroughly the courses of events which lead up to the illness, the effect of the illness on this particular child, and how the illness has influenced eventually the multiple causative or contributing factors." Absent such understanding, and treatment appropriate to it, "the child is then left prey to other harmful environmental factors, often without having the advantage of learning through experience anything about his own powers of adapting to environmental handicaps" (Washburn 1957, 59).

Skeptical voices, however, were now being raised in influential places, questioning the extent and quality of the fruits of the first generation of the longitudinal study of children. The National Institute of Mental Health, for instance, supported the thoughtful *Appraisal of the Longitudinal Approach to Studies in Growth and Development,* by Dankward Kodlin and Donovan J. Thompson, published as a Society for Research in Child Development monograph in 1958. That review notes that the underlying approach of the "whole-child" longitudinal studies is, in the natural-science vein, a first step, only appropriate to developing but not testing hypothesis. (Kodlin and Thompson 1958), a step that might perhaps have been better accomplished had founders' dreams not been so grandiose and had closer attention been paid to such niggling methodological problems as self-selection bias among participants in the longitudinal studies and the methodological implications of nonrandom disappearance from observation.

Even Alan Stone and Gloria Onqué's superb 1959 annotated bibliography of 288 longitudinal studies of children's personality expressed the difficulty of isolating a priori the proper causes of the outcomes of interest. "Consequently, many studies have accumulated incredible amounts of data which defy any degree of organized analysis" (Stone and Onqué 1959, xiii). Jerome Kagan, fresh from completing (with Howard A. Moss) the challenging task of hewing a book-length study from the data of a classic first-generation "whole-child" longitudinal project, the Fels Study, reported in 1964 to the Committee on Socialization and Social Structure of the Social Science Research Council on the state of longitudinal research. There he expressed severe doubts about the basic presumptions of most such work. "It is necessary that psychologists obtain more precise accounts of the developmental history of selected response systems. . . . For development is a cryptograph in which early appearing responses often lead to behaviors that are phenotypically unlike the original response but theoretically derived from the original habit" (Kagan 1964, 2).

Richard Q. Bell, of the National Institute of Mental Health, characterized prospective longitudinal study as an expensive purism, practical mainly for descriptive accounts of normative growth patterns, from which "a tremendous variety of results seemed to emerge, each variety associated with 'many complications' " on account of the homogeneity of the sample and the heterogeneity of the world (Bell 1960, 135). Five years later Bell asked whether, in view of the fact that longitudinally studied subjects had, even in the years since longitudinal method was introduced, changed detectably in physical growth, timing of maturity, linguistic development, and socialization practices, "developmental psychology can accumulate stable, replicable findings and superordinate principles faster than our subjects are changing" (Bell 1965, 2).[1] The solution would be found, if at all, in methods suitable for examining "multiple determinants"—that is, keeping changes in populations and environments in some way alive in the analysis itself rather than pretending that the individuals studied aged outside of historical process.

That is, in an odd fashion, the *only* way to use the old data on children as data on "children," rather than to disregard it as data on "children as they used to be," is to take advantage of its age to discuss the history in which it sat. In time, these challenges would be addressed within the field of developmental studies, Elder's radical approach—of operationalizing, and thereby problematizing, relevant elements of "history" in such a way that timeless laws are no longer anticipated save by higher-level synthesis—being one of the most heroic (see also Baltes, Reese, and Lipsitt 1980; Schaie and Hertzog 1982).

Lester Sontag, retiring after four decades as director of the Fels Longitudinal Study, offered a valedictory to the 1970 annual meeting of the American Psychological Association (APA) (Sontag 1971). He spoke, in a tone that was far short of triumphal, of the accomplishments to date of the pioneering American longitudinal studies of children's development (including the Fels Study) begun in the late 1920s and early 1930s. These studies, Sontag (1971, 989) noted, "differed immensely in the multidisciplinary nature of their research methodology and objectives, but they were all attacking primarily an area of inadequate knowledge, the development of children, rather than *concise problems* within that area."[2] Fine data had been created over the first two or three decades of longitudinal studies, Sontag noted, but these studies produced far less excellent research of a multidisciplinary sort than enthusiasts had anticipated.

Longitudinal study with a whole-child orientation did not work very well as a research approach for child developmentalists—in fact did not contribute much to the creation of an interdiscipline of child development—because studies in this vein lacked "adequate research design," employed "techniques which often were tools for clinical appraisal," and lacked both the reliability and the validity that developmental research really required. Longitudinal study was still needed, Sontag argued, but its goals and its measures would have to be better designed and more a priori. "Please do not misunderstand me," Sontag told the APA. "The importance of considering the child as a whole clinically cannot be denied. As a matter of fact, it was at about the time of the institution of the various centers for the longitudinal study of the whole child that the importance of considering the child as a whole began to seep into clinical medicine" (Sontag 1971, 989–90).

The latter decades of Sontag's forty-year directorship of the Fels Institute had been hard ones, and he had been able to save his challenged ship mainly by abandoning, piece by piece, the ambitions and finally even the whole of its psychological component, which initially was half the project. Research funding went elsewhere, generally to cross-sectional studies that rested on freshly gathered, freshly conceived data and often seemed directed to specific points of shared theoretical concern. Social and behavioral science in the heady two decades following World War II seemed *really* to be science, to conform to a Popperian model. Experiments, special-purpose survey research, and "the laboratory" were unquestionably the central tools of this science. Sontag's distinction between the clinical and the scientific captures the spirit of these decades

When the 1968 *International Encyclopedia of the Social Sciences* appeared, Harold Stevenson was responsible for the entry on developmental psychology. Noting the near-mortal weakening of the whole-child approach, Stevenson explained the logic of the coincident turning away from casewise analysis. "The descriptive approach in developmental psychology has been replaced by a variable-oriented approach. The adoption of systematic [subdisciplinary] positions dealing with developmental changes in children's behavior has led to an increased interest in determining children's responses to particular specifiable or manipulable variables and to a decreased interest in describing behavior in naturalistic or controlled settings" (Stevenson 1968, 139). Developmental psychology did not wholly abandon longitudinal study. Henceforth, it would examine within-variable trends over developmental time within different theoretically interesting subpopulations, seeking thus to infer what occurs within individuals variously situated within those populations—a leap that invited, on the one hand, a more systematic investigation of the role of context but, on the other, a far greater remoteness of empirical observation from theoretical process of development as most psychologists understood the term.

Stevenson's entry in the *International Encyclopedia* was not the only entry cross-referenced under longitudinal studies, for scholars in sociology (and political science) had experienced longitudinal study rather differently: theirs was the entry for panel studies, written by Bernard Levenson. Levenson's account explicitly distinguishes sociologists' and political scientists' interests in longitudinal analysis from those in psychology, which he characterizes as mathematically modeled accounts of repeated measures in a single dimension, whereas panel study "is non-experimental and descriptive. It emphasizes the interrelationships of many changing variables and is statistical, though not highly mathematical. There is considerable theoretical improvisation during the analysis of data" (Levenson 1968, 371).

The number of longitudinal studies in sociology had been growing, for sociologists were unburdened with a whole-person approach, looking instead at how population-based structures reproduce themselves and change. In 1963 *Sociological Abstracts* included only four studies published in 1963 that rested on prospective data on individuals or other changing entities, but over the years the number increased, and by the early 1970s large numbers of abstracts noted impatiently that longitudinal data was needed to answer the questions at hand *really right*. The several variants of the National Longitudinal Survey so well charted by Frank Mott for our conference were coming on line, as was a massive federally sponsored study of high schoolers, Project Talent, with its follow-up waves. Articles now began to appear employing longitudinal data sets of a size substantial enough to please sociologists, to allow them to examine far more securely such considerable multivariate models as the cohort-based model of pathways of intergenerational occupational mobility offered in 1967 in Peter Blau's and Otis Dudley Duncan's (1967) methodologically epochal *American Occupational Structure,* which itself rested partly on retrospection.

The definitive breakthrough in this process was probably the work of William H. Sewell, Robert Hauser, and David Featherman, based on statewide Wisconsin data, the first wave of which was gathered from high school seniors in 1957 (by a scholar with no idea of pursuing longitudinal research). Sewell's background in rural sociology had given him an interest in the impact of community upon the attitudes of those growing up there—notably, their educational aspirations—and by 1962, as the U.S. Bureau of the Census gathered the huge special cross-sectional supplement to the Current Population Survey on which *American Occupational Structure* would be based, he was already planning to take the Wisconsin data in a longitudinal direction, starting with a 1964 follow-up.

By 1975, when Sewell, Hauser, and Featherman published their monographic overview of the Wisconsin work, they could recognize that the direction of their longitudinal research had been to explore the impact of "a number of experiences that have an important bearing on post–high school educational outcomes. These include level of performance in high school, whether significant others encourage or discourage high educational and occupational aspirations, and whether or not the students actually develop these aspirations. All of these experiences intervene between the social origins, academic ability, and sex characteristics of the individual and his later achievements" (Sewell, Hauser, and Featherman 1976, 11). Context, as one can see, is central, and the psychological realm narrowly and rather statically defined; the individual-level progression examined is substantially external to the individual (occupation, educational achievement, and income) and readily ascertainable—and not obviously developmental in its formulation. (In the previous year, Glen Elder's *Children of the Great Depression* had appeared, far more developmental and far less demographic in its account of the life course, and resting on a profoundly fresh appreciation of archived longitudinal data.)

Enhanced computational capacity spurred ever more powerful statistical rubrics, and together these fed the appetite for inclusive models with inclusive samples that had been whetted for sociologists and others whose inherent interest was in supra-individual processes. When James S. Coleman (1974) described the current ferment in U.S. sociological methods for overseas colleagues in 1974, he cited prominently among the factors making for change multivariate methods for treating interval data, ready access to large micro-level data files for secondary analysis, and increased longitudinal data. Coleman had his finger on the pulse of the discipline. To work over clinically conceived longitudinal data in such a way that it would bear the kind of multivariate modeling that the new style of research demanded, however, would take the kind of combination of intellectual concentration, adventure, patience, and pure sweat that Elder and Laub and Sampson have written about in their papers for this book. For most sociologically inclined scholars, the older interpretive case-study tradition espoused by the pioneer American social psychologist W. I. Thomas (Elder 1994) was put aside in favor of the analyses that were remote from cases: variable centered and thoroughly multivariate, working out from cross sections toward short and then longer time sequences.

Where Do We Stand?

The trend toward multiple-use survey-based studies, and thus toward remotely designed and administered research instruments, reflects in part a widening and deepening faith in survey methodology. The faith, one might imagine, has been enhanced by the neat fit between the method and the computer, in permitting cheaper data collection by telephone, in permitting highly intricate sampling frames, in promoting happily unrestrictive initial coding schemes, and in inviting the undirected synergy that the widespread sharing of data encourages. Perhaps even more alluring is the proliferation of new statistical approaches to mass standardized data analysis and the algorithms that allow one to carry these out iteratively on one's desktop computer. Several of the papers presented at the Landmark Conference expressed or commented upon aspects of the expansion of confidence in surveys: increased credence in telephone interviews; pursuit of a "younger is better" sampling philosophy and a coupled readiness to credit children's responses and our ability to pose questions to them simply and with adequately uniform meanings; and a greater ease with the notion that theoretically interesting dimensions have been and can be measured in an unbiased way with relatively small batteries of questions, allowing large samples to overcome the effects of random noise.

To be sure, some of the essays are more uneasy than others with one or another element of this expanded confidence in the survey method-ology, but only the Cairns and Cairns paper explicitly resists survey method's expansiveness. The Cairnses maintain that "multiple levels of measurement are required rather than a focus upon single variables, single tests, or single contexts. One of the reasons is that the momentary features of relationships and contexts, for the most part, limit behaviors." Might this issue be located somewhere in the vicinity of the "traditional" split between psychology and sociology?

Against the smoothly flowing tide of our conference, too, and of this volume are the sharp concerns for the effects of endogeneity raised by David Weikart and Greg Duncan as they praise randomized-assignment experiments. These scholars, prepared to make considerable sacrifices to achieve security in asserting causality, are strongly informed by an ori-entation to policy and its implementation that perhaps demands greater sureness than does "pure" scientific cumulation.

This is an unusual position to take. It struck me repeatedly during the conference, although it was not said in so many words, that our experi-enced longitudinal scholars for the most part were rather eager to repo-sition social science's voice as a more exploratory one, less committed to the classical notion of science as the confirmation of explicitly hypothe-sized, deductively derived propositions. I could almost hear the words of R. G. Collingwood (1948), the idealist philosopher of history with whose formulations I was instructed as a graduate student, asserting imaginative reconstruction as the historical practitioner's goal. I wonder if, in fact, we cannot perhaps see in the leanings of many of our partici-pants in some of their less guarded moments an almost yielding look in the direction of interpretive social science (Rabinow and Sullivan 1979). Perhaps for at least some of our contributors there is a sense (not fully ar-ticulated, surely not fully explored or debated) that doing longitudinal research—at least, doing it *right*—leads the conscientious analyst willy-nilly through a phase of imaginative reconstruction, of self-conscious in-terpretation, perhaps even a direct if only auxiliary use of one's own subjectivity. No doubt this is middle-aged romanticization, on my part surely and on that of many of our contributors perhaps, but I certainly heard many invocations of "making sense" of lives, lives seen as some-thing real in that they were experienced really, and a wish to abandon the scientized distancing labels of "subject" and "respondent."

At moments, the question of what science is and should be was quite pointed. Frank Furstenberg's text is, in my reading, particularly inclined to decenter the way we see science (social and behavioral science, any-how). In it, he describes how the role of expert was thrust upon him long before he felt he knew anything in the neatly certain way "science" (or even "social science") was said to know. He also notes that he felt himself actually becoming an expert only when his view of social science was affected both by the growing relevance he found for his own work to larger political themes and by the triumphs he felt in his work as he saw that he knew "his" people better for having studied and restudied them. One cannot read Furstenberg's affecting account without recognizing that this is a scholar whose sense of social scientific knowledge has increasingly converged upon the usual sense of "wisdom."

Furstenberg's posture, however, both vis-à-vis science and vis-à-vis policy, was not that of everybody at the Landmark Conference. Weikart's hard-edged account of science is a striking contrast to Furstenberg's, as is the way he understands scientific expertise in the policy arena. Possibly more representative of the gathered scholars at the Landmark Conference than either Furstenberg or Weikart was Emmy Werner, whose research, in bringing her close to her subjects' lives, led her (for instance) to a powerfully resonant formulation of the notion of "resilience." Her scientific prickliness, however, turns her narrative immediately to thoughts of those unchartered acolytes whose purveyance of "resilience" is untested and possibly untestable, and her scientific recommendations to inquiry into both the "price" of this resilience and the limitations upon some children's lives imposed by their genetic heritage.

Werner expresses particularly eloquently a related perspective that is common to many, and perhaps most, of the contributors: that longitudinal analysis, both by the invariable repeated contact with the same individuals (if only to maintain rapport) and by the diffuse nature of understanding the complex, startling turns lifetimes take ("resilience," for instance), implies a moral engagement with the subjects of one's inquiry. That this is on the whole far truer for small-sample studies than large ones is obvious from the papers collected here, but what is more surprising is that the studies that rested on reanalysis of previously collected data reflected hardly less of this moral engagement than those studies in which respondents were actually seen in the flesh, year after year. Perhaps the subject of the study of lifetimes is, in the end, people and their experiences. A pleasing thought—but if it is, where exactly does this leave the study of intra-individual processes, and where does it leave the study of extraindividual structures? How might this fit the increased availability of massive, omnibus, longitudinal data sets and the computers and the techniques to exploit them?

Werner's kind of moral orientation often informs the discussion of casewise analysis, whether formal or informal. This is so, I think, in the less fervid but no less repeated refrain in Duncan's paper about the importance to him and to the Panel Study of Income Dynamics of checking the coding in a casewise rather than algorithmic fashion. It was important to Duncan, I think, because when he conscientiously confronted a single case, he called upon his humane imagination to make sense of responses that were not readily reconciled, and that imagination could not be stilled: every time he entered the magic basement at the Institute for Social Research, where the nationally representative sample of raw data was stored, he found himself impelled to make sense of the concrete pattern of a family's life, in the process of fitting the interviewer's highly constrained markings on the interview form together. The togetherness-on-a-page of the family's responses grabbed his imagination—Duncan's term is "making sense of the data, . . . observing the myriad events." He speaks of his "inability to anticipate the complexities of family economic life," which inability became, through a series of investigations that eventually approached the classical hypothesis-and-test format, one of the notions for which his work is best known and appreciated: the turbulence of economic life in contemporary American society.

Quite the same experience is reported by Laub and Sampson, who (with Elder's example before them) had the daunting task of making new sense of a mountain of systematically gathered research material that had not been miscoded but had been coded according to the somewhat idiosyncratic theoretical concerns and intellectual curiosities of a pair of scholars of a previous generation. Sheldon and Eleanor Glueck were both literally and figuratively dead and gone before Laub and Sampson happened upon their study data and wandered into the glorious quicksand. Thrashing their way through the mire they had voluntarily entered, they found that they would have to imaginatively revive the Gluecks to capture the logic of their ancient coding and data-gathering schemes so that these schemes could be transformed, allowing Laub and Sampson to answer their own questions (not uninfluenced by the process of rethinking the bygone Gluecks).

In the dialectic of forming the new codes, it is apparent that it was "making sense" of some of the lives, seen singly, that helped our contemporary scholars triangulate between where they found themselves, where the Gluecks had been, and where "the lives" had been. Sampson and Laub had to become, on a small scale and essentially as an intermediate and soon submerged research project, social biographers of some no-longer-young children. That is, they had to address casewise logic; and I cannot but wonder whether their having done so in the process of restructuring their data for variable-wise analysis did not lead them back to interviewing, and even schmoozing with, some of these superannuated "kids" later on.

Yet it was Sampson who took on Robert and Beverley Cairns directly at the conference when they argued so forcefully for casewise analysis. The inherent logic of conventional variable-centered analysis, the Cairnses argued, is the fine-grained analysis of the relationship of attributes within a population—and the too-distant inference to the person-level process or processes that would yield this pattern of distribution. The Cairnses advocated instead a configurational approach, whereby individual cases might be clustered inductively according to reasonably common patterns of early-life characteristics. This done, the Cairnses would ask, "How did they turn out?," looking to the different experience along the dimensions of developmental interest enjoyed by members of each of the inductively derived types. These relatively common pathways, in turn, might be illuminated by literally casewise examination of "prodigal" individuals from the various initial groups who, over time, did not do what "they should" have done (in a probabilistic, quantitative sense).

Sampson challenged the distinctiveness of this approach, asking whether subtly and thoughtfully applied variable-based methods would not accomplish the same end, since even a far more strictly clinical approach than that proposed by Cairns and Cairns would still rest upon the systematic observation and categorization of individuals by variables (their meaning derived from their position within the whole set of variables). If adequately theoretically specified beforehand, an adequate set of interactions among variables and multiple pathways can yield exactly the same picture. Sampson seeks this kind of a priori theoretical specification—rather than the almost clinical inductive mode of thinking and feeling that is the Cairnses' preferred way of proceeding—because, Sampson argues, this is the way theory building is most likely to proceed. Sampson asks, in effect, whether the Cairns and Cairns North Carolina data set (like most small-sample—and typically locally based—data sets, upon which casewise induction can be practiced) is going to yield the particular set of interactions and multiple pathways that one might find in another place, in another data set. If it does not, Sampson wonders, will the found relationship have been adequately theorized to draw us closer to parsimoniously organized knowledge?

Momentarily, two approaches to doing science confronted one another sharply at our conference. Had Cairns and Cairns asked Sampson why he privileges the national level (why not the international?), some of our deepest assumptions about what our work adds up to (or, at least, how it may be added up) might have been brought to the surface. Our momentum took us elsewhere, however.

Biography

The call for the Landmark Conference included the unusual invitation to participants to employ the form and spirit of an autobiography in discussing "their" own landmark contributions. Perhaps the organizers, inspired by a sense of generativity, warmed to the notion of having others discuss their innovative pathways through social and behavioral science, seeking by drawing these together to derive a clearer sense of who we longitudinal analysts, corporatively, are.

Never in the course of the conference did we discuss biography, however, nor the perhaps analogous and deeply out-of-fashion clinical case study. Fragments of our conversations, however, headed in this direction. Certainly our discussion of casewise analysis might have raised this idea. Certainly the repeated revelations of investigators seeking to "make sense" of individual records might have raised thoughts of biography in our minds. Certainly our extensive discussion of history might have, too, and even more so might the theoretically posed questions of how context blends with the innate, with early experience, and with agency. Perhaps some formal consideration of biography here will help clarify wherein the participants' offerings may have constituted an interesting, but risky, road not taken—surely not taken, at any rate, by our little fellowship of developmentalists.

The word "biography" raises for social and behavioral scientists the embarrassing question of generalization, for one thing. Biography has characteristically been of the exemplary individual rather than a representative set of individuals. As such, the characteristic developmentalist's question, "How did the child become the adult?," becomes for biographers, "What was so unusual about what the child was, or did, or experienced, to allow the extraordinary adult to emerge?" We may compare what the Cairnses referred to as "prodigal analysis," in which individuals' deviating pathways are explained against an explicit account of the usual, with the goal of showing wherein below the surface of events, at the level of process, the exceptional can be explained in terms that make sense of the usual.

What if we wrote "biographies" of typical as well as of prodigal cases and sought post facto to synthesize these? Are the most cumulatively useful things we can say about them, in essence, only about the incidence and the prevalence of the different types we can induce therein (Forrester 1996)? Is there a different approach, as the dissenting developmental psychologists, Kenneth and Mary Gergen (1984, 31), suggest?

> The developmental theorist can scarcely describe simple, disconnected events. . . . To do so would be considered pointless. If our analysis is correct, maximal intelligibility is achieved when the theorist includes in the analysis those events, and only those events, related to some evaluative endpoint. Ideally, these events should also be causally linked. In effect, to adhere to the characteristics of the well-formed narrative, the theoretical account must give unity, direction, and coherence to the life course. Further, this narrative is likely to draw from the pool of commonly accepted narratives within the culture. (See also Gergen and Gergen 1984; Rosenwald 1988.)

Note especially the last sentence, recalling the idea of clinical sensibility and how the clinical and the Gergens' biographical way of understanding are both similarly historically situated.

Narrative in general, and biography as an instance of it, is a genre of representation that seeks, through formal means, to convey the coherence of its subject. According to narrative theorists, however, it is not just a stylistic mode: it is also a mode of discovery of cohesiveness. (Autobiography, thus, is a mode, as well, of construction of cohesion in one's own life, a task we—we Westerners, anyway—spontaneously adopt in our own lives [Hermans 1992]). The storied world of human endeavor and experience, narrative theorists argue, is neither "out there," simply to be apprehended, nor simply "in here," to be imposed upon a random world "out there." Rather, human beings are story-telling animals. "Action, life, and historical existence are themselves structured narratively, independently of their presentation in literary form. . . . This structure is practical before it is aesthetic or cognitive" (Carr 1986, 185).

We tell stories about ourselves to ourselves in moments of reflection in order to make ourselves knowable to ourselves. We tell stories about ourselves to others so as to put forward a version of our self-accounting that allows us to assert our moral community with those to whom we tell our stories. We tell stories of others to evaluate and convey their moral worth and to evaluate and reassert our received sense of the moral. Our longitudinal accounts are all stories, of one sort or another, as soon as they move from a listing of antecedents and outcomes to the invocation of "pathways" or "risks" or "resilience." We are dependent upon story forms that are known to "work" within our culture in this sort of way. "The stories people hear and tell . . . shape in the most profound way the inner story of experience. We imbibe a sense of the meaning of our own baffling dramas from these stories, and this sense of its meaning in turn affects the form of a man's experience and the style of his action" (Crites 1971, 304; see also Bjorklund 1998). The value, or meaning, of biographical particulars depends in part upon the coherence of the whole story; at the same time the particulars contribute to that overall coherence their own preexistent, particular, local meaning, which rests on other stories.

Biographers' notions of the actor acknowledge intent derived in part from actors' looking ahead to an anticipated future, each both directing and constraining intent. Self—that is, as an emergent psychological entity exactly as it is the constructed subject of a literary genre—is what contemporary (even postmodern) biography is about. The story of the production of meritorious self by reflection upon agentic behavior in a world of possibility has been a consistent motif in American biography as in American culture for more than two centuries (Wilson 1991).

Our Landmark Conference participants were invited to reflect on their own professional and even personal experiences insofar as these might serve to clarify essential patterns in the unfolding of the longitudinal method for understanding the shape of lives and lifetimes. In fact, participants interpreted these instructions quite variously. To categorize how they did so is to risk great crudity and, perhaps, low reliability besides. Be this as it may, it is hard to escape the conclusion that Furstenberg enthusiastically took up the autobiographical invitation (that he himself had had a part in issuing), as did Duncan (urged on by me, he notes), Elder, Vaillant, Weikart, and Werner. In each of these papers there is a (somewhat stylized) "self" there in view, developing along with—and in some kind of a dialectical relation to—the developmental research that they were undertaking.

At the other extreme, perhaps because the autobiographical suggestion was an unusual one, several contributors have written papers that neither employ some account of their selves as a stylistic device, nor offer the kind of glimpses of personhood that invite one to understand the research in its terms, nor encourage one to look to the research to try to understand the man or woman who spoke at the conference or speaks through these papers. Mott and Entwisle, Alexander, and Olson are the straightforward cases in this category. I place Brunswick there as well, for she explicitly notes that she rejected a narrated autobiographical approach, favoring instead one that was "phenomenological," more nearly an account of moment-to-moment consciousness.

This leaves three cases at neither extreme. The Cairnses and Thornton, Freedman, and Axinn, I would say, have written similarly, interpreting the autobiographical invitation as a request for a more specifically professional autobiography, a narrated account of a career rather than of a developing person. Laub and Sampson, in my reading, also fit this in-between category in that they show a most exquisite commitment to the idea that the researcher's biography and the biographee's research are massively related, but they have chosen here to compose a biography of the Gluecks rather than of themselves.

If you have been willing to follow me along with this crude categorizing, perhaps you will also permit me a further crass coding, one in which the participants are ranked for the extent to which clinical intelligence is near the heart of the way they see and present their own best work (see table 14.1). (Recall that I am resting the "clinical" variable on the way the participants have presented their work in the present chapters rather than on a reading of their oeuvre, and so the correlation by my categorization may not be so surprising.)

I do find a consonance here. At minimum, it says that at a time when the scientized methodological prescriptions according to which our Landmark Conference participants were raised is undergoing challenge, those who are especially attracted to interpretive approaches—who seek to employ the clinical intelligence that they have developed over their professional lives—feel it suits their tastes to underline (perhaps explain in autobiographical terms) this deviation from their schooled learning. By

Table 14.1 Autobiographical Form by Clinical Mode of Reasoning

Employs Autobiography	Proclaims or Exemplifies the Clinical		
	Importantly	Incidentally	Not at All
Yes	Furstenberg Vaillant Werner	Duncan Elder	Weikart
Somewhat	Laub and Sampson	Cairns and Cairns	Thornton, Freedman, and Axinn
No			Brunswick Entwisle, Alexander, and Olson Mott

Source: Author's compilation.

and large, those who (in their presentations at the conference) emphasize scientific progress in their work did not develop for their readers an autobiographical persona.

For the overwhelming theme in the autobiographical accounts that were developed was that of the large role of quirkish curiosity, of the unintended, of contingency, of chance. Nowhere is this developed more strongly than in Furstenberg's story, for what better exemplar is there of the irrational element in life than "the family drama" of which he gives us a peek:

> My mother, a social worker in a newly established program for teenage mothers . . . , phoned me one day to ask if I would write some questions for a grant proposal to evaluate the program. She had volunteered the services of her son, the sociologist in training. . . . I patiently explained to my mother why I could not comply with her request. . . . Not deterred in the least by my professional scruples, my mother reappealed on grounds of filial piety. So I sent her a list of questions, accompanied by a letter replete with pedantic protest. The codirectors of the program . . . invited me to Baltimore to present a plan for evaluating the program, and thus the Baltimore study commenced.

If this is the way the enactment of social science occurs for one of our most distinguished longitudinal analysts, is it any wonder that he questions the ability of a priori analytic categories—even more so of standardized survey research protocols treated routinely—to capture the unfolding of the lives of those whose resources for getting done what they plan to get done are far more limited than his own? Or, to turn about the clauses, does it not in a sense follow that a man whose research data and research subjects have shown him adaptive capacities that have startled him will take the opportunity to offer an account of the chancy emergence of his own scientific self from the "baffling dramas" with which he has been beset?

Furstenberg's reflection, seen in this light, returns us to the question of generativity and identity and offers a reconciliation between the two. A narrative of the quest for identity, it appears to me, is what the conveners invited in offering participants the opportunity to employ the autobiographical form; and that is what, in a compressed way, Furstenberg and others have offered. The overwhelming tone of the autobiographies, however, as of the nonautobiographical papers, is one of generativity, an offering of both counsel and encouragement to those younger researchers courageous enough to set out upon such an uneven road.

For the papers offered here and the conversations that went forward at the Landmark Conference speak to a number of rather basic, unjoined questions that longitudinal researchers will wish to address as their own work goes forward, informed by our landmarks but without an orthodoxy in place to guide them. They offer almost as varied a sense of what the studied lifetime ought to look like as of suggestions for how to study it. We may hope that the generativity of the generation represented at our conference will serve to sponsor a quest for identity, as a part of its admirable legacy, among the generation of scholarship that follows.

Notes

1. In the same year, the classic exposition of the relationship of age, period, and cohort effects article (Schaie 1965) for developmental studies appeared, noting the danger that "history" poses to the validity of all quasi-experiments, the more so the more nearly "the whole child" is the subject.

2. Contrast the somber tone of this pronouncement with the bumptiousness of one of Sontag's Fels manifestos a quarter century earlier: "Our psychological program, while it includes cross-sectional studies of various sorts, studies of techniques, and longitudinal studies of individual differences, has as its final objective the interrelation of all this material into a study of the causes of individual differences in the psychological characteristics of children. How do urban children, for example, differ from those brought up in the country? . . . How does the child who is continually stimulated and 'pushed' to the limit differ from the child who is left to 'grow, like Topsy'?" (Sontag 1938).

References

Baltes, Paul B., Hayne W. Reese, and Lewis P. Lipsitt. 1980. "Life Span Developmental Psychology." *Annual Review of Psychology* 31: 65–110.

Bell, Richard Q. 1960. "Retrospective and Prospective Views of Early Personality Development." *Merrill-Palmer Quarterly* 6: 131–44.

————. 1965. "Developmental Psychology." *Annual Review of Psychology* 16: 1–38.

Bjorklund, Diane. 1998. *Interpreting the Self: Two Hundred Years of American Autobiography.* Chicago: University of Chicago Press.

Blau, Peter M., and Otis Dudley Duncan. 1967. *The American Occupational Structure.* New York: Wiley.

Carr, David. 1986. *Time, Narrative, and History.* Bloomington: Indiana University Press.

Coleman, James S. 1974. "Recent Developments in American Sociological Methods." *Polish Sociological Bulletin* 2: 11–23.

Collingwood, R. G. 1948. *The Idea of History.* Oxford: Clarendon Press.

Crites, Stephen. 1971. "The Narrative Quality of Experience." *Journal of the American Academy of Religion* 39: 291–311.

Elder, Glen H., Jr. 1994. "Time, Human Agency, and Social Change: Perspectives on the Life Course." *Social Psychology Quarterly* 57: 4–15.

Forrester, John. 1996. "If *p*, Then What? Thinking in Cases." *History of the Human Sciences* 9: 1–25.

Gergen, Kenneth J., and Mary M. Gergen. 1984. "The Social Construction of Narrative Accounts." In *Historical Social Psychology,* edited by Kenneth J. Gergen and Mary M. Gergen. Hillsdale, N.J.: Lawrence Erlbaum Associates.

————. 1986. "Narrative Form and the Construction of Psychological Science." In *Narrative Psychology,* edited by T. R. Sarbin. New York: Praeger.

Hermans, Herbert J. M. 1992. "Telling and Retelling One's Self-Narrative: A Contextual Approach to Life-Span Development." *Human Development* 35(6): 361–75.

Hughes, Byron O. 1958. "Dental Development and the Child as a Whole." *American Journal of Orthodontics* 44: 565–74.

Kagan, Jerome. 1964. "American Longitudinal Research on Psychological Development." *Child Development* 35: 1–32.

Kodlin, Dankward, and Donovan J. Thompson. 1958. "An Appraisal of the Longitudinal Approach to Studies in Growth and Development." *Monographs of the Society for Research in Child Development* 23(1): 1–47.

Levenson, Bernard. 1968. "Panel Studies." In *The International Encyclopedia of the Social Sciences,* edited by David L. Sills. New York: Macmillan.

Rabinow, Paul, and William M. Sullivan, eds. 1979. *Interpretive Social Science: A Reader.* Berkeley: University of California Press

Rosenwald, George C. 1988. "A Theory of Multiple-Case Research." *Journal of Personality* 56: 239–64.

Schaie, K. Warner. 1965. "A General Model for the Study of Developmental Problems." *Psychological Bulletin* 64: 92–107.

Schaie, K. Warner, and Christopher Hertzog. 1982. "Longitudinal Methods." In *Handbook of Developmental Psychology,* edited by Benjamin B. Wolman. Englewood Cliffs, N.J.: Prentice-Hall.

Sewell, William H., Robert M. Hauser, and David L. Featherman, eds. 1976. *Schooling and Achievement in American Society.* New York: Academic Press.

Sontag, Lester W. 1938. *The Samuel S. Fels Research Institute for the Study of Prenatal and Postnatal Environment.* Yellow Springs, Ohio: Antioch College.

————. 1971. "The History of Longitudinal Research: Implications for the Future." *Child Development* 42: 987–1002.

Stevenson, Harold. 1968. "Developmental Psychology." In *The International Encyclopedia of the Social Sciences*, edited by David L. Sills. New York: Macmillan.

Stone, Alan A., and Gloria Cochrane Onqué. 1959. *Longitudinal Studies of Child Personality*. Cambridge, Mass.: Harvard University Press for the Commonwealth Fund.

Washburn, Alfred H. 1957. "The Child as a Person Developing." *American Medical Association Journal of Diseases of Children* 94: 46–63.

Wilson, Rob. 1991. "Producing American Selves: The Form of American Biography." In *Contesting the Subject*, edited by William H. Epstein. West Lafayette: Purdue University Press.

Index

Boldface numbers refer to figures and tables

Temporary Assistance for Needy
Families (TANF), 153, 160*n*12, 310
Terman, Lewis, 116, 118–19, 129–30,
199
Terman study. *See* Life Cycle Study
of Children with High Ability
Thomas, W. I., 194, 196, 355
Thompson, Donovan J., 351
Thornberry, Terence, 305
Thorndike, Robert, 254
Thornton, Arland: autobiographical
invitation, reaction to, 362–63;
community-based samples, 350; personal and professional background/
activities, 24, 28–29, 315, 320, 331–33,
338; research findings, 19, 21
timing, 8; concepts of time and social
scales, 178–79; development of the
life-course perspective and, 18,
20–22; drug use and gender differences, 234–36; of the investigators,
27–29; of measurements, 177–78;
time overlaps, capitalizing on,
179–81
Tomlinson-Keasey, Carol, 7
Topkis, Gladys, 44

UJD. *See* Unraveling Juvenile Delinquency study
Unplanned Parenthood (Furstenberg),
44–45
Unraveling Juvenile Delinquency
(Glueck and Glueck), 89, 94, 96, 122
Unraveling Juvenile Delinquency
(UJD) study: age of study men on
selected dates, **95;** alcoholism,
125–26; follow-up study, 107–10;
intellectual context of, 92–94;
macro-level historical context,
95–98, 110–11; micro-level historical context, 98–104; military service, impact of, 209–10; original
case files, discovery of, 104–5; sample and procedures, 89–91, 122–24
U.S. National Surveys of Family
Growth, 316

Vaillant, Caroline, 117–18

Vaillant, George: archival research,
13, 349–50; autobiographical invitation, reaction to, 362–63; Boston
study, nondelinquents in, 89; Erick-
sonian notions, penchant for, 347;
Harvard study, 311 (*see also* Study
of Adult Development); methodology, 112*n*2; personal and professional background/activities, 28,
116–17; social policy and, 34
Vygotsky, Lev, 255

Walters, Richard, 270, 284
Webster, Murray, 168
Weikart, David: autobiographical invitation, reaction to, 362–63;
methodology, 356; personal and
professional background/activi-
ties, 22–24, 26, 28, 245–46, 255–59,
263; research findings, 10–11, 20;
science and social policy, 357; social policy and, 19, 22–23, 31
Weitzman, Lenore, 140
welfare: duration of poverty spells
and, 145–48; reform of, 147–48,
153–54, 310
Wellman, Beth Lucy, 247
Werner, Emmy: autobiographical invitation, reaction to, 362–63;
community-based samples, 350;
personal and professional back-
ground/activities, 27–28, 297–98;
research findings, 10, 20; science
and moral engagement, 357; social
policy and, 31, 34
Westoff, Charles, 66, 317
Wilson, Edwin B., 93
Wilson, James Q., 105
Wolfgang, Marvin, 305
women: data collection including,
67–70; Depression-era, studies of,
203–4; employment of, impact on
family life, 339; Harvard Law
School, treatment at, 112*n*7; Intergenerational Panel Study of Parents and Children (*see* Intergenerational Panel Study of Parents and
Children); success of, social factors